CW01067005

OLIVER GOLDSMITH IN CONTEXT

Oliver Goldsmith has a claim to be the only eighteenth-century author who wrote canonical works in prose fiction, poetry, and drama in English. An Irish writer working at the centre of the British and Irish Enlightenments, with all the rich complications of identity this entailed, he authored *The Vicar of Wakefield*, *The Deserted Village*, and *She Stoops to Conquer*, works that number among the greatest literary productions of the century. He was also a major historian, biographer, journalist, and translator operating at the heart of literary London.

Through four parts covering Goldsmith's Life and Career; Social, Cultural, and Intellectual Contexts; Literary Contexts; and Critical Fortunes and Afterlives, this volume engages with a wide range of illuminating topics that will allow both new and experienced readers of Goldsmith to understand more deeply the impact he had on his times and the powerful influence he exerted on subsequent literary culture.

MICHAEL GRIFFIN is Professor of English at the University of Limerick. He is General Editor, with David O'Shaughnessy, of *The Collected Works of Oliver Goldsmith* (2024–) and co-editor, also with O'Shaughnessy, of *The Letters of Oliver Goldsmith* (2018), both for Cambridge University Press. He is the author of *Enlightenment in Ruins: The Geographies of Oliver Goldsmith* (2013) and the editor of *The Selected Writings of Thomas Dermody* (2012) and *The Collected Poems of Laurence Whyte* (2016).

DAVID O'SHAUGHNESSY is Professor of Eighteenth-Century Studies at the University of Galway. He is General Editor, with Michael Griffin, of *The Collected Works of Oliver Goldsmith* (2024–) and co-editor, also with Griffin, of *The Letters of Oliver Goldsmith* (2018), both for Cambridge University Press. He is also the editor of *The Censorship of British Theatre: Playhouses and Prohibition, 1737–1843* (Cambridge University Press, 2023) and *Ireland, Enlightenment and the English Stage, 1740–1820* (Cambridge University Press, 2019).

OLIVER GOLDSMITH IN CONTEXT

EDITED BY

MICHAEL GRIFFIN

University of Limerick

DAVID O'SHAUGHNESSY

University of Galway

CAMBRIDGE
UNIVERSITY PRESS

Shaftesbury Road, Cambridge CB2 8EA, United Kingdom

One Liberty Plaza, 20th Floor, New York, NY 10006, USA

477 Williamstown Road, Port Melbourne, VIC 3207, Australia

314–321, 3rd Floor, Plot 3, Splendor Forum, Jasola District Centre,
New Delhi – 110025, India

103 Penang Road, #05–06/07, Visioncrest Commercial, Singapore 238467

Cambridge University Press is part of Cambridge University Press & Assessment,
a department of the University of Cambridge.

We share the University's mission to contribute to society through the pursuit of
education, learning and research at the highest international levels of excellence.

www.cambridge.org
Information on this title: www.cambridge.org/9781316518915

DOI: 10.1017/9781009004015

First published 2024

A catalogue record for this publication is available from the British Library.

A Cataloging-in-Publication data record for this book is available from the Library of Congress

ISBN 978-1-316-51891-5 Hardback

In memory of
Anne Griffin

Contents

Illustrations

Notes on Contributors

MELISSA BAILES is Associate Professor of English at Tulane University, specializing in British literature of the long eighteenth century, the history of science, and women's writing. Her book *Questioning Nature: British Women's Scientific Writing and Literary Originality, 1750–1830* (2017) won the British Society for Literature and Science Book Prize. Her second book, *Regenerating Romanticism: Botany, Sensibility, and Originality in British Literature, 1750–1830*, was published in 2023.

REBECCA ANNE BARR is Associate Professor in the Faculty of English, University of Cambridge, and a fellow of Jesus College. Her research focuses on gender, sexuality, and fiction in the long eighteenth century, with occasional forays into twentieth-century and contemporary culture. She has published widely on masculinity, sexual violence, and the history of the novel, and has also co-edited two collections of essays: *Ireland and Masculinities in History* (2019) and *Bellies, Bowels, and Entrails in the Eighteenth Century* (2018).

JOHN BERGIN is Adjunct Associate Professor in the School of History, University College Dublin. He has published on aspects of Irish history in the late seventeenth and eighteenth centuries. His special interests include Irish Catholic life in this period, Irish lobbying in London, and the Irish population of London.

WILL BOWERS is Senior Lecturer in Eighteenth-Century Literature and Thought at Queen Mary University of London. He has published essays on poets including Byron, Milton, Percy Bysshe Shelley, and William Wordsworth, and his first book, *The Italian Idea* (Cambridge University Press, 2020), won the European Society for the Study of English First Book Prize in 2022. He is an editor on the final two volumes of the Longman Annotated English Poets: Shelley series which will be published in 2024, and is currently editing William Cowper's *Poems, Hymns, and Letters.*

MICHAEL BROWN holds the Chair in Irish Scottish and Enlightenment History at the University of Aberdeen. He is the author of biographical studies of Francis Hutcheson and John Toland and of *The Irish Enlightenment* (2016). He is currently writing a study entitled *Making Up Britain in the Eighteenth Century.*

DAVID CLARE is Lecturer in Drama and Theatre Studies at Mary Immaculate College, University of Limerick. His books include the monographs *Bernard Shaw's Irish Outlook* (2016) and *Irish Anglican Literature and Drama: Hybridity and Discord* (2021) and the edited collections *The Gate Theatre, Dublin: Inspiration and Craft* (2018), *The Golden Thread: Irish Women Playwrights, 1716–2016*, 2 volumes (2021), and *Across Borders and Time: Jonathan Swift* (2022). He is also curator of the www.classicirishplays.com database funded by the Irish Research Council.

NORMA CLARKE is Emeritus Professor in English Literature at Kingston University. Her books include *Queen of the Wits: A Life of Laetitia Pilkington* (2008) and *Brothers of the Quill: Oliver Goldsmith in Grub Street* (2016). She published a family memoir, *Not Speaking*, in 2019 and continues to speak and write about memoir as a form. She is a regular reviewer for the *TLS*, the *Literary Review*, and other journals.

BEN DEW is Associate Professor of Cultural History at the Centre for Arts, Memory and Communities, Coventry University. His research is principally concerned with the history of historical writing in Britain. He is the author of *Commerce, Finance and Statecraft: Histories of England, 1600–1780* (2018) and the co-editor of *Historical Writing in Britain, 1688–1830* (2014) and *Polish Culture in Britain: Literature and History, 1772 to the Present* (2023).

AILEEN DOUGLAS is Professor of Eighteenth-Century Studies and a Fellow at Trinity College Dublin, where she teaches in the School of English. With Ian Campbell Ross she has co-edited *The Vicar of Wakefield* for *The Collected Works of Oliver Goldsmith* (Cambridge University Press, 2024). She has published widely on Irish writing of the long eighteenth century, most recently on Maria Edgeworth's writing for children; essays include '"What Follows": Maria Edgeworth's Works for Older Children', in *Women's Literary Education, 1690–1850*, edited by Jessica Lim and Louise Joy (2023). Other publications include *Work in Hand: Script, Print, and Writing, 1690–1840* (2017).

TIMOTHY ERWIN is Professor of English at the University of Nevada, Las Vegas, and the author of *Textual Vision: Augustan Design and the Invention of Eighteenth-Century British Culture* (2015), a study of visual imagery in Pope, Johnson, Hogarth, Fielding, Richardson, and Austen. Recent articles include 'Alexander Pope and a Carracci Venus at the Court of James II and Mary of Modena' in the *Huntington Library Quarterly* (2020), and 'Discours sur l'Œil: *Roméo et Juliette* et *Marriage A-la-Mode* de William Hogarth', in the *Actes des Congrès de la Société Française Shakespeare* (2022).

LYNN FESTA is Professor of English at Rutgers University. She is the author of *Fiction without Humanity: Person, Animal, Thing in Early Enlightenment Literature and Culture* (2019) and *Sentimental Figures of Empire in Eighteenth-Century Britain and France* (2006).

DAVID A. FLEMING is Senior Lecturer in History at the University of Limerick. His research concentrates on the social and political development of eighteenth-century Ireland, including politics, poverty, associational behaviour, and prostitution. He is the author of *Politics and Provincial People: Sligo and Limerick 1691–1761* (2010), *The University of Limerick: A History* (2012), and *Edmund Sexton Pery: The Politics of Virtue and Intrigue in Eighteenth-Century Ireland* (2023).

PAUL GORING is Professor of British Literature and Culture at the Norwegian University of Science and Technology in Trondheim. He specializes in eighteenth-century studies and has particular interests in theatre history, London-Irish theatre workers, news and its connections to imaginative literature, eighteenth-century lotteries, and the life and works of Laurence Sterne. He is the author of *The Rhetoric of Sensibility in Eighteenth-Century Culture* (Cambridge University Press, 2005) and *Eighteenth-Century Literature and Culture* (2008) and has edited many volumes including *Lives of Shakespearian Actors: Charles Macklin* (2008), *Travelling Chronicles: News and Newspapers from the Early Modern Period to the Eighteenth Century* (2018), Sterne's *A Sentimental Journey*, and Samuel Johnson's *Rasselas*.

DUSTIN GRIFFIN is Professor of English Emeritus at New York University. He is the author of eight books on English writers of the long eighteenth century. He previously wrote on Goldsmith in *Literary*

Patronage in England, 1650–1800 (Cambridge University Press, 1996), *Patriotism and Poetry in Eighteenth-Century Britain* (Cambridge University Press, 2002), and *Authorship in the Long Eighteenth Century* (2014).

MICHAEL GRIFFIN is Professor of English at the University of Limerick. He is the author of *Enlightenment in Ruins: The Geographies of Oliver Goldsmith* (2013) and the editor of *The Collected Poems of Laurence Whyte* (2016). With David O'Shaughnessy, he is co-editor of *The Letters of Oliver Goldsmith* (Cambridge University Press, 2018) and a General Editor of *The Collected Works of Oliver Goldsmith*, 8 volumes (Cambridge University Press, 2024–).

MAUREEN HARKIN is Professor and Chair of English at Reed College. Her primary research interests are eighteenth-century and Romantic-era literature, especially the work of Adam Smith, Henry Mackenzie, and Oliver Goldsmith. She is the author of numerous essays on Adam Smith, sentimental fiction, and eighteenth- and nineteenth-century literature and its contexts. She is the editor of Mackenzie's *The Man of Feeling* (2005) and is working on a study of Adam Smith's relation to eighteenth-century literary culture.

MOYRA HASLETT is Professor of Eighteenth-Century and Romantic Literature at Queen's University Belfast. Her most recent publications include two edited collections: *Irish Literature in Transition, 1700–1780* (Cambridge University Press, 2020) and *The Oxford Handbook of Irish Song, 1100–1850*, which she is co-editing with Conor Caldwell and Lillis O'Laoire. Her chapter on Goldsmith here (Chapter 29) comes out of that work on the cultures of Irish song up to and including the eighteenth century. Previously she acted as one of the general editors of the Four Courts Press Early Irish Fiction series, together with Aileen Douglas and Ian Campbell Ross, editing Thomas Amory's *The Life of John Buncle, Esq* (2011) for that series.

ROBERT W. JONES is Professor of Eighteenth-Century Studies at the University of Leeds. He is the author of several books and articles on the political and literary culture of Georgian Britain. His work has often explored ideas of empire and the responses of Irish writers and political figures, notably Edmund Burke, Richard Brinsley Sheridan, and Thomas Moore. His research interests are currently focused on an edition of *The Political Works of Richard Brinsley Sheridan* (co-edited with Martyn J. Powell), and a monograph, *The Theatre of Richard Brinsley Sheridan: Performance and Politics at Drury Lane.*

JARLATH KILLEEN is Professor in Victorian Literature in the School of English, Trinity College Dublin. His most recent monograph is *Imagining the Irish Child: Discourses of Childhood in Irish Anglican Writing of the Seventeenth and Eighteenth Centuries* (2023).

MEGAN KITCHING is a research assistant in the School of Arts at the University of Otago and an editorial assistant at Otago Polytechnic in Dunedin. She holds a PhD in eighteenth-century English literature from Queen Mary University of London. She has published on eighteenth-century philosophical poetry, landscape literature and aesthetics, and Oliver Goldsmith's prose personae.

MARÍA LOSADA-FRIEND is Senior Lecturer in the Department of Philology and Translation at the University Pablo de Olavide. Her lines of research within comparative literature studies focus on Irish, British, and American narratives of the eighteenth to the twentieth centuries and she has published a number of chapters and articles on Goldsmith. She co-edited *Dreaming the Future: New Horizons/Old Barriers in 21st-Century Ireland* (2011) and *Words of Crisis/Crisis of Words: Ireland and the Representation of Critical Times* (2016). A member of the Spanish Association of Irish Studies and the Spanish James Joyce Society, she was the coordinator of the 'Irish Studies in Spain' section in *Estudios Irlandeses/Journal of Irish Studies* (2018–20).

ALFRED LUTZ teaches in the English Department at Middle Tennessee State University. He is the author of essays on Oliver Goldsmith, Sarah Scott, Tobias Smollett, and W. G. Sebald in journals such as *Modern Language Quarterly, Studies in English Literature, Studies in Philology,* and *Studies in the Novel.*

EUN KYUNG MIN is Professor of English at Seoul National University. She is the author of *China and the Writing of English Literary Modernity, 1690–1770* (Cambridge University Press, 2018) and has published widely on eighteenth-century aesthetics, ethics, and cultural history. Her work has been supported by the International Society for Eighteenth-Century Studies, Lewis Walpole Library, Clark Library, Radcliffe Institute for Advanced Study, and Korea Research Foundation. She is currently working on theories of obligation and narratives of disappointment in seventeenth- and eighteenth-century English literature.

IAN NEWMAN is Associate Professor of English at the University of Notre Dame, and a fellow of the Keough-Naughton Institute for Irish Studies. He has published widely on eighteenth- and nineteenth-century British and Irish literature and culture. He is the author of *The Romantic Tavern: Literature and Conviviality in the Age of Revolution* (Cambridge University Press, 2019) and a co-editor of *Charles Dibdin and Late Georgian Culture* (2018), and (with David O'Shaughnessy) *Charles Macklin and the Theatres of London* (2022). His current research interests include various aspects of the song cultures of the eighteenth and nineteenth centuries.

DAVID O'SHAUGHNESSY is Professor of Eighteenth-Century Studies at the University of Galway. He is the author of *William Godwin and the Theatre* (2010) and has published widely on eighteenth-century theatre. Recent publications include the edited volumes *Ireland, Enlightenment and the English Stage, 1740–1820* (Cambridge University Press, 2019), *Charles Macklin and the Theatres of London* (with Ian Newman, 2022), and *The Censorship of Eighteenth-Century Theatre: Playhouses and Prohibition, 1737–1843* (Cambridge University Press, 2023). With Michael Griffin, he is the co-editor of *The Letters of Oliver Goldsmith* (Cambridge University Press, 2018) and a General Editor of *The Collected Works of Oliver Goldsmith*, 8 volumes (Cambridge University Press, 2024–).

MANUSHAG N. POWELL is Professor of English at Purdue University. She is the author of *Performing Authorship in Eighteenth-Century English Periodicals* (2012), co-author of *British Pirates in Print and Performance* (with Fred Burwick, 2015), and co-editor of *Women's Periodicals and Print Culture in Britain, 1690–1820* (with Jennie Batchelor, 2018). She edited the Broadview edition of Defoe's *Captain Singleton* (2019) and has published widely on pirates and periodicalists, usually not at the same time.

AMY PRENDERGAST is Assistant Professor in Eighteenth-Century Studies at Trinity College Dublin, having previously held the positions of Marie Skłodowska-Curie Research Fellow at Queen's University Belfast and Irish Research Council Postdoctoral Fellow and Teaching Fellow, also at Trinity. Her research expertise in the long eighteenth century centres on the areas of women's writing, life writing, writing from Ireland, and Franco-Irish connections and cultural transfers. She is author of *Literary Salons across Britain and Ireland in the Long Eighteenth Century* (2015), as well as articles and chapters in *European Journal of Life Writing, Life Writing, Women's Writing, Eighteenth-Century Ireland,* and *Irish Literature in Transition, 1700–1780* (Cambridge University Press, 2020). Her second monograph, *Mere Bagatelles: Women's Diaries in Ireland, 1760–1810,* is forthcoming.

JAMES BRYANT REEVES is Assistant Professor of English at Texas State University, where he teaches classes on mythology, satire, and eighteenth-century literature. His research focuses on religion in the long eighteenth century and has been published in *Eighteenth-Century Studies, Eighteenth-Century Fiction,* the *Keats-Shelley Journal,* and elsewhere. His first book, *Godless Fictions in the Eighteenth Century: A Literary History of Atheism,* was published in 2020 by Cambridge University Press.

IAN CAMPBELL ROSS is Emeritus Professor of Eighteenth-Century Studies at Trinity College Dublin. With Aileen Douglas, he has co-edited *The Vicar of Wakefield* (Cambridge University Press, 2024) for *The Collected Works of Oliver Goldsmith.* Other work includes essays in *Jonathan Swift in Context* (Cambridge University Press, 2024); the *Cambridge Guide to the Eighteenth-Century Novel 1660–1820* (forthcoming); 'Maria Edgeworth and the Culture of Improvement', in Fiorenzo Fantaccini and Raffaella Leproni, eds., *'Still Blundering into Sense': Maria Edgeworth, Her Context, Her Legacy* (2019); '"We Irish": Writing and Identity from Berkeley to Burke', in *Irish Literature in Transition 1700–1780* (Cambridge University Press, 2020); 'Crime Fiction', in the *Oxford Handbook to Modern Irish Fiction* (2020); and *Umbria: A Cultural History* (5th ed., 2020).

GILLIAN RUSSELL is Professor Emerita of Eighteenth-Century Literature at the University of York. She has written widely on the topics of theatre, sociability, gender, war, and print culture of the Georgian period. Her most recent book is *The Ephemeral Eighteenth Century: Print, Sociability and the Cultures of Collecting* (2020). She is currently working on a study of printed ephemera and radicalism post 1815 and on an edition of Charles Lamb's *Specimens of English Dramatic Poets,* general editor Gregory Dart.

KERRY SINANAN is Assistant Professor of Pre–1800 Global Literature and Culture at the University of Winnipeg. She specializes in the literature and culture of the Black Atlantic, Caribbean slavery and race, and the global dimensions of Black resistance and abolition up to the present.

She has published widely on these areas including a co-edited special issue for *Eighteenth-Century Fiction* on *The Woman of Colour* (1808) and the volume *Austen after 200: New Reading Spaces*. She has contributed two recent articles in special forums on Black and Indigenous literature, in *Studies in Romanticism*: 'Beads of Resistance: Reading Black Diasporic Indigeneity in the Black Atlantic' and 'Mary Prince's Back and her Critique of Anti-slavery Sympathy'. She is President of the Early Caribbean Society and her new edition of *The History of Mary Prince* (1831) is forthcoming.

RICHARD C. TAYLOR is the author of *Goldsmith as Journalist* (1993), as well as essays on Goldsmith's fiction and drama, eighteenth-century British culture, and postcolonial literatures. He taught a variety of courses in British literary history and directed programmes in transnational and multi-ethnic literatures at East Carolina University from 1989 until his retirement in 2021.

KATHERINE TURNER is Professor and Chair of English at Mary Baldwin University in Virginia. She has published widely on travel writing, women's writing, eighteenth-century poetry, and eighteenth-century afterlives. She has edited Laurence Sterne's *A Sentimental Journey* for Broadview Press and several volumes of women's memoirs for Pickering & Chatto. Recent articles include explorations of William Cowper and the newspapers, Cowper's influence on African American slave narratives, and Daphne du Maurier's historical fiction.

JAMES WARD is Lecturer in Eighteenth-Century Literature at Ulster University. He has published widely on Jonathan Swift and eighteenth-century literature, as well as on the reception and recreation of this period in modern screen, print, and performance media. Recent work includes *Memory and Enlightenment: Cultural Afterlives of the Long Eighteenth Century* (2018) and essays on the cultural representation of Irish psychiatric asylums and on Black Enlightenment lives in film and television.

JAMES WATT is Professor in the Department of English and Related Literature and the Centre for Eighteenth-Century Studies at the University of York, and is currently the director of the Centre. His latest book is *British Orientalisms, 1759–1835* (Cambridge University Press, 2019), and he is the editor of *The Citizen of the World* for *The Collected Works of Oliver Goldsmith* (Cambridge University Press, 2024).

NIGEL WOOD is Professor of Literature at Loughborough University. His publications in eighteenth-century studies include studies of Swift for the Harvester New Readings series (1986). He has edited the *Longman Critical Reader on Swift* (1999), a selection of Frances Burney's diaries and journals (1989), and an Oxford World's Classics edition of *She Stoops to Conquer and Other Comedies* (2008). His latest book is *Shakespeare and Reception Theory* (2020) and he is currently engaged on a life of Alexander Pope.

Preface

Oliver Goldsmith (1728–74) came to London in 1756 and over the remainder of his brief life he made one of the most substantial contributions to eighteenth-century writing. He began his career writing reviews and essays for periodicals such as the *Monthly Review* and the *Critical Review* before branching out into poetry, fiction, drama, history, and natural history writing. Few, if any, writers in English can claim to have written masterpieces, acknowledged as such then and now, in the major literary genres. His fictional tale *The Vicar of Wakefield* (1766) won admirers and imitators across Europe, his poems *The Traveller* (1764) and *The Deserted Village* (1770) have spawned a multitude of critical and creative responses, while *She Stoops to Conquer* (1773) remains one of the great comedies of the century and continues to be performed around the world today. Goldsmith was the first Professor of Ancient History at the Royal Academy; his histories of England, Rome, and Greece were read well into the nineteenth century. His *History of the Earth, and Animated Nature* was published posthumously in eight volumes and was regularly abridged in the decades that followed. He was a remarkably prolific writer, whose work across the genres has been celebrated.

Goldsmith came from the midlands of Ireland and was educated in Dublin, Edinburgh, and Leiden; he travelled through a number of European countries before he settled in England. Cultivating the acquaintance of Samuel Johnson, Joshua Reynolds, and Edmund Burke, among others, Goldsmith found himself as an Irishman with a European perspective at the very heart of London's world of letters. His contributions to literary culture emerged during the Seven Years' War (1756–63) and would reflect upon the Britain that would emerge in that conflict's wake as the major global state actor. His own ascent from impoverished hack writer struggling against prejudices to literary fame represented for many Irish the difficulties and possibilities that London offered. As a recognition of his achievements, his statue was erected outside the front gate of his alma mater, Trinity College Dublin, in 1864 alongside that of his friend Edmund Burke. Few Irish writers have had such a profound impact on British literary culture across three centuries.

This volume is divided into four parts that capture multiple aspects of his life and works. The first, 'Life and Career', assesses the biographical accounts we have of Goldsmith and the small body of correspondence he left behind. Literary lives are often marked by great friendships and mentorship as well as bitter feuds: Goldsmith's was no different and these are examined here. 'Social, Cultural, and Intellectual Contexts' looks at a range of topics, ideas, and institutions with which Goldsmith engaged. There are chapters on his social milieu, be it the Irish diaspora in London or Johnson's Literary Club. There are discussions of his university life, the library he left behind, and our sense of him as a writer engaged with cosmopolitanism and Enlightenment. Chapters look at how issues such as marriage, gender, religion, and race are treated in his works and do not shy away from revealing a more problematic Goldsmith to the modern reader. The context of the Seven Years' War and topics such as empire and liberty are also examined.

The third part of the volume, 'Literary Contexts', looks at a compendium of Goldsmith's literary contexts. From the major literary genres of poetry, drama, and fiction to his history writing, periodical reviewing, and translation, all aspects of Goldsmith's writing are covered. Orientalism, sentimentalism, and satire are major thematic strands of his oeuvre, but we also offer chapters that engage with music and song, and the sister arts. Our final part, 'Critical Fortunes and Afterlives', makes the rich afterlife of Goldsmith abundantly clear. Although he died in his mid-forties, his literary achievement was substantial, appreciation for his works sustained from the end of the eighteenth century right through to the twentieth and up to today. These final chapters convey the weight of Oliver Goldsmith's thought and art for our contemporary moment and are an appropriate confirmation of the need for a new and expanded scholarly edition of his works.

Chronology

1718 May: Anglican minister the
Reverend Charles Goldsmith (*c.*1693–
1747) marries Ann Jones (*c.*1697–
1770), daughter of the Reverend
Oliver Jones, after whom Goldsmith
is named.

1718 October: death of Thomas Parnell.
November: Voltaire, *Œdipe*.
December: War of the Quadruple
Alliance begins.

1719 March: Declaratory Act confirming
Westminster's powers in Ireland
passed. April: Daniel Defoe, *Robinson
Crusoe*. June: death of Joseph Addison.

1720 January: Spain joins Quadruple
Alliance and war with Spain ends.
October–November: South Sea
Company share prices collapse,
bringing financial ruin to many
investors.

1721 April: Walpole administration.

1722 January: Defoe, *Moll Flanders*.
March: Defoe, *A Journal of the Plague
Year*. May: Atterbury Jacobite plot
uncovered. Leading Jacobites
arrested. July: William Wood granted
patent to mint copper coins in
Ireland.

1724 March: first of Jonathan Swift's
Drapier's Letters responds to Wood's
halfpence. April: John Carteret
becomes Lord Lieutenant of Ireland.

1725 March: Alexander Pope's edition of
Shakespeare. April: Pope's translation
of Homer's *Odyssey*. September:
Wood's halfpence cancelled.

1726 October: *Gulliver's Travels*.

1727 February: conflict breaks out
between Britain and Spain. June:
death of George I, accession of
George II.

(cont.)

1728 November: Birth on 10 November of Oliver Goldsmith, probably at Pallas, Co. Westmeath, Ireland, fifth child and second son of Charles and Ann Goldsmith. Charles is appointed curate in Kilkenny West shortly after Oliver's birth. The Goldsmiths subsequently move to Lissoy, to the southeast of Pallas, along the Longford/Westmeath border.

1735–45 Goldsmith is educated through various diocesan schools in the Longford/Roscommon region.

1728 January: John Gay, *The Beggar's Opera.* May: Pope, *Dunciad.* October: Samuel Johnson enrols in Pembroke College, Oxford.

1729 April: Pope, *Dunciad Variorum.* October: Swift, *A Modest Proposal.*

1731 January: Edward Cave's *Gentleman's Magazine* begins.

1732 December: death of Gay.

1733 February: Pope, *Essay on Man*, 4 epistles–1734. May: Eliza Haywood, *The Opera of Operas.*

1734 November: George Faulkner's Dublin edition of Swift's *Works*, 4 vols.–1735.

1736 July: anti-Irish riots in East London.

1738 May: Johnson, *London: A Poem.*

1739 October: outbreak of War of Jenkins's Ear between Britain and Spain.

1740 November: Samuel Richardson, *Pamela, or Virtue Rewarded.* December: War of the Austrian Succession begins.

1741 April: Henry Fielding, *Shamela.* October: David Garrick's stage debut at Goodman's Fields Theatre as Richard III.

1742 January: William Collins, *Persian Eclogues.* February: Carteret administration; Fielding, *Joseph Andrews.* March: Pope, *The New Dunciad.* June: Edward Young, *The Complaint, or, Night Thoughts*, 9 parts–1745.

1744 February: Johnson, *Life of Savage.* March: France declares war on Britain. April: Haywood's *Female Spectator* begins. May: death of Pope; Sarah Fielding, *The Adventures of David Simple.* November: Pelham administration.

1745–50 Goldsmith studies at Trinity College Dublin. It is a largely unhappy experience but he graduates with a BA in February 1750.

1745 August: Jacobite Rebellion. October: death of Swift.

(*cont.*)

1746 February: Pelham administration resigns but quickly reforms. April: defeat of Jacobites at Culloden.

1747 April: Garrick and James Lacy acquire ownership of the patent for Drury Lane Theatre Royal; Thomas Warton, *The Pleasures of Melancholy*. November: Richardson, *Clarissa*, 7 vols.–1748.

1748 January: Tobias Smollett, *Roderick Random*; Robert Dodsley's *A Collection of Poems*. February: Laetitia Pilkington, *Memoirs*, 3 vols.–1754. April: Mary Leapor, *Poems upon Several Occasions*, 2 vols.–1751. November: Montesquieu, *L'Esprit des Lois*.

1749 January: Johnson, *The Vanity of Human Wishes*. February: Fielding, *Tom Jones*. May: Ralph Griffiths's *Monthly Review* begins. September: Buffon, *Histoire Naturelle*, 36 vols.–1804.

1750–2 Goldsmith works as a tutor in Roscommon. Various efforts are made to emigrate to America and to London but with no success.

1750 March: Johnson, *Rambler* begins. May: adoption of reformed Gregorian Calendar.

1751 February: Thomas Gray, *Elegy Written in a Country Churchyard*; Smollett, *Peregrine Pickle*. June: Denis Diderot commences the *Encyclopédie*. October: Haywood, *The History of Miss Betsy Thoughtless*.

1752–3 Goldsmith reads medicine at the University of Edinburgh with financial assistance from relatives, including brother-in-law Daniel Hodson and uncle Thomas Contarine.

1752 March: Charlotte Lennox, *The Female Quixote*.

1753 February: Smollett, *Ferdinand Count Fathom*. December: William Hogarth, *The Analysis of Beauty*.

1754–5 Goldsmith continues his medical studies at Leiden University in Holland.

1754 March: Newcastle administration. November: David Hume's *History of England*, 6 vols.–1762.

1755 April: Johnson's *Dictionary of the English Language*.

1755–6 Goldsmith journeys around Europe, largely on foot, debating and playing music to support himself. He visits Flanders, France, Germany, Switzerland, and Italy.

(*cont.*)

1756–7 Goldsmith arrives in London in February 1756. He works at various jobs: as an assistant to an apothecary, as a physician in Southwark, and as an usher at a boy's school in Peckham in Surrey. He may also have been a proofreader in Samuel Richardson's printing house. In April 1757 he begins work at the *Monthly Review*, edited by Ralph Griffiths.

1758 Goldsmith plans to travel to Coromandel, on the south-eastern coast of the Indian subcontinent, as a physician with the East India Company, but his application to work as a hospital mate is unsuccessful.

1759 He begins to contribute to Tobias Smollett's *Critical Review* in January. Meets Reverend Thomas Percy in February. Following the publication of *An Enquiry into the Present State of Polite Learning in Europe* in April, Goldsmith's literary acquaintance comes to include Edmund Burke and Samuel Johnson. However, the work is savagely reviewed by William Kenrick, the first attack of a long-running feud. Goldsmith seeks a number of Irish subscriptions for the *Enquiry*. He writes *The Bee*, his own periodical, in October and November.

1759–61 Goldsmith writes essays for a number of periodicals: the *Busy Body*, the *Weekly Magazine*, the *Royal Magazine*, and the *Lady's Magazine*. In January 1760 he begins his 'Chinese Letters' series in the *Public Ledger*, published by John Newbery. The series continues until August 1761.

1762 Goldsmith contributes essays to *Lloyd's Evening Post* in the first half of

1756 March: Smollett's *Critical Review* begins. April–May: Seven Years' War with France begins. May: Edmund Burke, *Vindication of Natural Society*. June: loss of Minorca. November: Pitt-Devonshire administration. December: Voltaire, *Essai sur les mœurs et l'esprit des nations*.

1757 April: Burke, *Enquiry into the Origin of our Ideas of the Sublime and the Beautiful*; Smollett, *A Complete History of England*, 9 vols.–1765. May: Horace Walpole, *Letter from Xo Ho*. July: Pitt-Newcastle administration.

1758 April: Johnson, *Idler* begins.

1759 January: Voltaire, *Candide*. April: Johnson, *Rasselas*. May: Young, *Conjectures on Original Composition*. December: Laurence Sterne, *Tristram Shandy*, 9 vols.–1767; Arthur Murphy, *The Orphan of China*.

1760 January: Smollett, *British Magazine* begins, featuring first instalment of his *Launcelot Greaves*. June: Macpherson, *Fragments of Ancient Poetry*. October: death of George II, accession of George III.

1761 March: Charles Churchill, *Rosciad*. July: death of Richardson. October: Bute-Newcastle administration.

1762 February: Frances Sheridan, *Memoirs of Miss Sidney Bidulph*. June:

the year. His 'Chinese Letters' are published as *The Citizen of the World* in May. Newbery contracts him to write what would become *A Survey of Experimental Philosophy*, eventually published two years after the author's death. This work signals a marked shift in his writing towards professional work in history and popular science. Between May and November Newbery publishes *Plutarch's Lives*, which Goldsmith had completed with translator Joseph Collyer, and in October *The Life of Richard Nash*. After some effort by Johnson, Newbery also acquires the rights for Goldsmith's novel *The Vicar of Wakefield*: he promptly resells a third share of the rights to Benjamin Collins and another third to William Strahan.

1764 In February Goldsmith becomes a founding member, with Samuel Johnson, David Garrick, Edmund Burke, Christopher Nugent, and others, of The Club. His *History of England, in a Series of Letters from a Nobleman to His Son* is published in June. Probably in the summer he composes an oratorio libretto titled *The Captivity*. Newbery publishes his major poem *The Traveller, or a Prospect of Society*, dedicated to his brother Henry, in December: it is the first work published under Goldsmith's own name.

1765 Revised editions of *The Traveller* appear from March to August, as does, in June, a collection of Goldsmith's *Essays*. An early version of his ballad *Edwin and Angelina* is privately printed for the Duchess of Northumberland.

1766 *The Vicar of Wakefield* is published in March. Goldsmith develops friendship with the Horneck sisters,

John Wilkes's *North Briton*, in which the Bute administration is attacked, begins. October: Sarah Scott, *Millenium Hall* (in which Goldsmith may have had an editorial hand).

1763 February: Treaty of Paris ends the Seven Years' War. April: Grenville administration; arrest warrant issued for Wilkes for attacking the king in *North Briton*. May: Mary Wortley Montagu, *Letters ... written during her travels in Europe, Asia, and Africa*. December: Wilkes goes into exile following publication of *An Essay on Woman*.

1764 May: James Grainger, *The Sugar-Cane*. July: Voltaire, *Dictionnaire Philosophique*. December: Horace Walpole, *Castle of Otranto*.

1765 January: Elizabeth Griffith, *The Platonic Wife*. February: Thomas Percy, *Reliques of Ancient English Poetry*. March: American Stamp Act. April: *The History of Goody Two Shoes* (in which Goldsmith may have had a hand). July: first Rockingham administration. October: Johnson's edition of Shakespeare.

1766 February: George Colman and Garrick, *The Clandestine Marriage*. March: repeal of Stamp Act. May:

(*cont.*)

Catherine and Mary, through Joshua Reynolds. A second edition of Goldsmith's *Essays* and his anthology *Poems for Young Ladies* appear, in April and December respectively.

1767 Goldsmith's comedy, *The Good Natur'd Man*, is submitted to George Colman after David Garrick is equivocal about the play's prospects. Goldsmith rebuts an accusation of plagiarism made by Kenrick in a letter to *St. James's Chronicle*. Goldsmith's anthology, *The Beauties of English Poesy*, appears in April.

1768 *The Good Natur'd Man* is first performed at Covent Garden on 29 January. Johnson supplies the prologue. William Griffin publishes the play in February. Goldsmith's brother Henry dies in May.

1769 William Griffin contracts Goldsmith to write a natural history in February. His *Roman History* is published in May. Thomas Davies contracts Goldsmith to write a history of England in June. He is appointed Professor of Ancient History at the Royal Academy in December.

1770 *The Deserted Village* is published in May. It is dedicated to Sir Joshua Reynolds. William Hodson, son of Daniel, arrives in London. Goldsmith tries to find his nephew a place. Goldsmith spends six weeks in France with the Horneck sisters and their mother. Goldsmith's life of the Irish poet Thomas Parnell is published in July, his life of Bolingbroke in December.

1771 January: Richard Cumberland, *The West Indian*. April: Henry Mackenzie, *The Man of Feeling*. June: Smollett, *Humphry Clinker*. September: death of Smollett.

Smollett, *Travels through France and Italy*. July: Chatham administration.

1767: June: duties imposed on import of tea into America. July: Sheridan, *The History of Nourjahad*; George Colman, Thomas Harris, John Rutherford, and William Powell acquire the patent to Covent Garden Theatre Royal.

1768 January: Hugh Kelly, *False Delicacy*. February: Sterne, *A Sentimental Journey through France and Italy*. March: Wilkes elected MP for Middlesex. May: Wilkes imprisoned for attacking the King in print. October: Grafton administration. December: death of Newbery.

1769 January: the letters of Junius (–1772), possibly by Sir Philip Francis, begin in the *Public Advertiser*. February: Wilkes expelled from Commons; Lennox, *The Sister*.
July: Wilkes reinstated.

1770 January: North administration; Kelly, *Word to the Wise*. March: Boston Massacre. April: Burke, *Thoughts on the Causes of the Present Discontents*.

1771 January: Richard Cumberland, *The West Indian*. April: Henry Mackenzie, *The Man of Feeling*. June: Smollett, *Humphry Clinker*. September: death of Smollett.

1772 May: William Chambers, *A Dissertation on Oriental Gardening*. June:

(*cont.*)

1772 Goldsmith's *Threnodia Augustalis*, in memory of the Princess Dowager, Augusta, is performed in February.

1773 *She Stoops to Conquer* is performed at Covent Garden on 15 March with David Garrick providing the prologue and John Quick as Tony Lumpkin. Later the same month he assaults Thomas Evans in response to an ad hominem attack in the *London Packet*. The success of *She Stoops* leads Goldsmith to write *The Grumbler*, a one-act comic afterpiece, for Quick's benefit night in May.

1774 Goldsmith dies on 4 April having suffered renal infection and fever. His poem *Retaliation*, a satiric riposte to some teasing he received at The Club earlier that year, is published a fortnight after his death. John Nourse publishes Goldsmith's *History of the Earth, and Animated Nature* in July. His *Grecian History* is published shortly after. The second edition of his *History of England* is announced in December.

1776 *The Haunch of Venison: A Poetical Epistle to Lord Clare* is published in May. Goldsmith's *Survey of Experimental Philosophy*, a two-volume compendium of science, is published in July. His friends arrange for a monument by Joseph Nollekens to be erected in his memory at Westminster Abbey.

Samuel Foote, *The Nabob*. July: William Kenrick, *Love in the Suds*.

1773 September: Phillis Wheatley, *Poems on Various Subjects*. December: Boston Tea Party protest against importation of East India Company tea into America.

1774 September: First Continental Congress in Philadelphia agrees to defy British coercion of America. August: George III proclaims rebellion in America.

1775 January: Johnson, *Journey to the Western Islands of Scotland*; Richard Brinsley Sheridan, *The Rivals*. May: Second Continental Congress in Philadelphia names George Washington commander-in-chief of American forces.

1776 January: Thomas Paine, *Common Sense*. February: Edward Gibbon, *History of the Decline and Fall of the Roman Empire*, 6 vols.–1788; Hannah Cowley, *The Runaway*. March: Adam Smith, *Wealth of Nations*. July: American Declaration of Independence.

Abbreviations

For frequently cited texts by Goldsmith, we give citations from editions used as copy-texts for the ongoing *Cambridge Edition of The Collected Works of Oliver Goldsmith*. For references to non-abbreviated sources in these chapters, publisher details are included only for post-1850 works.

Clarke, *Brothers of the Quill*	Norma Clarke, *Brothers of the Quill: Oliver Goldsmith in Grub Street*. Cambridge, MA: Harvard University Press, 2016.
Critical Heritage	*Oliver Goldsmith: The Critical Heritage*. London: Routledge, 1996.
Animated Nature	*An History of the Earth, and Animated Nature*, 8 vols. London: Printed for John Nourse, 1774.
Bee	*The Bee*. London: Printed for J. Wilkie, 1759.
Citizen	*The Citizen of the World; or, Letters from a Chinese Philosopher, Residing in London, to His friends in the East*, 2 vols. London: Printed for the Author and sold by J. Newbery, 1762.
Deserted Village	*The Deserted Village. The Fourth Edition*. London: Printed for W. Griffin, 1770.
Enquiry	*An Enquiry into the Present State of Polite Learning in Europe*. London: Printed for R. and J. Dodsley, 1759.
Good Natur'd Man	*The Good Natur'd Man: A Comedy*. London: Printed for W. Griffin, 1768.
Retaliation	*Retaliation: A Poem. Including Epitaphs on Some of the Most Distinguished Wits of This Metropolis. The Fifth Edition, Corrected*. London: Printed for G. Kearsly, 1774.

Stoops	*She Stoops to Conquer: Or, The Mistakes of a Night. A Comedy.* London: Printed for F. Newbery, 1773.
Survey	*A Survey of Experimental Philosophy.* London: Printed for T. Carnan and F. Newbery jun., 1776.
Traveller	*The Traveller; or, A Prospect of Society. The Sixth Edition Corrected.* London: Printed for T. Carnan and F. Newbery, jun., 1770.
Vicar	*The Vicar of Wakefield: A Tale.* Salisbury: Printed by B. Collins, for F. Newbery, 1766.
Ginger	John Ginger, *The Notable Man: The Life and Times of Oliver Goldsmith.* London: Hamish Hamilton, 1977.
Letters	*The Letters of Oliver Goldsmith*, ed. Michael Griffin and David O'Shaughnessy Cambridge: Cambridge University Press, 2018.
LOJ	James Boswell, *Life of Johnson*, ed. G. B. Hill and L. F. Powell, 6 vols. Oxford: Clarendon, 1934–64.
Prior, *Life*	James Prior, *The Life of Oliver Goldsmith, M. B. From a Variety of Original Sources*, 2 vols. London: John Murray, 1837.
Wardle	Ralph Wardle, *Oliver Goldsmith.* Lawrence: University of Kansas Press, 1957.

PART I

Life and Career

CHAPTER 1

Life

Michael Griffin

Published in the *Public Advertiser* one month after his death on 4 April 1774, An 'EPITAPH *on Dr.* GOLDSMITH' was a cruel amplification of many of the slights that Goldsmith had suffered from enemies (and indeed some ostensible friends) over the course of his writing life, slights concerning the discrepancy between his personal presence and his literary style, his lack of deep learning, his scientific and medical pretensions:

> HERE lies the Butt of all his Betters;
> The Riddle of the World of Letters;
> A *Man of Sense* of *no* discerning;
> A *Scholar* of *no greater* Learning:
> A *Bard*, whose Genius soar'd sublime
> A whole half Year to tag a Rhime;
> Made roar Box, Gallery, and Pit,
> Without one Grain of Mother-Wit;
> A *Man of Science* so profound,
> He'd prove a Square to be a *Round*;
> Would talk of *animated Nature*,
> As if himself had been Creator;
> Of Animation though bereft,
> His Right Hand oft forgot his Left:
> A mere *good natur'd Man* through Meekness,
> His *moral* Virtue, *natural* Weakness:
> A *Medic oft*, whose matchless Skill,
> In working Cures, was sure to kill;
> By his own Art who justly died
> A blundering, artless Suicide:
> Share, Earth-worms, share, since now he's
>   dead,
> His megrim, maggot-bitten Head.[1]

The inimical view, authored in all likelihood by his long-time arch-nemesis, William Kenrick, would be found more selectively and gently put, and balanced against his writerly virtues, in the accounts of others. Virginia Woolf remarked on the duality of Goldsmith's image handed down to us in biographical posterity by James Boswell. For all of his annoyance at Goldsmith's absurdity, writes Woolf, Boswell

> brings the other Goldsmith to the surface – he combines them both. He proves that the silver-tongued writer was no simple soul, gently floating through life from the honeysuckle to the hawthorn hedge. On the contrary, he was a complex man, a man full of troubles, without 'settled principle'; who lived from hand to mouth and from day to day; who wrote his loveliest sentences in a garret under pressure of poverty. And yet, so oddly are human faculties combined, he had only to take his pen and he was revenged upon Boswell, upon the fine gentleman who sneered at him, upon his own body and stumbling tongue. He had only to write and all was clear and melodious; he had only to write and he was among the angels, speaking with a silver tongue in a world where all is ordered, rational, and serene.[2]

Goldsmith's life story can be told along a spectrum between an affecting cautionary tale, even as a tragedy if the challenges he faced are amplified, or as a sort of absurdist comedy. Much depends on the temperament of the biographer and their empathy or otherwise with their subject. In fact, his life was not a particularly difficult one, all obstacles considered, and there were some: his incomplete education, his damaged looks, his impecunious habits. It could have been much worse: he could have had less talent. In fact, he was gifted and dexterous across the genres, and increasingly well paid for his work. Biographical posterity has him as a fool in life and a genius with a pen, but this duality cannot be fully true.

Goldsmith was born on 10 November, probably in 1728, either at Pallas near Ballymahon in Co. Longford or in Smith Hill near Elphin, Co. Roscommon, the second son and fifth child of the Rev. Charles Goldsmith (c.1690–1747) and Ann Jones (d.1770). Goldsmith's father was a clergyman of middling income who upon becoming rector at Kilkenny West moved to a dwelling near Lissoy, Co. Westmeath, the scene of much of Goldsmith's childhood and, to many, the 'Sweet Auburn' of his most famous poem, The Deserted Village (1770). His relatively peaceful childhood was, however, sorely interrupted by a dose of smallpox when he was eight or nine, which would leave him badly marked and a target of unkind remarks on his appearance for the rest of his life.

His education was a peripatetic affair, its earlier phase taking him around the towns and villages of the Irish midlands, its later – university – phase taking him from Dublin to Edinburgh, Leiden, Paris, and Padua.

His first teacher was a Mrs Elizabeth Delap, who was decidedly unenthused about his intellectual prospects. Goldsmith improved considerably, however, under the tutelage of Thomas Byrne, a veteran of the War of the Spanish Succession, who detected in his young charge a curiosity for languages, travel, and poetry. Goldsmith was then sent to the diocesan school in Elphin, previously run by his maternal grandfather and now under the successful stewardship of the Rev. Michael Griffin. He was then educated at Athlone and finally Edgeworthstown, where he attended the school of the Rev. Patrick Hughes. Hughes encouraged his interest in Latin.

Though his prospects for university education were endangered by his sister's careless early marriage, Goldsmith's beloved uncle Thomas Contarine subvented his enrolment at Trinity College Dublin between 1745 and 1750. Straitened circumstances dictated that he needed to enrol as a sizar, a student obliged to carry out menial tasks for wealthier students in lieu of a portion of his fees and board. It was intended that Goldsmith would proceed to a career in the clergy; an interview with the Bishop of Elphin, however, determined that he was not suitable for that vocation. After an abortive attempt to emigrate to America, and an equally abortive proposal that he study law at the Temple in London, he decided, or it was decided for him, to study medicine in Edinburgh, where he would reside from October 1752 until early 1754, after which point he went to Leiden to pursue further medical studies. From there he travelled to Paris and through central Europe. He would study further at Padua but the nature of his final medical qualification remains something of a mystery. The culture of the universities at which Goldsmith studied is described in Chapter 6 ('Universities') of this volume.

His continental studies occasioned a period of philosophically reflective travel, enabled by his linguistic dexterity and a serviceable talent in debating and in playing the flute. His entrepreneurial mode of travel informed his views of nations and national character and on the nature of travel and cultural comparison. These peregrinations he would later reimagine as those of a 'philosophical vagabond' in his famous novel *The Vicar of Wakefield* (1766); they would also inform his delineation of national advantages and disadvantages in his breakthrough poem, *The Traveller, or A Prospect of Society* (1764).

Goldsmith reached London, broke and professionally aimless, in February 1756. He worked at an apothecary's shop and tried for a spell to work as a physician, but his practice was unsuccessful: his hazy qualifications and Irish brogue may have discouraged monied clients, while the clients he did have were not monied enough to pay him. He wrote home to his brother-in-law Daniel Hodson on 27 December 1757 of his trials as a recently arrived immigrant 'in a Country where my being born an Irishman was sufficient to keep me [unem]ploy'd'. He was, he confided, just about able to 'make a shift to live' as a physician and as a writer (*Letters*, 21).

His first brush with the literary world was his acquaintance with Samuel Richardson, at whose print shop he worked as a proofreader. Subsequently he would become acquainted with Ralph Griffiths, to whom he was introduced by the Rev. John Milner, headmaster of a Peckham school where he worked as an usher. Griffiths was the proprietor of the *Monthly Review*, for whom Goldsmith would commence writing reviews (see Chapter 4, 'Booksellers and the Book Trade', and Chapter 23, 'Periodicals and Literary Reviewing'). Griffiths provided Goldsmith with an excellent apprenticeship, but the latter was very much cast in the role of menial dependent. Griffiths furnished him with room and board and an income at Paternoster Row, but the relationship was personally and intellectually stifling. Goldsmith would wriggle free of his connection to Griffiths in December 1758 – their relationship, and his relationship with the *Monthly Review*, soured considerably thereafter, though he would contribute one further review in October 1763.

After an attempt to emigrate to Coromandel as a ship's surgeon with the East India Company was stymied – he failed the Company's examination – Goldsmith would commit himself once again to a Grub Street existence, this time with Tobias Smollett's *Critical Review*. He would also publish his first book, *An Enquiry into the Present State of Polite Learning in Europe*, which drew upon his European travels and his reading, with Robert and James Dodsley, in April 1759. The book was not well reviewed by his erstwhile colleagues at the *Monthly Review*, nor was David Garrick impressed with Goldsmith's critique of contemporary theatre management. Goldsmith would revise *An Enquiry* and a second edition, controversial opinions on contemporary theatre subtracted, would be published four months after his death.

Goldsmith would go on to write for several periodicals in the years 1759–61. He piloted his own, the *Bee*, late in 1759. During this period he would become acquainted with Thomas Percy and Samuel Johnson, figures crucial to his career and to his biographical posterity. He would also fall under the relatively benign influence and management of John Newbery, for whose *Public Ledger* he would write the Chinese letters which would become *The Citizen of the World* (1762; see Chapter 11, 'Cosmopolitanism', and

Chapter 26, 'Orientalism'). Though his reputation was increasing amongst the literati, his works to this point were as yet published anonymously. Still, his income increased, allowing him to move from Green Arbour Court to better accommodation at Wine Office Court, near Fleet Street. The move was perhaps more than Goldsmith could manageably afford, however, and Johnson would have to intervene when Goldsmith was threatened with eviction in the autumn of 1762. Johnson assisted him in selling his manuscript of *The Vicar of Wakefield* to cover rent payments outstanding. The copyright was sold on 28 October 1762, though the novel itself would not be published until 1766. The threat of eviction prompted Goldsmith to reconsider his circumstances. He moved to Canonbury House in Islington, where John Newbery arranged for him to have his finances and domestic life managed by Elizabeth Fleming while he produced work for Newbery, including his *History of England, in a Series of Letters from a Nobleman to His Son*, which would be published (again anonymously) by Newbery in June 1764 (see Chapter 24, 'History Writing').

His status and anonymous Grub Street operations notwithstanding, Goldsmith's prose, and the esteem in which that prose was held, was such that he would be a charter member of the Literary Club founded by Joshua Reynolds which would meet at the Turk's Head Tavern in Soho (see Chapter 8, 'The Club'). Around this time he would move back from Islington into the heart of the city, taking up residence at King's Bench Walk in the Temple.

The confidence of Reynolds and Johnson would be justified in December 1764 with the publication of Goldsmith's long philosophical poem *The Traveller*, the first work which would have his name featured on the title page. The work was dedicated to his brother Henry and the dedication featured his thoughts on contemporary party politics and the decline of poetry (see Chapter 22, 'Prospect Poetry'). *The Traveller* was extremely well reviewed. Johnson, perhaps inappropriately – he had contributed key lines to the poem – proclaimed in the *Critical Review* that it was work of a standard not easily found 'since the death of Pope'.[3] Other reviews, including that in the *Monthly*, predictably were not as effusive, but generally the poem caused many onlookers, hitherto suspicious of what Goldsmith himself called his 'brogue [an]d his blunders', to reflect on their prejudices against him (*Letters*, 20). His fellow Irish midlander Robert Nugent, Viscount Clare, would upon reading *The Traveller* come to befriend and champion him. Anthony Chamier, knowing that Johnson had contributed some lines, admitted that he believed Goldsmith to have been the primary author of the work, and 'that', he asserted, 'is believing a great deal' (*LOJ*, 3:252). Mrs Cholmondeley, for her part, proclaimed upon reading it that she 'never more shall think Dr. Goldsmith ugly'.[4] Goldsmith's fame was consolidated fifteen months later: *The Vicar of Wakefield* (see Chapter 19, 'Fiction') was generally acclaimed also, though the author (as in the book's 'Advertisement') and reviewers alike admitted its somewhat chaotic structure.

The next phase of Goldsmith's career saw him venturing into the world of the theatre, a potentially lucrative line of writing (see Chapter 20, 'Theatre'). Though his first comedy, *The Good Natur'd Man*, was tepidly reviewed, it did well enough following its Covent Garden opening early in 1768 that Goldsmith was able to move to Brick Court in the Middle Temple. He was also in a position to rent a retreat along the Edgware Road, near Hyde, where he would work on his next major poem, *The Deserted Village* (see Chapter 21, 'Pastoral Poetry'), as well as a two-volume *Roman History*. The former, one of his best or best-known works, first appeared on 16 May 1770, the first edition of seven published in that year alone. *The Deserted Village* and the subsequent success on the stage of his brilliant comedy *She Stoops to Conquer* in March 1773, along with his earnings from histories and the eight-volume *History of the Earth, and Animated Nature* for which he had been handsomely contracted, meant that Goldsmith became one of the best earners in literary London over the last years of his life.

Unfortunately, he was also one of the most reckless with those earnings. He spent wildly on clothes and entertainments at Brick Court, to the extent that indebtedness was his default state. A neighbour and friend, the independently wealthy lawyer Edmund Bott, seems to have become the primary creditor for much of his extravagance. As his career progressed, and after leaving behind the personal stewardship of John Newbery, Goldsmith was increasingly in debt and inclined to focus on composing lucrative works and to neglect the sorts of writing which might have better enhanced his literary legacy. For all that he produced, however, he was never above the financial waterline.

As his health declined he tried to maintain sociability, but his engagement in a competition of wits amongst his friends at the St James's Coffeehouse was foreshortened by his rapid decline and death from renal failure on 4 April 1774. His unfinished poem *Retaliation*, submitted to the publisher George Kearsly by an unknown figure (possibly Bott, recouping debts Goldsmith owed by selling the last, uncontracted works among the papers left in the latter's rooms), was the product of his last round of sociability with an illustrious group which included Joshua Reynolds,

David Garrick, and Richard Cumberland, and a London Irish legal frater-
nity consisting of the Burkes (Edmund and Richard), John Ridge, and
Joseph Hickey, as well as the Dean of Derry, Thomas Barnard. This final
poem shows some of the best of Goldsmith's wit, just as its provocation
and reception demonstrated the less flattering perceptions that some of his
friends and all of his enemies had of him. He was certainly a figure of fun
to some, but he had a better capacity than is generally thought for
making fun of himself and turning a cutting line against his peers
when required or provoked. The *Retaliation* episode, and the comic
verse it produced, shows just how brilliant he could be, if not immedi-
ately in conversation, then certainly in the exquisitely marinated phrases
that he produced when alone with pen and paper.

Goldsmith put his life into his creative work in several ways; it is fair to
say, however, that he also put some creativity into his life story, for
wherever he recounted it to others, he invariably embellished matters to
the extent that biographers of the first generation found him a difficult
case. Goldsmith provided for Thomas Percy an autobiographical dictation
at the Duke of Northumberland's house on 28 April 1773; Percy, however,
found his account of his own personal and family history at times fanciful.
Percy's long-delayed biographical preface to Goldsmith's *Miscellaneous
Works* (1801), assisted by the interim research of Thomas Campbell,
Henry Boyd, and Samuel Rose, was an honourable if necessarily incomplete
effort.

James Prior's 1837 *Life of Oliver Goldsmith* was the first sustained attempt
to piece together the details of Goldsmith's formative years. It was, in its
way, a groundbreaking and pathfinding piece of work. Norma Clarke has
documented the fascinating story of the reception of Prior's biography, and
in particular the response of the biographer who would criticize and seek to
supplant it. In his early review in *The Examiner* John Forster complained
that Prior 'wanders away from his subject at every second or third page'.
Forster's 1848 biography sought also to overcome what he saw as an
unnecessary digressiveness and Irish emphasis in Prior's work, in accord-
ance with the hope, expressed in *The Examiner*, that in a future edition 'the
information will be plainly and simply put together, and that the reader
may be allowed to satisfy his interest about Goldsmith, without the penalty
of stumbling at every other page over Carolan the Irish bard, or Mr Burke
and his schoolfellows, or Mr Contarine and all his connections, or Mr
Lachlin Macleane', among other 'Misters and Doctors beside'.[5] Credited
with a far more focused achievement, Forster's biography went to several
editions. Prior's has never been reprinted.

The set-to between biographers captures for Clarke 'an important disagreement in early biographical practice'.[6] Prior thought it especially imperative that the life of a great Irish writer was properly investigated, which he proceeded to do by initiating correspondences with several figures in the Irish midlands with connections to Goldsmith and the Goldsmiths. Forster's biography was more impatient with Irish material and the Irish background is referred to throughout rather dismissively. Only upon his arrival in London, for Forster, does Goldsmith begin to be cultivated into the man of worth that he would become. In that sense Forster's biography, its first edition tellingly titled *The Life and Adventures of Oliver Goldsmith*, was a narrative of becoming, in some senses a romance with its own identifiable teleology, whereas Prior's was a more digressive work grounded in new and extensive primary research.

The second half of the twentieth century saw the publication of three full biographies which have been, to varying degrees, successful in putting Goldsmith in his contexts. Ralph Wardle (1957) augmented the nineteenth-century biographical tradition in the light of twentieth-century scholarship to that point. Arthur Lytton Sells's *Oliver Goldsmith: His Life and Works* (1974) emphasized Goldsmith's command of the French language and sources, while John Ginger's *The Notable Man: The Life and Times of Oliver Goldsmith* (1977) situated Goldsmith's career amidst the increasing cultural influence of the middle class.

Most recently, Norma Clarke (2016) has authored a compelling account of Goldsmith's writing life, beginning with his arrival in London in 1756. Clarke's account is a realistic one, acknowledging Goldsmith's considerable flaws and vulnerabilities without narrating those flaws and vulnerabilities as sources of unremitting calamity. Fully attuned to the biographical history and the pitfalls of romanticism, Clarke is not shy of depicting the prejudices Goldsmith faced, but recreates a three-dimensional person who was hard-nosed enough to get on with the business of writing across the genres and producing several classics in an evolving professional literary marketplace.

Notes

1. *Public Advertiser* (4 May 1774).
2. Virginia Woolf, 'Oliver Goldsmith', in *The Captain's Death and Other Essays* (London: Hogarth Press, 1950), 18.
3. Johnson, *Critical Review*, 18 (December 1764), 462.

4. *Johnsonian Miscellanies*, ed. George B. Hill, 2 vols. (Oxford: Clarendon, 1897), 2:268.
5. *The Examiner* (25 December 1836), 819.
6. Norma Clarke, '"More National (to Ireland) than Personal": James Prior's *Life of Oliver Goldsmith* (1837)', *Biography* 41.1 (2018), 49.

CHAPTER 2

Letters

David O'Shaughnessy

The correspondence of authors – 'the most direct material evidence for the inner life of their writers' – became increasingly recognized as a form of literary output throughout the eighteenth century.[1] As Louise Curran has observed, 'the eighteenth century has been identified as the great age of letter-writing, in terms of the number of letters that were written and printed, and the perceived mastery of proponents of the familiar style'.[2] When Alexander Pope included his letters in his multivolume editions from 1737 onwards, he recognized them as literary artefacts, as did his readership, and a new trend began in how a 'Works' should be assembled. Writers and their audiences understood that the epistolary 'converse of the pen', to take Bruce Redford's description, offered readers not only an insight into the mind of a writer but also a chance to immerse themselves into their creative process alongside the mechanics of literary publication, identify the corollaries between these exchanges and their published (and unpublished) oeuvre, and assess how their contemporaries viewed them, all in helpfully chronological and multinodal format. Given this context, as an eighteenth-century author increased in fame, the performativity of their epistolary personae tended to increase as the judgement of posterity began to loom larger in their minds. William Godwin, to take one example from the end of the century, used a letter-copying machine, courtesy of Thomas Wedgwood, to make duplicates of his outgoing correspondence.[3] Never shy about his legacy-to-be, Godwin anticipated correctly that his letters would be understood as essential paratext to the understanding of his contribution to eighteenth-century thought. All of these considerations are true to some extent for Oliver Goldsmith; however, although he was one of the most prolific writers of his age and one who wrote across multiple genres, posterity has been left with very few letters on which we can draw to better understand the man and the writing. His first biographer, James Prior, lamented to John Mitford:

It is astonishing how few [autobiographical documents] there are available to the biographer. My search has been very extensive and unremitting for fourteen months; and though certainly I have gleaned a great deal, and found much new matter in [Goldsmith's] literary history and many press and political pieces not acknowledged by him, but unquestionably genuine, I find much difficulty in seeing letters of his which exist.[4]

If we compare this epistolary archive to those of his contemporaries in the Literary Club, Goldsmith's pales into quantitative insignificance. The editors of Burke's correspondence put the number of extant letters at more than 1,900 and estimate he had 1,200 or so individual correspondents.[5] Samuel Johnson's letters need a full five volumes to contain them; David Garrick's three.[6] Oliver Goldsmith's known corpus of letters amounts to 67 letters and can be largely found in a single slim – albeit elegant – volume.[7]

There are a number of contributing factors to this relatively paltry output – outside of the standard vicissitudes of eighteenth-century archival incompletion – profile, geography and self-confidence among them. Goldsmith was notoriously shy and his circle of friends was small. He worked for many years after his arrival in London in 1756 in relative anonymity, achieving fame only after the publication of *The Traveller* in late 1764. Living where he did, in the west end of the city, close by the bookshops and theatres that formed the infrastructure of his social and professional life, meant that much of his daily business could be carried out in person. His low profile in his early London years meant Goldsmith had negligible opportunity to cultivate a network beyond these narrow confines. It also meant there was little inducement for correspondents to retain his letters, unlikely as it seemed during the years of hack work that they would become literary artefacts in due course (there is no surviving letter to Samuel Johnson, for instance, and only one to a member of the London Irish community with whom he was long associated).[8] Dying as young as he did in 1774 at the age of only forty-five meant he had only a few years of the considerable literary profile that his major literary success would give him. Goldsmith's epistolary habits in London had only a brief time to move past using letters as 'a functional instrument of communication – a stopgap method of conducting business, requesting a favour, answering an invitation, or perpetuating a friendship'.[9] While Johnson had the time to grow into an 'epistolary vocation', Goldsmith's letters never had much of a chance of developing beyond the diurnal grind of 'writing for bread'.[10]

Nonetheless, the letters that have survived have valuable information about Goldsmith's life, works, and the world in which he operated.

The earliest known letter dates from late 1752 when he was studying in Edinburgh and the final one was sent around March 1774 in London, just weeks before he died. He corresponded with his family, giving us the best access available to an interior Goldsmith in both his formative and later years, but also with many of the leading male cultural figures of his period: Joshua Reynolds, James Boswell, David Garrick, Charles Burney, and George Colman. And both the outgoing and incoming letters to Goldsmith can help us chart Goldsmith's rise from the garrets of Grub Street to literary celebrity.

Goldsmith's letters might be usefully approached in clusters: there are six letters in the period 1752–4 when Goldsmith travelled to Edinburgh and Leiden; seven in the years 1757–9 that cover Goldsmith's initial arrival in London as he tried to get his writing career off the ground; and a substantial body of thirty from 1771 to 1774 which relate to the composition and performance of *She Stoops to Conquer* and the 'public' Goldsmith that emerged as a consequence. While there are some strays and indeed intriguing mini-clusters that fall outside these three group-ings, this trio provides a useful means to think about what the epistolary archive offers Goldsmith studies. This chapter will suggest not only that Goldsmith did not have the opportunity to develop an 'epistolary voca-tion', but that the archive that we have suggests that he would never have done so in any case.

Goldsmith's letter to Daniel Hodson in October–November 1752 (Figure 2.1) is the first of six letters that give us some sense of Goldsmith's life as a medical student in Edinburgh and Leiden. Balderston observed that these letters were 'filled with reminiscent tender-ness' and the recipients were all significant figures in his life: Hodson was his brother-in-law; Robert Bryanton, a school friend and fellow under-graduate at Trinity College Dublin; and the Reverend Thomas Contarine was his uncle by marriage and a stalwart financial supporter.[11] The letters, as a body, give us a fascinating window into the routine of university life in Edinburgh in the period. Goldsmith provides a tantalizing snapshot of his teachers at one of the centres of European Enlightenment as well as the trivialities of the day-to-day (see Chapter 6, 'Universities'). Notably, the missives to Bryanton (Letter 3) and Contarine (Letters 2, 4, 6) are among the lengthiest in the archive. They relay an inquisitive and observant mind as well as containing the seeds of future literary projects – Goldsmith's peripatetic pedagogy across European countries leads him in these letters to think about cultural and topographical differences and national identity, features that would mark much of his early work from *Enquiry into the*

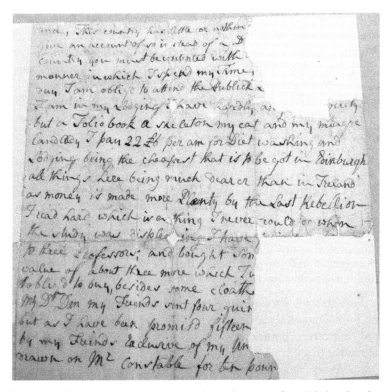

Figure 2.1 The earliest known letter by Goldsmith, written from Edinburgh to his brother-in-law Daniel Hodson in 1752. Huntington MS, HM 118. The Huntington Library, San Marino, California

Present State of Polite Learning in Europe (1759) and *The Citizen of the World* (1762) to *The Traveller* (1764):

[The Leideners] sail in coverd boats drawn by horses and in these you are sure to meet people of all nations here the Dutch slumber the French chatter and the English play cards, any man who likes company may have them to his Taste for my part I generally detachd myself from all society and was wholy Taken up in observing the face of the country, nothing can Equall its beauty wherever I turn my Eye fine houses elegant gardens statues grottoes vistas present themselvs but enter their Towns and you are charmd beyond description no no[th]ing can be more clean [or beau]tifull. (Letter 6)

What is striking about these letters is their length and the degree to which Goldsmith opens up, especially to his good friend Robert Bryanton, to whom he ruefully reflects 'an ugly and poor man is society for himself'

(Letter 3). Alongside this raw self-examination, there is an eager expansiveness that peters out as his career progresses.[12] We can also detect his ambivalent love for Ireland in these letters, another feature of his later work and one indeed which emerges most explicitly in his first known letter home after his arrival in London in 1756. A letter to brother-in-law Daniel Hodson (Letter 7) foreshadows his account of the state of English authorship in his *Enquiry into the Present State of Polite Learning in Europe* (1759):[13]

> but whether I eat or starve, live in a first floor or four pair of stairs [attic] high, I still remember [my Irish friends] with ardour, nay my ve[ry coun]try comes in for a share of my affection. Unaccountable [fond]ness for country, this maladie du Pays, as the french [call] it. Unaccountable, that he should still have an affec[tion for] a place, who never received when in it above civil [contemp]t, who never brought out of it, except his brogue [an]d his blunders; sure my affection is equally ridiculous with the Scotchman's, who refused to be cured of the itch, because it made him unco'thoughtful of his wife and bonny Inverary.

Sadly, this is the only remaining letter from that immediate initial period of settling into London, a challenging task for an impecunious Irishman in the mid eighteenth century.[14] We have to wait until August 1758 for his next letter, the first of a new cluster surrounding the publication of *Enquiry into the Present State of Polite Learning in Europe* (see Chapter 25, 'Authorship'). At this stage of his career, Goldsmith had been employed as a writer for the *Monthly Review* under Ralph Griffiths before moving on to write for the *Critical Review*. While planning to pursue a medical career in India with the East India Company, he agreed to write the *Enquiry*. Wary of pirated copies appearing in Dublin – a common practice in the period – Goldsmith drew on his familial connections in order to 'disappoint their avarice' (Letter 8) as best he could and asking them to circulate proposals to their acquaintance.

The letters to cousins and friends are an intriguing melange of reprimand, request, and reflection. He queries Bryanton as to 'why in so long an absence was I never made a partner in your concerns' (Letter 9) and chastises his cousin, Jane Lawder, plaintively sighing that he had 'endeavoured to forget them whom I could not but look upon as forgetting me' (Letter 10). These letters bespeak a continuance of his longing for Ireland and while the intimacy they strive to generate cannot be divorced from his commercial motivations, there is a fervour in his demand for news of home that strikes the reader as sincere:

I beg you and Dan would put your hands to the oar and fill me a sheet with somewhat or other, if you can't get quite throu your selves lend Billy or Nancy the pen and let the dear little things give me their nonsense. Talk all about yourselves and nothing about me. You see I do so, I know not how my desire of seeing Ireland which has so long slept has again revivd with so much ardour. (Letter 11)

These lengthy missives, particularly to Bryanton and Hodson, where he is asking for help, in his biggest commercial venture to date, from friends and family with whom he has been lengthily separated by both distance and time, bestir an interiority unique in the Goldsmith archive. His immediate precarity, alongside his belief he was India-bound, provoke a wry but bitter self-examination of his situation and prospects, particularly in terms of his venture to become a public intellectual:

> God's curse Sir, who am I? Eh! What am I? Do you know whom you have offended? A man whose character may one of these days be mentioned with profound respect in a German Comment or Dutch Dictionary. Whose name you will probably hear ushered in by a Doctissimus Doctissimorum, or heelpiec'd with a long lattin termination. Think how Goldsmithius, or Gubblegurchius or some such sound as rough as a nutmeg grater, will become me? Think of that. God's curse, Sir who am I? (Letter 9)

Such access to Goldsmith's feelings are absent when we come to the last and most substantial cluster of letters. In the wake of *The Traveller* and *The Vicar of Wakefield*, Goldsmith had become a public figure, one clear indication of which are his letters to the London newspapers (Letters 18, 25, 53). He now felt obliged to defend himself through public forums against charges of literary impropriety. Although there are letters to close friends such as Joshua Reynolds (Letters 32, 33) and Catherine Bunbury (Letters 64) that perform a confident swagger and literary self-consciousness, indeed playfulness, there is nothing of the introspective vulnerability of his earlier letters.

> Pray madam where did you ever find the Epithet good applied to the title of Doctor? Had you calld me learned Doctor, or grave Doctor or Noble Doctor it might be allowable because these belong to the profession. But not to cavil at triffles; you talk of my spring velvet coat and advise me to wear it the first day in the year, that is in the middle of winter. A spring velvet in the middle of winter?!! That would be a solecism indeed. And yet to increase the inconsistence, in another part of the letter you call me a beau. Now on one side or other you must be wrong. If Im a beau I can never think of wearing a spring velvet in winter, and if I be not a beau – why – then – that explains itself. (Letter 64)

Certainly, the letters related to *She Stoops to Conquer* betray his misgivings and uncertainties regarding the project, even Letter 37 to Bennet Langton in 1771 when he first mentions the play, but these are typical of the nerve-jangling experience that was eighteenth-century dramatic writing. Having already gone through this with his 1768 *The Good Natur'd Man* (Letters 23, 24) did not make it any easier the second time round; the desperation in his appeal to Covent Garden manager George Colman is manifest:

> I entreat you'l relieve me from that state of suspense in which I have been kept for a long time. Whatever objections you have made or shall make to my play I will endeavour to remove and not argue about them. To bring in any new judges either of its merit or faults I can never submit to. . . . For God sake take the play and let us make the best of it, and let me have the same measure at least which you have given as bad plays as mine. (Letter 47)

As we know, Goldsmith's play confirmed his reputation as one of the leading writers of his generation (see Chapter 20, 'Theatre'). His letters to the Duke of Northumberland (Letter 50), architect William Chambers (Letters 51, 52), and James Boswell (Letter 54) are helpful in adumbrating the immediate acclaim with which his second comedy was greeted. Intriguingly, Boswell's initial letter of congratulations appears to have been deliberately misleading in order to elicit a response – which it did. Writing from Scotland, Boswell implied he would not be in London for some time whereas he in fact travelled there the following day; he also appended insistently, 'Pray write directly. Write as if in Repartee.'

Boswell does not paint a flattering picture of Goldsmith in his *Life of Johnson*. But here, one of the great literary chroniclers of the century insists that the Irishman has 'not a warmer friend or a steadier admirer', so eager is he for a Goldsmith-penned missive for his personal collection. Goldsmith's response is detailed and friendly but it is equally brisk and businesslike: 'I have been three days ago most horridly abused in a newspaper, so like a fool as I was I went and thrashd the Editor. I could not help it. He is going to take the law of me' (Letter 54). Goldsmith's reference to his assault on Thomas Evans, a bookseller who had published a typically vitriolic piece by his long-time nemesis William Kenrick, is matter-of-fact despite the threat of legal action (see Chapter 3, 'Friendships and Feuds'). On the one hand, it might suggest that Goldsmith felt relatively secure now that he was the darling of London; on the other, it may betray an exhaustion, a deadening of spirit at yet another misfortune in a long litany of misfortunes. But what is clear is that he felt no confidence that Boswell, despite their Literary Club intimacy, offered an outlet for Goldsmith to unburden himself at a moment where his remarkable theatrical triumph had been cut short by the viciousness of the dogged Kenrick.

The contrast between these later letters and those from the earlier periods in his life are consequential. Certainly, we get a better sense of his literary range, ambitions, and acquaintance with letters to Hester Thrale (Letter 55), Thomas Percy (Letter 56), bookseller John Nourse (Letters 57, 65), and Charles Burney (Letter 59), among a number of others. We can glean rich and suggestive details about ongoing and planned projects in both Ireland and England from his letters. But this 'public' Goldsmith is emotionally and psychologically taciturn. His years of being privately mocked by the Johnson circle and public ad hominem attacks by Kenrick and others crippled him with social complexes, awkwardness, and outright wariness (see Chapter 8, 'The Club'). If his more fluent and breezily confident friends such as Burke, Garrick, and Johnson developed epistolary vocations, Goldsmith never did; the raw promise of his earlier correspondence to Irish intimates had long dissipated and his cumulative sense of unjust treatment now dominated. Whether this was an overegged sense of grievance or a fair assessment of sustained unpleasant bullying is up for discussion, but the archive suggests that Goldsmith would never have regained the epistolary flow of his earlier correspondence even if he had lived a longer life.

Notes

1. Ian Watt, *The Rise of the Novel: Studies in Defoe, Richardson and Fielding* (Harmondsworth: Penguin, 1963), 217.
2. Louise Curran, *Samuel Richardson and the Art of Letter-Writing* (Cambridge University Press, 2016), 2.
3. *The Letters of William Godwin Volume I: 1778–1797*, ed. Pamela Clemit (Oxford University Press, 2011), xxxii–xxxiv.
4. James Prior to John Mitford, 26 January 1832. John Mitford Collection, Yale University Library, Osborn FC76 1/38, 39.
5. *The Correspondence of Edmund Burke*, ed. Thomas W. Copeland et al., 10 vols. (Cambridge University Press, 1958–78), 1:ix; 10:48.
6. *The Letters of Samuel Johnson*, ed. Bruce Redford, 5 vols. (Oxford: Clarendon, 1992–4).
7. *The Letters of Oliver Goldsmith*, ed. Michael Griffin and David O'Shaughnessy (Cambridge University Press, 2018) contains sixty-six of his letters. A smaller corpus of letters was previously available in *The Collected Letters of Oliver Goldsmith*, ed. Katharine Balderston (Cambridge University Press, 1928). A previously unknown letter to Benjamin Collins (dated 7 November 1759) came to light at auction in 2023.

8. Goldsmith had close ties to the London Irish community, particularly the legal set that congregated around the Temple Exchange Coffee-house. For more on Irish legal students in London, see Craig Bailey, *Irish London: Middle-Class Migration in the Global Eighteenth Century* (Liverpool University Press, 2013), especially chapter 2.

9. *Letters of Samuel Johnson*, ed. Redford, 1:ix.

10. 'Oh Gods Gods! here in a Garret writing for bread, and expecting to be dunned for a milk score!'. Letter to Robert Bryanton, 14 August 1758. *Letters*, 30.

11. *The Collected Letters of Oliver Goldsmith*, ed. Balderston, ix.

12. See Taylin Nelson's discussion of Goldsmith's use of animal metaphors to describe his initial tribulations in the London literary world. 'Labouring Bodies: Work Animals and Hack Writers in Oliver Goldsmith's Letters', in *Letters and the Body, 1700–1830*, ed. Sarah Goldsmith, Sheryllynne Haggerty, and Karen Harvey (New York: Routledge, 2023), 212–35.

13. See also Letter 11 to Hodson.

14. See my 'Tolerably Numerous: Recovering the London Irish of the Eighteenth Century', *Eighteenth-Century Life* 39.1 (2015), 1–13.

CHAPTER 3

Friendships and Feuds

Norma Clarke

Oliver Goldsmith was a man who took sociability seriously. In his writings he reached out to the widest possible audience, seeking to entertain as well as inform, and he did so, too, in the many friendships that filled his life. Convivial and talkative, he liked to be amongst all sorts of people: not only writers, but also actors and musicians, painters and politicians, and the artisans and shopkeepers, ex-soldiers, footmen, lawyers' clerks, porters, knife-grinders, and chair menders who thronged the streets, gathered in taverns and coffee-houses and formed the audiences for his plays. With some of these he gambled and lost money: we know little about the friends and acquaintances with whom Goldsmith played cards, and not much more about those who tapped him for money knowing that he was generous, soft-hearted, and keen to oblige. With some he walked out on what he called his 'shoemaker's holidays' to drink tea in Islington, or host a breakfast party, or visit the pleasure gardens of Ranelagh and Vauxhall. Talking often led to singing, playing the flute, or dancing (see Chapter 29, 'Music and Song'). It depended on the company. Since most of our information about Goldsmith comes from the professional men who encountered him in London as his fame grew, and who observed him amongst the self-conscious literati, it is easy to forget how much of Goldsmith's social life remains unknown. He left no journals and only a few letters and other sources that help us understand what he felt about the people with whom he mixed (see Chapter 2, 'Letters'). There is nothing that throws light on his relations with women, no *London Journal* such as Boswell kept, telling of encounters with women on the streets; no wife whose family would have been, in the eighteenth-century meaning of the word, Goldsmith's 'friends'.

Goldsmith's career took off quickly after he arrived in London in 1756 and he was admitted into the company of other noted writers. His name became known to editors of periodicals and booksellers looking for capable authors (see Chapter 4, 'Booksellers and the Book Trade', and Chapter 23,

'Periodicals and Literary Reviewing'). A bookseller like John Newbery who employed Goldsmith to write for a range of publications over a period of almost ten years (Newbery died 1767) and who arranged accommodation for him including in his own house in Canonbury, and of whom Goldsmith left an affectionate humorous portrait in *The Vicar of Wakefield*, was one kind of friend; a struggling Irishman like Edward Purdon, with whom Goldsmith wrote and concocted literary schemes, another. A popular anecdote that circulated after Goldsmith's death tells of him being duped out of his watch and some guineas by John Carteret Pilkington, also an Irishman trying to live by literature (see Chapter 9, 'Irish London'). Goldsmith himself used to tell the story of the watch, the guineas (and two white mice) as an after-dinner entertainment. He was amused by Pilkington and sympathetic towards his plight, elements of which fed into *The Vicar of Wakefield* and other writings, but he eventually lost patience with him.

Goldsmith's first modern biographer, Ralph Wardle, suggested that the friends Goldsmith made in London literary circles often failed to understand his humour. With men like Purdon and Pilkington, and, later, with his patron Robert Nugent, Goldsmith enjoyed 'good Irish fun' (Wardle, 5). Goldsmith himself characterized the Irish as remarkable for 'the gaiety and levity of their dispositions' (Wardle, 6). Insofar as he participated in that characterization he was often at odds with the mood of those who gathered for conversation in clubs like the Club, founded in 1764. The Club's aims were serious: members met on a weekly basis at the Turk's Head Tavern in pursuit of mutual improvement. There was food, drink, talk, and laughter, but not levity. Leo Damrosch dubs the Club 'a constellation of talent that has rarely if ever been equalled', including as it did Joshua Reynolds, Samuel Johnson, Edmund Burke, Adam Smith, Edward Gibbon, David Garrick, and James Boswell (see Chapter 8, 'The Club').[1] Boswell had not at first been admitted, being considered too lightweight, but once in he set about recording the exchanges as material for his *Life of Johnson*. His ambition was to produce a monument to Johnson's magisterial conversational talents. This meant showing Johnson exposing the weaknesses of other people's arguments, and for these purposes Goldsmith served Boswell well. Goldsmith features frequently in Boswell's *Life of Johnson*, and all the references are belittling ones.

Boswell was rivalrous towards Goldsmith, whose friendship with Johnson predated his own. Also, Goldsmith was a successful writer and Boswell was not. In his pre-Johnson days, Boswell had been at the opening night of Mrs Sheridan's *The Discovery* and realized that Goldsmith was sitting behind him, talking to a companion: 'His conversation revived in my mind the true ideas of London authors', Boswell wrote, 'which are to me something curious, and, as it were, mystical'.² Boswell's 'true ideas' about authorship were romantic as well as mystical, and Goldsmith was the least mystical of writers. But they did become friends of a sort, with the admixture of ambivalence that Boswell always felt and was revealed in his *Life of Johnson*.

Joshua Reynolds was proud to be Goldsmith's intimate friend. Between them there was no ambivalence: they 'unbosomed their minds freely to each other'. According to Reynolds, their conversations often turned on the friends they shared, in the Club and elsewhere, and the meaning of friendship and sociability. Reynolds agreed with Goldsmith that it was not 'superior parts, or wisdom, or knowledge that made men beloved – that men do not go into company with a desire of receiving instruction, but to be amused – that people naturally avoid that society where their minds are to be kept on the stretch'.

Attempting to counter derogatory views of Goldsmith, Reynolds left a sensitive account of what others considered his friend's 'absurdity'. He admitted that what were called blunders, or socially inappropriate behaviour, often arose from attention-seeking, from Goldsmith's 'horror ... of being overlooked by the company'. He also acknowledged that 'a man seldom acquires the character of absurd without deserving it', even if, as another friend remarked, what Goldsmith said in jest was often 'mistaken ... for earnest'.³

Nor does a man acquire a reputation for enviousness without cause. Goldsmith was certainly envious of those who were rewarded with praise and pensions. He resentfully wondered why James Beattie, whose *Essay on Truth* was extravagantly praised, should get a pension for one book when he, ill and in debt, had written several. He was not resentful of Johnson, who was a friend as Beattie was not, and whose pension was obviously deserved, but he was jealous. Johnson held Goldsmith in high regard as a writer and Goldsmith must have known this even if he could not always feel it. His jealousy of Johnson was a complex mix of admiration, respect, and annoyance at knowing that their association led to him being regarded as a lesser light, Dr Minor to Dr Major. Johnson's habit of correcting Goldsmith or criticizing him, as recorded by Boswell, reinforced this attitude.

It was to the other members of the Club on a night when Goldsmith was not present that Johnson insisted on his merits. Johnson declared

Goldsmith 'a man of the most distinguished abilities'. *She Stoops to Conquer* was a deserved success. *The Traveller* was 'a very fine performance'. As an historian Goldsmith stood 'in the first class'. Boswell queried this. What about Hume and Robertson? Johnson did not budge. 'Goldsmith tells you shortly all you want to know ... No man will read Robertson's cumbrous detail a second time; but Goldsmith's plain narrative will please again and again'.[4] These judgements underscore the well-known story of Johnson's intervention when Goldsmith was in debt to his landlady and unable to leave his rooms. Johnson took the manuscript of *The Vicar of Wakefield* and sold it. He had faith that whatever Goldsmith had written, be it poetry, prose, comic drama, or history, was of value.

Johnson was the most admired critic of his day and to have his friendship was a mark of status which Goldsmith well understood. In literary circles friendship often meant helping a career progress – be it by reading and commenting on manuscripts or recommending an author to a bookseller or puffing a book in the coffee shops. From his early days as a writer Goldsmith helped and was helped by others in this way. He aided Thomas Percy in finding a publisher and it was to him that he dictated a brief memorandum of his life, hoping Percy would become his biographer. James Grainger was a colleague on the *Monthly Review* and *Critical Review*. Tobias Smollett edited the *Critical Review*. Smollett made a habit of entertaining authors at his house in Chelsea and wrote a satirical account in *Humphrey Clinker* of one such Sunday. It is easy to imagine Goldsmith with his 'merry-making disposition' enjoying the mix of chancers and pranksters, professors of Greek and sober churchmen found at Smollett's table.

But it was not all merrymaking. Literature was an insecure profession, and attacking other authors a recognized way of getting on. William Kenrick, who succeeded Goldsmith as a critic on the *Monthly Review*, penned savage anonymous reviews. The proprietor of the *Monthly*, Ralph Griffiths, resentful at having lost Goldsmith or cannily aware that fomenting rivalry with the competitor *Critical Review* was good for business, encouraged him. Plagiarism was common, and a common accusation: 'The republic of letters is ever in a state of civil warfare', Kenrick declared, and 'every man, being an enemy to his neighbour, takes the spoil of his goods for lawful plunder'.[5] Kenrick became Goldsmith's enemy. Hugh Kelly was a fellow Irishman with whom Goldsmith had an amicable working relationship. Goldsmith contributed to Kelly's series of essays, the *Babler*, probably on several occasions and certainly when he wrote, ironically as it now seems, an essay on the theme of friendship. The men fell out in 1768 when Kelly's first play, *False Delicacy*, was a hit at Drury

Lane in the same season that Goldsmith's first play, *The Good Natur'd Man*, was staged at Covent Garden.

The rift with Kelly illustrates the complexities of friendship for those who lived by the arts. Garrick had not rushed to accept *The Good Natur'd Man* for Drury Lane and his enthusiasm for Kelly, whose play brought in healthy profits, cannot have improved Goldsmith's mood. On the opening night of *The Good Natur'd Man*, the Club rallied to support their friend, making visits to the green room and carrying Goldsmith off for a celebratory supper after. The bailiff scene had been hissed, however, and although Goldsmith put on a show of cheer he broke down in tears when all his friends except Johnson had left.

The bailiff scene had been hissed because it was considered 'low'. Bailiffs, and all that they implied about lives lived on the edge of financial crisis, were unwelcome on stage. But Goldsmith knew about debt and indebtedness. The life he made for himself in London amidst friends who admired him was a precarious one. He earned well but spent hugely, not least because it was necessary to look the part of a successful writer. He loved to buy new clothes; he loved to entertain lavishly in well-furnished lodgings. His favoured self-image was that of the good-natured man, benevolent, disbursing the funds that came his way to those in need, becoming, in imagination, friend to everyone.

The publication of *The Traveller* in 1764 transformed Goldsmith's life (see Chapter 22, 'Prospect Poetry'). He was famous. The poem, wrote Joshua Reynolds, 'produced an eagerness unparalleled to see the author. He was sought after with greediness'.[6] Those seeking Goldsmith's acquaintance included persons of the highest rank and among them one at least became a firm friend: Robert Nugent, Lord Clare, a Lord of the Treasury, Vice-Treasurer of Ireland, with a country seat at Gosfield in Essex and a house in Great George Street, Westminster. Nugent was a worldly, jovial Irishman and soon Goldsmith was absorbed into the domestic routines of his household, staying at Gosfield where he helped build an icehouse, dining in Westminster, allowing Nugent's young daughter Mary to play tricks on him (Goldsmith was always good with children) and – in more sober vein – accompanying Nugent's dying son to Bath. In 1771, a correspondent told Smollett that Goldsmith 'now generally lives with his countryman, Lord Clare'. While certainly an exaggeration, the report nonetheless conveys the strength of Goldsmith's friendship and the comfort his presence could provide. *The Haunch of Venison*, a poetic epistle written to thank Lord Clare for a gift of venison, gives a lively sense of the shared humour between the men.

With an expanded circle of friends and a flow of commissioned work, Goldsmith also needed to make space and time for writing. In summer 1768 he thought of accepting Percy's offer to stay at his rectory in Northamptonshire. He sent a list of queries: would he be a nuisance? Would he be able to transport his books? Could he easily get milk, meat, and tea? And, above all, were there 'troublesome neighbours' (*Letters*, 78)? In the end he took a cottage near Edgware, sharing the tenancy with Edmund Bott, a young barrister who had rooms across the hall from him in Brick Court in the Temple. Bott had independent means; when Goldsmith died a few years later £2,000 in debt the principal creditor was Bott. Little is known of the friendship but one anecdote survives to suggest that they enjoyed evenings in town and that either or both were a little drunk on their return journeys.

Goldsmith was never isolated in his country retreats. Friends made the journey out from town to dine with him; for all his fears of 'troublesome neighbours' he was more likely than not to befriend the locals. By contrast, his relations with his family back home in Ireland were marred by distance (he never returned, and did not keep up a regular correspondence) and complicated by layers of guilt and fear. His older brother whom he loved died in 1768; from his mother he was alienated and when she died he wore only half mourning. He seems to have been nervous that his younger brothers would sponge off him: while generous towards other indigent Irishmen who turned up in London, he discouraged his brothers' tentative plans to come over and settle. He was, however, helpful to his nephew William Hodson.

Goldsmith could be irritable and peevish but there is no evidence that he wished to conduct feuds, as William Kenrick certainly did, nor that he viewed the republic of letters in Kenrick's terms, as a 'civil war'. Stung by an attack in the *London Packet* after the success of *She Stoops to Conquer* in 1773, he went to the office and started a fight with the publisher Thomas Evans. They were separated by Kenrick, who probably wrote the article. It was uncharacteristic behaviour except that it gave others opportunity to consider him a fool when the whole story featured in the *Packet* a few days later, angled to Goldsmith's disadvantage, and when Evans threatened to sue.

Goldsmith's working life made huge demands and his ability to balance the stresses of major commissions like *History of the Earth, and Animated Nature* in eight volumes and successful plays like *She Stoops to Conquer* (stage success was 'great cry and little wool . . . the dirtiest money that ever poor poet put in his pocket', Goldsmith told Boswell) with increasing social demands was limited (*Letters*, 125). But his best work emerged from his intense sociability. It is somehow appropriate that in one of his last poems, the posthumously published *Retaliation*, he addressed his friends. He was invited to write the poem as an answer back to those who, dining at the St James's Coffee-house, had proposed to write mock epitaphs on him. Edmund Burke, David Garrick, and Joshua Reynolds are among those Goldsmith characterized in largely affectionate but also shrewd and quite biting couplets. Only Reynolds (the 'lamb') escapes censure, the wisest and best friend of a writer whose epitaph for himself was a single line: 'Magnanimous Goldsmith, a gooseberry fool' (*Retaliation*, 7).

Since most of our information about Goldsmith comes from the professional men who encountered him in London, and who observed him among the self-conscious literati, it is easy to forget how much of Goldsmith's social life remains unknown. We can say with confidence that he took sociability seriously, was loved by many, and was ever the least solitary of men.

Notes

1. Leo Damrosch, *The Club: Johnson, Boswell, and the Friends Who Shaped an Age* (New Haven, CT: Yale University Press, 2019), 135.
2. *Boswell's London Journal, 1762–63*, ed. Frederick A. Pottle (London: William Heinemann, 1974), 176.
3. *Portraits by Sir Joshua Reynolds*, ed. Frederick W. Hilles (McGraw-Hill, 1952), 44–59; Prior, *Life*, 2:379–80.
4. James Boswell, *Life of Johnson* (Oxford World's Classics), 527–8.
5. John Ginger, *The Notable Man: The Life and Times of Oliver Goldsmith* (London: Hamish Hamilton, 1977), 300.
6. *Portraits by Sir Joshua Reynolds*, 41.

CHAPTER 4

Booksellers and the Book Trade

Richard C. Taylor

Newly arrived in London in his late twenties, Oliver Goldsmith may have seemed the least likely to succeed among the aspirants to literary fame in the capital. With an undistinguished academic background and the burden of facing the snobbery and bigotry of the English literati towards the Irish, he added his own personal demons – most obviously an ever-enthralling debt – to the challenge of finding a ticket for the 'fame coach', as he called it in an essay for his miscellany the *Bee* (3 November 1759, 153). His timing, however – for a writer humble enough to work anonymously for pennies and bold enough to put his writing before the 'fierce tribunal' of critical scrutiny – was extraordinary, and his remarkable and varied literary career was very much a product of a series of dramatic changes transforming the world of *belles-lettres*.

Goldsmith's arrival in the city corresponded with the beginning of the Seven Years' War, the 'Great War for Empire' as some call it. His essays for the *Public Ledger* under the guise of a Chinese observer of British customs offered a satirical look at the Orientalist craze then at its height and the public appetite for all things foreign (see Chapter 11, 'Cosmopolitanism', and Chapter 26, 'Orientalism'). As a 'hack' working for many of the best-known booksellers of the period, he became for a time a kind of fictional foreign correspondent: a pretend eyewitness culling the latest gossip from France and other more 'exotic' locales while remaining in the confines of his employer's garret.

He was lucky to arrive at the doorsteps of booksellers – a term signifying the multifaceted roles of those who edited, promoted, printed, and sold books and periodicals – at a time of a developing press infrastructure, of which public literary discourse was a surprisingly prominent part. A growing reading public demanded to be fed, and booksellers and their anonymous employees like Goldsmith met the demand with an explosion in literary and miscellaneous periodicals: daily, weekly, and monthly accounts of the literary and related cultural news – often reviewing and advertising their own authors' book publications (see Chapter 23, 'Periodicals and Literary Reviewing').

Goldsmith's first prominent employer was the bookseller Ralph Griffiths, somewhat notorious for publishing John Cleland's *Fanny Hill, or Memoirs of a Woman of Pleasure* (1750). In 1749, Griffiths had co-founded the *Monthly Review*, perhaps the first important book review journal in English. Books had usually received summary treatment in the earlier periodical press, often with little or no critical assessment. Griffiths's enterprise offered regular, detailed, and fairly sophisticated literary criticism from his assemblage of little-known contributors. The work was a foot in the door for Goldsmith in 1757, but it also supplied free books to an impoverished writer – no insignificant benefit – and a chance to develop his own critical sensibilities. He also contributed to Tobias Smollett's *Critical Review* – the rivalry a surprisingly public sensation in the late 1750s (see, for example, *The Battle of the Reviews*, published anonymously in 1760).

Branching out from review work, Goldsmith took advantage of the increasing number of venues for public literary, dramatic, and other cultural discourse. A variety of new journals employing the talents of writers like Samuel Johnson published more extensive discussions of the state of literature, and Goldsmith developed and published essays about the state of poetry, the theatre, fashion, courtship, and politics. Precisely how genuinely 'anonymous' these essays were remains open for debate, but Goldsmith's facility for producing thoughtful and entertaining reflections on British culture brought him an increasing amount of journalistic work, and eventually the notice of fellow writers and artists and the reading public. Book reviewing and periodical essay writing laid a foundation for Goldsmith's career, even if it apparently never fully rescued him from debt.

Among the 'catchpenny' assignments he took on were projects under the direction of John Newbery, of Newbery Prize fame, who published 'moral tales' such as 'Jack the Giant Killer' for children. Goldsmith supplied Newbery with prefaces for a variety of books and may have written 'The History of Little Goody Two-Shoes' (1765), although authorship attribution problems remain sticky for most of the published writing in the period (see Chapter 25, 'Authorship').

As Goldsmith struggled to contribute to the newly changing world of *belles-lettres*, a broader debate was ongoing in the press about the status of authorship itself. Goldsmith's professional debut corresponded with increasing disdain for the patronage system which had dominated publishing. Booksellers and their trade became so successful so relatively quickly that the older system of wealthy or aristocratic sponsorship was replaced by a system that measured success by popular approval and commercial sales. The change had become largely a fait accompli by the 1760s when Goldsmith's career was at its height. James Ralph's book *The Case of Authors by Profession or Trade* (1758) captures much of this change as the literary world reconsiders the role of authorship at a time when it was performed almost entirely invisibly. The acceptance of authorship as a respectable undertaking, let alone as an acknowledged profession, was a much slower process than its commercialization, but it created in Goldsmith and his contemporaries a self-consciousness about their roles as writers and, increasingly, as public figures.

A case could be made that the works for which Goldsmith is most celebrated were directly or indirectly a product of his early work for the booksellers. I've argued, for example, that Goldsmith's magazine story 'The History of Miss Stanton', written for *The British Magazine* (a publication in which both Smollett and Newbery were involved), became in a later incarnation his novel *The Vicar of Wakefield.*[1] The contemporary periodical *The Connoisseur* supplied Goldsmith with the idea for the character of Tony Lumpkin in his most successful play, *She Stoops to Conquer.*[2]

Goldsmith's career working with the booksellers was double-sided: it brought him access and a degree of celebrity among the literary and artistic elite of London, but it meant (at least in James Boswell's estimation) playing the fool – Dr Minor – to Samuel Johnson's Dr Major. His remarkably diverse productivity bought him a ticket on the 'Fame Coach', but it probably never rescued him from the poverty and the anxiety of insurmountable debt. He is one of the early products of the newly established British commercial press, and he embodies the new, still ambiguous status of the 'professional author' – to risk anachronism – relying on the approval of the public and the finances of his booksellers for survival.

Even those who particularly admire Goldsmith, who rank him among the major writers of the 'High Georgian' period rather than among the 'major minors', have found little interest in his reviewing work, which launched his career as a writer for hire. Critics have argued that his reviews are too sketchy, too formulaic, too much a product of time and editorial constraint to be taken seriously. Slight as many of the reviews are, though, they reveal a great deal about Goldsmith's developing sensibilities, and they have the virtue of being positively attributable to Goldsmith, unlike some of his essay work. Further, Goldsmith reviewed at a fascinating time in journalistic history, when for the first time two London review journals were competing for readers and adopting a variety of innovations. Even though the pieces Goldsmith wrote for Ralph Griffiths's *Monthly Review* were often fragmentary and unsophisticated, they provide insight into *Goldsmith's* development as a writer in the context of an evolving infrastructure involving the book and periodical trade.

Goldsmith and Johnson were both in their mid-twenties when they began their authorial careers. Both writers received their first employment from a leading London periodical editor, engaged in a rivalry with another journal for readership: Johnson first approached Edward Cave, publisher of the *Gentleman's Magazine*, in 1737, when the journal was engaged in a 'magazine war' with the *London Magazine*.[3] Twenty years later Goldsmith was hired by Griffiths, whose *Monthly Review* was being challenged by its rival, the *Critical Review*. The writers' initial approaches to their first appointments, however, were vastly different: Johnson pursued his prospective employer aggressively – tactlessly, Thomas Kaminski suggests.[4] By contrast, Goldsmith's hiring was serendipitous; by all accounts, he stumbled upon his first journalistic position.

Why should Griffiths hire a man with an inauspicious background as 'vagabond', failed physician, and temporary schoolmaster? Having little documentary evidence, scholars have resorted to speculation. For example, Elizabeth Eaton Kent fictionalizes: 'As Dr. Milner at times contributed to the *Monthly Review*, the conversation turned to literary criticism, and Goldsmith's remarks attracted the attention of Griffiths, who asked the usher for some specimens of his critical writing.'[5] In fact, we have no evidence to suggest that Milner contributed to the *Monthly*. We do know, however, that Griffiths had reviewed a collection of Milner's sermons in the journal.[6] Benjamin Christie Nangle identifies the authorship, with reasonable reliability, of all attributable, full-length *Monthly* reviews during this period. Several contextual factors, however, help clarify the issue and make this event seem somewhat less extraordinary than it has seemed in the past. One contributing factor must have been Milner's strong recommendation. More than a year after the editor and his reviewer terminated their agreement, Griffiths threatened Goldsmith with prison for failing to repay a loan. Though Griffiths's accusatory letter is no longer extant, Goldsmith's reply suggested that the editor had blamed Milner for misrepresenting Goldsmith's character: 'You seem to think Doctor Milner knew me not. Perhaps so; but he was a man I shall ever honour' (*Letters*, 49).

The timing of Goldsmith's hiring is a relevant consideration: he spent all of his first stint with the *Monthly* during the journalistic off-season, when Parliament was not in session and the amount of published ephemera declined. John Brewer remarks on this pattern as it continued into the 1760s: 'December to March was the most popular time of year for reviewing (and, by inference) for publication, while precious few pamphlets at all were discussed between July and October.'[7] A new *Monthly* employee hired to begin in April would presumably enjoy seven relatively 'slow' months to adjust. Goldsmith later remarked on this tendency in one of his many satires on bookselling for the *Public Ledger* which would be published later in *The Citizen of the World*: 'Nothing in [a bookseller's] way goes off in summer, except very light goods indeed. A review, a magazine, or a sessions paper, may amuse a summer reader; but all our stock of value we reserve for a spring and winter trade' (*Citizen*, 1:219).

Goldsmith's approaches to his assignments were almost as varied as the materials themselves: from a sharp, one-sentence dismissal of a novel included in the Monthly Catalogue to a thorough summary and critical response to Edmund Burke's *Philosophical Enquiry into the Origin of Our Ideas of the Sublime and the Beautiful* in May 1757, to a seven-page extract from a translation to which he added only a three-sentence preface and a one-line conclusion the following month. Some of his reviews justify William Black's complaint: 'They are somewhat laboured performances. They are almost devoid of the sly and delicate humour that afterwards marked Goldsmith's best prose work.'[8] Others, such as his delightfully ironic response to the diatribe against theatregoing, support the case Robert Hopkins makes concerning Goldsmith's satiric techniques.[9] The humour he displayed, both genial and savage, certainly provides an important exception to Ricardo Quintana's claim that the *Monthly* was 'staid in tone'.[10]

Though he may, indeed, have been well suited for his new position, Goldsmith apparently despised his work for Griffiths. Although he seldom made written reference to his reviewing career, he did include a bitter summary in his autobiographical testimony to Bishop Percy. Percy records: 'In this Thraldom ["Thraldom" is excised and "situation" substituted] he lived 7 or 8 Months Griffith and his wife continually objecting to everything he wrote & insisting on his implicitly submitting to their corrections ... & since Dr. Goldsmith lived with Griffith & his wife during this intercourse the Dr. and he thought it incumbt. to drudge for his Pay constantly from 9 o'clock till 2.'[11] In spite of his often-repeated misgivings about writing for pay and his apologies for the 'catchpenny' nature of his work, Goldsmith began a productive journalistic career with a highly successful editor and a well-established, influential periodical. A survey of the types of tasks he performed as a reviewer suggests that his damning account of working for the *Monthly* may have been hyperbolic.

More than most of his colleagues, Goldsmith displayed remarkable diversity in his full-length reviewing. His assignments included important works in philology, drama, periodical writing, philosophy, history, travel literature, satire, and natural history – most of the genres popular in the late 1750s. He was either fortunate enough or sufficiently perspicacious to review several of the most controversial and influential works of 1757, written by some of England's foremost authors. An anonymous 'hack', with no known previous experience either as author or critic, he found himself on the staff of London's best established review and assigned the task of judging the likes of Edmund Burke, John Home, Tobias Smollett, David Hume, Thomas Gray, George Colman, and other leading literary lights.

In establishing a role for himself as a contributor to a variety of London periodicals, Goldsmith frequently assumed the fictional 'foreign correspondent' role first created for him by Griffiths as he laboured on his Catalogue notices. Like most other reviewers he had been assigned a diverse assortment of newly published works – from medical treatises to poetry collections – but the number of foreign works to which he was assigned clearly distinguished Goldsmith's work from that of his peers. He brought this same diversity to his essay career; like his predecessors he tried his hand at a variety of essay types: light social satire in the manner of Addison, moral and literary criticism reminiscent of Johnson and John Hawkesworth's contributions to the *Adventurer*, and dramatic theory similar to Murphy's for the *Gray's-Inn Journal*. But the most prominent and distinguishing essay form in which Goldsmith worked was the 'foreign correspondent' type. By continuing this persona, Goldsmith could apply what he had learned in his earlier European travels, he could maintain the illusion of distance from the periodical trade and its political infighting, and he could appeal to a clearly established public appetite for foreign news and cultural comparison. The frequency with which he assumed this role and his attendant success best differentiates Goldsmith's journalistic work from that of his contemporaries.

Goldsmith's critical analyses and comparisons of the nations of the world provided an outlet for his own critique of British culture, as well as that of the nation's rivals. The genial 'Citizen of the World', though endowed (as Goldsmith admits in his preface) with the author's own colloquial ease, nevertheless furnished Goldsmith with another persona to effect specious cultural comparison and sincere social criticism. The essay series also established an important source of assignments for Goldsmith in the 1760s as he provided a central feature of Newbery's periodical the *Public Ledger*. Newbery was an important source of 'hack work', and Goldsmith likely contributed – albeit anonymously – to one of the most important innovations of the press of this period: the idea, promoted by Newbery and his staff, of children's literature as a discrete genre for which there was a strong public appetite.

James Raven cites the 'vast increase in publications' as well as the 'new diversity of printed materials' as contributing to a period of explosive growth, innovation, and specialization among booksellers – all of which shaped Goldsmith's career and at least made conceivable the idea of authorship as an occupation, if not a recognized profession. The number and range of new publications, along with the new methods of circulation Raven cites, provided opportunities for anonymous 'hacks' to develop as writers and make the commercial connections that could sustain a 'living' (although hardly a lucrative or steady one).[12] The developing industry provided an alternative to the increasingly archaic patronage system.

Goldsmith's literary apprenticeship with the periodicals also led him to the personal connections that facilitated his best-known works and brought him fame. While reviewing for Griffiths and later Smollett, Goldsmith found in the prestigious booksellers Robert and James Dodsley a publisher for *An Enquiry into the Present State of Polite Learning* (1759), an underappreciated forerunner of his non-fiction work. After Robert's retirement, James Dodsley became one of a number of publishers contracting Goldsmith for his miscellaneous prose – the histories and life writing that would help provide for Goldsmith during the later 1760s and early 1770s, when he was afflicted by his legendary financial problems and, increasingly, ill health.

His publishing connections, including John Newbery, led him to 'the Club', Johnson's notice and literary mentorship, and the publication of *The Vicar of Wakefield* (1766) by Francis Newbery, nephew of John, who also printed Goldsmith's best-known play, *She Stoops to Conquer* (1773), and his poem *The Traveller* (1764). Some have argued for Goldsmith's authorship of *The History of Little Goody Two Shoes* (1765); he certainly contributed moralizing prefaces and other such 'catchpennies' as a part of Newbery's foundational work in children's literature. William Griffin, reputedly a patron of Irish authors, collected Goldsmith's essays in a volume that appeared in 1765, and then offered him a publication venue for natural history and other miscellaneous prose. He also published Goldsmith's best-known poem, *The Deserted Village* (1770). George Colman and Thomas Davies represented crossover figures: the playwright Colman produced *The Good Natur'd Man* in 1768, and the actor and bookseller Thomas Davies published Goldsmith's *History of Rome* (1768). The first part of Goldsmith's career – as a literary journalist in an exploding market – set up the second part, in which as an increasingly public figure (his name appearing titularly in much of his writing from the mid 1760s on) and a prominent part of the Johnson circle, he earned the fame he sought, if not the financial security.

Goldsmith's essay contributions to fields as varied as natural history and biography demonstrate his range and diligence as a writer in an emerging publishing industry dominated by booksellers and their 'authors for hire' such as Henry Fielding and Johnson who found in periodical work a kind of chaotic literary nursery. Goldsmith appeared at a time when the notion of authorship as a legitimate occupation – even a profession – was at least being entertained by some. A quickly evolving literary infrastructure, including a few well-known booksellers and many more who remain obscure, offered a path to literary acclaim and emergence from the anonymity of the 'hack' by trade.

Notes

1. Richard C. Taylor, 'Goldsmith's First Vicar', *Review of English Studies* 41 (March 1990): 91–9.
2. Richard C. Taylor, 'A Source for Goldsmith's Tony Lumpkin in *The Connoisseur*' *English Language Notes* 26 (March 1989): 30–6.
3. See *History and Sources of Percy's Memoir of Goldsmith*, ed. Katharine C. Balderston (Cambridge University Press, 1926), 16. Ralph Wardle follows biographers who have written that the agreement was to include a salary of one hundred pounds (Wardle, 76). In the manuscript of Goldsmith's biographical narration to Bishop Percy (28 April 1773), however, '100 Pd. per annum' is overwritten with 'some pecuniary stipend'.
4. For a discussion of this 'war' and Johnson's first contacts with Cave, see Thomas Kaminski, *The Early Career of Samuel Johnson* (New York: Oxford University Press, 1987), 3–23.
5. Elizabeth Eaton Kent, *Goldsmith and His Booksellers* (Ithaca, NY: Cornell University Press, 1933), 22.
6. Benjamin Christie Nangle, *The Monthly Review, First Series, 1749–1789: Indexes of Contributors and Articles* (Oxford: Clarendon, 1934), 159.
7. John Brewer, *Party, Ideology, and Popular Politics at the Accession of George III* (Cambridge University Press, 1976), 143.
8. William Black, *Goldsmith* (London: Macmillan, 1909), 29.
9. See Robert Hopkins, *The True Genius of Oliver Goldsmith* (Baltimore, MD: Johns Hopkins University Press, 1969).

10. Ricardo Quintana, *Oliver Goldsmith: A Georgian Study* (New York: Macmillan, 1967), 21.
11. *History and Sources of Percy's Memoirs of Goldsmith*, 16.
12. James Raven, *The Business of Books: Booksellers and the English Book Trade 1450–1850* (New Haven, CT: Yale University Press, 2007), 221–2.

PART II

Social, Cultural, and Intellectual Contexts

CHAPTER 5

Enlightenments

Michael Brown

Was Oliver Goldsmith representative of the Enlightenment? To ask the question as directly as this seems to require a direct answer; one that asserts or denies his affiliation with an intellectual movement. Or perhaps it requires a genealogical mapping of the relationships that bind the Irish-born writer to the bickering family that makes up Peter Gay's 'party of humanity'.[1] Goldsmith is certainly a candidate for such clan membership. He was committed to a literary career which, while blighted by financial hardship (much of it of his own making), both resembles the low Enlightenment Robert Darnton documented in the Parisian setting and expresses the Grub Street entrepreneurialism Pat Rogers associated with its London sibling.[2] In his manifold appearances as journalist, dramatist, novelist, and translator, Goldsmith was fundamentally a man of letters, making his way on the wit and wisdom of his pen. And as an amiable commentator on the parochialism and snobbery of his urbane society, he was a critic in the fashion of the French *philosophes*, using fashionable ideas for subtle polemical ends.

To write of Goldsmith's relationship to the Enlightenment is to enter a debate around the very concept of the Enlightenment itself. It begins with the use of the definite article: 'the' Enlightenment. While recent accounts by Jonathan Israel, Ritchie Robertson, and Anthony Pagden have all sought to reassert the movement's unitary character, the Enlightenment remains a hotly contested nomenclature.[3] Even while recognizing that it is a neologism retrospectively applied to the period, allowing historians to group particular sets of ideas under one term of art, the term has remained volatile and prone to fragmentation.[4]

The common manoeuvre to escape these criticisms has been to place an adjective before the noun. Far from asserting a singular unitary Enlightenment, then, historians have increasingly narrowed their claim to identifying a certain kind of Enlightenment. Even Israel is eager to defend a 'radical' Enlightenment, while he accepts that it existed on a spectrum that also involved a moderate Enlightenment and counter-Enlightenment voices. The inflection point is to be found in numerous studies. For Margaret Jacob, the Enlightenment is secular; for David Sorkin, it is religious. Ulrich Lerner sketches out a Catholic Enlightenment; Shumel Feiner maps a Jewish one.[5] And in the work of J. G. A. Pocock, the fine-grained theology of Protestantism permits him to identify an Arminian Enlightenment at work in the Church of England which contrasts to the Enlightened Calvinism that informed the Scottish Enlightenment.[6]

As this last coinage suggests, also in circulation is a series of explicitly national Enlightenments that give the movement a distinct local currency. Inspired by the 1981 collection edited by Roy Porter and Mikulas Teich, the concept of the Enlightenment in national context has permitted a multiplication of political Enlightenments grounded on claims of regional sovereignty.[7] Moving beyond the paradigmatic forms of the French and German Enlightenments, a Scottish Enlightenment has been revived and revisited since the late 1960s, and essays and books have sought to sketch out national variations as distinctive as the Italian Enlightenment, the Polish Enlightenment, the Danish Enlightenment, and the Spanish Enlightenment, amongst others.[8] Particularly pertinent to Goldsmith, there is also a case to be made for an Irish Enlightenment.[9]

However, this identification of multiple Enlightenments with multiple national contexts runs the danger of replicating the error of falsely stabilizing a neologism of its own by making the nation state the presiding context. The problem can be conceived of in two distinct ways. Granted there was a vibrant and raucous, sometimes rancorous discourse of national difference and of chauvinistic pride. But how far this aligns with ideas concerning the nation state and the ideological commitment to national self-governance is hotly debated in the scholarly literature. Here primordialists assert the nation state's heritage over and against modernists who attach the ideology firmly to the industrialized state of the nineteenth century. More recent approaches have tried to reach a resolution by tracking how the cultural imaginary transformed national identity into nationalist ideology. But this ethno-symbolist approach has only added to a cacophony of competing claims about the validity of the nation as a historically meaningful category.[10]

Second is the way in which political identity itself has become pluralized. While national identity has remained pre-eminent in these discussions, both regional and supranational political commitments have been brought increasingly into focus in recent interventions. Colin Kidd has written of an Ayrshire Enlightenment in explicating the writings of Robert Burns, while Jon Mee has propounded the existence of a trans-Pennine Enlightenment in his work on the Lunar Club and associated luminaries.[11] Comparing national Enlightenments has, in contrast, enabled a distillation of what these distinctive movements shared, such as the concern for political economy in John Robertson's study of Scotland and Naples, returning us to the puzzle of whether the Enlightenment was fundamentally a single European intellectual movement.[12] And with the globalizing turn in the wider study of the period, an Atlantic Enlightenment comes into focus.[13]

How then might we answer our apparently direct question: was Oliver Goldsmith representative of the Enlightenment? In offering an answer it might be useful to note the parallels in the two debates I have sketched. Both the discussions of the Enlightenment and of political identity have sought to reconcile their position by pluralizing and ranking them by scale of reach. And in applying these methods to the case at hand, we can perceive Goldsmith evincing multiple political identities and through this committing himself to multiple Enlightenments. Indeed, scaling up the first involves a multiplication of the second.

Let us begin with the local. Goldsmith spent most of his adult life in London, making his rather haphazard way through the Grub Street culture of occasional journalism and hack writing (see Chapter 23, 'Periodical and Literary Reviewing'). As Norma Clarke has documented, his writing was largely piecework, generated by commissions and projecting, rather than being coloured by the life of leisure enjoyed by Alexander Pope or, in other circumstances, Jonathan Swift. Goldsmith was fundamentally reliant on his pen for his fortune. In that, his life was spent actively engaged in what Jürgen Habermas influentially termed the literary public sphere.[14] The public sphere was enlightened to the extent that it engaged in debate, in criticism, and in often satiric commentary on the events of the day. Take, for example, the *Bee*, a failed essayistic periodical in the tradition of Addison and Steele's *Spectator* which Goldsmith headed up for eight issues in late 1759. As with the *Spectator*'s disavowal of politics, the *Bee* steered away from commenting on the ongoing Seven Years' War; nor did Goldsmith allude to political scandal. Instead he offered more whimsical fare, often reflecting on the condition of writing itself. Thus in 'An Account of the Augustan Age in England' he identified the reign of Queen Anne as the high point of literary creativity.

But Goldsmith was multifaceted in his deployment of dialects of Enlightenment. In this, he was of course not alone. He shared this flexibility with his contemporaries Richard Brinsley Sheridan and

Edmund Burke. And like them he suffered from having his Irish origins occluded by his incorporation into the more dominant strain of English debate. But what enabled this engagement with the English tradition was the existence of a shared platform on which Irish, English, and indeed Scottish writers could engage in controversy and constructive dialogue: namely an asymmetrical, rather spasmodic British Enlightenment concerned precisely with questions of personal identity, the integration of intellectual life, and the spread of British imperial influence overseas.

If Britain, then, is a central context for Goldsmith's dialects of Enlightenment, so, too, can we find direct evidence for his engagement with the continental European Enlightenment, notably that of France. His journalism was shot through with references to the great literary figures of the French Enlightenment, Voltaire and Montesquieu most notably (see Chapter 30, 'France and French Writing'). His European concern also found an outlet in his early poem *The Traveller*, the subtitle of which – 'A Prospect of Society' – speaks to its Enlightenment ambitions (see Chapter 22, 'Prospect Poetry'). Goldsmith makes the ambition of the work explicit in his statement of dedication. In a passage that carries loud echoes of Montesquieu's ambitions in *The Spirit of Laws* (1749), Goldsmith declared, 'My aims are right. Without espousing the cause of any party, I have attempted to moderate the rage of all. I have endeavoured to shew, that there may be equal happiness in states that are differently governed from our own; that every state has a particular principle of happiness, and that this principle in each may be carried to a mischievous excess' (*Traveller*, iii–iv). As he then versifies the sentiment:

> Such is the patriot's boast, where'er we roam,
> His first, best country ever is, at home.
> And yet, perhaps, if countries we compare,
> And estimate the blessings which they share;
> Tho' patriots flatter, still shall wisdom find
> An equal portion dealt to all mankind,
> As different good, by Art or Nature given,
> To different nations makes their blessings even.
>
> (*Traveller*, 5)

The Citizen of the World (1762) was similarly an intellectual offspring of Montesquieu's *Persian Letters* and Voltaire's *Letters on England* (see Chapter 11, 'Cosmopolitanism', and Chapter 26, 'Orientalism'). First appearing as a series of 'Chinese Letters' in the *Public Ledger*, it was compiled two years later under its more open title. Framed as a fictitious travelogue, the series of letters effected an occasional critique of British society and mores. Much has been made of the fact that the term the 'citizen of the world' appears only twice in the letter sequence. Yet this is to miss the point of the epithet. It is not that the fictitious Chinese author is positioned outside of national or racial identity; rather his position as an outsider to English society provides him with a distance from his surrounds, one that comes from his liminal standing between cultures. In doing so the author's alienation was a creative one, suggestive of a greater level of sophistication and cultivation to be found abroad. His presence was disruptive of the self-satisfaction of the home-bred patriot, such as that of the philosophic cobbler on which the Chinese correspondent reported in letter LXV. On being asked whether he had ever travelled, the cobbler retorted: 'I have lived, said he, a wandering sort of life now five and fifty years ... [but] I have never left the parish in which I was born but three times in my life that I can remember: but then there is not a street in the whole neighbourhood that I have not lived in, at some time or another' (*Citizen*, 1: 285).

In its defence of travel and the wider view it affords, the letter foreshadows the moral energy of *The Traveller*. And in framing the work as containing the insight of a traveller from China, Goldsmith moved his imagination beyond Europe and actively globalized his writing. The cosmopolitanism he promulgated was an imaginative one; it was to ask citizens to keep in mind a global context and to reckon with the local in that light. But the Chinese author remains an outsider to English society, and is recalcitrant in his commitment to his Chinese origins. What makes him cosmopolitan is not his desire or ability to shed one culture for another, but to learn from one culture what might be improved in the other: this is a cosmopolitanism of comparison, not one of sublimation.

Yet while this kind of cosmopolitanism may seem self-limiting, it was also in this early work that Goldsmith set out his vision of totalizing Enlightenment, one with both global ramifications and local applications. It might be suggested that for all their variety and the pecunious nature of their origins, his works were written in service to this vision. Goldsmith, then, is an Enlightenment figure, but one who tells us something discreet and important about the nature of the Enlightenment. To that we now turn.

The case of Oliver Goldsmith suggests that multiple Enlightenments can align with multiple political identities. Just as Goldsmith was capable of authoring significant works in numerous genres – a novel, plays, poetry, history, and journalism – so his political identity could encompass a variety of inflections. His loyalties reached from Ireland to England, to Britain, to

Europe, and even contained some globalizing tendencies. He was, in this specific sense, a product of the emergent British state with its asymmetrical unions and complex interweave of ethnicities.[15]

In that, Goldsmith was a shapeshifter capable of metamorphosis and able to speak in many tongues. He was at once able to work within the given locality of London and draw on his national origins in Ireland; to contribute to the national debate within England while availing of the stage a British context provided. He kept in his sight line the desire for a more Enlightened age in Europe while remaining aware of the globalizing impulse of imperial endeavour. In scaling up through this variety of geographic contexts for his Enlightenment vision he was at once mindful of the audiences for his works – readers of newspapers and periodicals, audiences in the playhouse, avid readers of literary fiction and travel writing. He was as at ease with genre-switching as he was with the crossing of political boundaries in his imaginative life.

This flexibility of intellectual ambit also extended beyond his array of political idioms to his capacity to deploy numerous Enlightenment dialects: Irish, English, British, European, and even global. But for all this fluidity, there was a coherence and consistency to his articulation of Enlightenment ideas. If we accept the spectrum of ideas that ran from counter-Enlightenment thought to the radical manifestations of freethinking, Goldsmith was a devoted exponent of the Moderate Enlightenment, one grounded in empirical methodology and sceptical of the attraction of radical change. He was also an exponent of a latitudinarian approach to religious questions, which spanned the churches of England, Scotland, and Ireland, as well as finding followers in the Dutch Republic (see Chapter 15, 'Religion'). And he was a committed participant in the republic of letters, reimagined by Clifford Siskin and William Warner as characterized by modes and forms of mediation.[16]

In his commitment to these values, Goldsmith finally tells us something of the Enlightenment's own nature. His writing relies on the possibility that the Enlightenment can be conceived of as a utopian project, imagining a 'no place' of perfectibility and tranquillity. He is engaged in what Lyman Tower Sargent calls 'social dreaming' and in thinking through the consequences of social 'estrangement' which Darko Suvin sees as central to the utopian condition. He is also part of the tradition of eighteenth-century Irish utopianism sketched by Deirdre Ní Chuanacháin.[17] His work might also be included in the utopias of the British Enlightenment collected by Gregory Claeys.[18] But Goldsmith's imagination ultimately occupies that no place which is the defining characteristic of the Enlightenment's concern with an improved futurity. It is this imaginative location which allows him to move across the boundaries that defined much of the literary landscape of his time, and which permits him to speak so fluently to our time and place.

Notes

1. Peter Gay, *The Party of Humanity: Essays on the French Enlightenment* (New York: Alfred A. Knopf, 1964).
2. Robert Darnton, 'The High Enlightenment and the Low Life of Literature', in *The Literary Underground of the Old Regime* (Cambridge, MA: Harvard University Press, 1982), 1–40; Pat Rogers, *Grub Street: Studies in a Subculture* (London: Methuen, 1972).
3. Jonathan Israel, *A Revolution of the Mind: Radical Enlightenment and the Intellectual Origins of Modern Democracy* (Princeton University Press, 2009); Ritchie Robertson, *The Enlightenment: The Pursuit of Happiness, 1680–1790* (London: Allen Lane, 2020); Anthony Pagden, *The Enlightenment and Why It Still Matters* (Oxford University Press, 2013).
4. For a thoughtful analysis of the historiography surrounding the term, see Vincenzo Ferrone, *The Enlightenment: History of an Idea* (Princeton University Press, 2010).
5. Margaret C. Jacob, *The Secular Enlightenment* (Princeton University Press, 2019); David Sorkin, *The Religious Enlightenment: Protestants, Jews, and Catholics from London to Vienna* (Princeton University Press, 2008); Ulrich Lerner, *The Catholic Enlightenment: The Forgotten History of a Global Movement* (Oxford University Press, 2016); Shumel Feiner, *The Jewish Enlightenment* (University of Pennsylvania Press, 2004).
6. J. G. A. Pocock, *Barbarism and Religion, Volume One: The Enlightenments of Edward Gibbon* (Cambridge University Press, 1999), 50–71.
7. Roy Porter and Mikulas Teich, eds., *The Enlightenment in National Context* (Cambridge University Press, 1981).
8. See for instance the essays in Richard Butterwick, Simon Davies, and Gabriel Sánchez Espinosa, eds., *Peripheries of the Enlightenment, SVEC* (Oxford University Press, 2008).
9. Michael Brown, *The Irish Enlightenment* (Cambridge, MA: Harvard University Press, 2016). On Goldsmith, see pages 339–43.
10. Umut Özkirimli, *Theories of Nationalism: A Critical Introduction* (London: Palgrave, 2017).
11. Colin Kidd, 'Satire, Hypocrisy and the Ayrshire–Renfrewshire Enlightenment', in *The International Companion to John Galt*, ed. Gerard Carruthers and Colin Kidd (Glasgow: Association for Scottish Literary Studies, 2017), 15–33; Jon Mee, 'Transpennine Enlightenment: The Literary and Philosophical Societies and Knowledge Networks in the North, 1781–1830', *Journal for Eighteenth-Century Studies*, 38 (2015), 599–612.

12. John Robertson, *The Case for the Enlightenment: Scotland and Naples, 1680–1760* (Cambridge University Press, 2005).

13. Francis D. Cogliano and Susan Manning, *The Atlantic Enlightenment* (London: Routledge, 2008). On the global context for the Enlightenment, see Sebastian Conrad, 'Enlightenment in Global History: A Historiographic Critique', *American Historical Review*, 117 (2012), 999–1027, and David T. Gies and Cynthia Wall, eds., *The Eighteenth Centuries: Global Networks of Enlightenment* (Charlottesville: University of Virginia Press, 2018).

14. Jürgen Habermas, *The Structural Transformation of the Public Sphere: An Inquiry into a Category of Bourgeois Society* (Cambridge: Polity Press, 1989).

15. See Ian McBride and Tony Claydon, eds., *Protestantism and National Identity, Britain and Ireland, c.1650–c.1850* (Cambridge University Press, 1998).

16. Clifford Siskin and William Warner, eds., *This Is Enlightenment* (University of Chicago Press, 2010).

17. Deirdre Ní Chuanacháin, *Utopianism in Eighteenth-Century Ireland* (Cork University Press, 2016). Sargent is cited on page 12; Suvin on page 21.

18. Gregory Claeys, ed., *Utopias of the British Enlightenment* (Cambridge University Press, 1990).

CHAPTER 6

Universities

David A. Fleming

There were about 130 universities in Europe when Goldsmith was born, most founded in the preceding 200 years. The largest concentration was in France, Spain, and Italy, which resulted in nearly three quarters of all universities having a Catholic affiliation. Most of the Protestant institutions were found in the German states and the United Provinces (now the Netherlands), many emerging as Lutheran or Calvinist establishments following the confessional divisions of the sixteenth and seventeenth centuries. The four universities in Scotland (Aberdeen, Edinburgh, Glasgow, and St Andrews) were all Presbyterian, while the two in England (Oxford and Cambridge) and the one in Ireland (Trinity College) were Anglican, reflecting the established churches within those kingdoms (see Chapter 15, 'Religion'). Although many universities still served their original purpose of educating clergymen, lawyers, and doctors, their function had expanded by the early modern period to embrace the broader education of men. To what extent they advanced or even embraced the new scientific, cultural, and philosophical ideas emerging during the Renaissance and later the Enlightenment has been a matter of debate, but recent research suggests that the nature of the early modern university was complex and varied. Some adapted to the new ideas and were active in promoting them, while others ignored or resisted the challenge that seemed to threaten established notions of what was taught in these institutions and how. Even within institutions, individuals might be divided on these new ideas. This contrasting experience was evident in Britain and Ireland. While the English and Irish universities played little or no role in embracing or advancing the new thinking of the eighteenth century, those in Scotland facilitated the emergence of a distinctly Scottish Enlightenment (see Chapter 5, 'Enlightenments'). But for students these longer developments may have gone unnoticed: most were interested in the immediate task of obtaining the necessary qualification for a career in the church, law, or medicine, or simply to have acquired the learning expected of a gentleman.

Irishmen who sought a university education typically attended only one institution. For some, such as lawyers, attendance at an Inn of Court was required once an initial university degree had been obtained. Goldsmith's experience was unusual in that he formally attended three universities: Dublin, Edinburgh, and Leiden. This path was a consequence, perhaps, of vocational uncertainty as he pondered what his future might hold. Attendance at university implied social status as so few either attained the prerequisite learning or had the necessary financial means to pay fees and maintain themselves. As the son of a clergyman who had himself acquired a university education in order to minister in the established Church of Ireland, the young Goldsmith was schooled from an early age with the expectation, perhaps, that he too would be educated at Dublin. But the family's pecuniary circumstances limited his prospects. He might never have been admitted were it not for the fact that Trinity College accepted students who could prove their academic ability and were willing to perform menial work in the institution in lieu of fees. Thus when the seventeen-year-old Goldsmith matriculated on 11 June 1745, he was admitted as one of the seven 'sizars' or students whose fees were paid in return for their labour. In all seventy students were admitted in that year, of whom fifty-five paid their own way and were termed 'pensioners', seven fellow-commoners who were entitled to certain privileges, and one noble-man's son.

Having obtained a bachelor of arts degree in 1750, Goldsmith travelled to Edinburgh to study medicine. His path there and ultimately to Leiden was not atypical. Although he might have studied medicine in Ireland at the College of Physicians in Dublin, founded in 1692, doing so in Scotland would result in a quicker qualification and perhaps was more attractive to a young man eager to see the world. Most Irishmen who practised medicine in Ireland, particularly those Catholics and Presbyterians unwilling to take the religious test for entry into the Irish College of Physicians, travelled to the continent for medical training. Leiden, and increasingly Edinburgh, appealed as medical training there seemed more practical and engaging. Between 1575 and 1875, 236 Irish students matriculated to study medicine in Leiden, to which must be added those like Goldsmith whose names were not recorded in the register.

Goldsmith arrived in Edinburgh in October 1752. There was already a significant Irish presence in the university as many Ulstermen, particularly Presbyterians, found it both practical and convenient to study in

Scotland. Goldsmith spent two years there before deciding to complete his education at the medical school at the University of Paris, but in the end determined to do so at Leiden. This decision followed a long-trodden path for many Scottish medical students, who typically moved to Leiden to complete their education. Unlike at most other universities across Europe, no religious test was required of students entering Leiden. As a result, the place attracted students of various faiths and nationalities. But this traffic between Scotland and the United Provinces was in decline by the 1740s as Edinburgh's reputation for medicine began to outrival that of Leiden and other schools. From the second half of the eighteenth century Edinburgh reversed the trend, attracting ever more international students to Scotland.

Although Goldsmith is not recorded among the 173 students who matriculated at Leiden in 1754, we can be sure from his correspondence that he began his studies there in that year. It was not unusual for some to attend lectures but not matriculate. Some were well-to-do visitors, there for a term or more before moving on. Others, like Goldsmith, may have been unable to stump up the necessary fees. Goldsmith recalled only four 'British' students in Leiden when he was there. In reality, six from Britain and Ireland were admitted in 1754, and a handful of others who had matriculated in the years preceding must have been there too. All were there to study medicine. The only other Irishman admitted in 1754 was his friend from Trinity and Edinburgh, Thomas Ellis. A year later, William Broughton of Dublin followed exactly the same route.

Each university had a distinctive character defined by its age, its religious ethos, its governance structures, its architecture, and its curriculum. When Goldsmith entered Trinity College, it was 153 years in existence, founded in 1592. Leiden and Edinburgh were not much older, established in 1575 and 1582 respectively. Although universities may have all seemed similar in function and purpose, early modern institutions developed in different ways. Trinity modelled itself on Oxford and Cambridge, each espousing Anglican principles under the patronage of the monarch, who appointed a chancellor as nominal head of the institution. Edinburgh and Leiden had a different character. Though they had been established by the state and had a distinctly Calvinist religious ethos, the city authorities in both cases had a significant say over university appointments and finances. In Edinburgh the town council were the College's patrons and during Goldsmith's time made appointments and oversaw its finances. In Leiden a board of governors formed by three appointees from the states making up the United Provinces and four drawn from those who had been burgomasters of the city took an active part in the university's administration.

The early modern university was small in comparison to its modern successor. In Trinity a provost, twenty fellows, five professors, and six lecturers catered for about 360 students during Goldsmith's residence there. The provost was appointed for life by the king's deputy in Ireland, the lord lieutenant, and was, until 1774, drawn from the fellows or from Oxford or Cambridge. By 1750, Edinburgh's student numbers, at about 600, were nearly twice those of Dublin, of which half pursued medicine. At its head was a principal, appointed for life by the city's corporation. As in Dublin the principal was typically a clergyman. At Leiden the head of the university was the rector, who was chosen annually by the board of governors from amongst its sixteen statutory professors, making it a less powerful position compared to Dublin and Edinburgh where incumbents tended to wield influence over appointments. Besides professors and assessors, Leiden employed several supernumerary professors for its roughly 650 students.

Notions of hierarchy and place typified these universities. Just as the student body was stratified according to status and means, staff too observed distinctions amongst themselves. In Dublin each distinction among the fellowship and between scholar, fellow-commoner, pensioner and sizar was reflected in the various gowns and trimmings students were required to don each day. It is not surprising therefore that Goldsmith would later resent his time as an undergraduate in labouring alongside the college's servants. Leiden was the least affected by outward signs of hierarchy, there being no requirement for either professors or students to wear gowns on a regular basis. But some students set themselves apart by choosing to wear a distinctive oriental dressing gown, which remained fashionable for most of the eighteenth century, much to the disgust of some visitors to the city.

Most medieval universities had been established in monastic settings, with buildings formed around a quadrangle for dining, sleeping, and safeguarding books. Others developed a distinctive architectural arrangement over time, often leasing buildings initially and allowing students to board privately. To any young man from the Irish provinces, Trinity College and Dublin more generally must have made an impression. Just opposite the College a sumptuous, neoclassical parliament building of white Portland stone had been completed in 1731. The College proper had a mixture of seventeenth- and eighteenth-century buildings around two large and two small quadrangles or 'squares', with a number of gardens and open spaces to the west and south. The grandest and most imposing was the three-storey new library, completed in 1732, which was reserved for fellows and graduates. In the year Goldsmith left Dublin, the College's principal, west façade, which with the parliament building formed College Green, was taken down and work began on a new building completed in 1759. Overall, the ensemble gave an impression of modernity and stature, befitting the city's claim to be second only to London in the Hanoverian dominions.

Edinburgh and Leiden were much smaller cities. Edinburgh's university buildings were 'more convenient than magnificent', as one 1755 account described them. Located away from the city's main thoroughfare, in the southern part of the city, its buildings, some dating prior to its foundation, were arranged around an irregular square. Unlike at Dublin, neither students or professors were required to reside within the university, many taking private lodgings. Goldsmith found a room in Trunk Close north of the university, just off the city's main street and a ten-minute walk away. As a result the character of the university was very different from the more collegial, though confined atmosphere at Dublin.

Unlike Edinburgh and Dublin, Leiden's buildings were not concentrated in any one particular area of the still fortified city. Its most prominent was the sixteenth-century gothic Academy building located in the south-west part of the city. Just behind it was one of Europe's oldest and best-stocked botanical gardens, laid out in 1590. Its library and anatomical theatre, built in 1595, were located in a neighbouring street, separated from the Academy Building by a canal. By the eighteenth century the anatomical theatre was more of a curiosity for travellers than anything else, with its collection of human and animal skeletons and preserved remains, including Egyptian mummies. Medical students learned by attending patients at a hospital located in a converted monastery several streets away to the north. As at Edinburgh, students at Leiden generally resided in private lodgings, very often made up of compatriots. Goldsmith initially found lodgings from Emerentia Henrietta Kechler, the widow of Jean Alliaume, on Pieterskerkgracht, in the heart of the city and close to the principal church, St Pieter's. If Edinburgh lacked a collegial character, Leiden was certainly defined by its university. With a population of 38,000, it was much smaller than Dublin and Edinburgh, and therefore more intimate, and had a much more diverse population.

Goldsmith's education at Dublin was based on a curriculum established more than 100 years before, where students were required to spend four years in study before they might receive a degree. The daily routine was divided between classics and what contemporaries called science, or what today is referred to as mathematics, physics, and philosophy. Once matriculated each student was given a tutor to provide instruction in all disciplines. Goldsmith was allotted to Rev. Theaker Wilder, who had been appointed one of the junior fellows in the same year Goldsmith arrived. Regardless of the formal curriculum, universities such as Trinity were to inculcate notions of discipline, respect, and moral values. In this regard, the tutor played a pivotal role. Wilder seems to have been as much concerned with Goldsmith's behaviour as he was with his studies.

The course of lectures in classics prescribed most of the major Greek and Roman works, including the *Aeneid* and *Georgics*, the *Iliad*, and the *Odyssey*, besides the works of Juvenal, Livy, Lucien, Sallust, Suetonius, Tacitus, and Xenophon, among others. What emphasis might be placed on one or other depended much on the attitude of the tutor and professor. In the science course, logic was studied in the first two years, natural science in the third, and ethics in the fourth. The junior freshman year was devoted to Franco Petri Burgersdijk's *Institutionum logicarum* (1626), while the senior freshmen studied Jean Le Clerc's *Logica, sive ars ratiocinandi* (1692) and extracts from the Polish Jesuit Martinus Smiglecius's *Logica* (1618). Although these were old works by the time Goldsmith was introduced to them, they were nevertheless considered useful well into the second half of the eighteenth century. Both Burgersdijk and Smiglecius extolled the Aristotelian approach to learning philosophy, which by Goldsmith's time was largely outdated and had been replaced in other European universities by a mechanical philosophy of understanding natural phenomena. But if these works might be considered old-fashioned, they were somewhat balanced by those of Le Clerc, a French Protestant and theologian influenced by the work of the English physician and philosopher John Locke.

When Goldsmith reached his third year, when natural science was studied, he was expected to read Le Clerc's *Physics* (1696), Edward Wells's *Young Gentleman's Astronomy* (1712), Bernhardt Varen's *Universal Geography* (1650), and that part of Jean-Baptiste du Hamel's *Philosophia Vetus et Nova ad Usum Scholæ Accommodata* (1678) which dealt with general physics and which had been commissioned by Jacques-Nicolas Colbert, archbishop of Rouen as a textbook for universities throughout France. In the final year, students at Dublin were to study ethics and metaphysics.

This curriculum was delivered by way of lecture and tutorial instruction and examined by disputation every year. Students were either commended for their diligence in attending lectures or cautioned for neglecting to do so. Goldsmith's first year seems unremarkable in this regard: he featured in neither list. But in his second and third years he was both commended and admonished for attendance or lack of it. Much worse, on 9 May 1748 he was 'turned down' during the term examinations and not permitted to progress into the next year. Only a handful of students were ever 'turned down', making his situation atypical. He would, however, go on to obtain a degree.

Unlike Dublin, Leiden and Edinburgh had made great strides in advancing a modern curriculum and method of teaching. Both too had professors who made significant contributions to intellectual enquiry, evident in the publications emanating from them, which would not be evident in Dublin until much later. One of the major differences between Dublin and the Scottish and Dutch universities was in the method of instruction. In Edinburgh and Leiden specialist professors and lecturers taught their own disciplines, contrasting the experience in Dublin where the tutor was expected to cover the entire curriculum, with the professor providing regular lectures.

Leiden's reputation had been built on the scholarship and teaching of the likes of Justus Lipsius (1547–1606), Joseph Scaliger (1540–1609), and the medic Herman Boerhaave (1668–1738). Boerhaave's approach placed emphasis on practical training along with disputation and the traditional lecture. Besides learning about the theory and nature of the body from classical authors, students were instructed through anatomical dissection and inspection, as well as practical classes in botany and chemistry. Since the mid seventeenth century students had presented themselves in the city's hospital to receive tuition by the bedside. In the first decades of the eighteenth century Boerhaave's approach to teaching, which reduced the subject to its basic elements by removing irrelevant, usually antiquated ideas, won widespread acclaim. He also advocated an incremental curriculum which first introduced students to the basics of mathematics, chemistry, and mechanics (influenced by the ideas of Isaac Newton), before examining medical theory in the following year, and ultimately the study of disease and remedies in the next. Apart from those practical classes in the hospital, students were required to attend lectures, though by Goldsmith's time many were being offered by the professors in their own lodgings and for additional fees.

Edinburgh consciously modelled itself on Leiden, particularly from the beginning of the eighteenth century when reforms aimed to broaden its largely theological curriculum into other areas such as medicine, anatomy, botany, history, and law, and thereby appeal to Scotland's country and city elites. The three Scottish professors associated with medicine that Goldsmith mentions in his correspondence (Alexander Munro, Andrew Plummer, and Charles Alston) had all studied at Leiden before returning to Edinburgh. The emergence of a distinguished school of medicine modelled on Boerhaave's ideas was seen as one of the most important consequences of these developments. Perhaps reflecting these changes, the young Goldsmith in 1754 thought that medicine was not taught as well in Leiden as it was in Edinburgh and that most of his Dutch professors were 'lazy', excepting the professor of chemistry, Jerome David Gaubius (1705–80).

Nearly all universities in early modern Europe were chartered or corporate bodies providing special privileges for those who were members of them. In Leiden students were exempted from paying certain taxes on wine and could be reprimanded for wrongdoing only by the university rather than the civic authorities. Although such legal exemptions did not exist in Dublin, there was nevertheless an idea that the university and its members were distinct and therefore beyond the normal reach of the law in certain circumstances. In particular students and staff believed that the civic authorities had no jurisdiction within the College. During Goldsmith's time in Dublin a head porter refused to admit the lord mayor into the College while wearing his regalia of office, indicating in a real sense that the city's authority did not extend there.

It is within this context that Goldsmith's involvement in a student-provoked attack on a city bailiff in 1747 can be understood. In May that year, Goldsmith and at least nine other senior freshmen seized a bailiff who had arrested a student for debt within the College. Upset by this breach of their presumed privilege, a number of students dowsed the bailiff with water. They then proceeded to mobilize a crowd of citizens to rescue their imprisoned compatriot, which resulted in two deaths when the prison authorities fired on the mob. Significantly, the College itself rather than the civil authorities reprimanded the students. Had the students been civilly prosecuted, it might have inflamed student sentiment further. Five students were expelled, while Goldsmith and four others were admonished for the support they gave to them.

Goldsmith's own views on universities and the education they provided were given not long after his college years had concluded in *An Enquiry into the Present State of Polite Learning in Europe* (1759; see Chapter 25, 'Authorship'). Here he divided institutions into three types. The first were those of the 'old scholastic establishment where the pupils are immured, talk nothing but Latin, and support every day syllogistical disputations in school philosophy', which he decried. The second were those where students 'are under few restrictions, where all scholastic jargon is banished, where they take a degree when they think proper, and live not in the college but the city'. Here he placed Edinburgh and Leiden, and perhaps best reflected his own experience. The third was 'a mixture of the two former, where the pupils are restrained but not confined, where many, though not all, the absurdities of scholastic philosophy are suppressed and where the first degree is taken after four years matriculation', giving Dublin, Oxford, and Cambridge as examples (*Enquiry*, 185–6). For Goldsmith, Edinburgh and Leiden had offered freedom from the restrictions and servitude he had experienced in Dublin and the practical knowledge he hoped to acquire. Yet, notwithstanding his own trajectory, he believed that universities like Oxford produced the best learned men by which society was enriched. Overall, Goldsmith approved of universities, though could not help reflect that 'the only true school of improvement' was experience of the world itself (*Enquiry*, 189).

CHAPTER 7

Libraries

Paul Goring

Among the marble busts of philosophers and authors in the magnificent Long Room Library of Trinity College Dublin, is one of Oliver Goldsmith, sculpted in the 1820s by William Behnes, showing him looking pensive but with head turned, as though glancing to see what company might be entering the room. The Long Room provides a fitting setting for a depiction of Goldsmith, not only because of his eminent marble companions who, by association, silently vouch for his significance in the world of letters, but also because his short life was lived during a great age of libraries and much of his published output was facilitated by evolving habits and systems of book collecting and knowledge circulation. Goldsmith indeed must have walked – and, more importantly, read – in the very space where his monument stands today; the construction of the Long Room was completed a dozen years before he went up to study at Trinity College in 1745 (see Chapter 6, 'Universities'). That building work was just one development of a library amongst many in the eighteenth century, as institutional, commercial, and private book collections were expanded, newly gathered, combined, catalogued, and shelved in repurposed or specially designed spaces for the benefit of both scholarly readers and the broader reading public, a growth witnessed in almost all European countries and beyond.

The founding of the British Museum Library in London in 1753 is emblematic of the expansion of Britain's library culture that was ongoing in Goldsmith's lifetime. It was based on a vast private collection of books and manuscripts owned by Sir Hans Sloane which was acquired for the nation and then augmented with other collections, notably around 9,000 volumes given by George II. The library was opened to the public in 1759, by which time Goldsmith had settled in London. With a small reading room and a ticketing system for access, the library limited the number of readers, but still it was London's first major library open to the public and it gave a new availability to materials that were formerly in private hands.[1] At the same time, for those with the means to pay for reading matter, commercial circulating libraries were being established across Britain. There were proprietary libraries, owned collectively by shareholding readers, as well as subscription libraries charging membership or borrowing fees. Such enterprises varied greatly in terms of ownership, size, type of content, cost of borrowing, and locale, with some collections housed in dedicated premises while others were adjuncts to clubs, meeting rooms, and coffee-houses. Collectively, though, they point to the growing public appetite for books and to the inventiveness of entrepreneurs focused on both creating and satisfying demand.[2]

Personal ownership of books, at many levels of society, was also increasing markedly during this period. A modest collection of books filling a shelf or two became a common feature of eighteenth-century households supported by middling incomes, whilst wealthier collectors established larger collections, sometimes involving the designation or building of dedicated library rooms. Some private collections, in fact, came to rival major institutional libraries. One of the largest and most renowned in Goldsmith's time was gathered by Topham Beauclerk, a friend of Samuel Johnson and, like Goldsmith, a founding member of the Literary Club (see Chapter 8, 'The Club'). 'Everybody goes to see it', Horace Walpole wrote of Beauclerk's library. 'It's put the [British] Museum's nose quite out of joint.'[3]

Goldsmith himself was not a collector on this scale, but he too assembled a notable personal library of which a revealing record survives in the form of an auction catalogue. It was common for books to be disposed of through auction – second-hand books were valuable commodities – and after Goldsmith died his books and other possessions were sold in this way, having been listed in a published *Catalogue of the Houshold Furniture, With the Select Collection of Scarce, Curious and Valuable Books, in English, Latin, Greek, French, Italian, and Other Languages, Late the Library of Dr. Goldsmith, Deceased*. The catalogue is reproduced in *Sale Catalogues of Libraries of Eminent Persons, Volume 7: Poets and Men of Letters*, edited by Hugh Amory. The cataloguing is sometimes slipshod; the auctioneer, George Good, was primarily a trader in second-hand furniture, leading Amory to describe the catalogue as 'what we would expect of an upholsterer, for whom books are merely another form of interior decoration'.[4] It would have served its purpose for buyers, though, and many (perhaps most) of the titles – which are shortened but usually given with dates and numbers of volumes – can be linked to known publications. Auction catalogues rarely provide definitive insights into what a book collection might have meant for its owner and how that collection was used, but a cautious examination of the contours of Goldsmith's library can nonetheless add texture to our understanding of him as a figure whose authorship rested on wide and immensely varied reading and of how he accessed his reading matter.[5]

The catalogue groups Goldsmith's books into 162 lots according to book size – 30 lots of folios, 26 of quartos, and 106 of octavos and duodecimos. Many of the lots were bundles rather than single titles, and altogether the catalogue presents around 300 named titles, including numerous multi-volume works. The collection also included around 110 further works, which are recorded in the catalogue without the titles given. The first lot of octavos and duodecimos, for example, included 'Voyages to Bengal and Buenos Ayres. Three odd volumes of Plays. Epistles of Aristaenetus and 4 more'.[6] Which plays were found in those odd volumes and which four titles were deemed unworthy of full listing can never be known; the catalogue, then, offers an incomplete picture of Goldsmith's collection – and with the unspecified titles it does not allow firm conclusions to be drawn about books that Goldsmith did *not* possess. But from the titles that are listed the outlines of the collection can be charted and some patterns in Goldsmith's acquisition of books and reading can be inferred.

Like most intellectuals of the period, Goldsmith was a multilingual reader, and this is reflected in the collection, which included around as many French books as English books, together with numerous works in Latin and others in Italian, German, and Greek. There is no significant body of Dutch publications, but in terms of origin all the major publication centres of Europe are represented. Even the most cursory survey of the titles shows it to be the collection of an intellectual keen to be in tune with the currents of European thought. The titles cover the breadth of the natural sciences, with luxury editions of classic works, such as a Latin folio edition of Francis Bacon's works from 1665 ('Baconi Opera, *Franc.* 1665'; folios: 3), as well as more recent works such as John Hill's *The History of Fossils* (1748) (folios: 27). As a professional author, Goldsmith had many literary skills, some of which lay in extracting material from multiple sources and synthesizing it to produce new works – he possessed, as the editors of his letters put it, an 'indefatigable and painstaking talent for compilation and assembly' – and in his library some of his sources may be traced (*Letters*, lxi–lxii). The collection, for example, would have provided Goldsmith with valuable material when he was compiling his mammoth work of geographical and natural history, *A History of the Earth, and Animated Nature* (1774). He had three multivolume works by Karl von

Linné, all in Latin (octavos: 100, 101, 102), Charles de Geer's *Mémoires pour Servir à l'Histoire des Insectes* (1752–78) (quartos: 18), and Antoine Gouan's *Histoire des Poissons* (1770) (quartos: 3), as well as a volume on quadrupeds from Konrad von Gesner's venerable *Historia Animalium* from 1551 (folios: 3). It is known that Goldsmith drew directly on all of these works when composing his *Animated Nature*, and there are further works in the collection – notably the transactions of the leading scientific societies of France, Germany, and England – which he also consulted (see Chapter 16, 'Natural History and Science').[7] Among the lots of smaller-format books is one offering the 'Histoire de L'Académie Royale' in fifteen volumes, but with 'the 11th wanting' – the gap in the run perhaps a sign of carelessness or maybe of his willingness to lend books to aid the circulation of knowledge. We know from his letters that Goldsmith had a liberal and sometimes casual attitude towards books. 'I did not know what were the volumes I sent', he wrote to Hester Thrale in 1773, 'but sent what I had' (*Letters*, 127).

Extending the collection of learned works were numerous volumes of philosophy, with works by the French *philosophes* and *encyclopédistes* particularly well represented. The final quarto lot is comprised of twenty-five volumes of the *Encyclopédie ou Dictionnaire Raisonné des Sciences, des Arts et des Métiers*, dated 1770 (quartos: 26), and, suggesting his attentiveness to philosophical debate, he also had responses to the *Encyclopédie*: Voltaire's 'Questions sur L'Encyclopédie, 2 tom, 1771' (octavos: 80) and 'Dictionnaire Critique Pittoresque & Sentencieux' by Louis-Antoine de Caraccioli, from 1768 (octavos: 39). There are other French-language reference works, such as the 'Dictionnaire Littéraire' from 1768 (octavos: 38) and *Dictionnaire de Littérature* from 1770 (octavos: 49), while among the single-authored French intellectual works are runs of volumes by Voltaire, Fontenelle, and Montesquieu (octavos: 57, 58, 89), and the 'Chefs d'Oeuvres de Marmontel' (quartos: 4). This last work was published in Paris in 1773, the year before Goldsmith died, and generally the collection suggests that he was keeping up to date with the very latest philosophical interventions and also that, in his final decade, he had sufficient funds to buy new publications (see Chapter 30, 'France and French Writing').[8] The catalogue lists a small number of works from the sixteenth century – books which were antiquarian in his own day – and there are more from the seventeenth century – but it was predominantly a library of modern and relatively modern publications. It included ancient writers, though, and Goldsmith had to hand most of the classical authors whose presence was de rigueur in an eighteenth-century scholarly library.

The catalogue lists a significant stock of travel works, both old and more recent. This content in his library is, of course, in tune with Goldsmith's fundamentally cosmopolitan perspective; such books are fitting for the shelves of a man who had wandered extensively in Europe, who addressed geographical topics in his writing, and who chose a 'citizen of the world' as one of his authorial personae. He also had 'Lettres de Montesquieu' (octavos: 4) – in other words, *Lettres Persanes* (1721), Montesquieu's fictional travelogue which, with its oriental perspective and epistolary form, was one of the more significant precursors to the *Letters from a Chinese Philosopher* that Goldsmith offered in his *Citizen of the World* (1762; see Chapter 11, 'Cosmopolitanism', and Chapter 26, 'Orientalism').

There were many other literary works in the collection. Austin Dobson, surveying the catalogue in the nineteenth century, observed that it was particularly rich 'in French minstrels and playwrights', and there are indeed numerous French literary works, although here the vagaries of the catalogue impede the uncovering of a finely detailed picture.[9] In two adjacent lots, for example, are found 'Four odd vols. of Cornelle's [*sic*] Plays, and 7 more French books' and 'French Plays by Avis. Ditto by Grange. Ditto by Champmelé. Theatre de la Foire. Ditto by Favart, and 5 more' (octavos: 4 and 5). But with other lots showing that he had, for example, the works of the playwrights Louis de Boissy, David-Augustin de Brueys, and Florent Carton (known as Dancourt) (octavos: 10 and 36), there is little doubt that Goldsmith took a deep interest in the French dramatic tradition. He also had French novels, including *Thérèse Philosophe* (1748), a hybrid of philosophy and pornography by the Marquis d'Argens (octavos: 62), and other continental prose works by José Francisco de Isla and Pietro Chiari, leading Hugh Amory to conclude, with some primness, that Goldsmith had a 'highly unusual taste in novels'.[10]

The library was also stocked with English-language playwrights and poets: Chaucer, Milton, Waller, Davenant, Vanbrugh, Dryden, Rowe, Prior, Pope, Gay, Percy , and others. Among the more recent poetic works is John Leslie's *Killarney*, published in Dublin in 1772 (quartos: 22). The presence of this notable Irish topographical poem – one which probes the position of Ireland within the world and in relation to empire – is suggestive of Goldsmith's ongoing interest in the politics and culture of Ireland as well as in a poetic genre in which he himself had excelled with *The Deserted Village* (1770; see Chapter 21, 'Pastoral Poetry', and Chapter 22, 'Prospect Poetry').[11] Regarding poetic composition, he had two copies of Edward Bysshe's *The Art of English Poetry* (1702) (octavos: 22

and 23) – perhaps he consulted this work and mined its dictionary of rhymes when writing his own verse.

Among the English-language prose works are periodicals – *The Spectator, The World, The Idler,* and *The Connoisseur* (octavos: 17, 23, 3, and 24) – as well as some novels. He had two volumes of 'D'Foe's Works', apparently in French translation,[12] and twelve volumes of 'Fielding's Works', as well as *A Series of Genuine Letters between Henry and Frances* (1757), a genre-blurring sentimental work blending fact and fiction by Elizabeth and Richard Griffith (octavos: 14, 21, and 2). The listed titles, though, include relatively little English-language prose fiction – more might be expected in the library of the author of *The Vicar of Wakefield* (1766).

Given Goldsmith's studies and aspirations to practice as a doctor, the paucity of medical books in the library may also appear surprising. He had a copy of Jean Astruc's *A Treatise of the Venereal Disease* from 1754 (quartos: 14), but there are basically very few medical titles. Some of the unspecified 'others' may have been medical books, but regarding the absence of content that might be expected in the collection, two points should be made: firstly, Goldsmith had almost certainly shed countless books during his financially unstable and, for a time, peripatetic life; secondly, much of his reading would have been of books that he did not own. Amory notes that 'it may well be that the improvident poet had formed and pawned several libraries previously', and it does seem that Goldsmith's bibliophilia was not of a kind that made parting with books difficult.[13] As a student in Dublin, for example, he apparently sold his books to facilitate a trip to Cork (see Ginger, 56). More important, though, is the fact that Goldsmith's personal library, whatever it contained at different points in his life, was just one of many collections of reading matter and source material which he must have accessed as a reader and researcher.

Examining the sources of Goldsmith's *Animated Nature,* Winifred Lynskey observed that the scientific works he drew upon most liberally, such as the Comte de Buffon's encyclopaedic *Histoire Naturelle* (1762–8), are in fact not listed in the auction catalogue.[14] With a wider focus, Amory notes that the books sold at the auction 'do not seem to represent Goldsmith's reading very adequately or even his intellectual debts'.[15] Clearly he read widely beyond his own collection, enjoying the many opportunities he would have had to consult books he did not own. As a student in Dublin, Edinburgh, and Leiden he would have had access to the university libraries, and when he arrived in London in 1756 the positions he took on were of a kind that would have afforded access to books. As a reviewer for Ralph Griffiths's *Monthly Review* – with lodgings at the premises of the magazine – he would have been immersed in a stream of the very latest publications and, as a London resident, he would, if he could afford the fee, also have had reading opportunities at many of the coffee-houses which kept up-to-date and often very extensive libraries for the use of their clientele.[16] As he became established in the city, his widening network of social connections opened up opportunities for using personal libraries that were far better stocked than his own. In his last years, for example, it appears he was a regular visitor to the home of Topham Beauclerk. 'I see Mr Beauclerc very often both in town and country,' he reported in a letter in 1771 (*Letters*, 98). Some of the research for *Animated Nature* was almost certainly undertaken in Beauclerk's vast library.[17]

Goldsmith was known to handle books very roughly. Sir John Hawkins recalled Goldsmith tearing 'out of a printed book six leaves' to save the trouble of transcribing the content, and other anecdotes point to him, with his focus on the intellectual substance of a publication, having a carefree attitude to books as material objects.[18] He may not always have been the most welcome reader of other people's books, then, but there is little doubt that he read many more than he owned. The auction catalogue of his collection is certainly an illuminating and suggestive document. As a window into Goldsmith's reading, though, the catalogue needs to be seen in the context of a broader network of libraries, smaller book collections, and informal reading opportunities that presented themselves to or were sought out by a figure whose work as a writer across diverse genres clearly rested upon a voracious and lifelong consumption of a heterogeneous mass of printed matter.

Notes

1. P. R. Harris, 'The First Century of the British Museum Library', in *The Cambridge History of Libraries in Britain and Ireland, Volume II: 1640–1850*, ed. Giles Mandelbrote and K. A. Manley (Cambridge University Press, 2006), 405–21. Goldsmith is not included in Harris's list of 'various well-known people [who] made use of the Reading Room', but several of his friends and acquaintances, including Edmund Burke and Edmund Gibbon are listed (407).
2. James Raven, 'Libraries for Sociability: The Advance of the Subscription Library', in *The Cambridge History of Libraries*, 241–63. Raven dates the start of the proliferation of commercial circulating libraries to the mid eighteenth century (242).

3. *Horace Walpole's Correspondence with the Countess of Upper Ossory II: Vol. 33* in *The Yale Edition of Horace Walpole's Correspondence*, ed. W. S. Lewis and A. Dayle Wallace (New Haven, CT: Yale University Press, 1965), 136.

4. *Sale Catalogues of Libraries of Eminent Persons, Volume 7: Poets and Men of Letters*, ed. Hugh Amory (London: Mansell, 1973), 228. For Goldsmith's library, see pages 235–46. Amory provides a useful introduction to the catalogue (227–33). An earlier treatment, imagining the sale of both the furniture and books, is given in Austin Dobson, 'Goldsmith's Library', in *Eighteenth Century Vignettes* (London: Chatto and Windus, 1892), 166–75.

5. On the limitations of auction catalogues as sources, see Arthur der Weduwen, Andrew Pettegree and Graeme Kemp, 'Book Trade Catalogues: From Bookselling Tool to Book Historical Source', in *Book Trade Catalogues in Early Modern Europe* (Leiden: Brill, 2021), 3–32 (30–1). https://doi.org/10.11 63/9789004422247_002.

6. Amory, *Sale Catalogues*, 241. Hereafter titles in quotation marks are as they appear in the catalogue while those in italics have been normalized. References are given in the text by catalogue section and lot number.

7. Winifred Lynskey, 'The Scientific Sources of Goldsmith's *Animated Nature*', *Studies in Philology* 40:1 (1943), 33–57 (47–8).

8. Amory connects the newer books in the collection with the 'relative affluence' that Goldsmith enjoyed from the 1760s (*Sale Catalogues*, 228).

9. Dobson, 'Goldsmith's Library', 170.

10. Amory, *Sale Catalogues*, 229.

11. On the politics of *Killarney*, see Julia M. Wright, *Representing the National Landscape in Irish Romanticism* (Syracuse, NY: Syracuse University Press, 2014), 1–46.

12. The Defoe volumes are listed as '2 tom' whereas for the works in English 'vol.' is used.

13. Amory, *Sale Catalogues*, 228.

14. Lynskey, 'Scientific Sources', 45.

15. Amory, *Sale Catalogues*, 229.

16. Markman Ellis, 'Coffee-House Libraries in Mid-Eighteenth-Century London', *The Library*, 10:1 (2009), 3–40.

17. David Noy, *Dr Johnson's Friend and Robert Adam's Client: Topham Beauclerk* (Newcastle upon Tyne: Cambridge Scholars, 2016), 132.

18. John Hawkins, *The Life of Samuel Johnson* (London, 1787), 420.

CHAPTER 8

The Club

Ian Newman

The Literary Club, often simply known as 'The Club', was founded by
Samuel Johnson and Joshua Reynolds in 1764. The Club has, quite rightly,
been understood as the very epitome of a certain, familiar strain of
Enlightenment clubbability, modelling earlier eighteenth-century ideals
of conversation and channelling them into a new form of argument-as-
sport (see Chapter 5, 'Enlightenments'). Most frequently, this venture has
been cast in heroic terms as a battle of wits in which erudition and logic
across a vast range of subjects was the model of conversation. There is
unquestionably something compelling about the idea of the greatest minds
of a generation gathering together for the purposes of robust, eloquent
argument – and many of the people who gathered in the club became,
sometimes on their own terms and sometimes because of their club
membership, among the most admired, sometimes idolized, figures of
the second half of the eighteenth century. Leo Damrosch has described
the club's members, without much exaggeration, as 'the Friends that
shaped an Age'.[1]

The extraordinary influence club members wielded across a wide array
of cultural fields lends itself to the kinds of breathless admiration in which
it has been frequently described, but when viewed through the lens of
Goldsmith's participation, a different narrative begins to emerge, one that
exposes something else about the Club, and about the culture of mid-
century conviviality more broadly (see Chapter 3, 'Friendships and Feuds').
Goldsmith was routinely ridiculed at the Club – by Johnson in particular.
For a person like Goldsmith who had been derided for his appearance
throughout his life, this could not have been a pleasant experience.
Goldsmith, then, can help balance heroic accounts of the club by fore-
grounding a sense of the cruelty of this celebrated institution. The purpose
of this chapter is to provide a more balanced account of the Club than we
are used to, one that insists on Goldsmith's centrality to its activities, not
only as a founding member and successful product of its cultural

networking, but also as a figure who exposes the dual nature of the Club: both admirably influential and, at times, vicious.

The idea for the Club was Joshua Reynolds's, suggested one evening by the fireside as a way to cheer up Johnson, who had been suffering from debilitating depression triggered by his inability to complete his edition of Shakespeare.[2] Reynolds was among the best-known artists in Britain, specializing in portraiture. Frances Burney described Reynolds as 'pleasant, unaffected and agreeable', and she said of him that there was 'no one among those who have celebrity, I can converse with so easily and comfortably'.[3] He was also a serious drinker and a member of a number of clubs, including several notoriously heavy-drinking societies, such as the gambling club Almack's and the Society of Dilettanti, which met at the Thatched House Tavern in St James's Street, and about which Horace Walpole wrote that it was a club for which 'the nominal qualification is having been in Italy, and the real one being drunk'.[4] Johnson, though prone to occasional bouts of self-flagellating sobriety, could also drink heavily, declaring that he was capable of abstinence but not of temperance.[5] It is little surprise, then, that when the Club was formed it was resolved they would meet in a tavern, The Turk's Head, at 9, Gerrard Street, Soho.

Club meetings took place in an upper room of The Turk's Head, where members were served dinner and plentiful quantities of wine. But the main purpose and attraction of the Club was conversation – an art highly valued in the eighteenth century. John Hawkins, another of the club's original members, recorded Samuel Johnson saying, 'As soon as I enter the door of a tavern I experience an oblivion of care and a freedom from solicitude ... wine there exhilarates my spirits, and prompts me to free conversation and an interchange of discourse with those who I most love.'[6] For Johnson the tavern represented a secure space characterized by its freedoms. Taverns were spaces in which thoughts, ideas, and opinions, stimulated by wine and urged on by affectionate company, could be given free reign and tested out without fear of repercussion. By encouraging stimulating conversation, taverns enabled aspiring writers, actors, artists, and politicians, through their networked interests and the interchange of ideas, to develop a sense of themselves *as* writers, actors, artists, and politicians. This undertaking was a reflexive exercise in self-definition, allowing members to partici-pate in a culture of learned men in order to understand themselves as worthy of impressive company and encouraging them to recognize themselves as 'literary men'.[7]

When the Club was first established the number of members was purposefully restricted. Initially only nine men were permitted: Joshua Reynolds, Samuel Johnson, Edmund Burke, Oliver Goldsmith, Topham Beauclerk, Bennet Langton, John Hawkins, Anthony Chamier, and Christopher Nugent. Later Charles Burney wrote, 'it was Johnson's wish that our Club should be composed of the heads of every liberal and literary profession, that we might not talk nonsense on any subject that might be started, but have somebody to refer to in our doubts and discussions, by whose Science we might be enlightened'.[8] Burney understood the club explicitly as an Enlightenment project intended to encourage and promote knowledge and to expand the possibilities of understanding, and (importantly) to make learning the province of men of the professional classes.

The membership grew steadily, initially in small increments of twos and threes, and then with increasing numbers. In 1765, Samuel Dyer and Thomas Percy were admitted, in 1768 George Colman and Robert Chambers became members, and in 1773 they were joined by James Boswell, David Garrick (whose admission was not unrelated to his agreeing to stage *She Stoops to Conquer*), William Jones, Lord Charlemont, and Agmondesham Vesey. The numbers kept swelling, with Edward Gibbon, Charles James Fox, George Steevens, Adam Smith, Richard Brinsley Sheridan, Joseph Banks, and Charles Burney becoming among the more notable members who joined during Johnson's lifetime. When, by 1777, the membership had increased to thirty, Johnson grew dissatisfied and set up the Essex Head Club instead with a membership limited to twenty-four, though by that point the need of the Club for Johnson's mental health had been significantly reduced by a circle of friends in Streatham, notably Henry Thrale and his wife, Hester.

As Johnson's dissatisfaction suggests, the Club was explicitly an *exclusive* club of men who formed a tight network of outsized cultural influence. Members encouraged and competed with one another and became prominent figures across a dazzling array of cultural products, including economics (Adam Smith), literary criticism (Johnson), the theatre (Garrick, Goldsmith), ballad scholarship (Percy), musicology (Burney), poetry and novel writing (Goldsmith), biography (Gibbon, Boswell), art (Reynolds), and politics (Burke). The idea of competition was central to the conception of the Club. Jon Mee has written about the way the club had a 'masculine ethos of competition' with 'an emphasis on 'manly' or 'solid' conversation rather than the flashing puns of other clubs of its era.[9] There was a seriousness of purpose to Johnson's Club and the style of conversation Johnson preferred, which Boswell described as 'talking for victory' (*LOJ*, 2:100).

Boswell's *Life of Johnson*, through its idiosyncratic collection of anecdotes and *bon mots*, consistently emphasized that, at the Club, the best argument would win the day, an idea that proved central to Habermas's theorization of the rise of public opinion.[10] But other accounts of Johnson's conversation emphasize more the brusque bullying to which Johnson subjected his conversational opponents. Reynolds, for example, expressed his surprise that a man whom he knew to be gentle in private could be so violent in company: 'In mixed company he fought on every occasion as if his whole reputation depended upon the victory of the minute, and he fought with all the weapons. If he was foiled in an argument he had recourse to abuse and rudeness.'[11] But while Johnson's conversational tone could at times be overbearing, the project of the Club itself seemed to unite 'manly' conversation with pleasure and forms of levity. At one point during a trip to Scotland Boswell and Johnson playfully discussed the possibility that the 'club should come and set up in St. Andrew's, as a college, to teach all that each of us can, in the several departments of learning and taste'. This 'project', which Johnson 'entered fully into the spirit of' (*LOJ*, 5:108), suggests not only the seriousness with which the club members valued each others' intellects, but also the spirit of play that presided over the conversation. It was competitive and serious, but could also be light-hearted.

This perhaps helps us to understand Goldsmith's role in the club, which has frequently been understood in somewhat pitying terms. One oft-retold anecdote tells of Goldsmith's suggestion to expand the club's membership, as they had all talked together so much that 'there can now be nothing new among us: we have travelled over one another's minds'. Johnson retorted, 'Sir, you have not travelled over my mind, I promise you' (*LOJ*, 4:183). This anecdote has often been cited as an example of Johnson's quick wit and felicity with a well-turned phrase, but has also been used to suggest what it must have been like to be Goldsmith in these exchanges. Hester Lynch (Thrale) Piozzi, citing this story among others, wrote in sympathy with Goldsmith that 'many such mortifications arose in the course of their intimacy'.[12] In Piozzi's account Johnson was able to disregard abuse, but Goldsmith was much more sensitive to it. She offers a telling instance of an occasion when a performance of *The Good Natur'd Man* had been hissed. That night Goldsmith attended the Club and 'chatted gaily among his friends, as if nothing had happened amiss'. She continues:

> to impress them still more forcibly with an idea of his magnanimity, he even sung his favourite song about an old woman tossed in a blanket seventeen

times as high as the moon, but all this while I was suffering horrid tortures (said he), and verily believe that if I had put a bit into my mouth it would have strangled me on the spot, I was so excessively ill; but I made more noise than usual to cover all that, and so they never perceived my not eating, nor I believe at all imaged to themselves the anguish of my heart.[13]

This story provides some enticing details about the social pressures of conviviality and good humour expected at the club, and the importance of maintaining the 'social virtues' in spite of inner turmoil. But there's another aspect to the story that reveals something further about the nature of Johnson and Goldsmith's relationship. Piozzi's story continues, quoting Goldsmith:

> but when all were gone except Johnson, I burst out a-crying, and even swore by —— that I would never write again. 'All which, Doctor (says Mr. Johnson, amazed at his odd frankness), I thought had been a secret between you and me; and I am sure I would not have said anything about it for the world. Now see . . . what a figure a man makes who thus unaccountably chuses to be the frigid narrator of his own disgrace'.[14]

In this anecdote, Goldsmith's display of emotion in front of Piozzi alarms Johnson, and characteristically he feels compelled to draw a moral lesson from the spectacle, telling Goldsmith that he should keep 'such mortifications to himself' unless he desired 'to be meanly thought of by all'. This assertion of a moral lesson that takes precedence over the claims of sympathy suggests the degree to which those who knew Johnson and recalled his conversation understood that moral truth was Johnson's priority. But it is also testimony to the profound intimacy between the two men. While Goldsmith felt the need to perform in front of the Literary Club, he could be open with Johnson in private – something that needs to be taken into account as we consider Goldsmith's relationship to the Club.

As John Ginger points out, the fact that Goldsmith was one of the initial nine members of the Club – given preference over the likes of Thomas Percy and David Garrick, whom Johnson had known much longer – suggests the high esteem in which Johnson held him (Ginger, 188). The account of the Club given by Percy (who became a member in 1765) indicates the respect in which Johnson held Goldsmith. Percy, attempting to correct the accounts of the Club provided by Hawkins and Piozzi already discussed, reported that Johnson 'intended the Club should consist of Such men, as that if only Two of them chanced to meet, they should be able to entertain each other without wanting the addition of more Company to pass the Evening agreeably'.[15] In this account Johnson's admiration for Goldsmith is more clear – and the anecdotes that demonstrate the kinds of cruelty to which Goldsmith was subject should be seen against this more generally favourable background.

Simon Dickie's discussion of the kinds of cruelty that were routine in eighteenth-century metropolitan culture provides another important context for understanding Goldsmith's role in the Club. Dickie's larger claims concern the way historians of the eighteenth century have relied too heavily on discussions of polite manners and forms of genteel conversation recommended in conduct literature. His attention instead relies on 'The snatches of real conversation that have come down to us', that are 'full of open jokes about sickness and deformity'. Goldsmith, famously unattractive as he was, provides Dickie with one of his key examples, 'with a face scarred by childhood smallpox, a protruding forehead, receding chin, and noticeably awkward physique'.[16] Consistently cruel references to his 'monkey face' and 'grotesque orang-outang figure' are littered throughout his biographies. Dickie's point is not simply that these forms of cruelty need to correct the emphasis on genteel conversation that we have inherited, but that cruelty was both acceptable and indeed had a kind of social currency, with a 'value to everyday readjustments of the social pecking order'.[17]

It is within this context that Goldsmith's value to the Club might best be understood. The treatment of Goldsmith at the Club, the forms of abuse to which he was subject, were entirely normalized within eighteenth-century culture. This is not to say that Goldsmith would have been immune to the cruelty, but it is to suggest that it was entirely possible for Goldsmith to have been a highly respected, intellectually valued member of the Club, to whom Johnson was fiercely loyal, *and also* the butt of everyone's joke. What might seem like a contradiction to us in fact exposes our distance from the values of eighteenth-century conversational culture.

To be clear: it is not my intention to dismiss the forms of abuse to which Goldsmith was subject at the Club, or to suggest that it was somehow all just harmless fun. These kinds of abuse had lasting and powerful consequences – well illustrated by Piozzi's story of Goldsmith breaking down in tears after his play had been hissed. Clearly there were forms of psychological turmoil attendant on the culture of cruelty, which themselves had physical repercussions in terms of Goldsmith's ability to write, to earn a living, and ultimately to house and feed himself. What I do want to suggest, however, is that eighteenth-century club life involved a complex calculus of advantages and hardship.

Fiscally, the calculations would have been complex. Many anecdotes relating to Goldsmith centre on his penury, and in *Brothers of the Quill*

Norma Clarke has given us a fine account of the precarity of eighteenth-century authors that Goldsmith endured for much of his life. The weekly cost of dinner at The Turk's Head would have been a considerable expense, and even Boswell, the son of a Scottish laird, looked on tavern dining as a luxury in which he could indulge only sparely.[18] Goldsmith must have calculated that the long-term benefits – economic, social, and moral – of weekly tavern dinners would outweigh the immediate hardships to his pocket. He would undoubtedly have been extremely flattered to have been asked to join such elevated company as that assembled by Johnson and Reynolds. He would have understood the cultural capital that being a member of the Club gained him, not to mention the more tangible benefits friendship with these men bought, such as interventions with publishers to get payment for works and members' attendance at performances of his plays.[19] The Club was profoundly useful, and the abuse endured must have been a cost Goldsmith was willing to pay. But it indicates too that for all the abuse, and the overbearing moral conviction Club members had to endure, something profoundly enjoyable remained about conversation with these men. The image of Goldsmith singing his favourite ballad of the old woman tossed in a blanket, performing levity, while enduring anguish of the heart, perhaps remains a fitting image of the complexities of Club membership.

Notes

1. Leo Damrosch, *The Club: Johnson, Boswell, and the Friends Who Shaped an Age* (New Haven, CT: Yale University Press, 2019).
2. W. Jackson Bate, *Samuel Johnson* (New York: Harcourt Brace, 1975), 366.
3. *The Early Journals and Letters of Fanny Burney*, ed. Lars E. Troide and Stewart J. Cook, 5 vols. (Oxford: Clarendon, 2012), 5:213.
4. Horace Walpole, *Correspondence*, ed. W. S. Lewis, 48 vols. (New Haven, CT: Yale University Press, 1937–83), 18:211.
5. William Roberts, *Memoirs of the Life and Correspondence of Mrs Hannah More*, 2 vols. (New York, 1834), 1:146.
6. John Hawkins, *Life of Samuel Johnson, LLD* (London, 1787), 87.
7. For more detail on Johnson's conception of a tavern, see Ian Newman, *The Romantic Tavern: Literature, Politics and Conviviality* (Cambridge University Press, 2019), 23–4.
8. *The Correspondence and Other Papers of James Boswell relating to the Making of the 'Life of Johnson'*, ed. Marshall Waingrow (New Haven, CT: Yale University Press, 2016), 311.
9. Jon Mee, *Conversable Worlds: Literature, Contention and Community, 1762 to 1830* (Oxford University Press, 2011), 90–1.

10. Jürgen Habermas, *The Structural Transformation of the Public Sphere: An Inquiry into a Category of Bourgeois Society*, trans. Thomas Burger (Cambridge, MA: MIT Press, 1991).

11. Charles Leslie and Tom Taylor, *The Life and Times of Sir Joshua Reynolds*, 2 vols. (London: John Murray, 1865), 2:462.

12. Hester Lynch Piozzi, *Anecdotes of the Late Samuel Johnson, LLD during the Last Twenty Years of His Life* (London, 1786), 180.

13. Piozzi, *Anecdotes*, 245.

14. Piozzi, *Anecdotes*, 246.

15. Waingrow, *Correspondence relating to the 'Life of Johnson'*, ed. Marshall Waingrow, 209.

16. Simon Dickie, *Cruelty and Laughter: Forgotten Comic Literature and the Unsentimental Eighteenth Century* (University of Chicago Press, 2011), 85.

17. Dickie, *Cruelty and Laughter*, 85.

18. Newman, *The Romantic Tavern*, 23.

19. For an account of Johnson's intervention with a bookseller so Goldsmith could pay his rent, see Piozzi, *Anecdotes*, 119. For an account of Johnson's intervention with Colman to put on *She Stoops to Conquer*, and the friends who provided moral courage by attending the opening night, see Richard Cumberland, *Memoirs of Richard Cumberland Written by Himself*, 2 vols. (London, 1807) 1:364–9.

CHAPTER 9

Irish London

John Bergin

In 1756, aged about twenty-eight, Oliver Goldsmith arrived in London, where he would live almost without interruption until his death eighteen years later. He arrived in a city already well-established as a magnet for Irish people of every social class, religion, and ethnic origin. It has been estimated that the Irish comprised 3 per cent of London's population during the eighteenth century, and it has been suggested that the Irish middle class, both permanent and temporary residents, comprised about 1,000 members at the end of the century.[1]

Direct evidence of Goldsmith's social life and friendships is all too scarce, but we can say that the Irish were considerably better represented in his social and professional circles than in London as a whole. During his early years of hackwork his associates (and rivals) included Isaac Bickerstaff, Samuel Derrick, John Pilkington, Charles Macklin, Edward Purdon, and Paul Hiffernan (see Chapter 3, 'Friendships and Feuds'). More established figures included Arthur Murphy, Edmund Burke (and his brother, Richard), and Robert Nugent, Viscount Clare. Other acquaintances of some eminence included the attorney Joseph Hickey and the painter James Barry. There are also minor figures of whom relatively little is known and who would be forgotten but for their association with Goldsmith, such as Fergus MacVeagh. Most of Goldsmith's Irish associates were, like himself, born into the Church of Ireland, but some were Catholics, converts to Protestantism, or Protestants from mixed religious backgrounds (see Chapter 15, 'Religion').

Until very recently, the conventional picture of the Irish in eighteenth-century London has been of a small, wealthy, and nearly entirely Protestant class and a larger, uncounted and nameless class of poor Irish Catholics who lived in neighbourhoods the names of which, like St Giles, were bywords for squalor. Recent research, however, has begun to reveal a more extensive and more complex Irish presence. The highest social tier was a mix of permanent residents and seasonal visitors of fashion drawn from the ranks of the peerage and gentry. These were in large measure the 'absentee' class, living off rental income from their Irish properties. Another contingent of Irish, small in number but sometimes very wealthy, were owners of West Indian slave plantations who, once they had made their fortunes, chose to retire to London.[2] At the other extreme were poor Irish vagrants and a considerable number of Irish, including domestic servants, porters, and chairmen, labouring in more or less unskilled occupations.

But Irish were also found in the many intermediate layers of metropolitan society. They included shopkeepers, tradesmen, and skilled artisans (Irish peruke makers seem to have been quite numerous, for example, a fact perhaps connected with the trade in imported human hair from Ireland). In the City of London, Europe's pre-eminent commercial and financial centre, there were Irish merchants and bankers; some of these were eminent and wealthy figures, but the greater number were entrepreneurs on a relatively modest scale. Their commercial 'houses' often employed other Irish as domestic servants, clerks, bookkeepers, and packers of goods. The Irish were active in various branches of the legal profession and in medical practice. Irish politicians, property owners, and litigants frequently visited London, which was the home of the royal court, the privy council, government ministers, Parliament, and law courts and was the ultimate seat of power for Ireland. Those who did not visit in person could pay to have their interests represented by professional agents, who were themselves often Irish-born lawyers, in London. A few Irishmen – including Edmund Burke and Robert Nugent – even made careers in English politics. The extent, complexity, and degree of integration of the Irish in the middling layers of London society, long overlooked, has received more scholarly attention of late.[3]

Of course, public expressions of dislike of or at least condescension towards the Irish are easy to find. There are concrete examples of outright hostility towards the Irish, particularly the poor who were sometimes resented as competitors for employment. An extreme instance was the anti-Irish riots of 1736, when national antipathy was mixed with anti-Catholic feeling; the poorer Irish were of course overwhelmingly Catholic.[4] However, it has not always been realized that Catholics were present at every level of the Irish-born population of London, including the wealthiest, even if the propertied Irish elite were predominantly members of the established Church of Ireland. Among the professional Irish too, including the milieu in which Goldsmith would make his career, Catholics were represented in numbers which were far from negligible.

Many immigrants to London would experience failure and disappointment, but the city was nonetheless relatively open to talented and energetic outsiders. Goldsmith himself wrote in the trying early period of his life in London that 'my being born an Irishman was sufficient to keep me [unem]ploy'd' (*Letters*, 21). Yet his own later career rather disproves this assertion, as do many examples of Irish professional success in London. Even Irish Catholics, who undoubtedly faced more prejudice than Anglicans such as Goldsmith, often thrived. For example, Charles Molloy (d. 1767), editor of the journal *Common-Sense*, found his nationality no barrier to success in journalism, despite some implicit sneering at his being 'an *Irish Roman-Catholick*'.[5]

Goldsmith, a committed if undemonstrative Protestant, seems to have been quite devoid of sectarian feeling in his friendships and social life; indeed, his own family background was partly Catholic (*Letters*, xvii–xviii). The Irish of all denominations, in their encounters abroad, seem to have found themselves more conscious of common nationality. Sectarian and political tensions and the consequent social discomfort between Irish Protestants and Catholics were less acute in cosmopolitan London than in Ireland.

Goldsmith's Irish friends and associates naturally included literary figures, but also scions of aristocratic families, the landed gentry, merchants, physicians, legal students, and lawyers. They were a wide spectrum of the London Irish, at least those of some education and culture; some of the latter were poor enough and were known to impose on the good nature of their literary countryman. His relations with other Irish are generally known through circumstantial evidence or the accounts of third parties, collected by James Prior long after his death. No letters remain, however, 'to throw light on his relationships with Samuel Derrick, Jack Pilkington, Paul Hiffernan or Edward Purdon, all Irish figures involved in the machinations of London's Grub Street' (*Letters*, xlix).

If some of Goldsmith's Irish associates such as Paul Hiffernan were Catholic, others such as Arthur Murphy and Robert Nugent were born into Catholic families but conformed to the established church as young men. Edmund Burke, the great Protestant advocate of Catholic relief, had a Catholic mother and sister and was married to the daughter of his Irish Catholic physician, Christopher Nugent. Burke and Christopher Nugent were of course, with Goldsmith, among the founding members of the Literary Club. The Cork-born painter James Barry was, like Burke, the child of a Protestant father and a Catholic mother, but unlike Burke he had been raised a Catholic. Hickey was a Protestant who was proud of his Gaelic ancestry and had Catholic friends in Ireland.

In the relative prosperity of his last years Goldsmith lived in the Middle Temple, described as 'a favourite abode . . . of several men of letters' (Prior, *Life*, 2:136) and 'a fashionable address for a bachelor' (Clarke, *Brothers of the Quill*, 316). The Inns of Court were of course legal institutions, populated largely by lawyers and students of the law. They had an important Irish dimension: it was necessary, before being called to the bar in Ireland, to 'keep terms' at one of the Inns of Court. Irish students attended all four of the Inns, but at this period they favoured the Middle Temple above the rest. Goldsmith himself was, according to his sister's account, once intended for the law: 'His uncle Contarine . . . resolved to send him to the Temple, that he might make the law his profession. But in his way to London, he met at Dublin with a sharper, who . . . emptied his pockets of fifty pounds, with which he had been furnished for his voyage and journey'.[6] It is a little curious that Goldsmith, thwarted in his plans to study the law at the Temple, should ultimately take up residence in an institution which was the destination of many Irish legal students. However, like the other Inns, the Middle Temple was more than simply an institution for training barristers. Some students attended as part of their 'finishing' as young gentlemen. Catholics, effectively excluded from the universities, were freely admitted to all of the Inns. Though only Protestants could be called to the Irish or English bar, Catholics could practise in some specialized niches of the law in both countries. These professional specialisms and the Inns of Court in general were milieux where Irish Protestants and Catholics mixed freely.

Among Irishmen admitted to the Middle Temple were Charles Molloy (in 1716), though he is better known as a journalist than as a lawyer. Catholics were excluded from pleading in the courts but colonized and developed the specialized field of property conveyancing. They could practise from their consulting chambers, generally in the Inns of Court, serving clients both Catholic and Protestant, in Ireland and England. David Murphy, a native of County Kerry admitted in 1729, was one of these Catholic 'chamber counsel', living and practising the law in the Middle Temple during Goldsmith's time there. There is no evidence that Goldsmith knew Murphy, but he did know Joseph Hickey, and Murphy and Hickey were both known to have frequented the King's Arms in Pall Mall. This tavern was a resort of the fashionable Irish, some of them Catholics and suspected Jacobite plotters.[7]

Edmund Burke had been admitted to the Middle Temple in 1750, but his time there was over before Goldsmith knew him or took up residence there himself. However, Goldsmith came to know several Irish Protestant students at the Middle Temple, including Robert Day (admitted 1764), later an eminent judge, as well as Day's friend Henry Grattan (1767) and the playwright Hugh Kelly (1768). Day, whom Goldsmith befriended, later recalled how Goldsmith 'much frequented the Grecian Coffeehouse, then the favourite resort of the Irish and Lancashire Templars' (Prior, *Life*, 2:357), while a modern account demonstrates that the Grecian was 'an Irish space'.[8]

Goldsmith, while at the Middle Temple, had a chance encounter, but a revealing one, with a young Irishman called Fergus MacVeagh, 'from a poor but respectable Roman Catholic family in the north of Ireland' (Prior, *Life*, 2:342). MacVeagh had no connection with the Inns; having attended a Jesuit school in France, he found himself adrift in London without money or friends and was sitting reading in Temple Gardens when Goldsmith initiated a conversation with him. Many decades later, MacVeagh (after he had taken the additional surname McDonnell and enjoyed a successful career as a physician) gave Prior an account of their friendship. He was still deeply attached to the memory of Goldsmith, who had given him practical assistance by employing him to translate material from French for his *Natural History*. Goldsmith's own continental travels, undertaken after his studies at Leiden, probably facilitated the bond he formed with MacVeagh. Vague though the details of his itinerary are, Goldsmith certainly visited some important institutions frequented by Irish Catholics, such as the university of Louvain. More than most Irish Protestants of his day, he would have had knowledge of, and probably sympathy with, the experiences of Irish Catholics educated on the Continent, such as MacVeagh, Paul Hiffernan, and indeed even converts such as Arthur Murphy, who had attended the Jesuit school at St Omer in France before becoming a Protestant.

MacVeagh told Prior that, having been abroad when Goldsmith died, on his return to London he 'had frequent opportunities of hearing much of my old patron from several of his surviving acquaintance whom I met at the house of Dr Prendergast, an Irish physician, then resident at Richmond, who had made a fortune in Jamaica'.[9] Two members of this circle named by MacVeagh were well-known Irish friends of Goldsmith, namely Richard Burke (brother of Edmund) and the attorney Joseph Hickey. Prendergast, nowhere else mentioned in the scholarly literature, was himself presumably a friend of Goldsmith's. He is evidently 'Dr John

Prendergast of Richmond in Surrey', whose wife's death was reported in 1789.[10] He appears at various dates as a member of the Medical Societies of Edinburgh and London. In 1791, when he disposed of substantial property in Jamaica, he was said to be of the City of London.[11] He was an active member of the charity concerned with the Irish poor in London, the Benevolent Society of St Patrick, which elected him to the post of physician in 1791.[12]

Another Irish physician among Goldsmith's friends was William Redmond, 'who having resided several years in France where he had been acquainted with the poet, had come to try his success in England' (Prior, *Life*, 1:461). Movement back and forth between France and London was not uncommon among the Irish, especially Catholic merchants and professionals. Redmond, who evidently arrived in London on a rather more secure footing than MacVeagh, dined with Goldsmith in 1763 during his sojourn at Islington. He appears as a member of the Society for the Encouragement of Arts, Manufactures and Commerce from 1760, when he became embroiled in a prolonged and public dispute over the Society's decision not to award him a premium for his discoveries in relation to antimony. Redmond appeared frequently in London newspapers of the 1760s on account of his dispute with the Society, as the author of some pieces of verse, and as a practising physician, notably for his treatments of cancers of the breast.

Redmond furthermore had a link with a very specific niche in London, that of the embassies of the Catholic states. Their chapels were the only places of Catholic worship entirely free from official harassment, and these embassies often played host to Irish lobbying and intrigue. Redmond was physician to Count Haslang, the Bavarian minister in London, which connects him to another anecdote in Prior, who described how Goldsmith was gulled by 'a foreigner at this time in London, countenanced by the Bavarian Ambassador and others, under the name of Colonel Chevalier de Champigny, soliciting subscriptions for a History of England in French, partly translated and partly original' (Prior, *Life*, 2:142).[13] Champigny appears to have been a friend of Redmond, whose treatise of 1762 he translated into French as *Essai sur les principes de l'antimoine* (1765). Champigny's newspaper advertisements in 1766 encouraging subscriptions for his history named those who had already subscribed, including Haslang and Redmond, though not Goldsmith.[14] The history would not be published until 1777, but Champigny seems to have been a more substantial figure than Prior believed, publishing various translations into French and compositions of his own. His *Mémoires de*

Miss Fanny Palmer (1769) has been described as 'a perfect specimen of the pseudo-English fiction which was produced by, and also fed, the growing anglomania of the French reading public of its time'.[15] Its list of subscribers includes 'Mr. Redmond, Docteur en Médecine' and 'Mr. le Docteur Goldsmith'.

Some members of Goldsmith's circle are reasonably well known in their own right, even if their association with him is only known from passing mentions. One such was 'Mr Thomas Fitzmaurice, a relative of a noble Irish family'; he was a son of the earl of Shelburne and a member of the British Parliament. It might be noted too that he had attended the Middle Temple before being called to the bar there in 1768. Other Irish make brief appearances in Prior: Mr Roach, a 'commercial' man, and 'Mr Seguin, a mercantile man of some literary tastes', who enjoyed a 'considerable intimacy' with the poet. Goldsmith undertook a considerable favour for 'Mr and Mrs Pollard, of Castle Pollard', in introducing them to Dr Johnson (Prior, *Life*, 2:440, 159, 192). The Pollards are not known to have had any special distinction, but as their estate was in County Westmeath they perhaps had some acquaintance with Goldsmith's family.

Future scholarship will doubtless add to our understanding of the eighteenth-century London Irish. Even if a good deal may never be known about some of these Irish as individuals, we can say that collectively they were an essential part of the fabric of Goldsmith's life in London.

Notes

1. Jerry White, *London in the Eighteenth Century* (London, 2012), 157; Craig Bailey, *Irish London: Middle Class Migration in the Global Eighteenth Century* (Liverpool University Press, 2013), 5–7.

2. Nini Rodgers, *Ireland, Slavery and Anti-slavery, 1612–1865* (Basingstoke: Palgrave Macmillan, 2009), 61–7.

3. David O'Shaughnessy, ed., 'Networks of Aspiration: The London Irish of the Eighteenth Century', a special issue of *Eighteenth-Century Life* 39:1 (2015), 1–235; Bailey, *Irish London*.

4. Jerry White, *London in the Eighteenth Century*, 158 ff.

5. *An Historical View of the Principles, Characters, Persons, &c. of the Political Writers of Great Britain* (London, 1740), 16.

6. Thomas Percy, 'The Life of Dr. Oliver Goldsmith', *The Miscellaneous Works of Oliver Goldsmith, M.B.*, 4 vols. (London, 1801), 1:13–14.

7. Bailey, *Irish London*, especially 113–14.

8. Bailey, *Irish London*, 79.

9. Prior, *Life*, 1:23; 2:342–9. For MacVeagh, see also W. Innes Addison, *A Roll of the Graduates of the University of Glasgow* (Glasgow: McLehose & Sons, 1898), 363; The National Archives of the UK, WO 25/766/184, services of officers on full and half pay, 1828; PROB 11/1801/317, will of Doctor Fergus Mac Veagh McDonnell, signed 1831, proved 1832.

10. *The World*, 21 January 1789.

11. *Caribbeana*, ed. Vere Langford Oliver, 6 vols. (London: Mitchell, Hughes and Clarke, 1910–19), 3:23–4.

12. *Public Advertiser*, 7 November 1791, where his address is given as London Street (in the City); *Oracle*, 7 March 1794.

13. Compare *Reports of Cases Argued and Adjudged in the Court of King's Bench*, 5 vols. ([1766]–80), 3:458–9.

14. *Public Advertiser*, 7 November 1766.

15. Josephine Grieder, 'Eighteenth-Century French Anglomania and Champigny's *Mémoires de Miss Fanny Palmer*', *Journal of the Rutgers University Libraries*, 50.2 (1988), 115–19.

CHAPTER 10

Liberty

Nigel Wood

The term 'Liberty' was much used (and abused) by Goldsmith's contemporaries. Its political charge stemmed from the impulse to take due notice of the consequences of the Revolution Settlement (1688–9), whereby the sacred bases of monarchical authority were challenged by forms of popular consent and contract. These gestures towards libertarian beliefs were in fact varied when it came to a consideration of their objectives and Goldsmith was well aware of how potentially hackneyed the gestures towards Liberty had become. In *She Stoops to Conquer*, Jeremy's drunken praise of 'liberty and Fleet-street for ever!' (*Stoops*, 70) associates the term with riot and a site of factional strife and Goldsmith was apt to regard the cry as a rather empty slogan. George Primrose in *The Vicar of Wakefield* has aspirations to gain fame by writing, but his objective to write free of market pressures comes to nothing as his literary talents are crowded out by hirelings who stoop to provide 'essays on liberty, eastern tales, and cures for the bite of a mad dog' (*Vicar*, 2:10). Indeed, Lien Chi Altangi, in *The Citizen of the World*, regards as the very 'dullest' of writers those who take liberty and virtue as their topics (*Citizen*, 2:47).

For Goldsmith, however, a serious inspection of the term had become timely and necessary. Taken in semantic isolation, 'Liberty' carried positive connotations, yet by mid-century the term had taken on a partisan colouring. Sir Robert Filmer's ultra-Tory ideal in his posthumous *Patriarcha, or The Natural Power of Kings* (1680) heralded the idea of a divinely ordained monarch placed at the apex of authority and instituted by birthright. This figure could set aside common and statute law – even if enshrined in tradition – and adjudicate even matters that could have been said to derive from a sense of natural right or contract. Authority stemmed from a patriarchal line of inheritance first enjoyed by Adam: 'For as *Adam* was Lord of his Children, so his Children under him had a command over their own Children, but still with subordination to the First Parent, who is Lord-Paramount over his Children's Children to all Generations, as being the *Grand-Father* of his People.'¹ Subjects are locked into subordination to monarchical judgement and thereby order is promised and perhaps maintained.²

The theory foundered somewhat on the fact that there had been multiple interruptions to primogeniture, the most obvious being the deviation from the Stuart line with the abdication of James II in 1688 and then the Hanoverian solution to the hiatus in 1714 with the demise of Queen Anne. God could have willed this providentially working through history, but this was to strain the idea almost to breaking point; if subjects could arrange matters so as to provide continuity – and no evident crisis – then the door was left open for other explanations. The cogency of this view was stamped in the thinking behind the Jacobite insurrections of both 1715 and 1745, in appeals to resurrect the true Stuart line. With John Locke's *Two Treatises of Government* (1690), the distrust of Filmer's location of indefeasible authority gathered pace; especially in the first Treatise, he questioned the equation of any civil subject with the biological link between a child and father. Subjects had to be won over by consent, leaving an option of dissent if a monarch's actions were questionable – perhaps an affront either to an ancient constitution or a social contract. For Locke, there was arbitrary tyranny or, on the other hand, a reasonable alternative according to a law of nature that imposed duties and limits at the same time as it allowed a measure of free will; liberty was not license:

> The Freedom then of Man, and Liberty of acting, according to his own Will, is grounded on his having Reason, which is able to instruct him in that Law he is to govern himself by, and make him know how far he is left to the freedom of his own will. To turn him loose to an unrestrain'd Liberty, before he has Reason to guide him, is not the allowing him the priviledge of his Nature, to be free; but to thrust him out amongst Brutes, and abandon him to a state as wretched, and as much beneath that of a Man, as theirs.³

The Revolution Settlement was not only a pragmatic fix to ensure regal succession, but also a more wide-reaching revision of how liberty might appear in a maturing civil government.⁴

This set of distinctions between obedience and freedom had undergone significant modification since 1690. The argument that an original state of responsible liberty was embedded in classical times was indeed rather hackneyed by the time Goldsmith compiled his own two-volume *A History of England, in a Series of Letters from a Nobleman to His Son* (1764), but his own chronology took in a need to embrace religious freedom as the basis for ethical rectitude and a sustainable constitution.

In Letter II, ancient Grecian and Roman republican thought supplied a valuable template yet one that served vastly different times. It was now the turn of the English to educate the world in tracing 'progressive steps from barbarity to social refinement, from society to the highest pitch of well constituted freedom' (see Chapter 24, 'History Writing'). This 'happy region' provided a shining example of 'liberty and ... happiness'.[5] A detailed history of the nation illustrated such prosperity – the inexorable growth of refinement in the arts and sciences alongside Lockean reasonableness. When surveying *The Beauties of English Poesy* (1767), Goldsmith noted Joseph Addison's achievement in his *A Letter from Italy: To The Right Honourable Charles, Lord Halifax* (1701) and praised it for its 'strain of political thinking that was, at that time, new in our poetry'.[6] The *Letter* as a prospect poem serves as an analogue to similar surveys that are only apparently above political tumult – and probably served as a model for Goldsmith's *The Traveller, or A Prospect of Society* (1764), his own glance at futurity (see Chapter 22, 'Prospect Poetry'). Addison's panoptic vision was addressed to Charles Montagu, the first Earl of Halifax, who had served as one of the Whig Junto and in 1704 was a target of the incoming Tory government on the accession of Queen Anne; its Whig sympathies – and its insistence that these would be protected by progressive legislation and the prolongation of the Spanish Succession conflict – are heralded. Liberty promised plenty and a removal of poverty, and was particularly evident in 'Britain's stormy Isle' (l. 56; 5), a quality that 'makes her barren Rocks and her bleak Mountains smile' (l. 140; 7). This virtuous power adds force to the nation's status as Europe's bellicose peacemaker, a 'Care to watch o'er Europe's Fate, / And hold in Balance each contending State' (ll.145–6; 8). This is not to claim that Goldsmith's Liberty derives its power from contemporary political considerations, but rather that the most current associations of the Prospect vision contained a tincture of Whiggish optimism.[7] This utopian gesture was also insistent in James Thomson's *Liberty* (1735–6)[8], where the Goddess oversaw previous decline only to herald in the present an efflorescence in 'Britannia'. Greece had forfeited the 'solid Base' of free thought constructed by Lycurgus that promoted

> ... equal Life, [and] so well a temper'd State;
> Where mix'd each Government, in such just Poise
> Each Power so checking, and supporting

that liberty is possible (17). The mind is where true freedom lies, but where the present is concerned it is allied to free trade, "a daring Canvas" on which there is 'pour'd with every Tide/A golden Flood' (49–50). Peering into the future, Thomson contemplates thereby an enduring establishment of the sciences, fine arts, and public works that allows a confidence to escape the lures of theocratic corruption.[9]

The Traveller only appears to echo this confidence but proves to be a warning against complacency. Art promotes a cluster of glorious civic virtues ('Wealth, commerce, honour, liberty, content'), yet when these are brought into any public sphere, there is contention, not equipoise: 'Yet these each other's power so strong contest,/That either seems destructive of the rest' (*Traveller*, 6). Commerce alone cannot promote happiness. Indeed freedom can be illusory and dwindle into a breaking of the 'social tie', where we cannot thrive with too much independence. Society might rely too much on the 'fictitious bonds' of wealth and law (*Traveller*, 19) and we forget to aspire to spiritual qualities wherein 'Our own felicity we make or find' in a 'secret course' of 'domestic joy' (*Traveller*, 23). Bathed in nostalgia for a lost organic community, he was to lament in *The Deserted Village* (1770) the depopulation that results from rapacious commerce, wherein 'trade's unfeeling train/Usurp[s] the land and dispossess[es] the swain' (*Deserted Village*, 4). There is thus a bifocal perspective at play in Goldsmith's travelling; at its macro level, political unity is always under threat once individualism thrives unchecked, and at the micro level – though seen in the rear-view mirror – there is the 'Sweet Auburn' of memory and vision.[10]

The balancing act required in achieving the successful state interests him and we should not be too distracted by the charge of sentimentalism often attached to his writing. Indeed his persona of the nomadic outsider, an amalgam of an Irish self with an immigrant's Englishness, provides a peculiar variety of libertarian assumption mitigated by a drive to soften the pain of isolation and personal doubt. In Letter II prefacing his 1764 *History of England, in a Series of Letters*, he views a constitution as our bulwark against these ills, a notional extension of how the one and the many might be reconciled. Indeed the aim of the project of tracing the development of the modern English state is not quite the one beloved of Whig optimists:

> Every person, residing here, has a share in the liberties of this kingdom; as the generality of the people are ultimately invested with the legislation. It is therefore every man's duty to know the constitution, which, by his birthright, he is called to govern; a freeholder, in a free kingdom, should certainly be instructed in the original of that agreement, by which he holds so precious a tenure.[11]

The one term that resonates here is that claim to be a 'freeholder'. The history of that term is complex. It takes in Filmer's *The Freeholder's Grand Inquest* (1648) that underscores the need for unquestioning civil obedience and *The Freeholder's Plea against Stock-Jobbing Elections of Parliament Men* (1701), usually attributed to Daniel Defoe, that argued the opposite – a rationale for resistance to the opportunism of a traditional franchise. It is likely, however, that the most prominent associations clinging to that term derive from Addison, whose periodical, *The Freeholder* (1715–16), was incisive in its definition of the term and the status of its application to a political class. Ownership brings with it a respect for the item owned, and this has salutary results, for if one has a claim in and on the state then a social compact (under a monarchy) has a role: 'A Free-Holder of *Great Britain*, is bred with an Aversion to every Thing that tends to bring him under a Subjection to the arbitrary Will of another.'[12] This leads to a species of political participation wherein one possesses a 'remote Voice in every Law that was enacted'.[13] Much like representation in the Roman Senate via tribunes – as allowed in ancient Roman governance – there is ensured thereby a link between the populace and governors. This structural limit on both authority and liberty is probably what Goldsmith had in mind when he noted Voltaire's motivation for visiting England, his 'admiration' for a 'government in which subordination and liberty were blended in . . . just proportions', adding up to 'the finest model of civil society' (*Memoirs of M. De Voltaire* [1761]; III:246–7).[14]

This, though, is Goldsmith at his most optimistic, for the traveller's view looks beyond the façades of ritual and self-satisfaction. In his 'The Revolution in Low Life' that appeared in *Lloyd's Evening Post* (14–16 June, 1762), there are several passages where an appearance of liberty is closely examined and found to be unevenly distributed. Foreign trade does promote the attractions of luxury yet 'as it can be managed only by a few' will therefore only make a few prosperous: 'it is calculated rather to make individuals rich, [more] than to make the aggregate happy'. The result – often hidden from public life – is an unbridgeable gulf between rich and poor: 'The Great . . . boast of their liberties . . . and they have liberty. The poor boast of liberty too; but, alas, they groan under the most rigorous oppression.' Liberty is thus something of a mirage, for if one were to inspect the social structure closely, then inequality is built into the system. The Vicar is clear on this, for just as he praises liberty as the 'attribute of Gods', he also finds it merely 'the theme of modern declamation'. As soon as one accepts the fact that all would be kings, it follows that not all can lead – some will be more advantageously placed to start with or some would be too cunning in exploiting others. Better to identify where there is potential for tyranny (in a monarchy) and limit it than search for it amongst a hydra-headed multitude. The poor will always be with us yet it is down to the middle order to regulate this divide between the entitled and destitute: 'In such a state . . . all that the middle order has left, is to preserve the prerogative and privileges of the one principal tyrant with the most sacred circumspection' (*Vicar*, 1:205). It is certainly the view of the 'philosophic vagabond' that the Vicar's son has become that a monarchy 'was the best government for the poor to live in, and commonwealths for the rich' (*Vicar*, 2: 31). To make this successful, therefore, one has to acknowledge, along with Lien Chi Altangi, that some are 'born to teach, and others to receive instruction', just as any organization is the more successful, as the serpent in the fable exemplifies, if there is 'one head and many tails' rather than the other way about (*Citizen*, 2:146; see Chapter 11, 'Cosmopolitanism', and Chapter 26, 'Orientalism').

The crucial qualification, however, is that 'sacred circumspection' that keeps in check unbridled freedom, not only as concerns aristocratic privilege but also the desperation of the dispossessed. Goldsmith was not alone in attempting to codify a liberty secured within a civil society, and the most influential effort early in his century was Anthony Ashley Cooper, Earl of Shaftesbury's 'An Enquiry concerning Virtue, or Merit', to be found in his *Characteristicks* (1711), wherein virtue could be made useful to all, especially where there remains a tincture of self-worth nurtured to resist tyranny through the generations. This is a support against the encroachment of slavery, wherein 'despotick Rule' might be sustained free from any challenge by agreed laws or 'a just Administration'. '*Example*' is the best regulator of behaviour, passed down from any 'virtuous Administration' to create 'Virtue in the Magistrate' and also – to counter Filmer's Adamic line of genealogical authority – an esteem of liberty within '*private Familys*'.[15] For Goldsmith's Vicar, such paternal concern dwells in a generosity of spirit that does not distrust liberty (see Chapter 19, 'Fiction').[16]

The English pat themselves on their collective back whenever 'Liberty' is the topic, but by 1762 and Lien Chi Altangi's reflections on freedom, there is the clear suspicion that this is not enjoyed universally. As a slogan, the claim that the English pre-eminently have achieved a peak of liberty is actually just self-confirming; Goldsmith did concur in viewing the English state as aiming at a sustainable and equable constitution, but with the proviso that one might enjoy 'all the advantages of democracy with this superior prerogative borrowed from monarchy, *that the severity of their laws may be relaxed without endangering the constitution*' (*Citizen*, 1:215). Populist governments tend to adhere to literal legal interpretations, but these are brittle arrangements and leave the door open to wrangles and short-term fixes; only when authority has the 'strength of [an English] native oak' combined with the 'flexibility of the bending tamarisk' might the public – in reality – be protected, for any public zeal for an 'imaginary freedom' is the basis of myth, whereby there was the mirage that by abridging monarchy one might increase native privileges: 'every jewel plucked from the crown of majesty would only be made use of as a bribe to corruption' (*Citizen*, 1:218).

The experience of travelling is for Goldsmith not merely a narrative or poetic trope but derives from his own condition – unrooted and unsure of any instinctive allegiance. His desire to interrogate any feelings of his own freedom is motivated by a countervailing comprehension that this should be diluted by belonging and adherence. This was so from the first in his publishing career but gathered pace once he gained a measure of celebrity. As early as 1759, in the first issue of the *Bee* (6 October), his account of Poland brought him back to the realization that English life guarded liberty with some reward – everyday life free from constraint and angry compulsion (1:371). Nationalist pride was only one half of the equation, for it could be carried to a dangerous excess, as Wilkinson – the upstart butler – in Chapter XIX in *The Vicar of Wakefield* did. Calculated to evoke John Wilkes's shrill libertarian impulses, Wilkinson's outlook stands in stark contrast to the espousing of careful continuity and generous regard for limited monarchical power expressed by the Vicar. As he testified in his letter to Bennet Langton (7 September 1771), his *History*, although originally calculated to tread a careful middle-of-the-road path, could be mistaken for a denial of civil freedoms, as he was 'abused in the newspapers for betraying the liberties of the people' (*Letters*, 99). This could be taken as, in part, a rather disingenuous defence, given the contemporary context, yet there is also – in a longer view – an innocence in his attempt to stand clear of partisan cries for freedom: a hope that there might be sufficient common ground to ensure a balanced concern for all.

Notes

1. *Patriarcha, or, The Natural Power of Kings by the Learned Sir Robert Filmer, Baronet* (London, 1680), 12.
2. See H. T. Dickinson's account in his *Liberty and Property: Political Ideology in Eighteenth-Century Britain* (London: Weidenfeld and Nicolson, 1977), 22–35, supplemented by Cesare Cuttica's 'Reputation versus Context in the Interpretation of Sir Robert Filmer's *Patriarcha*', *History of Political Thought*, 33 (2012), 231–57.

3. John Locke, *Two Treatises of Government in the Former, the False Principles and Foundation of Sir Robert Filmer and His Followers Are Detected and Overthrown, the Latter Is an Essay concerning the True Original, Extent, and End of Civil Government* (London, 1690, 2:vi, 281).

4. See Richard Ashcraft and M. M. Goldsmith, 'Locke, Revolution Principles, and the Formation of Whig Ideology', *The Historical Journal*, 26.4 (1983), 773–800; Charles D. Tarlton, 'Reason and History in Locke's *Second Treatise*', *Philosophy*, 79 (2004), 247–79; and Ronald Marden, '"Who Shall be Judge?" John Locke's *Two Treatises of Government* and the Problem of Sovereignty', *Contributions to the History of Concepts*, 2.1 (2006), 59–81.

5. Oliver Goldsmith, *An History of England, in a Series of Letters from a Nobleman to His Son*, 2 vols. (London, 1764), 1:8.

6. Oliver Goldsmith, *The Beauties of English Poesy*, 2 vols. (London, 1767), 1:111. See Joseph Addison, *A Letter from Italy: To the Right Honourable Charles Montagu, Lord Halifax* (London, 1701).

7. See Ingrid Horrocks, '"Circling Eye" and "Houseless Stranger": The New Eighteenth-Century Wanderer (Thomson to Goldsmith)', *English Literary History*, 77 (2010), 665–87.

8. *The Works of Mr. Thomson. Volume the Second. Containing, Liberty, a Poem in Five Parts . . .* (London, 1736), Part II, 'Greece'.

9. See William Levine, 'Collins, Thomson, and the Whig Progress of Liberty', *Studies in English Literature, 1500–1900*, 34 (1994), 553–77.

10. See the overview of Richard Helgerson in his 'The Two Worlds of Oliver Goldsmith', *Studies in English Literature, 1500–1900*, 13 (1973), 516–34, Robert A. Bataille, 'City and Country in *The Vicar of Wakefield*', *Eighteenth-Century Life*, 3 (1977), 112–14 and Michael Griffin, 'Delicate Allegories, Deceitful Mazes: Goldsmith's Landscapes', *Eighteenth-Century Ireland / Iris an Dá Chultúr*, 16 (2001), 104–17.

11. *History of England, in a Series of Letters*, 1:12.

12. *The Freeholder* 1 (23 December 1715), 4.

13. *The Free-Holder, or Political Essays* (London, 1716), 2.

14. See Graham Gargett, 'Oliver Goldsmith and Voltaire's *Lettres Philosophiques*', *Modern Language Review*, 96 (2001), 952–63.

15. Anthony Ashley Cooper, *Characteristicks of Men, Manners, Opinions, Times. In Three Volumes* (London, 1711), 2:63–5. See the interpretation offered by Michael Meehan in his *Liberty and Poetics in Eighteenth Century England* (London: Croom Helm, 1986), 22–41.

16. See James P. Carson, '"The Little Republic" of the Family: Goldsmith's Politics of Nostalgia', *Eighteenth-Century Fiction*, 16.2 (2004), 174–96.

CHAPTER II

Cosmopolitanism

James Watt

In her essay 'The New Cosmopolitanism and the Eighteenth Century', Mary Helen McMurran discusses the twenty-first-century revival of cosmopolitan thinking among public intellectuals aiming to counter 'new malignant strains of patriotism eroding rights and tolerance on the world-political stage'.[1] This 'cosmopolitan turn' has in turn prompted attention to the historical provenance of the ideal, which is rooted in classical antiquity ('cosmopolitan' derives from the Greek *kosmopolitēs*, meaning 'citizen of the world') and customarily associated with the French Enlightenment. In a parallel recent development, the label 'cosmopolitan' has come to be stigmatized by conservative politicians of various stripes seeking to gain advantage through differentiating the 'ordinary' people to whom they appeal from a 'liberal elite' – comprising 'citizens of nowhere' – that is too detached from any sense of local belonging to be able to recognize the strength of supposedly popular concerns. This chapter will consider both the importance of cosmopolitanism for Goldsmith and the way in which he interrogated the ideal and sometimes pre-emptively challenged the terms of such an 'anti-elite' backlash against it.

Although (as McMurran notes) 'cosmopolitanism' itself is seldom referred to in eighteenth-century writing, Goldsmith often used cognate terms or phrases, as, for example, in his *Enquiry into the Present State of Polite Learning in Europe* (1759), which presents 'the wearing off national prejudices, and the finding nothing ridiculous in national peculiarities' as among the beneficial consequences of overseas travel (*Enquiry*, 182). In *The Citizen of the World* (1762) the Chinese philosopher Lien Chi Altangi identifies as a 'Cosmopolite' with a 'regard to mankind' who imagines 'the world being but one city' (*Citizen*, 2:178, 2:85, 2:238). His first reference to the honorific of Goldsmith's title comes in Letter 20, when he writes of how 'Confucius observes that it is the duty of the learned to unite society more closely, and to persuade men to become citizens of the world' (*Citizen*, 1:73). In Letter 23 Altangi tells of how a contributor to a subscription fund to support French prisoners of war described himself both as '*an Englishman*' and as '*a citizen of the world*' (*Citizen*, 1:89), and the work often in this way poses cosmopolitan self-identification against the narrow sense of patriotic attachment that helped to sustain hostilities during the ongoing Seven Years' War. Goldsmith's editorial persona asserts that 'the Chinese and we are pretty much alike', and as in Letter 7 Altangi invokes an essential 'human heart' behind the 'differences which result from climate, religion, education, prejudice, and partiality' (*Citizen*, 1:iv, 1:23). 'From Zerdusht [Zoroaster] down to him of Tyanea [Apollonius]', he declares, 'I honour all those great men who endeavoured to unite the world by their travels; such men who grew wiser as well as better, the farther they departed from home, and seemed like rivers, whose streams are not only encreased, but refined, as they travel from their source' (*Citizen*, 1:24; see Chapter 26, 'Orientalism').

Whereas Altangi in this quotation affirms human commonality and interconnection, in Letter 108 he rather differently presents cosmopolitan openness as affording a potentially transformative encounter with the new and unknown. After lamenting the ignorance of previous European travellers in Asia who had been 'influenced either by motives of commerce or piety', he imagines the 'variety of knowledge and useful improvement' that an unprejudiced traveller 'would . . . bring back in exchange' (*Citizen*, 2:169, 2:170). Altangi here appeals to a model of 'daring' curiosity exemplified by the English pioneer of scientific method Francis Bacon, and when he goes on to ask why learned societies have not yet sent 'one of their members into the most eastern parts of Asia, to make what discoveries he was able' (*Citizen*, 2:171), he may also allude to the German philosopher Gottfried Leibniz's call for a reciprocal 'commerce of light' between Europe and China.[2] In the same letter Altangi cites 'an . . . observation of *Boyle*, the English chymist' (*Citizen*, 2:172) regarding the innovations identified by artisans specializing in a particular trade, while elsewhere he refers to English intellectuals such as Shaftesbury and John Locke, diverse Greek and Roman authors, and French *philosophes* including Voltaire.[3] To some extent, therefore, Goldsmith's reference points in *The Citizen of the World* are indeed those of a cultural elite that could readily identify with the idea of a cosmopolitan European literary sphere and thus think of itself as detached from or elevated above popular prejudice (see Chapter 5, 'Enlightenments').

Denis Diderot wrote in a letter to David Hume that 'I flatter myself I am like you, a citizen of the great city of the world', and Altangi sometimes conceives of 'the world' in comparable terms, as 'but one city'.[4] At the

outset, though, Altangi also presents himself as a 'poor philosophic wan-
derer' (*Citizen*, 1:2), and this self-description echoes that of the 'Traveller'
in the first number of the *Bee* (1759), who states that 'out of my own
country, the highest character I can ever acquire, is that of . . . a philosophic
vagabond' (*Bee*, 27). Goldsmith's biographers often emphasize the forma-
tive nature of his experience of undertaking menial duties for financial
support at Trinity College Dublin, and much of what he wrote is
imprinted by the straitened circumstances of his early life (see Chapter 1,
'Life', and Chapter 2, 'Letters'). Altangi is one of many mobile personae
evident across Goldsmith's work, and even as he demonstrates his facility
of reference to Enlightenment thinkers, he also acknowledges the harsh
conditions of his overland journey to Europe and the painfulness of his
distance from home and family (*Citizen*, 1:3). Throughout his writing too,
however, Goldsmith often suggests that mobility, even where it is
a function of penury, offers an enhanced sense of critical perspective: as
he writes in his *Enquiry*, 'A man who is whirled through Europe in a post
chaise, and the pilgrim who walks the grand tour on foot, will form very
different conclusions' (*Enquiry*, 181). In Letter 67 of *The Citizen of the
World*, Altangi privileges the 'experience' that is gained from social inter-
course, stating (in a caricature of Rousseau) that one 'who has . . . spent his
life among books' is 'utterly unqualified for a journey through life' and
liable to become a 'man-hater' consumed by spleen and resentment
(*Citizen*, 2:7, 2:10).

In Letter 10, Altangi says more about his journey to Europe and how he at
one point passed through 'Xaixigar' – probably Kashgar, formerly a trading
post on the Silk Road between China and Europe. Together with his
reference to the Russian caravan which takes his letters from Moscow to
Beijing, this allusion to the Silk Road suggestively connects Altangi's mobil-
ity with established networks of global commerce. Altangi claims in Letter
108 that previous travellers to Asia had been impelled by 'motives of com-
merce or of piety', as already mentioned, and here and elsewhere Goldsmith
can be seen to distinguish between disinterestedly 'philosophical' and overtly
instrumental understandings of travel. In his essay 'Upon Political Frugality'
in the *Bee*, Goldsmith laments that profit-driven commercial innovation
outpaces other forms of improvement that cross-cultural contact might make
possible: 'We are arrived at a perfect imitation of Porcelaine', he states, but
'let us endeavour to imitate the good to society that our neighbours are found
to practise, and let our neighbours also imitate those parts of duty in which
we excel' (*Bee*, 136). If Goldsmith sometimes thus seeks to differentiate
cosmopolitanism from 'globalization', an advanced stage of capitalism,

however, he also recognizes the precariousness of any such distinction, and the difficulty of securing a critical vantage point that is not implicated in the workings of commercial society: in his preface to *The Citizen of the World* Goldsmith's editorial persona presents 'Chinese morality' as itself a commodity as he imagines taking a 'small cargoe' of it to sell at the Frost Fair on the frozen River Thames, only for the ice to break beneath his wheelbarrow (*Citizen*, 1:vi).

While Altangi imagines the 'variety of knowledge and useful improvement' that a Bacon-inspired traveller to Asia 'would ... bring back in exchange' (*Citizen*, 2:170), in other letters he acknowledges the economic imperatives that currently govern cross-cultural exchange, which he accordingly depicts in less utopian terms. Bacon's argument in support of extending humankind's dominion over nature was consequent upon (among other things) the European discovery of the Americas, and in Letter 17 Altangi offers an Olympian perspective on the contest between Britain and France for territory and wealth across the Atlantic: in Britain's case, he states, this involves 'an exchange of her best and bravest subjects for raw silk, hemp, and tobacco' (*Citizen*, 1:62).[5] Goldsmith's work here implicitly juxtaposes the peaceful ideal of global commerce articulated in Joseph Addison's *Spectator* 69 (19 May 1711), in which Mr Spectator at the Royal Exchange imagines himself as 'a Citizen of the World', with the violent competition over distant resources between rival colonial powers.[6] It again contrasts ideal and reality in its often sceptical reference to the 'republic of letters' – a phrase translated from Latin to French by the philosopher Pierre Bayle, and often (if wishfully) invoked as an open and inclusive community of intellectual exchange across national boundaries. While Goldsmith demonstrates the extent of his own reading, he also via Altangi rehearses what Eun Kyung Min calls a 'Popean vision of the London press as a confederacy of dunces rather than a cosmopolitan commonwealth of letters'.[7] Altangi's description of the 'club of authors' in Letters 29 and 30 and the 'company of philosophers and learned men' in Letter 58 accentuates the gulf between appealing theory and debased practice (*Citizen*, 1:119, 1:250).

Goldsmith remained serious about the cosmopolitan ideal, and he may have petitioned Lord Bute in 1761 to propose himself for the kind of expedition to Asia which Altangi calls for at the end of Letter 108: 'To send out a traveller, properly qualified ... might be an object of national concern; it would in some measure repair the breaches made by ambition; and might shew that there were still some who boasted a greater name than that of patriots, who professed themselves lovers of men' (*Citizen*, 2:172–3).

The phrase 'that there were still some' is telling here, however, because it suggests that 'lovers of men' are exceptions to the general (non-cosmopolitan) rule: Altangi has a kind of alliance with the man in black, whom he first meets at Westminster Abbey in Letter 13, but this friendship is partly built on their both being eccentric outsiders. In the frequently cited Letters 14 and 33, Altangi's description of being summoned to visit 'ladies of distinction' emphasizes that those who are most intrigued by him are little interested in any notion of cultural exchange and in fact misrecognize the content of his difference, such is the strength of their exoticizing assumptions (see Chapter 26, 'Orientalism'). As well as thus questioning the extent of investment in the cosmopolitan ideal in contemporary Britain, by acknowledging the sway of false consciousness (which grips Altangi too), Goldsmith's work also at times undercuts itself by playing Altangi's cosmopolitanism for laughs. In Letter 85, for example, Altangi insists that 'my regard to mankind fills me with concern for their contentions' and that 'I am an enemy to nothing in this good world but war; I hate fighting between rival states', only then to trivialize these claims through his reference to the rivalry between the actresses Isabella Vincent and Charlotte Brent: 'I hate fighting even between women!' (*Citizen*, 2:85).

This kind of comedy is apparent elsewhere too, as, for example, towards the end of Altangi's 'Indian tale' in Letter 85, when he refers to the figure of the 'black-eyed Princess', whose sobriquet is a marker not of her exotic beauty but instead of the 'two black eyes she had received in her youth, being a little addicted to boxing in her liquor' (*Citizen*, 2:101). *The Citizen of the World* conjoins frivolity and seriousness throughout, however, and another index of the latter, in addition to the work's commentary on the Seven Years' War, is the extent of its somewhat underappreciated historical and geographical reference (see Chapter 17, 'War and Empire'). This aspect of Goldsmith's cosmopolitanism goes beyond his effort to establish a persona and backstory for his Chinese philosopher, and it is evident when, in Letter 87, Altangi's friend Fum Hoam notes the troubling populousness of Qing China's Russian neighbour then reflects on how 'migrations of men' ('Goths, Huns, Vandals, Saracens, Turks, Tartars') have been a driving force behind the rise and fall of Asiatic and European empires (*Citizen*, 2:96). The passage in question draws on Buffon's *Natural History* (1749–1804) – intellectual ambition and derivativeness (verging on plagiarism) is another conjunction characteristic of *The Citizen of the World* – but it nonetheless offers, albeit in miniature, a foray into global history that may additionally be inflected by Goldsmith's Irishness and his experience of mobility, which arguably made him especially attentive to the determining significance of the movements of others.

Premised on the idea of 'the world being but one city to me', as Altangi puts it in the work's final paragraph, *The Citizen of the World* belongs to a particular moment in Goldsmith's career as a writer: in subsequent works, as has often been argued, his attention shifts from the city to the country, and from seeing through the eyes of one who considers himself a 'stranger nowhere' to focusing on more overtly exiled figures who are 'at home nowhere'. In comparison with a contemporary such as Hume, who celebrates the eighteenth-century metropolis as a locus of cosmopolitan sociability, Goldsmith is less sanguine about the city, not least because he remains exercised by the uneasy relationship between commercial prosperity and national well-being. *The Citizen of the World* is indeed a notably reflexive work which stages both the possibilities and the limitations of cosmopolitanism – on the one hand by presenting the ideal as offering an impartial detachment from the national antagonisms prolonging the Seven Years' War, and on the other by showing it as embedded nonetheless in instrumental forms of cross-cultural connection, and as a minority concern, either of the privileged or marginal, in any case.

Another measure of the complexity of Goldsmith's engagement with difference is that his mediation of Enlightenment thinking involves an appeal to emergent constructions of race, as when Altangi in Letter 10, describing his overland journey across Central Asia to Europe, refers to the figure of 'the brown Tartar [who] wanders for a precarious subsistence, with an heart that never felt pity, himself more hideous than the wilderness he makes' (*Citizen*, 1:31); a comparable typification of others is evident in Goldsmith's series of essays 'A Comparative View of Races and Nations' (1760) as well as in *The Traveller* (1764). This kind of reference ostensibly represents the antithesis of cosmopolitanism, but it derives from the expansive classificatory schema of Buffon and Linnaeus, pioneers in the field of natural history, and it also demonstrates Goldsmith's position as an innovator in his own right: as Roxann Wheeler points out, in his *History of the Earth, and Animated Nature* (1774) Goldsmith would be 'among the first to single [skin colour] out above all other characteristics by which humans were distinguished' (see Chapter 14, 'Race', and Chapter 16, 'Natural History and Science').[8] It is important to recognize as well, however, that there are numerous other 'Tartars' in *The Citizen of the World*, and sometimes, as in Letter 32's account of the consumption of hallucinogenic mushrooms by the 'Tartars of Koreki' (the 'poorer sort' drink the urine of 'rich Tartars', in what Altangi presents as an analogue of rituals of obeisance in Britain), ideas of ethnic and cultural difference primarily seem to provide a way of thinking about social distinction at home (*Citizen*, 1:133).

I will conclude by briefly considering a letter from *The Citizen of the World* in which Goldsmith not only addresses the condition of the poor but also interrogates the opposition between cosmopolitanism and localism which I alluded to at the outset. Even as Goldsmith uses Altangi to offer an Olympian view of the politics of the Seven Years' War, above the fray of competing national interests, he also presents him encountering individuals such as the 'disabled soldier' (in Letter 119), who, irrespective of his own sufferings, continues to celebrate his Englishness and denigrate the French. Altangi's framing of the veteran's narrative invites us to see him as among the unacknowledged 'many' who, literally 'citizens of nowhere', 'are obliged to wander without a friend to comfort or assist them, find enmity in every law, and are too poor to obtain even justice' (*Citizen*, 2:217). Rather than straightforwardly pose the false consciousness of the bellicose patriot against the enlightenment of the detached observer, Goldsmith in this letter complicates any such distinction by suggesting that a foreignness – in the form of unknown or unrecognized stories – is to be found in everyday life at home too. David Simpson writes of Romantic-period authors whose work is 'in the business of asking us to notice things we might not otherwise notice about our immediate environments', and (sometimes at least) Goldsmith's self-critical reflection on the meaning of cosmopolitanism can comparably be seen to approach this familiar yet elusive concept in 'prospective' terms – in other words, as referring to an ongoing challenge of comprehension and ethical engagement rather than an achieved or achievable state.[9]

Notes

1. Mary Helen McMurran, 'The New Cosmopolitanism and the Eighteenth Century', *Eighteenth-Century Studies*, 47.1 (2013), 19–38 (19).
2. Lawrence Williams, 'Anglo-Chinese Caresses: Civility, Friendship and Trade in English Representations of China, 1760–1800', *Journal for Eighteenth-Century Studies*, 38.2 (2015), 277–96 (283).
3. Boyle was Irish.
4. Cited in McMurran, 'New Cosmopolitanism', 28.
5. Carolyn Merchant, 'Secrets of Nature: The Bacon Debates Revisited', *Journal of the History of Ideas*, 69.1 (2008), 147–62.
6. *The Spectator*, ed. Donald F. Bond, 5 vols. (Oxford: Clarendon, 1965), 1:294.

7. Eun Kyung Min, *China and the Writing of English Literary Modernity* (Cambridge University Press, 2018), 162.

8. Roxann Wheeler, *The Complexion of Race: Categories of Difference in Eighteenth-Century British Culture* (University of Pennsylvania Press, 2000), 180.

9. David Simpson, 'The Limits of Cosmopolitanism and the Case for Translation', *European Romantic Review*, 16.2 (2005), 141–52 (150).

CHAPTER 12

Marriage

Aileen Douglas

In 1768 Frances Burney was reading *The Vicar of Wakefield* (1766). The sixteen-year-old recorded how she had been 'surprised into tears' and felt it to 'be impossible any person could read this book thro' with a dry eye', but her first impressions had not been at all favourable.[1] Burney had come to Goldsmith's work from the sentimental correspondence of the married writers Elizabeth and Richard Griffith, published as *A Series of Genuine Letters between Henry and Frances* (1757), which she admired for its tenderness and elegance; *The Vicar of Wakefield* suffered in comparison. In particular, Burney recorded how 'disgusted' she was by the way the Vicar talked about his wife: 'such indifference – such contempt'.[2] Undoubtedly, the shock to Burney's readerly expectations was of a kind that Goldsmith might have predicted, indeed, even set out to provoke. A persistent theme in his work across genres – including fiction, periodical writings, and reviews – is the dissonance between marriage as a narrative convention and marriage as lived experience and social institution; or, to state the case more baldly, the misrepresentation of marriage in fiction (see Chapter 19, 'Fiction'). In 1757, commenting on a translation of a French novel, Goldsmith wearily wrote that it concluded, 'as they all do', with a narrator in conjugal bliss, 'Beloved by my family, and more especially so by a wife, whose lover I am, as well as a husband'. To which Goldsmith expostulated: 'Reader, if thou hast ever known such perfect happiness, as these romance-writers can so liberally dispense, thou hast enjoyed greater pleasure than has ever fallen to our lot. How deceitful are these imaginary pictures of felicity!'[3] Any reader comparing these emphatic statements with the picture of felicity with which, just a few years later, Goldsmith concluded *The Vicar of Wakefield* – a double wedding and the validation of a third – might feel an explanation is called for.

The marriages with which *The Vicar of Wakefield* concludes are but one aspect of a work that is fundamentally and variously concerned throughout with marriage. Moreover, *The Vicar's* representation of marriage maps onto a temporal framework, reaching into the past, engaging with the present, and projecting into the future. Some of the Vicar's own arcane, idiosyncratic views on marriage drive the plot and are a source of comedy while looking back to an esoteric and dated clerical controversy. More topically, and in social and political contexts, *The Vicar* participates in debates initiated by the Hardwicke Marriage Act of 1753 and articulates some of the arguments opponents made against its passage. Then, looking forward into the future, its realized portrait of marriage as the basis of affective family life can be seen as both original and significant in the development of domestic fiction.

The Vicar of Wakefield begins with the Primrose family affluent and contented, and anticipating the marriage of the eldest son, George, to the beautiful and wealthy Arabella Wilmot. In the series of disasters that soon beset the family the pride the Vicar takes in his pugnaciously held views on marriage play a notable part.

> Matrimony was always one of my favourite topics, and I wrote several sermons to prove its utility and happiness: but there was a peculiar tenet which I made a point of supporting; for I maintained with Whiston, that it was unlawful for a priest of the church of England, after the death of his first wife, to take a second, or to express it in one word, I valued myself upon being a strict monogamist. (*Vicar*, 1:10)

William Whiston (1667–1752), clergyman and natural philosopher, was in 1710 expelled from his post as professor of mathematics at the University of Cambridge for heretical views regarding the Trinity. He became increasingly attached to a form of primitive Christianity which included the belief that clerical remarriage should be prohibited.[4] Dr Primrose's energetic promulgation of his Whistonian views to his son's prospective father-in-law – a clergyman who, unknown to the Vicar, is about to wed his fourth wife – precipitates a quarrel that puts an end to his son's engagement and, together with the Vicar's simultaneous and substantial financial losses, begins his family's series of reversals. Subsequently, the pride the Vicar takes in his stature as a 'strict monogamist' makes him an easy dupe and leads to further financial loss. Attempting to sell the family's broken-down horse at a fair to realize ready money, the Vicar is hailed by the trickster Ephraim Jenkinson as 'the great Primrose, that couragious monogamist, who had been the bulwark of the church' (*Vicar*, 1:135). The 'rapture' the Vicar feels at this characterization completely disarms him, makes Jenkinson the owner of the horse, and leaves the Vicar with only a worthless bond. Jokes at the expense of the Vicar's peculiar views and his monomaniacal promotion of them continue into the second volume when, reunited with his son George, who has been attempting to earn his living as a hack writer, the Vicar hopes that he did not, in his publications, 'pass over the importance' of hierarchical monogamy (*Vicar*, 2:6).

The Vicar's quirks would have prompted comparison with several contemporary fictions. Henry Fielding's Parson Adams in *Joseph Andrews* (1742) is another naïve cleric whose taste for publication is gently mocked. Additionally, while Goldsmith may have been critical of Laurence Sterne's *Tristram Shandy* (1759–67), describing it as a 'pert and obscene novel', there is no denying that the Vicar's stance on marriage is a hobby horse akin to Uncle Toby's war games and Walter Shandy's *Tristrapædia*.[5] Certain twentieth-century readings of *The Vicar of Wakefield* argue that the Vicar's backward-looking preoccupation with the 'graveyard of clerical tracts', with its associated vanity and complacency, make him an object of satire.[6] The Vicar's foibles do not, however, interfere with his fundamental Christianity, most clearly seen in his pursuit of Olivia and his insistence that his seduced and repentant daughter be received once again in the family home.[7] Such charitable and loving treatment of a 'fallen' woman by a paternal figure is unusual in eighteenth-century fiction, as is the Vicar's exception to a dominant understanding of women as a form of property to be exchanged between fathers and husbands in marriage.

On the very particular issue of clerical marriage the Vicar's views may be backward looking, but his understanding of how marriage might work in the general population is more topical. *The Vicar of Wakefield* participates directly in what had become, by 1766, a long-running public debate over the measures of Hardwicke's Marriage Act, or to give the law its full title, An Act for the Better Preventing of Clandestine Marriages, 1753, 26 Geo II.[8] The main provisions of the Act required that all marriages be performed by an Anglican clergyman in a church or chapel in the couple's parish, that banns be called for three Sundays prior to the wedding, and that minors obtain parental consent. Only Jews, Quakers, and the royal family were exempted from the law, which meant that Catholics and all other Dissenters became legally obliged to marry in a church to which they did not belong (see Chapter 15, 'Religion'). The necessity to call banns could be eliminated through the purchase of a licence from a bishop. Those opposing the Act argued that it worsened the condition of women because it made them vulnerable to promises of marriage that could not be enforced, that it gave parents tyrannical powers over their minor children, that it restricted class mobility, and that it increased the power of the state vis-à-vis the church.[9] Although it has recently been argued the '1753 Act did not constitute such a radical break with the past as has been claimed', much academic opinion has tended to see the Act as a watershed in the history of the legal regulation of marriage 'marking the change from a pluralistic system, in which multiple forms of marriage were accepted, to a more restrictive, prescriptive approach'.[10]

Certainly public debate continued after the passage of the Act, with periodic attempts at repeal, with Goldsmith expressing opposition in several literary forms. In *The Citizen of the World* (1762), letters originally published in the *Public Ledger* in 1760–1, Lien Chi Altangi, a Chinese 'Philosopher' visiting London, writes home in mock credulity about 'laws made, which even forbid the peoples marrying each other' (*Citizen*, 2:31; see Chapter 11, 'Cosmopolitanism', and Chapter 26, 'Orientalism'). The letter then facetiously describes the Act's various provisions. The need for parental consent is described as 'a clog upon matrimony' because it is 'more difficult for the lover to please three than one'. Other provisions cause even more difficulty: the delay caused by the necessity to call the banns is 'a very great clog', and the attendant publicity 'a severe clog' (*Citizen*, 2:32). In Letter CXI, Altangi returned to his theme: 'The laws of this country are finely calculated to promote all commerce, but the commerce between the sexes. Their encouragements for propagating hemp, madder and tobacco, are indeed admirable! Marriages are the only commodity that meet with none' (*Citizen*, 2:195–6).

If the Vicar's hobby horse is 'strict monogamy', Lien Chi Altangi is preoccupied by low marriage rates. He rehearses standard oppositional positions on the Marriage Act as part of what he perceives as a broader social problem: that London is full of the aged unmarried (fussy spinsters and timid bachelors) and that marriage is 'not sufficiently encouraged' and 'out of fashion' (*Citizen*, 1:112, 2:98).

In *The Vicar of Wakefield* the Marriage Act also comes in for adverse comment, but for the reason that it hinders class mobility. Travelling in search of his 'lost child', Olivia, the Vicar is invited to dine by a man he believes to be a country gentleman (in fact, he is a butler impersonating his absent master). In the ensuing political discussion the Vicar gives a long and impassioned speech outlining his views on monarchy and governance, his warm exposition delineating how wealth accumulates in commercial states and increases the tendency towards the 'aristocratical': 'Besides this, the very laws of a country may contribute to the accumulation of wealth; as when those natural ties that bind the rich and poor together are broken, and it is ordained that the rich shall only marry among each other' (*Vicar*, 1:203).

Here the provisions of the Act are seen as destructive of the 'natural ties' between classes and of the possibility of marriage permitting the circulation of wealth outside a narrow, restricted social group. In the Vicar's broader analysis, the restriction that 'the rich shall only marry among each other' does not simply concentrate wealth; it also concentrates power to the detriment of the general good (see Chapter 10, 'Liberty'). The Vicar's theoretical view on marriage and the desirability of class mobility is clear enough, but he does not consistently apply it – if at all. After an early encounter with Squire Thornhill he warns his family that 'Disproportioned friendships ever terminate in disgust' and enjoins keeping to 'companions of our own rank' (*Vicar*, 1:47). Later he frets over the apparent attraction between his daughter Sophia and Mr Burchell, whose personal qualities he admires but whom he understands to be a 'man of broken fortune' (*Vicar*, 1:80).

The Vicar of Wakefield represents the new era of regulation after the Marriage Act in a number of important ways. Certain provisions of the Marriage Act – the requirements as to place of ceremony and the calling of the banns over a period of several weeks – were designed to ensure publicity and hence reduce the risk of coerced marriages. Yet the Act also allowed publicity to be evaded: a licence purchased from a bishop absolved the requirement to call banns, and a licence purchased from the Archbishop of Canterbury allowed a marriage to occur at a place and time of the couple's choosing. Significantly, all of the marriages that occur in *The Vicar of Wakefield* involve licences. Burchell, now revealed to be Sir William Thornhill, overnight obtains the licence for his own marriage to Sophia and for George's marriage to Arabella. The licence is also key to the marriage between Olivia and Squire Thornhill. A bleakly comic exchange between Olivia and her father after their reunion reveals tensions between secular and religious understandings of the regulation of marriage, and the Vicar's adherence to a pre–Marriage Act sense of legitimacy. Olivia admits that she knew her wedding 'privately performed by a popish priest, was no way binding' (*Vicar*, 2:48). The Vicar is delighted, however, if only momentarily, exclaiming that if the marriage has been performed by a priest in orders then Olivia is now Thornhill's wife 'to all intents and purposes; nor can all the laws of man, tho' written upon tables of adamant, lessen the force of that sacred connexion' (*Vicar*, 2:49). In asserting the primacy of sacred religious rite over merely man-made law the Vicar is at one with opponents of the Marriage Act who believed that marriage was properly the concern of the Church rather than the State. The Vicar's flash of confidence is, however, immediately extinguished when his daughter discloses that Thornhill 'has been married already, by the same priest, to six or eight wives more, whom, like me, he has deceived and abandoned' (*Vicar*, 2:49). Only at the very end of the tale is the marriage between Olivia and Thornhill revealed to be legitimate, as, in an eleventh-hour twist, the 'licence' which Thornhill understood to be false and procured to aid in his deception of Olivia turns out to be valid. Though, ultimately, there is no sham marriage in *The Vicar of Wakefield*, the tale does nothing to suggest the efficiency of the Act in preventing such marriages.

The tale ends with the marriages of two of the Vicar's children and the marriage of a third validated. Undoubtedly, this is a particularly gratifying outcome for a father whose narration begins with his long-standing opinion that 'the honest man who married and brought up a large family, did more service than he who continued single, and only talked of population' (*Vicar*, 1.[1]), mercantilist language in which family is equated with population – and population is a source of wealth. The second thing we learn about the Vicar is of his own early marriage to a wife he chose as 'she did her wedding gown, not for a fine glossy surface, but such qualities as would wear well' (*Vicar*, 1.[1]). It was just such pragmatic, 'indifferent' references to the Vicar's wife which so disgusted Frances Burney. Once Burney read on, however, 'the description of his rural felicity, his simple, unaffected contentment – and family domestic happiness, gave me much pleasure'.[11] Later readers concurred. In the early nineteenth century the 'great charm' of *The Vicar* was understood to reside in its 'fire-side picture' of domestic affections.[12] A feature of *The Vicar of Wakefield* is the presence throughout not only of the Vicar's older, marriageable children, but also of the younger ones: performing their party pieces during evenings at home, eating gingerbread, and – in more dramatic and sentimental scenes – being rescued from the fire and sturdily unafraid to be with their father in the prison. *The Vicar of Wakefield* represents the family as a site of struggle between faltering paternal authority and fatherly affection, a tension encapsulated by the Vicar when he accedes to a request from his older daughters because 'I was tired of being always wise' and 'loved to see them happy' (*Vicar*, 1:90).[13]

That *The Vicar of Wakefield* ends with a double wedding may be seen as Goldsmith's subtly ironic undermining, through exaggeration, of the conventions of contemporary prose fiction. The point is reinforced by the marked contrast with Goldsmith's treatment of marriage in the 'laughing comedy' *She Stoops to Conquer* (1773), where Mr Hardcastle may believe he has been 'pretty fond of an old wife' (*Stoops*, 2), but the bickering of the play's elders does not indicate contented companionability, nor does the brilliant role-playing which constitutes the courtship of Kate Hardcastle and Charles Marlowe allow any sense of how their marriage might look once the role-playing is cast aside (see Chapter 13, 'Gender', and Chapter 20, 'Theatre').[14] More importantly, marriage in the tale is not solely about a sense of an ending. Goldsmith's 'pictures of family life' represented 'a new strain in fiction'.[15] His use of 'a family setting, and the problem of marriage, produced a new and original form'.[16] The representation of marriage in *The Vicar of Wakefield* does not merely look sideways to Hardwicke's Marriage Act but, much more importantly, forward to so much fiction of later times, bringing to mind sentiments George Eliot would express in the 'Finale' of *Middlemarch* (1871–2): 'Marriage, which has been the bourne of so many narratives, is still a great beginning . . . the beginning of the home epic.'[17]

Notes

1. *The Early Journals and Letters of Fanny Burney, 1768–1773*, ed. Lars E. Troide (Oxford: Clarendon, 1988), 12.
2. Burney, *Early Journals and Letters*, 12.
3. *Monthly Review*, 16 (May 1757), 45.
4. See *Whiston's Primitive Christianity Reviv'd: In Four Parts*, 4 vols. (London, 1712), II, [np]. Book VI, §347.
5. *Public Ledger*, 30 June 1760, reprinted as Letter LI in *Citizen*, 1:229–33.
6. See Robert H. Hopkins, *The True Genius of Oliver Goldsmith* (Baltimore, MD: Johns Hopkins University Press, 1969), 174–5.
7. Oliver W. Ferguson, 'Dr. Primrose and Goldsmith's Clerical Ideal', *Philological Quarterly* 54.1 (1975), 323–32.
8. Lisa O'Connell discusses *The Vicar of Wakefield* as the 'last important novel to engage with the marriage debate directly' and notes that the period in which the novel was written coincided with efforts to repeal the Act, and with Goldsmith's own close association with Robert Nugent, who led parliamentary opposition to it: O'Connell, *The Origins of the English Marriage Plot: Literature, Politics and Religion in the Eighteenth Century* (Cambridge University Press, 2019), 173–4.
9. On opposition to the Act see O'Connell, *English Marriage Plot*, 26–8.
10. Rebecca Probert, *Marriage Law and Practice in the Long Eighteenth Century: A Reassessment* (Cambridge University Press, 2009), 2, 5.
11. Burney, *Early Journals and Letters*, 12.
12. *New Annual Register, or, General Repository of History, Politics, and Literature* (January 1817), 56, 443.

13. See Raymond F. Hillard, 'The Redemption of Fatherhood in *The Vicar of Wakefield*', *Studies in English Literature, 1500–1900*, 23.3 (1983), 465–80.

14. James Phillips argues the play celebrates bourgeois marriage 'without being able to represent it'; 'Oliver Goldsmith's *She Stoops to Conquer*: The Stakes of Shame and the Prospects of Politeness', *English Literary History*, 87.4 (2020): 999–1023 (999).

15. Ricardo Quintana, *Oliver Goldsmith: A Georgian Study* (London: Weidenfeld and Nicolson, 1967), 105.

16. Ronald Paulson, *Satire and the Novel in Eighteenth-Century England* (New Haven, CT: Yale University Press, 1967), 274.

17. George Eliot, *Middlemarch*, ed. David Carroll (Oxford: Clarendon, 1986), 818; John Francis Waller terms the Vicar a 'domestic epic' in the introduction to *Works of Goldsmith* (London: Cassell, Petter, & Galpin, 1864), 2.

CHAPTER 13

Gender

Rebecca Anne Barr

Goldsmith's reputation is strangely respectable. Henry James, attempting to grasp the peculiar perfections of *The Vicar of Wakefield*, admits its oddity. It is 'the spoiled child of our literature': lovable, infantile, unaccountable.[1] For David Garrick too Goldsmith's compound of contradictions defies explanation:

> A great love of truth; yet a mind turn'd to fictions;
> Now mix these ingredients, which warm'd in the baking,
> Turn to learning, and gaming, religion and raking.
> With the love of a wench, let his writings be chaste;
> Tip his tongue with strange matter, his pen with fine taste; . . .
> For the joy of each sex, on the world I'll bestow it:
> This Scholar, Rake, Christian, Dupe, Gamester and Poet.[2]

The author and his works fuse in a figure of comic eccentricity. But 'odd' (a word that Garrick uses twice to describe Goldsmith), is also synonymous with 'queer'. Samuel Johnson parses odd as 'particular; uncouth; extraordinary . . . Strange; unaccountable; fantastical; unlucky, unlikely; in appearance improper'.[3] Oddness suggests opacity and illegibility, an excess that lies aslant the explicable or rational and inherently English norms.

Delightfully comic rather than morally suspect, Garrick's portrait of droll incongruity coasts on Goldsmith's unmentioned but implicit Irishness. Goldsmith's not-quite-Englishness had to be sufficiently plausible to placate and please English audiences. Goldsmith managed it – some of the time. But even as his plays and novel kowtow to patriarchal plots and metropolitan prejudices, they also demonstrate ambivalence about eighteenth-century norms of gender and sexuality.

Goldsmith's literary career maps onto the era of sensibility and sentiment – terms denoting sympathetic bodily feeling and the moral knowledge inherent in such feeling. But this aspirational model of gender was inextricable from international conflict and aggressive colonial expansion. He arrived in London at the beginning of the Seven Years' War when Georgian Britain's commercial and cultural wealth was fuelled by imperial expansion (see Chapter 17, 'War and Empire'). The mid-century expansion of the novel had staked a market claim for the reformative power of refined feeling. The tropes of 'virtue in distress' provided by Samuel Richardson's virginal heroines, Pamela and Clarissa, extracted money and tears from paying audiences. Women's sensitivity, modesty, and gentility were touted as positive social forces capable of reforming men and improving manners.[4] Feminine appetites supposedly fuelled a globalized market which depicted trade as a 'soft power' disseminating the beneficial effects of British enlightenment. The tensions in this discourse were manifested in the 'feminization debate' – British discourse which trumpeted the progressive effects of women on modern society while seeking to condemn perceived transgressions of an increasingly binary gender order.[5] Cultural concern about the ascendancy of 'masculinized' women over 'effeminate' men thus correlated with British warfare: a calibration of maximally efficient national gender norms.

The eighteenth-century theatre was a significant site for the negotiation of genders (see Chapter 20, 'Theatre'). It also had 'a particular force . . . for the eighteenth-century London Irish', who worked as authors, actors, and managers.[6] As Lisa Freeman has shown, the stage was 'a critical site for social exchange in eighteenth-century English culture . . . where identity itself could be understood as a public property rather than as the private or privatized concern of the subject'.[7] As a platform where Irish 'good nature' and wit could be performed for a literary profit, Goldsmith's dramas explicate the gendered paradoxes in his writing. His 'Essay on the Theatre' (1773) rhetorically overstates the tide of 'sentimental comedies' in order to assert a family resemblance between his 'laughing comedy' and the early-eighteenth-century stage, denouncing French drama to manoeuvre his plays closer to a 'manly' English humour. But Goldsmith's plays are as much a product of sentiment as of wit, ridicule, and satire. Indeed, the inherently performative qualities of Richardsonian sensibility spawned many comedies, helping to 'revive theatrical culture' following the Licensing Act of 1737.[8] Despite his promotion of Anglo masculinity, reading for gender in Goldsmith reveals 'eighteenth-century Anglophone culture [as] already inherently queer', illuminating the odd, unaccountable, or other as constituent parts of mainstream literary culture.[9] Goldsmith's works, as James Kim observes, display a 'striking ambivalence toward the new sexual economy, a curious and recurrent discontent with the prospect of bourgeois matrimony and its promise of heterosexual intercourse'.[10] The 'odd fellows' of Goldsmith's works evince persistent disinclinations towards both marriage and women, insinuating queer strains of gender and sexuality. In *The Vicar of Wakefield*, the polyphilo-progenitive Primrose is more enamoured of almost every man he meets than of his own wife and daughters. In *The Good Natur'd Man* (1768), the sentimental hero is a reluctant lover, preferring the pleasures of assisting other men. In *She Stoops to Conquer* (1773), Marlow's sexual phobia of 'modest' women emasculates him around prospective spouses, libidinally curtailed to lower-rank women who are conveniently unsuitable for marriage (see Chapter 12, 'Marriage'). Crucially, instead of subverting or disrupting gender or genre, these figures instead 'anchor emergent norms' by their conscription into nuptial happy endings and their indictment of women's unruly passions.[11] These works elevate homosociability above the conjugal heterosexuality their plots rhetorically affirm.

The chaste self-effacement of Goldsmith's heroes might seem an improvement on the sexual aggression of the aristocratic libertine, but their misogyny is merely more sly. Instead of conventionally virile masculine authority figures Goldsmith focuses on seemingly marginal or subordinated masculinities: financially dependent, romantically averse, and charmingly hapless fools. However, potential subversiveness is neutralized by the heteronormative frameworks that surround them. As 'the entire array of polarized taxonomies that organize compulsory heterosexuality', heteronormativity is responsible for generating the 'aura of obviousness' and inescapability of heterosexuality.[12] So although they do not embody culturally dominant forms of masculinity, these genial men are complicit with and ultimately rewarded by heteronormative patriarchy. While heroines like Pamela Andrews have *their* virtue rewarded only after punitive sexual trials, the idiosyncratic inadequacies of Goldsmith's milksops are overcompensated by a 'patriarchal dividend'.[13] Thus, inadequate father Primrose is saved from penury by a 'nobilis ex machina', the powerful and discreet Squire Thornhill; romantically averse Honeywood has his debts dissolved by a discreet woman without having to submit to the self-abasement of courtship rituals and is exonerated by his surrogate father; Marlow's performance anxiety is solved by a rank-appropriate woman prepared to role-play a barmaid.[14] Goldsmith gives men more than their due, lubricating the patriarchal dividend with laughter and genial self-effacement.

The Good-Natur'd Man models the key aspects that unite all Goldsmith's odd heroes, flirting with the conflation of text, author, and eponymous character. 'In the propensities of Honeywood', Elizabeth Inchbald asserted, 'the author turned a conscious glance upon the infirmities to which *he* was subject; and ... he made this portrait both bold and natural, from having viewed *himself*'.[15] The play is an 'auto-critique' of complicity: 'a disposition which, though inclined to right, had not the courage to condemn the wrong – those splendid errors, that still took the name from some neighbouring duty – charity, that was but injustice; benevolence, that was but weakness; and friendship, that was but credulity'.[16] In Inchbald's radical reckoning, self-awareness does not excuse moral deficiency. It is no accident that the insipid incel and white sentimentalist of *The Woman of Colour* (1808) is named for Goldsmith's hero. Sir William, Honeywood's uncle and benefactor, arrives to deliver a reformatory shock to his heir, whose refined sensibility and willingness to oblige anyone has led to debt and the depreciation of his own character. Though he stage-manages the hero's arrest, Sir William takes paternal pride in Honeywood's flaws. 'A delicate hand' must be used to chastise his nephew since 'there are some faults so nearly allied to excellence, that we can scarce weed out one without eradicating the virtue' (*Good Natur'd Man*, 3). Honeywood's weakness is not women but men. 'Too good natur'd ... too much every man's man' (1), Honeywood's homosocial disposition leaves him open to unscrupulous propositions. His servants bilk and exploit him; he sponsors his friend's elopement despite being under house arrest for debt; self-interested modern politician Lofty passes himself off as his saviour and claims interest on the lie by getting the hero to woo Miss Richland – the hero's supposed love object – on his behalf. Honeywood's is a cluelessly nostalgic version of civic virtue, a malfunctioning relic of a masculinist past that, like Harley in Henry MacKenzie's *Man of Feeling* (1773), cannot function properly in commercial society. Lacking reformative agency, both characters resort to incontinent spending as an auto-erotic sop to their consciences, mistaking financial incontinence for benevolent largesse: 'he calls his extravagance, generosity; and his trusting everybody, universal benevolence' (2). But while Harley tends to spend around weeping maidens, the recipients of Honeywood's cash and sympathy are men.

The heroes' 'asexual possibility' creates plots whose tendency to inertia can be resolved only by gendered substitution and surrogation: the creation of characters whose dynastic or heterosexual desire makes things happen – whether the hero wants them to or not.[17] Honeywood's interest, like Goldsmith's, lies beyond the contours of the romance plot. As Norma Clarke notes, though 'he utilised the conventions of love, there is no serious love interest in any of his writings, no love scenes and no bawdy'.[18] In *The Good Natur'd Man*, this leads to flat, 'uninteresting ... and inanimate' women characters.[19] The purported love object Miss Richland is almost allegorical: a sexual solution to financial crisis. But the marriage that 'would set all things to rights again' is unimaginable to the hero. Honeywood's deference to her engenders selfless idolization and chivalric obedience: anachronistic and non-propulsive modes which tend toward inconclusive and sexually unconsummated relationships. Honeywood defines friendship as 'disinterested commerce between equals', a superior bond to the 'abject intercourse between tyrants and slaves' found in romantic love (10). But this misrecognition of 'the commerce of everyday life' ultimately makes Honeywood 'a voluntary slave of all' (72). Honeywood's sexual passivity overthrows anti-Irish stereotypes of the penurious Irish fortune hunter of the period, who sells himself for financially advantageous (and generally loveless) marriage. Miss Richland ultimately proposes to him, discharging his debts and surrendering herself – and her wealth – to him.

Content in philanthropic bachelorhood, Honeywood's absence of desire spurs everyone else into action. His 'good nature' can be read not as sensitivity but as 'stagnant *insensibility*', what one contemporary review called the 'selfish compromises of an indolent spirit' (*Critical Heritage*, 73). Such erotic lethargy means women have to do the legwork to generate marriage plots against poor odds. Miss Richland's savvy develops into Kate Hardcastle's enterprising management; poor Mrs Hardcastle desperately tries to matchmake her boorish son, Tony Lumpkin. In both plays, women's pragmatic agency supplements a lack in the heroes: their moral delicacy confirmed by the play's sentimental irony and sympathetic humour. It is Kate's demand that the suitor her father chooses also be attractive and sexually capable that finally aligns Marlow's sexual proclivities with his rank status. But Kate's agency is not necessarily progressive. Though an avid novel reader she is clearly unchanged by Richardsonian attempts to reshape romance. Her preferences are clear: a 'reserved lover' is a turn-off. 'Young, handsome ... I put [these traits] foremost. Sensible, good-natured; I like all that. But then reserved, and sheepish, that's much against him' (*Stoops*, 8). Kate's calculus of desire is fairly unreconstructed: she doesn't expect a soulmate in a spouse. Goldsmith insinuates that the basic instincts of women of quality make Marlow's deference as unappealing as that of *Clarissa*'s good Mr Hickman, who is 'so *generally* meek ... so naturally fitted for rebuke' that women don't know 'whether to pity or laugh at him'.[20] Unlike the virginal Hickman, Goldsmith's good man *can* perform with 'creatures of another stamp' (8).

Gender is spatially and relationally coded rather than of fixed value. When they arrive in the rustic tavern of the Three Pigeons, Marlow and Hasting's à la mode fashion contrasts with the coarse manliness of Tony Lumpkin, who 'misrecognizes' them as Frenchmen. His xenophobia suggests that national character is hard to read. This categorical confusion is echoed in Marlow's anxiety that he will be mistaken as 'the Dullissimo Maccaroni' (*Stoops*, 82). This artificial amalgam situates the play within the 'Macaroni craze' of the 1770s, when Italian fashion invaded the British metropole.[21] 'Macaroni' fashion reveals gender identity as artifice, refusing polite moderation for flamboyant performance. Marlow and Hastings are merely 'vestamentary fops' whose fine dress attests to high taste and feminine refinement rather than queer desires.[22] The homosocial space of the inn imposes a kind of 'temporal drag' on the norms of modern refinement: estranging contemporary politeness so that its 'unnatural' quality becomes apparent.[23] Not merely a masculine foil, Lumpkin as good-natured lord of misrule is also characteristic of genial stage Irishman. Multiple modes of masculinity are set against one another, showing how gender identities are not fixed but plural and mobile, dependent on context and relation.

Goldsmith makes Marlow the product of competing gender codes of politeness. His shyness around women of quality is 'the Englishman's malady', a hallmark of English deference to rank. By sequestering men within homosocial networks they fail to acquire the polish that comes from conversing with the 'fair sex'.

> Where could I learn that assurance you talk of? [Marlow laments] My life has been chiefly spent in a college, or an inn, in seclusion from that lovely part of the creation that chiefly teach men confidence. I don't know that I was ever familiarly acquainted with a single modest women – except my mother – But among females of another class you know –
> *Hastings*: Ay, among them you are impudent enough of all conscience.
> *Marlow*: They are of *us* you know. (*Stoops*, 20)

Sexual inhibition authenticates Marlow's deeply entrenched rank consciousness, his amatory incapacity signalling his traditional values. Emasculated by the women on whose modesty English politeness depends, Goldsmith's Marlow suggests that sexuality is culturally acquired rather than innate: his failures are those of nurture rather than nature. But though he laments his victimhood, nowhere is privilege more visible than in his inability to be moved by women's charms. Marlow's insensibility 'sets everything in motion by not being subject to motion itself': his lack of

stimulation makes others work to get attention, an obduracy that manu-
factures the conditions for bourgeois marriage.[24] The disjunction between
Marlow's 'real' worth and his socially sanctioned hypocrisy is designed to
generate 'sentimental irony'. 'Doom'd to adore the sex, and yet to converse
with the only part I despise !'(22) he laments. But *She Stoops to Conquer*
implicitly accepts that rank inferiority makes some women fair game.
Marlow's sexual disgust at the 'milliner's 'prentice' or 'dutchesses of
Drury Lane' (22) is designed to imply his comparative quality: as a 'good
man' he is entitled to better.

   She Stoops to Conquer ironizes the gender assumptions underpinning
sentimentalism. Unlike the consecrated innocence of eighteenth-century
girlhood, Kate is sexually knowing and deploys her wit not to reform the
man, but to bag one whom she can effectively dominate. But not merely
are women characters tasked with the performative labour needed to keep
the plot advancing (role play, smart repartee, loving and match-making
dreadful sons, stage-managing grumpy fathers); their success in such work
also reinscribes old tenets of misogynist satire. Kate's facility with disguise
recalls parodies of Richardson's *Pamela*, which suggested that virtue was
mere masquerade and that women (specifically in the guise of attractive
serving girls) are adept at self-interested performance. Goldsmith's drama
of 'impudence rewarded' irreverently recalls Henry Giffard's *Pamela:
A Comedy* (1741): a saucy and farcical adaption of Richardson's novel.
A sexist counterpose is formulated by theatricalizing the anti-Pamellist
stance: 'an impudent fellow may counterfeit modesty, but I'll be hanged if
a modest man can ever counterfeit impudence' (*Stoops*, 21). In laughing
comedy, men's inability to 'rise' to the occasion and perform on demand
testifies to superior integrity: their modesty, unlike women's, cannot be
faked.

   She Stoops to Conquer's misogynist satire is made explicit in the epilogue.
A metacommentary on women's life as 'a play, compos'd to please',
femininity is construed as a sequence of gendered performances designed
to exploit men and gratify women's appetites. The increasing worldliness
of an initially 'harmless and young' blushing maid diminishes both her
attractiveness and her morality. 'Unblushing', she begins to 'talk loud,
coquet the guests, and scold the waiters'. Taken to town, she plies her trade
as 'the chop-house toast of ogling connoisseurs': a self-conscious feast for
the male gaze. Revelling in her sexual power, she 'broils her lovers' hearts'
on 'the gridiron'. Rewarded by a socially advantageous marriage, the
erstwhile barmaid pretends to taste and quality, trilling at operettas and
dancing in public: pitiable affectations that expose her to ridicule.

Too old for sexual gratification, all that is left is the petty pleasure of cards. At the end of a play seemingly about a good man's shyness and a smart woman's ingenuity, the laugh is turned against woman's hypocrisy and affectation by Goldsmith's prosecuting 'female barrister'.

But while Goldsmith's drama evinces contempt for the women who keep his slight plots moving, there is ample evidence of men's preference for each other's company. The ultimate premise for *She Stoops to Conquer* is two men's desires to make 'our personal friendships hereditary' (*Stoops*, 79) by having their children intermarry. In *The Good Natur'd Man*, the miser Croaker (comically mismatched with a jolly wife) laments his friend, 'Dick Doleful' whose suicide leaves him bereft.

> Indeed, Mr Honeywood, I never see you but you put me in mind of poor – Dick. Ah, there was merit neglected for you! And so true a friend; we lov'd each other for thirty years, and yet he never asked me to lend him a single farthing.
> *Honeyw.* Pray what could induce him to commit so rash an action at last?
> *Croaker.* I don't know, some people were malicious enough to say it was keeping company with me; because we used to meet now and then and open our hearts to each other ... he used to say Croaker rhimed to joker; and so we us'd to laugh! (*Good Natur'd Man*, 8)

Croaker and Dick are an odd couple: his claim that 'we lov'd each other' is the closest thing to romance in the play. Comic incongruity teeters on the brink of queerness. In Goldsmith's work passionate prepossession takes place *only* between men. Primrose's encounter with the counterfeiter Ephraim Jenkinson is no less than a scene of homoerotic seduction. Primrose testifies that he 'never in my life saw a figure that prepossessed me more favourably ... Never did my heart feel sincerer rapture than at that moment ... no lovers in romance ever cemented a more instantaneous friendship' (*Vicar*, 1:134–7). Primrose's passion has never been moved this way by a woman. In works structured by heterosexuality, moments of comic pleasure are found in the 'form of giddily expressed homosocial desire'.[25]

Goldsmith's genial humour licenses nostalgic gender politics. The blithe contentment of his otherworldly heroes suggest an asexual possibility at odds with 'the comic imperative of ensuring marital exchange', a yearning for pastoral homosociality which shades toward heterophobia even as it submits to the inevitability of marriage.[26] Balancing the effeminate tendencies of his modern men are representatives of the ancien régime order of manliness: bluff soldiers like Squire Hardcastle, who might seem outdated but whose property and firm English lineage anchor the insecure gender identity of Goldsmith's man of feeling. Goldsmith's dramas play with a quintessentially Irish opacity of character and an incipient queerness or fluidity of gender identity. Both sentimental and satirical, Goldsmith's comically divided protagonists suggest that eighteenth-century gender identity was a set of fungible conventions deployed in differing ways, to multiple audiences, and (for better or worse) freed from essential interiority. His characters may pine for a past where patriarchal hierarchy was stable and certain, but their likeably labile gender identities are the inevitable product (and saving grace) of modern commercial society. Like Irish plays of the early eighteenth century, Goldsmith's dramas stage a form of heteronormative 'Irish entryism' whose conservative gender politics are designed to 'win the confidence of . . . the English gentry' through comic geniality.[27] Through the comic quiescence of queer masculinity, Goldsmith's dramas commit to the preservation of a cultural and heteronormative order from which his heroes hope to benefit.

Notes

1. Henry James, 'Introduction to the Vicar of Wakefield 1900', *Critical Heritage*, 65.
2. David Garrick, 'Jupiter and Mercury: A Fable', in *The Poetical Works* (London, 1785), 532–3.
3. Samuel Johnson, 'odd, adj.1755', in *A Dictionary of the English Language* (1755). https://johnsonsdictionaryonline.com/1755/odd_adj. Accessed 22 April 2023.
4. See Soile Ylivuori, *Women and Politeness in Eighteenth-Century England: Bodies, Identities, and Power* (New York: Routledge, 2018).
5. See E. J. Clery, *The Feminization Debate in Eighteenth-Century England: Literature, Commerce and Luxury* (Basingstoke: Palgrave, 2004).
6. David O'Shaughnessy, 'Introduction: Staging an Irish Enlightenment', in *Ireland, Enlightenment and the English Stage, 1740–1820* (Cambridge University Press, 2019), 1–27 (2).
7. Lisa A. Freeman, *Character's Theater: Genre and Identity on the Eighteenth-Century English Stage* (University of Pennsylvania Press, 2001), 237.
8. Thomas Keymer and Peter Sabor, *'Pamela' in the Marketplace: Literary Controversy and Print Culture in Eighteenth-Century Britain and Ireland* (Cambridge University Press, 2005), 114.
9. Declan Kavanagh, 'Queering Eighteenth-Century Irish Writing: Yahoo, Fribble, Freke', *Irish Literature in Transition, 1700–1780*, ed. Moyra Haslett (Cambridge University Press, 2020), 244–62 (247).
10. James Kim, 'Goldsmith's Manhood: Hegemonic Masculinity and Sentimental Irony in *The Vicar of Wakefield*', *The Eighteenth Century*, 59.1 (2018), 21–44 (24).
11. Kavanagh, 'Queering Eighteenth-Century Irish Writing', 246.

12. Ana de Freitas Boe and Abby Coykendall, 'Introduction', in *Heteronormativity in Eighteenth-Century Literature and Culture*, ed. Ana de Freitas Boe and Abby Coykendall (Farnham: Ashgate, 2014), 1–22 (7).

13. J. W. Messerschmidt, *Hegemonic Masculinity: Formulation, Reformulation, and Amplification* (Lanham, MD: Rowman and Littlefield, 2018), 29.

14. Marshall Brown, *Preromanticism* (Stanford, CA: Stanford University Press, 1994), 149.

15. Elizabeth Inchbald, *The Goodnatured Man . . . With Remarks by Mrs Inchbald* (London, 1808), 5.

16. Terry Eagleton, *Crazy John and the Bishop and Other Essays on Irish Culture* (South Bend: University of Notre Dame Press, 1998), 107; Inchbald, *The Goodnatured Man*, 5.

17. Elizabeth Hanna Hanson, 'Making Something Out of Nothing: Asexuality and Narrative' (Loyola University, Chicago, IL: Unpublished dissertation, 2013), 5.

18. Norma Clarke, *Brothers of the Quill: Oliver Goldsmith in Grub Street* (Cambridge, MA: Harvard University Press, 2016), 323.

19. Inchbald, *The Goodnatured Man*, 4.

20. Samuel Richardson, *Clarissa, or, The History of a Young Lady*, ed. Angus Ross (Harmondsworth: Penguin, 1984), 209.

21. See James Evans, '"The Dullissimo Maccaroni": Masculinities in *She Stoops to Conquer*', *Philological Quarterly*, 9.1 (2011), 45–65.

22. Susan Staves, 'A Few Kind Words for the Fop', *Studies in English Literature, 1500–1900*, 22.3 (1982), 413–28.

23. Elizabeth Freeman, *Time Binds: Queer Temporalities, Queer Histories* (Durham, NC: Duke University Press, 2010), xxiii, 59.

24. Wendy Anne Lee, *Failures of Feeling: Insensibility and the Novel* (Stanford, CA: Stanford University Press, 2019), 55.

25. Kim, 'Goldsmith's Manhood', 25.

26. Lisa A. Freeman, 'The Social Life of Eighteenth-Century Comedy', *The Cambridge Companion to British Theatre, 1730–1830*, ed. Jane Moody and Daniel O'Quinn (Cambridge University Press, 2006), 75.

27. Helen Burke, 'Crossing Acts: Irish Drama from George Farquhar to Charles Macklin', in *Blackwell Companion to Irish Literature*, ed. Julia M. Wright (Oxford: Blackwell, 2010), 125–41 (131, 140).

CHAPTER 14

Race

Kerry Sinanan

Chain of Being and Buffonian racial classification suffuse eighteenth-century literature as part of the Enlightenment project of ordering and rationalizing the world and its living things, including humans (see Chapter 5, 'Enlightenments', and Chapter 16, 'Natural History and Science'). As Arthur Lovejoy states, 'It was in the eighteenth century that the conception of the universe as a Chain of Being, and the principles which underlay this conception – plenitude, continuity, gradation – attained their widest diffusion and acceptance'.[1] Race was made through these gradations of human difference that, since the early modern period, had been described by male travellers in the service of colonialism and transatlantic slavery. As Jennifer Morgan details, the forging of race has a long history, extending from even before Christopher Columbus and Walter Raleigh, through to Richard Ligon, Samuel Purchas, and the enslavers William Snelgrave and Edward Long, to name a few: 'Travel accounts produced in Europe and available in England provided a corpus from which subsequent writers borrowed freely, reproducing images of Native American and African women that resonated with readers' to create 'monstrous' others.[2] In the hands of enslavers, travellers, and colonists Lockean empiricism legitimized an observationally based reality in which descriptions of racialized others by white men could be repeated as apparent fact.[3] Race was made throughout proliferating texts that were multi-generic, comprising 'discovery' narratives, enslavers' journals, early histories, and first-hand accounts, which together intensified the making of indigeneity and blackness as 'savage' and inferior within the context of racial capitalism, ultimately to justify genocide, conquest, and the theft of labour.

Alongside these myriad narrative texts, race was forged in colonial law to maintain white power as in the 1662 *partus sequitur ventrem* Virginia Act, which tied slave status to Black mothers,[4] and in the 1682 Christian Parentage Virginia Slave Act, which transformed racialized others, overwhelmingly Black people, into the property of free white men:

Act I. It is enacted that all servants . . . which [*sic*] shall be imported into this country either by sea or by land, whether Negroes, Moors [Muslim North Africans], mulattoes or Indians who and whose parentage and native countries are not Christian at the time of their first purchase by some Christian . . . and all Indians, which shall be sold by our neighboring Indians, or any other trafficking with us for slaves, are hereby adjudged, deemed and taken to be slaves to all intents and purposes any law, usage, or custom to the contrary notwithstanding.[5]

Race was thus made through multiple discursive acts as 'a fungible assemblage rather than a coherent preconstituted entity' in order to sanction devastating degrees of power centred in the hands of colonial institutions and states.[6] In a chapter, 'On the Varieties in the Human Race', from the second volume of his eight-volume *An History of the Earth, and Animated Nature* (1774) Goldsmith actively promotes and enhances a racist, systemic classification based on the writings of others, including those of George Louis Leclerc, Comte de Buffon, that situates white people at the top of a Chain of Being hierarchy and Black people at the bottom. Using his Grub Street hack-writer skills, Goldsmith expanded a readable, popular collection of the white supremacist myths produced by colonial culture: such hack work underlies the making of race in what is called the 'information revolution' of the eighteenth century.[7]

Through the Chain of Being 'race' becomes naturalized, almost invisibly, in the literature of the eighteenth century, presenting itself in terms of travel, politeness, liberalism, sociability, and putative cosmopolitanism that engaged the world, ironically often without the need for actual travel to be undertaken by either the writer or the reader.[8] Goldsmith plays a significant part in forging this Euro-supremacy in the wider literary culture; as Winifred Lynskey notes, 'Goldsmith's place is as important as that of Pope . . . or of Johnson . . . Goldsmith's chain of being is unique in the eighteenth century.'[9] Lynskey asserts Goldsmith's uniqueness on the grounds of his totalizing, detailed schema that brought an intensity of description and discursive expansion to taxonomy, making it more readable and plausible. Yet Chain of Being discourse is less readily recognized in eighteenth-century studies as participating in race's devastating dynamics because it describes gradations of difference under a universalist, monogenist umbrella: universalism supposedly rescues race-making from the egregious argument that humans comprise different species. As Lovejoy lists, a wide range of Enlightenment thinkers made race under monogenism not only an acceptable schema, but an apparently natural one:

'Addison, King, Bolingbroke, Pope, Haller, Thomson, Akenside, Buffon, Bonnet, Goldsmith, Diderot, Kant, Lambert, Herder, Schiller' all expanded Chain of Being discourse.[10] Polygenists like Edward Long and Samuel Estwick are regarded broadly as outliers to the mainstream of Enlightenment thought on human difference, but it is vital to note that supremacy is also fundamental to Chain of Being ordering: the links that connect are also hierarchical separations within a constructed, gradational scale. As Lynskey notes, 'In the system of both Buffon and Goldsmith, man has a proud position at the head of all created beings. All creatures ascend in the scale according to various relationships which they bear to man.'[11] Therefore, as Stuart Hall states, the Enlightenment, while ending polygenist orderings of the human, makes 'a new type of binary structure of representation, between the West and its others, which requires a more exquisitely differentiated and continuously sustained marking of various grades, degrees, and levels within an overall system of human difference'.[12] These differences lead to overwhelming material oppression wielded by Europeans within the context of colonial power and slavery.

In 'An History of Animals', Goldsmith delineates a white supremacist account of 'human variety' that forges 'distinct', biological race while invoking the tools of Enlightenment empiricism to naturalize apparently observable reality: a reality that he himself never observed. And Goldsmith places white people at the top of a pyramid of being:

> That we have all sprung from one common parent, we are taught both by reason and religion to believe; and we have good reason also to think that the Europeans resemble him more than any of the rest of his children. However, it must not be concealed that the olive-coloured Asiatic, and even the jet-black negro, claim this honour of hereditary resemblance; and assert that white men are mere deviations from original perfection. Odd as this opinion may seem, they have Linnaeus, the celebrated naturalist, on their side; who supposes man a native of the tropical climates, and only a sojourner more to the north. But not to enter into a controversy upon a matter of very remote speculation, I think one argument alone will suffice to prove the contrary, and show that the white man is the original source from whence the other varieties have sprung. (*Animated Nature*, 2:239–40)

Goldsmith asserts an imagined proposition as rational fact: white men are closest to the 'image' of God and therefore superior to other humans. While we know today that Africa is the source of *Homo sapiens*, Black people are made in Goldsmith's European race discourse, not as being outside of humanity, but as the lowest form of a 'racial telos' of humans in the Enlightenment.[13] In the context of eighteenth-century transatlantic slavery, it is this positionality that legitimizes their exploitation and that lays the ground for the antiblackness of imperial eugenics.

Out of this humanist supremacy, in which man dominates all other life on earth, comes white supremacy, delineated clearly by Goldsmith in his chapter 'Of the Varieties in the Human Race', in which he states, 'It should seem, consequently, that man is naturally white' (*Animated Nature*, 2:233). From this pinnacle, other races descend in Goldsmith's schema, including 'Laplanders', 'Tartars', that include the Chinese and Japanese, who have 'no religion' and 'no morality, no decency of behaviour' (*Animated Nature*, 2:221), 'the southern Asiatics' (*Animated Nature*, 2:223), 'the Negroes of Africa' (*Animated Nature*, 2:226), and 'Americans', who are the Indigenous peoples of the Americas. Having described 'Asiatics', Goldsmith moves to describe African people: 'this gloomy race of mankind is found to blacken all the southern parts of Africa' (*Animated Nature*, 2:228). Goldsmith notes that 'different nations' produce variety amongst African people yet ultimately it is epidermal blackness, 'a black colour, with a smooth soft skin', that unifies them (*Animated Nature*, 2:226). While all the races Goldsmith delineates are described with pejorative terms, there is an implicit schematic gradation down to the people of Guinea as 'extremely ugly' and having 'an insupportable scent' (*Animated Nature*, 2:226). It is no coincidence that in Guinea the foremost slave-trading ports had long been established and Goldsmith regurgitates much from enslavers themselves. This empirical detail, touch, sight, and smell, is all imagined by him in a virtual, discursive construction of race that comes to have materially devastating force. Crucially, these assertions were asserted in the same year by the highly influential polygenist Edward Long in his 1774 *History of Jamaica*. Long asserts that human species variety between white and Black people is due to a layer of blackness under the skin of the latter: 'It is likewise presumed, upon reasonable grounds, that the different casts of complexion, observable among the different species of men, derive their various tints principally, if not entirely, from the colour of their reticula.'[14] And in his list of 'evidence' of Black people's different species status Long puts forth that they have 'a bestial or fetid smell'.[15] Long's position as a Jamaican planter ensures his stake in asserting the inferiority of Black people whose unfree labour he depends on and illustrates why it is vital to read Goldsmith's racist discourse in the context of slavery and racial capitalism which required a recycling of hierarchical human difference that does not greatly differ in its assertions between the mono and polygenists.

Goldsmith continues to assert that the physical and mental inferiority, supposedly characteristic of Black people, is linked to the geography of Africa itself, a space for descent and degeneration:

> [T]he climate seems to relax their mental powers still more than those of the body: they are, therefore, in general, found to be stupid, indolent, and mischievous. The Arabians themselves, many colonies of whom have migrated southward into the most inland parts of Africa, seem to have degenerated from their ancestors: and forgetting their ancient learning, with their beauty, have become a race scarce any way distinguishable from the original inhabitants. (*Animated Nature*, 2:228)

Goldsmith's account also ties race to gender in his repetition of the travel-writing myth of Black women's long breasts which, he tells us, 'after bearing one child, hang below the navel' (*Animated Nature*, 2:228). As Morgan asserts, it is Black women who bear the lowest status in the discourse of early travellers who repeatedly assert the 'sagging breasts' of Black women. 'African women's Africanness became contingent on the linkages between sexuality and a savagery that fitted them for both productive and reproductive labor.'[16] Goldsmith participates in the bestialization of African mothers and reproduces an image of them familiar throughout the eighteenth century that provides a discursive correlation to *partus sequitur ventrem*. In opposition to the descent of Africanness, Europeans are described as the race in which, Goldsmith tells us, the pinnacle of human achievement has been realized: 'Those arts which might have had their invention among other races of mankind, have come to perfection there' (*Animated Nature*, 2:231). Europe is an expansive space but Goldsmith asserts that while 'The inhabitants of these countries differ a good deal from each other ... they generally agree in the colour of their bodies, beauty of their complexions, the largeness of their limbs, and the vigour of their understandings' (*Animated Nature*, 2:230–1).

It is in this way that, as Charles Mills tells us, race-making in the Enlightenment world creates the unacknowledged political global system of white supremacy, namely the 'racial contract':

> Ironically, the most important political system of recent global history – the system of domination by which white people have historically ruled over and, in certain important ways, continue to rule over nonwhite people – is not seen as a political system at all. It is just taken for granted; it is the background against which other systems, which we are to see as political are highlighted.[17]

Goldsmith's role in making race, and therefore the racial contract, was in his ability to repeat, synthesize, and stylistically improve upon the large body of writings by many naturalists of the period, and indeed was promoted as part of his value to English culture that continued into the Victorian period when his work would become part of a broader eugenicist consensus underpinning empire. As the Publisher's Advertisement to an 1855 edition states,

> It is true, he cannot be classed with a Buffon, a Linnaeus, a Cuvier, and other great naturalists; yet if it may not be affirmed of him that he added much to the science itself, it must nevertheless be allowed that he was the first English writer who, by the inimitable graces of his style and manner, threw a charm over the subject which was new to the English reader, and the effect of which, in rendering the science of Natural History popular, has been great and extensive.[18]

Animated Nature would go through dozens of reprints, carrying its influence into the late nineteenth century as a vessel of what passed for Enlightenment knowledge about the natural world. George Eliot's Maggie Tulliver in *The Mill on the Floss* (1860) reads to her brother Luke from *Animated Nature* describing 'elephants, and kangaroos, and the civet cat, and the sun-fish, and a bird sitting on its tail' (Book 1, Ch. 4), testifying to the influence of a book that was widely disseminated and became a household natural history long after its first publication. *Animated Nature* also gained credence from the popularity of Goldsmith's *The Vicar of Wakefield* (1766), which itself would become one of the most widely read novels of the nineteenth century (see Chapter 34, 'Afterlives 1: The Victorian *Vicar*'). The fact that what Goldsmith wrote in his influential *Animated Nature* was at most second-hand and highly embellished fiction speaks to the power that myths of race and classification gained in the height of imperial and colonial rule.

Goldsmith did of course encounter Black people in London. Michael Bundock details accounts of Goldsmith's meeting with Francis Barber, a Jamaican man enslaved by Colonel Richard Bathurst, a friend of Samuel Johnson. The *Town and Country Magazine* in April 1771 describes 'Dr. Goldsmith, meeting Dr. Johnson with his little lacquey behind him, for whom he has a sort of parental affection, asked his learned friend if he intended to bring him up a scholar? "Yes," replied Dr. Johnson'.[19] Barber was the 'lacquey' and another retelling of the tale a few months later labels him as Johnson's 'young Negro'. As Bundock notes, Goldsmith, unlike Johnson, did not adjust what he had to say about Black people from his real-life encounters despite the fact that Barber was educated, genial, and clearly respected by Johnson.

Goldsmith and other liberal thinkers are often exonerated from being racist for refusing to use a Buffonian schema and for asserting, in contrast to polygenist models of species being, a connected 'universalism'. Michael Griffin reads Goldsmith as an 'enlightenment anti-imperialist' asserting that 'the imaginative geographies of enlightenment are not necessarily or completely in league with imperialism'.[20] Such a view arguably attempts to absolve an Irish writer from white supremacist thinking, focusing on location, rather than on the very explicit race-making work that Goldsmith does, work that was fundamental to licensing empire. Caution against libertarian excess is not inherently anti-racist and, within the racial contract, in fact seeks to protect white rights. Along with Griffin, James Watt reads the 'universalism' in Goldsmith as contradictory to the classificatory race emerging in Buffonian natural history. What such assessments sidestep, however, is how racialized being, that is very close to species being, is ushered in through the back door of 'variety' within universalism, as depicted clearly in Figure 14.1, that clearly draws on eugenicist racism.[21]

While this plate claims to objectively present an observable reality, as Devin J. Vartija notes, 'there is nothing "natural" about using physical features to classify humanity and, given that the so-called races of humanity are not natural kinds, issues of power and social control are intimately bound up with how we conceptualize the human'.[22] But this descriptive force in the service of hierarchized being, epitomized by Goldsmith, served a powerful function to legitimize systemic white supremacy. Thomas Jefferson was bequeathed a copy of *Animated Nature* printed in the US in 1795, listed in his inventory of Wythes Library which he then sold to the Library of Congress.[23] It is not difficult to see the connections between the racist systems epitomized by Goldsmith that are then reproduced by Jefferson in his *Notes on the State of Virginia* in which he fully asserts colour as a hierarchical characteristic to justify the ongoing enslavement of African Americans: 'It is not against experience to suppose, that different Species of the same genus, or varieties of the same species, may possess different qualifications ... This unfortunate difference of colour, and perhaps of faculty, is a powerful obstacle to the emancipation of these people.'[24] These profound evils of Enlightenment are the legacy of Goldsmith's Chain of Being hierarchies in reality, notwithstanding the putative claims of 'liberty' and 'universalism' asserted by white men of the period. As Emmanuel Chukwdui Eze makes clear, 'Enlightenment philosophy was instrumental in codifying both the scientific and popular European perceptions of the

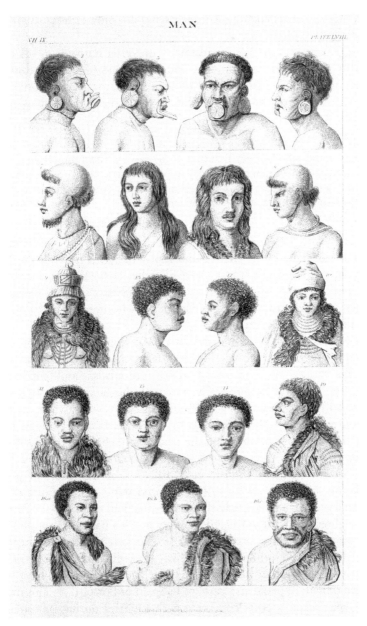

Figure 14.1 'Varieties of Human Race no. LVI', *A History of the Earth and Animated Nature* (Glasgow, 1857), volume 1 of 2. Huntington Library, RB 498067. The Huntington Library, San Marino, California

human race ... in articulating Europe's sense not only of its cultural but also *racial* superiority.'[25]

Criticism that emphasizes Goldsmith's universal humanism, his concern with geographies and empire, and his drawing on other sources, ignores a wholesale construction of biological race that clearly concludes in the superiority of those with 'white skin', something he does most emphatically:

> Of all the colours by which mankind is diversified, it is easy to perceive that ours is not only the most beautiful to the eye, but the most advantageous. The fair complexion seems, if I may so express it, as a transparent covering to the soul; all the variations of the passions, every expression of joy or sorrow, flows to the cheek, and, without language marks the mind. (*Animated Nature*, 2:232)

As Roxann Wheeler states: 'Although Linnaeus and Buffon both emphasized color differences in their delineations of humans, Goldsmith is among the first to single it out above all other characteristics by which humans were distinguished.'[26] Via this white supremacism, anti-blackness becomes the end product of Goldsmith's environmental and cultural explanation of human difference.

In these ways, Goldsmith's derivative drawing on the histories of enslavers, planters, and colonial thinkers constructs a devastating hierarchy of human 'variety' in service of a European colonialism and empire (see Chapter 17, 'War and Empire'). The wider ramifications, for Irish Studies more broadly, of understanding Goldsmith as a purveyor of white supremacy, have yet to be fully dealt with by the field. Because Ireland itself experienced intensive colonization the tendency has been to read its liberal philosophy within the context of imperial geographies and, as I have shown, to draw on universalism as a palliation of the forces of global domination. However, owing to its colonized status, and because of the sectarian legacies from having itself been planted and settled by the British, by the eighteenth century, Ireland was very much a partner in empire and in the white supremacist project. Black people were visible in eighteenth-century Ireland and although, as William Hart discusses, no census was taken, the proportion of Black people in Ireland was 'likely to have been exceeded only in England and perhaps in Spain or Portugal'.[27] This makes sense given Ireland's ports and trade with England during transatlantic slavery, and given the fact that many Anglo-Irish were themselves enslavers. Hart and Nini Rodgers also both discuss the fact that Olaudah Equiano, the formerly enslaved African abolitionist activist, was able to

successfully tour Ireland and gather support from Catholic emancipation-
ists and Protestant anti-slavery communities.[28] At the same time, as Hart
details, anti-black racism and chattel slavery were indeed part of eight-
eenth-century Irish life as the upper classes, like their British counterparts,
bought and sold Black people as servants and status markers:

> That a number of these black servants were in effect slaves cannot be in
> doubt. They are so described in newspaper advertisements for runaways,
> and even, in a few cases, in advertisements offering them for sale ... There is
> no disguising the existence of slavery in Ireland at this time, nor that it was
> restricted, in practice, to black people from Africa and the East Indies.[29]

Irish Studies is beginning to reckon with the frequent collusion of Irish
history and culture with the very forces of empire that enveloped it. But
much more remains to be done and Goldsmith's role at the heart of tying
Irish intellectual history into Europe's white supremacy project deserves
fuller consideration.

Notes

1. Arthur O. Lovejoy, *The Great Chain of Being* (Cambridge, MA: Harvard
   University Press, 1936), 183.
2. Jennifer L. Morgan, *Laboring Women: Reproduction and Gender in New World
   Slavery* (University of Pennsylvania Press, 2011), 15, 16. While Morgan focuses
   on the intersection of race and gender, she also provides an overall history of
   racist travel and colonial writing in 'Some Could Suckle Over Their Shoulder':
   Male Travelers, Female Bodies and the Gendering of Racial Ideology 1500–
   1770', *William and Mary Quarterly*, 54.1 (1997), 167–92. There are several
   discussions on race in the Enlightenment but they differ widely in their aims
   and ideological underpinnings. Roxann Wheeler emphasizes religion and
   custom as the main definers of 'human difference' and argues that skin colour
   as a definer of 'race' was not general until the later eighteenth century:

   > The third quarter of the eighteenth century is especially crucial to consolidating
   > complexion as a significant visible human difference, partly because of the impact of
   > Buffon's *Natural History* and because of Linnaeus's several revised editions of his
   > *General System of Nature* (1735) joined with the emergence of 'homegrown' British
   > systems of natural history in the 1770s, most notably Oliver Goldsmith's, they all
   > signpost a burgeoning conviction that there were myriad differences, physical and
   > cultural among humans. (*Complexion of Race: Categories of Difference in Eighteenth-
   > Century British Culture* (University of Pennsylvania Press, 2000), 29)

3. There is a large body of writing on the question of the racism and empiricism of
   Western philosophers and of John Locke in particular. Andrew Valls argues
   that methodology does not necessarily dictate if a philosopher is racist: 'Rather
   than focusing on whether "empiricism" facilitates racism, perhaps we should
   ask whether Locke's or Hume's does' (*Racism in Modern Philosophy*, ed.

Andrew Valls (Ithaca, NY: Cornell University Press, 2005), 4). See also *Philosophers on Race: Critical Essays*, ed. Julie K. Ward and Tommy L. Lott (London: Blackwell, 2002). Many of these discussions fail to engage with critical race theory or Black studies and depend on Western modes of critique to assess white supremacy. In this way, they repeat the dynamics of early modern and Enlightenment travel writing that centre white reading. As Charles Mills argues,

> Liberal enlightenment presumes an objective perception of things as they are and as they should be, factually and morally, for political communities characterized by reciprocally respecting relations among equally recognized persons in agreement on the fair terms for the appropriation of the world. But racial domination interferes with objective cognition, denies equal racial personhood, and generated rationalizations of unjust *white acquisition*. (*Black Rights/White Wrongs: The Critique of Racial Liberalism* (Oxford University Press, 2017), xvi)

4. Jennifer L. Morgan, '*Partus sequitur ventrem*: Law, Race, and Reproduction in Colonial Slavery', *Small Axe*, 22.1 (2018), 1–17.

5. General Assembly, 'An Act to Repeale a Former Law Makeing Indians and Others Ffree' (1682). *Encyclopedia Virginia*. https://encyclopediavirginia.org/entries/an-act-to-repeale-a-former-law-makeing-indians-and-others-ffree-1682. Accessed 4 February 2023.

6. Nikhil Pal Singh, *Race and America's Long War* (University of California Press, 2017), xvi.

7. Michael Griffin, *Enlightenment in Ruins: The Geographies of Oliver Goldsmith* (Lewisburg, PA: Bucknell University Press, 2013), 18. Goldsmith's recycling and plagiarism are also well-documented by Michael Griffin. See 'Oliver Goldsmith and François-Ignace Espiard de la Borde: An Instance of Plagiarism', *Review of English Studies: New Series*, 50.197 (February 1999), 59–63.

8. Michael Griffin offers a defence of Goldsmith's cosmopolitanism: 'Equally, Goldsmith's famous cosmopolitanism, his expressed citizenship of the world, was one which appreciated, as did Swift and Johnson, the ironic possibilities of cultural encounter, and included a pronounced commitment to cultural respect and reciprocity' (*Enlightenment in Ruins*, 9). White supremacy as delineated in Goldsmith is, however, predicated on hierarchy and superiority, frequently asserting the inferiority of those he discursively racializes.

9. Winifred Lynskey, 'Goldsmith and the Chain of Being', *Journal of the History of Ideas* 6.3 (1945), 363–74 (363).

10. Lovejoy, *The Great Chain of Being*, 183–4.

11. Lynskey, 'Goldsmith and the Chain of Being', 364.

12. Stuart Hall, *The Fateful Triangle: Race, Ethnicity, Nation*. ed. Kobena Mercer (Cambridge, MA: Harvard University Press, 2017), 55.

13. Zakiyyah Iman Jackson, *Becoming Human: Matter and Meaning in an Antiblack World* (New York University Press, 2020), 20.

14. Edward Long, *The History of Jamaica or, General Survey of the Antient and Modern State of That Island: With Reflections on Its Situation, Settlements,*

Inhabitants, Climate, Products, Commerce, Laws, and Government, 3 vols. (London, 1774), 2:49.

15. Long, *The History of Jamaica*, 352.
16. Morgan, *Laboring Women*, 36.
17. Charles Mills, *The Racial Contract* (Ithaca, NY: Cornell University Press, 1997), 1–2.
18. Oliver Goldsmith, *A History of the Earth and Animated Nature*, vol. 1 (Edinburgh: A. Fullarton and Company, 1855).
19. Michael Bundock, *The Fortunes of Frances Barber: The True Story of the Jamaican Slave Who Became Samuel Johnson's Heir* (New Haven, CT: Yale University Press, 2015), 129.
20. Griffin, *Enlightenment in Ruins*, 6.
21. Oliver Goldsmith, *A History of the Earth and Animated Nature: With Numerous Notes from the Works of the Most Distinguished British and Foreign Naturalists. Illustrated, etc.* (Glasgow: Blackie & Son, 1857).
22. Devin J. Vartija, *The Color of Equality: Race and Common Humanity in Enlightenment Thought* (University of Pennsylvania Press, 2021), 16–17.
23. William and Mary Digital Archive. https://digitalarchive.wm.edu/handle/10 288/13433. Accessed 21 April 2023.
24. Thomas Jefferson, *Notes on the State of Virginia* (London, 1787), 230–40.
25. Emmanuel Chukwdui Eze, ed., *Race and the Enlightenment: A Reader* (London: Blackwell, 1997), 6.
26. Wheeler, *Complexion of Race*, 180.
27. William Hart, 'Africans in Eighteenth-Century Ireland', *Irish Historical Studies*, 33.129 (2002), 19–32 (21).
28. Nini Rodgers, *Equiano and Anti-slavery in Eighteenth-Century Belfast* (Belfast: The Belfast Society, 2000).
29. Hart, 'Africans in Eighteenth-Century Ireland', 24.

CHAPTER 15

Religion

James Bryant Reeves

Although eighteenth-century Ireland was (as it remains today) predominantly Catholic, Oliver Goldsmith was born into the country's Protestant Ascendancy, the relatively small number of Anglican priests and politicians who ruled Ireland throughout the seventeenth and eighteenth centuries. From his earliest days, therefore, Goldsmith's religious leanings were informed by an Anglican religious culture that emphasized religion's practical, moral function over and above doctrine or theological speculation. For eighteenth-century Anglicans like Goldsmith, religious belief was thoroughly embedded in the world. Although Goldsmith held to 'common sense' Christian doctrines like the divinity of Christ and the supernatural origin of the New Testament, his religion was not defined primarily by theological niceties or intellectual conviction but by the rhythms of Anglican ritual and everyday acts of reverence, piety, and benevolence. While 'belief' was increasingly associated with intellectual conviction and individual experience in the latter half of the eighteenth century – by thinkers as diverse as the Methodist John Wesley (1703–91), on one hand, and the deistic philosopher David Hume (1711–76), on the other – for Anglicans like Goldsmith it remained largely communal, ritualistic, and grounded in practice.

Echoing the first definition of 'Religion' provided in Johnson's *Dictionary* (1755), Goldsmith's writings consistently equate religion with 'Virtue'.[1] For example, in his various literary tributes to his brother, Henry (*c.*1722–68), and their father, Charles (*c.*1690–1747), both of whom served as parish priests in the Church of Ireland, Goldsmith praises his clerical idols for their compassion, benevolence, and active charity. In *The Traveller* (1764), which Goldsmith dedicated to his 'dear brother', Henry's home is an 'abode, where want and pain repair', a house of 'pity' where Henry teaches his guests the 'luxury of doing good' (*Traveller*, 2). Similarly, *The Deserted Village*'s (1770) 'preacher', famously modelled on Goldsmith's deceased father, was 'More skilled to raise the wretched than to rise' himself (see Chapter 21, 'Pastoral Poetry'). The 'good man' relieved the indigent and the downtrodden, forgetting 'their vices in their woe', and 'he prayed and felt, for all'. While the preacher's doctrine was steadfast – he was not moved by 'doctrines fashioned to the varying hour' – Goldsmith's focus throughout the poem is on the priest's piety and 'steady zeal'; we are never told which exact doctrines constitute the 'Truth' that 'the pious man' preached on Sundays (*Deserted Village*, 8–11).

Goldsmith's other major paean to his father, *The Vicar of Wakefield* (1766), likewise depicts Anglicanism as a religion defined chiefly by its ethical impulses, and the novel's doctrinal commitments might best be described as vaguely theistic (see Chapter 19, 'Fiction'). Indeed, the Reverend Charles Primrose is admirable because he attends to his clerical duties without relying on a curate, because he cares intensely for his parishioners, and because he is, like Goldsmith himself, relentlessly (even naively) charitable. His benevolent actions, not his doctrines or intellectual convictions, make him a commendable priest. It is worth noting too that his friends consider his one theological hobby horse – his promotion of 'strict' monogamy and his consequent participation in the Whistonian controversy – his 'weak side' (*Vicar*, 1:10; see Chapter 12, 'Marriage'). In sum, Goldsmith's ideal clergyman, and thus his ideal religion, avoids doctrinaire theology and dogmatism in favour of charity, generosity, and tolerance.

The Vicar of Wakefield makes this commitment to practice over precepts explicit in its treatment of scepticism and irreligion. Convinced that Mr Thornhill means to court his daughter Olivia, Primrose declares early in the novel that 'no free-thinker shall ever have a child of mine' (*Vicar*, 1:63). Given Thornhill's superficial wit and his desire to outshine others in conversation, Primrose suspects that the young squire is irreligious. Moreover, by calling Thornhill a 'free-thinker', Primrose associates him with the growing number of eighteenth-century individuals who questioned key Christian tenets, such as Christ's resurrection, the possibility of miracles, or the divine origin of scripture. Authors and philosophers like Hume, Matthew Tindal (1657–1733), and Henry St John, 1st Viscount Bolingbroke (1678–1751) challenged traditional Christian notions of God and the supernatural, and, as a result, many Christians – Anglicans, dissenters, and Catholics alike – worried that, in the words of Goldsmith's Anglo-Irish literary predecessor Jonathan Swift, '*Knavery and Atheism*' were as '*Epidemick as the Pox*'.[2]

Yet *The Vicar of Wakefield* seems entirely unbothered by freethinking critiques of Christianity. In response to Primrose's strictures against Thornhill, his young son Moses declares:

> Sure, father, . . . you are too severe in this; for heaven will never arraign him
> for what he thinks, but for what he does. Every man has a thousand vicious
> thoughts, which arise without his power to suppress. Thinking freely of
> religion, may be involuntary with this gentleman: so that allowing his
> sentiments to be wrong, yet as he is purely passive in their reception, he is
> no more to be blamed for their incursions than the governor of a city
> without walls for the shelter he is obliged to afford an invading enemy.
> (*Vicar*, 1:64)

Primrose concurs with his son's assessment while also insisting that free-
thinkers are nonetheless culpable if they wilfully ignore 'the proofs' that
support Christianity's veracity (*Vicar*, 1:64). Primrose is, of course, correct
that Thornhill is depraved and untrustworthy – he abducts young Olivia,
effectively consigns Primrose to debtors' prison, and tries to marry George
Primrose's love, Arabella, in order to secure her fortune. At the same time,
Thornhill *does* marry Olivia at the novel's end, implicitly endorsing
Deborah Primrose's opinion that freethinking is nothing more than
a phase men inevitably leave behind when they marry and their wives
'make converts' of them (*Vicar*, 1:65). Freethinking is certainly an error
(Moses describes it as 'vicious', after all), but irreligious tenets are not
a great concern for Goldsmith. Ultimately, Thornhill is arraigned for his
'vicious' behaviour and not for his 'vicious thoughts'.

In fact, real-world deists and religious sceptics like Voltaire (1694–1778)
and Bolingbroke earned Goldsmith's praise if he considered their lives and
writings moderate, reasonable, and virtuous. For example, in his *Life of
Henry St John, Lord Viscount Bolingbroke* (1770), Goldsmith praises the
Tory statesman and philosopher at length while mentioning his heterodox
religious principles only briefly. Goldsmith notes that, in conversation and
in his letters on the proper uses of history, Bolingbroke 'freely' gave his
opinion 'upon the subject of the divine original of the sacred books, which
he supposes to have no such foundation'.[3] For Goldsmith, Bolingbroke's
doubts about the Bible's divine inspiration didn't align with the philo-
sopher's 'acuteness or his learning'. However, Bolingbroke doubted not
because he was immoral but because he only trifled in theology; he simply
didn't take the time to consider religion seriously. Rather than condemn-
ing Bolingbroke's irreligion, Goldsmith portrays it as a regrettable yet
relatively insignificant deviation from Bolingbroke's characteristic 'genius
and understanding'.[4]

Goldsmith's writings likewise reflect his tolerance for certain non-
Christian religions. Although he was committed to the Anglican Church
in which he was raised, Goldsmith deliberately avoided being '*bigotedly*

attached to any particular system of faith, or to any particular mode of worship'.[5] His sympathy extended, for instance, to England's historically oppressed Jewish population: in *The History of England* (1771), Goldsmith rebukes Edward I's 'prejudices' and 'severity' against Jews, lamenting that they 'were the only part of [Edward's] subjects who were refused that equal justice which the king made boast of distributing' (see Chapter 24, 'History Writing').[6] The fictional, monotheistic Confucians of *The Citizen of the World* (1762) are also depicted as worthy of respect and esteem (see Chapter 11, 'Cosmopolitanism', and Chapter 26, 'Orientalism'). Lien Chi Altangi and his primary correspondent Fum Hoam are honourable and 'rational', and, like moderate eighteenth-century Anglicans, they 'believe one eternal intelligent cause of all' (*Citizen*, 1:32). Their religion is theologically vague; it is defined by 'the love of virtue', which its adherents pursue out of gratitude to 'the giver of all' (*Citizen*, 1:34). In this way, Goldsmith's Confucians reflect the contemporary Eurocentric assumption that, despite their distinct, variegated doctrines and practices, Eastern religions were ultimately grounded in an ancient, pan-Asian monotheism that was congruent with central Christian teachings.[7]

As these examples indicate, Goldsmith's cosmopolitan, sympathetic impulses were extensive. At the same time, they were also severely compromised. For, while he conforms the complicated contours of Confucianism to his own moderate Anglicanism in *The Citizen of the World*, he simultaneously denounces Buddhism, Islam, and the 'religion of the Daures' (a shamanist religion of the Mongolic people of north-eastern China) for their adherents' supposed fanaticism, irrationality, and 'absurd[ity]' (*Citizen*, 1:32). In *The History of England*, moreover, he perpetuates anti-Semitic stereotypes about Jewish 'usury and extortion', even as he denounces Edward I's 'prejudice'.[8] In addition, by depicting Anglicanism as a practical religion committed to sympathy and compassion, Goldsmith simultaneously positions the established Church as a reasonable middle ground between the perceived excesses of Catholicism and nonconformist 'enthusiasm'. That is, by portraying Anglicanism as theologically generous and tolerant of difference, he paradoxically condemns Catholics and non-Anglican Protestants for their supposed lack of tolerance.

On one hand, Catholicism was, according to Goldsmith, a superstitious religion that had degenerated from Christianity's early purity and simplicity. While his *History of England* praises individual Catholics like Sir Thomas More (1478–1535), it predictably criticizes the Roman Church for requiring auricular confession, mandating clerical celibacy, promoting 'frauds and avarice', amassing 'numberless reliques' and supposed miracles that 'delude[d]' the people, and persecuting its adversaries with unrelenting severity.[9] Goldsmith firmly supported the English Reformation of the 1530s, despite Henry VIII's ruthlessness. *The History of England* therefore claims that 'the most noble designs' are sometimes 'brought about by the most vicious instruments; for we see even that cruelty and injustice were thought necessary to be employed in our holy redemption'.[10] By the eighteenth century, however, the English Church was thoroughly Protestant. Indeed, after the Catholic James II was driven from the throne in 1688 and Parliament subsequently passed the Act of Settlement in 1701, which stipulated that all future British monarchs would be Protestant, the Anglican Church's political foothold was secured. The Church of England was hegemonic in the eighteenth century and its cultural, political prominence allowed authors like Goldsmith to portray Anglicanism as a calm, comfortable, compassionate alternative to the supposed intemperance and 'ancient superstition' of Roman Catholicism (while necessarily downplaying Anglicanism's suppression of other Christian sects and denominations).[11]

On the other hand, the Church of England was considered a bulwark against overzealous, fanatical forms of Protestantism. In the seventeenth and eighteenth centuries, growing numbers of dissenters (Presbyterians, Puritans, Baptists, Quakers, and other sectaries who weren't members of the established Church) and Anglicans who participated in John Wesley's Methodist movement contributed to an emergent evangelical movement that advocated intensely personal, heartfelt forms of devotion. Eighteenth-century evangelicals emphasized the need for Christians not simply to follow church rituals or practices unfeelingly but to have a personal, often emotional conversion experience and to experience God working in their individual hearts. In this regard, evangelicalism made faith a very personal affair; it was not necessarily about Church practices or sacraments but about personal conviction and devotion. Finally, evangelicals proselytized, meaning they tried to spread their faith and to convert others – even those who already considered themselves Christians – to the experiential, evangelical faith.

Anglican toleration of dissenting sects was officially codified in the 1689 Toleration Act, which granted all Trinitarian Christians the freedom to worship as they saw fit. At the same time, many Anglicans wished to maintain the Church of England's hegemonic status in British culture and were consistently troubled by evangelicalism's seeming disregard of history, tradition, and ritual in favour of what they considered navel-gazing individualism. Anglicans suspicious of evangelicalism often aligned it with 'enthusiasm', the period's favourite pejorative term for those who considered their own feelings and emotions evidence of God's presence. Thus Goldsmith's Lien Chi Altangi marvels that religious sects 'in England are far more numerous than in China' before facetiously claiming that evangelical spirituality is a 'good bargain' (*Citizen*, 2:182). By emphasizing God's personal grace over good works, English 'enthusiasts' attempt to reach 'Paradise at as small expense as possible'. They are not virtuous, in other words; they are spiritual cheats. Lien Chi Altangi singles out Methodists, who ostensibly agree with the 'established religion' in points of doctrine, for their ridiculous behaviour: they 'weep' for 'amusement', fill their worship services with 'sighs and groans', and 'Laughter is their aversion' (*Citizen*, 2:183). In other words, they attempt to appear more serious and more spiritual than they actually are. Such overzealous, 'enthusiastic' forms of spirituality were, for Goldsmith, objects 'of ridicule'. Conversely, proper spirituality was characterized by moderation, restraint, and 'the light of reason' (*Citizen*, 2:184).

Thus, Goldsmith responded to the religious issues of his day by depicting Anglicanism as a winsome middle ground between the perceived excesses of Catholicism and nonconformist or Methodist 'enthusiasm'. Insisting that Anglicanism's denominational rivals were often intolerant, immoral, or irrational, he advocated his religion as theologically generous and tolerant of difference. Ironically aware of doctrinal minutiae and the impossibility of attaining certainty in theological matters, Goldsmith conceived of religion as something to live and to embody, not to debate.[12] While Goldsmith's religion was limited by the prejudices of his time, it nonetheless aspired to an (unachieved) ideal of openness, sincerity, and generosity.

As the son of a priest who revered the clergymen in his own family, Goldsmith might have been expected to enter holy orders himself. Despite his lack of fit for the priesthood – the apocryphal story is that Goldsmith's ordination was rejected when he wore red breeches to see Bishop Synge in the late 1740s – Goldsmith held religion in high esteem and thought its moral dictates and its promises of life hereafter conducive to virtuous living. It might be too much to say, as one of his early twentieth-century biographers did, that Goldsmith 'had the pure spirit of the pastor' and was 'a veritable minister of God'.[13] Still, for Goldsmith, religion was entangled with all facets of life, including his own writing. With this in mind, the religion/secular divide that permeates much of our contemporary thinking must be abandoned when we approach Goldsmith's writing. His engagement with religion should be assessed not according to the doctrines he explicitly espoused (or failed to espouse), but according to religion's practical function within his literary corpus.

Notes

1. Johnson's complete definition is 'Virtue, as founded upon reverence of God, and expectation of future rewards and punishments'. See the entry for 'Religion' in Samuel Johnson, *A Dictionary of the English Language*, vol. 2 (London, 1755).

2. Jonathan Swift, *A Tale of a Tub and Other Works*, ed. Marcus Walsh (Cambridge University Press, 2010), 31.

3. Oliver Goldsmith, *The Life of Henry St John, Lord Viscount Bolingbroke* (London, 1770), 103.

4. Goldsmith, *The Life of Henry St John, Lord Viscount Bolingbroke*, 6.

5. John Evans, 'Prefatory Address to *The Traveller*', in *The Poetical Works of Oliver Goldsmith* (London, 1804), quoted in Edward. H. Mikhail, ed., *Goldsmith: Interviews and Recollections* (New York: St. Martin's Press, 1993), 23. Emphasis added.

6. Oliver Goldsmith, *The History of England, from the Earliest Times to the Death of George II*, vol. 2 (London, 1771), 8.

7. For more on eighteenth-century European understandings of Eastern religion, see Urs App, *The Birth of Orientalism* (University of Pennsylvania Press, 2010).

8. Goldsmith, *The History of England*, 2:9.

9. Goldsmith, *The History of England*, 2:374.

10. Goldsmith, *The History of England*, 2:419.

11. Goldsmith, *The History of England*, 3:16.

12. In this context, see Liem Chi Altangi's claim that Europe's 'priests, by neglecting morality for opinion, have mistaken the interests of society' (*Citizen*, 1:180).

13. E. S. Lang Buckland, *Oliver Goldsmith* (London: G. Bell & Sons, 1910), 14.

CHAPTER 16

Natural History and Science

Melissa Bailes

In the late seventeenth and eighteenth centuries what we now call 'science' was often known as natural history (including the developing fields of botany, zoology, and geology) and natural or experimental philosophy (especially physics). This era saw tremendous scientific advancement within the first scientific revolution and organization of the Royal Society, as well as the researches of British thinkers including Robert Boyle, John Ray, Isaac Barrow, Robert Hooke, John Flamsteed, and John Wallis, and Continental natural philosophers such as Descartes, Galileo, Kepler, and Huyghens. Moreover, Isaac Newton's conjoining of empirical observation with mathematical method in his *Philosophiae Naturalis Principia Mathematica* (1686) represented the triumph of scientific thought in the minds of numerous British poets, philosophers, theologians, and other scientists of the era (see Chapter 5, 'Enlightenments'). Additionally, during this period, various scientific voyages and expeditions to locales around the globe greatly aided the efforts of collectors and classifiers by returning with countless specimens hitherto unknown to Western naturalists and readers. For example, in 1768–71, Captain James Cook's first of three major explorations of the Pacific included the naturalists Daniel Carl Solander and Joseph Banks, who returned with thousands of 'new' species of plants, preserved fish, birds, insects, and hundreds of drawings. British and European naturalists rapidly organized such discoveries through taxonomies, especially those of the Swedish naturalist Carl Linnaeus. Yet, some other naturalists, including the French Georges Louis Leclerc, Comte de Buffon, challenged Linnaean principles as too abstract and failing to account for the vastness and multiplicity of the natural environment. Buffon's writings extended the earth's geological timescale, and his massive *Histoire Naturelle*, begun in 1749 and still uncompleted at his death in 1788, attempted to offer a full account of the natural world.

Collections gathered within expeditions throughout the era helped estab-
lish museums, including the Ashmolean at Oxford in 1683 and the British
Museum in 1759. Public lectures and demonstrations further encouraged
popular interest in science. Although traditionally composed in Latin, books
published in Britain about natural history and natural philosophy increas-
ingly were written or translated in English and considerably rose in popular-
ity in the mid eighteenth century and succeeding decades as they targeted
a wider audience.[1] Indeed, during this period, the British botanist Peter
Collinson enthused that natural history sold 'the *best of any books* in
England'.[2] Oliver Goldsmith published two works specifically contributing
to his era's fascination with these fields of science: his *History of the Earth, and
Animated Nature* (1774) and *A Survey of Experimental Philosophy* (1776), both
of which were published posthumously. Impressively, as Roy Porter sug-
gests, *Animated Nature* was 'probably the most popular work of natural
history in Enlightenment Britain'.[3]

Goldsmith's *Animated Nature* provides a comprehensive natural history
that synthesizes and skilfully compares arguments and information from
various naturalists, including Linnaeus and Buffon. Goldsmith viewed the
enhancement of science's stylistic appeal as his chief contribution to such
works and enlivened his borrowings with engaging descriptions and per-
sonal observations of the natural world. His incorporation of these other
writers' theories and classifications participates in the collective, collabora-
tive mode of natural history, a science that invited the participation of non-
specialists and revision during this era. Since the period's naturalists often
corrected their own work in successive editions as new information or
discoveries became available, science's resulting sense of flux sometimes put
the line between fact and fiction in doubt, blurring the division between
literature and the sciences. Of course, previous to science's professionaliza-
tion during the early decades of the nineteenth century, the term 'science'
could constitute any branch of knowledge including literature. Thus, as
Michael Griffin and David O'Shaughnessy note, 'Goldsmith must have
seen in [his *Animated Nature*] an opportunity to bring together his literary
brilliance with his indefatigable and painstaking talent for compilation and
assembly' (*Letters*, lxi–lxii). In fact, Goldsmith may have developed plans
to write his natural history as early as 1763, after penning prefaces for
Richard Brookes's *New and Accurate System of Natural History*, as
Goldsmith undertook extensive readings and domestic travels in the sub-
sequent decade aiding the composition of his scientific work. He signed
a contract with the publisher William Griffin for *Animated Nature* in 1769,
yet Griffin sold the entire copyright to John Nourse in 1772 (*Letters*, 141). In

a February 1774 letter to Nourse, Goldsmith wrote that he had thoughts of extending *Animated Nature* to include both botany and fossils; however, the author died two months later, in April 1774, at the age of forty-five (*Letters*, 142). His friends organized a monument in Westminster Abbey, for which Samuel Johnson wrote a Latin inscription celebrating Goldsmith's authorial breadth as a 'Poet, Natural Philosopher, Historian / Who left no species of writing untouched' (*Letters*, lxii).

Nevertheless, during his lifetime Goldsmith's friends denigrated his knowledge of the natural sciences, attributing his choice to write *Animated Nature* solely to his financial needs. Richard Cumberland, for instance, wrote that Goldsmith 'hardly knew an ass from a mule, nor a turkey from a goose, but when he saw it on the table. But publishers hate poetry, and Paternoster Row is not Parnassus'.[4] Johnson similarly remarked that Goldsmith would make his scientific work 'as entertaining as a Persian tale' and 'give us a very fine book on the subject; but if he can distinguish a cow from a horse, that I believe may be the extent of his knowledge of Natural History'.[5] In their estimations of *Animated Nature*, Johnson and Cumberland echo Goldsmith's own modest claim that authorial style rather than knowledge would constitute his contribution to scientific novelty. However, Washington Irving declares in his biography of Goldsmith, 'Cumberland was mistaken ... in his notion of Goldsmith's ignorance and lack of observation as to the characteristics of animals. On the contrary he was a minute and shrewd observer of them; but he observed them with the eye of a poet and moralist as well as a naturalist.'[6] Indeed, just as Goldsmith's poetic vision shapes his scientific observations, his natural history also informed some of his poetry and other works and thus provides an important context for understanding his oeuvre.[7]

Goldsmith's eight-volume *Animated Nature* (1774) went through at least twenty editions and abridgments over the next century, with the latest edition dated 1876.[8] Within the work's original edition, its first volume focuses on the earth sciences or geology, primarily recounting Buffon's theories on these subjects while additionally reviewing various other naturalists' hypotheses regarding the earth's formation as well as descriptions of its surface, water, air, volcanoes, earthquakes, winds, meteors, and other associated phenomena.[9] In the second volume, Goldsmith continues to follow Buffon's theoretical frameworks, here discussing topics related to zoology and anthropology as well as overlaps between these areas of study, with chapter headings including 'A Comparison of Animals with the Inferior Ranks of Creation', 'Of Sleep and Hunger', 'Of Old Age and

Death', 'Of the Varieties of the Human Race', and 'Of Monsters'. Assessing naturalists' hypotheses on the 'varieties of the human race', Goldsmith claims that there are 'six distinct varieties in the human species ... But there is nothing in the shape, nothing in the faculties, that shows their coming from different originals; and the varieties of climate, of nourishment, and custom, are sufficient to produce every change' (*Animated Nature*, 2:212–13). As Katy L. Chiles has shown, during the eighteenth century race 'was thought to be an exterior bodily trait, incrementally produced by environmental factors (such as climate, food, and mode of living) and continuously subject to change'.[10] Buffon, expressing his Eurocentrism, wrote that 'if, by any great revolution, man were forced to abandon those climates which he has invaded, and to return to his native country, he would, in the progress of time, resume his original features, his primitive stature, and his natural color. But the mixture of races would produce this effect much sooner', and '150, or 200 years, are sufficient to bleach the skin of a Negro' (see Chapter 14, 'Race').[11]

Goldsmith's remaining volumes of *Animated Nature* describe individual biological species, so that volumes three and four largely adhere to Buffon's discussions of animals, volume five and part of volume six focus on birds, the rest of volume six and the beginning of volume seven turn to fish, and the remainder of volume seven and half of volume eight combine studies of frogs, lizards, serpents, and insects, leaving the remainder of volume eight for the work's index. Goldsmith claims that Buffon's studies only aided his first four volumes, and he was 'left to my own reading alone to make out the history of birds, fishes, and insects' and thus 'taxed my scanty circumstances in procuring books which are on this subject [i.e., natural history], of all others, the most expensive' (*Animated Nature*, 1:xii). In addition to citing naturalists such as Buffon, Linnaeus, Ray, William Derham, George Edwards, Francis Willughby, and Thomas Pennant, he also employs numerous voyages and works of travel writing.[12] Moreover, he quotes or references classical writers including Pliny, Ovid, Aristophanes, Virgil, and Hesiod, as well as British authors such as Shakespeare, Milton, Waller, Thomson, and Pope (see Chapter 7, 'Libraries').

According to Goldsmith, natural history has two aims: 'First, that of discovering, ascertaining, and naming all the various productions of nature' and 'Secondly, that of describing the properties, manners, and relations, which they bear to us, and to each other' (*Animated Nature*, 1:i). Enticing his readers to the study of natural history, he assures that 'The mere uninformed spectator passes on in gloomy solitude; but the naturalist, in every plant, in every insect, and every pebble, finds something to entertain his curiosity, and excite his speculation' (1:vi). Goldsmith specifies that his natural history 'is written with only such an attention to system [or classification] as serves to remove the reader's embarrassments and allure him to proceed', and is arranged 'by the greatest obvious distinction that ['nature'] herself seems to have made' (1:ix). By this means, 'the reader, being already possessed of the name of any animal, shall find here a short, though satisfactory history of its habitudes, its subsistence, its manners, its friendships and hostilities' (1:ix). Goldsmith thus loosely follows Buffon, for example, in classifying quadrupeds, but divides these animals into fourteen classes, including the Horse Kind, the Cow Kind, the Sheep Kind, the Deer Kind, the Hog Kind, the Cat Kind, the Dog Kind, and so on, allowing him 'to draw together both domestic and wild varieties of the same animal, while Buffon usually separates them'.[13] *Animated Nature* additionally contains a large number of illustrations especially of less familiar quadrupeds, some of which are copied from Buffon's *Histoire Naturelle*. Notably, rather than considering natural history as 'a useful science', Goldsmith suggests that 'it is the occupation of the idle and the speculative, more than of the busy and the ambitious part of mankind' (*Animated Nature*, 1:xiv). Thus, arguably aligning his natural history with the knowledge and pleasure associated with reading literature, he asserts that Buffon's works convinced him that, stylistically, it is best 'to write from our own feelings, and to imitate nature' (1:xiv).

In fact, Goldsmith's descriptions of animals are often striking and imaginative, sometimes privileging literary skill and appeal despite questioning a report's scientific accuracy. For instance, in one of his most memorable accounts he portrays the American rattlesnake charming or mesmerizing to its death an unfortunate bird or squirrel even as he admits some naturalists' incredulity regarding this phenomenon.

> The snake is often seen basking at the foot of a tree, where birds and squirrels make their residence. There, coiled upon its tail, its jaws extended, and its eyes shining like fire, the rattlesnake levels its dreadful glare upon one of the little animals above. The bird or the squirrel, which ever it may be, too plainly perceives the mischief meditating against it, and hops from branch to branch, with a timorous plaintive sound, wishing to avoid, yet incapable of breaking through the fascination: thus it continues for some time its feeble efforts and complaints, but is still seen approaching lower and lower towards the bottom branches of the tree, until, at last, as if overcome by the potency of its fears, it jumps down from the tree directly into the throat of its frightful destroyer. (*Animated Nature*, 7:213–14)

Goldsmith's dramatic account thus not only evokes a mixture of sympathy and horror from the reader, but also creates its own sense of 'fascination', inducing the reader to continue his or her studies in natural history. In addition to his era's conventions of sensibility, he also engages with concepts of improvement and their potential paradox regarding humanity's domestication of certain animals. Again, Goldsmith's arguments follow Buffon, who claims that 'degeneration' and 'improvement' are essentially the same in the view of 'Nature' because both indicate a change from that species' original form.[14] Likewise, Buffon sometimes deems instances of 'improvements' in domesticated animals as more likely to be degenerations for the animals as species. In this vein, Goldsmith explains:

> THOSE animals that take refuge under the protection of man, in a few generations become indolent and helpless. Having lost the habit of self-defence, they seem to lose also the instincts of nature. The sheep, in its present domestic state, is of all animals the most defenseless and inoffensive. With its liberty it seems to have been deprived of its swiftness and cunning; . . . Loaded with an heavy fleece, deprived of the defence of its horns, and rendered heavy, slow, and feeble, it can have no other safety but what it finds from man. This animal is now, therefore, obliged to rely solely upon that art for protection to which it originally owes its degradation. (*Animated Nature*, 3:38–9)

Although Goldsmith generalizes these thoughts on domestication, claiming that 'In all countries, as man is civilized and improved, the lower ranks of animals are repressed and degraded,' he nevertheless suggests value in such alterations and concludes regarding the sheep that 'Human industry has therefore destroyed its grace to improve its utility' (*Animated Nature*, 4:157; 3:51). If this statement of utility mitigates his earlier refusal to consider natural history as a 'useful science', he harbours other concerns for natural or experimental philosophy.

Goldsmith's two-volume compendium of science, *A Survey of Experimental Philosophy*, became his final published work, appearing in 1776 and thus two years after his death. Despite its late publication date, the project was initially contracted with the publisher John Newbery in 1762 and therefore before *Animated Nature*, helping to prompt 'a shift in his writing towards history and popular science' (*Letters*, lxvi). Here, Goldsmith particularly draws on natural philosophers who wrote about aspects of physics in the late seventeenth and eighteenth centuries; he references the theories of, for example, Newton, Boyle, Hooke, Edmond Halley, Herman Boerhaave, Benjamin Franklin, Nicolas Malebranche, and Richard Helsham. This work's first volume includes chapters on topics such as matter, magnetism, electricity, gravity, elasticity, and hydraulics, while the second volume discusses subjects including fire, cold, light, the refraction of light, sight, colours, and the rainbow. The volumes also contain several engraved plates illustrating experiments involving, for instance, magnets, velocity, and conducting electricity. In his introduction to this work, Goldsmith sometimes highlights the violent and gendered imagery long employed within this science, stating that natural philosophers 'torture Nature by Experiments, and oblige her to give up those secrets, which she had hitherto kept concealed' (*Survey*, 1:4).

According to Goldsmith, the progress of natural philosophy 'from enjoyment, proceeds to *conjecture*; from thence to *observation of facts*, which from their paucity give birth to *hypothetical* system, which is succeeded by experimental investigation, and this at length gives rise to the true *Experimental* system, which, though still defective, is yet built upon the surest foundation' (*Survey*, 1:4). Displaying nationalism, he relates that the 'English philosopher', Newton, 'first effected what his predecessors had hitherto only aimed at' and 'had the pleasure of seeing his countrymen at once seize the truths he revealed to mankind', and although the French 'continued to teach the opinions of their countryman Descartes', the 'Truth [of Newton's theories] ... at length prevailed' (*Survey*, 1:13, 14). Nevertheless, Goldsmith also indicates that, since the time of Newton, natural philosophers have made slow progress. He asserts that 'it is rather to accidental experiments, than to painful inductions, that we are indebted for the modern discoveries in' some properties of, for example, 'electricity, magnetism, and congelation' (*Survey*, 1:16). Thus, recounting and assessing his contemporaries' hypotheses pertaining to physics, Goldsmith admits that although 'In the last age it was fashionable to suppose that we could satisfactorily account for every appearance around us: at present, the real philosopher seems to rest satisfied that there is much in this science yet to be discovered, and that what he already knows bears no proportion to what remains unknown' (*Survey*, 1:16–17).

Notes

1. See also, for example, Melissa Bailes, *Questioning Nature: British Women's Scientific Writing and Literary Originality, 1750–1830* (Charlottesville: University of Virginia Press, 2017), 7.
2. Quoted in Jacqueline Pearson, *Women's Reading in Britain, 1750–1835: A Dangerous Recreation* (Cambridge University Press, 1999), 67.

3. Roy Porter, *The Making of Geology: Earth Science in Britain, 1660–1815* (Cambridge University Press, 2008), 110–11.

4. Quoted in Edward H. Mikhail, ed., *Goldsmith: Interviews and Recollections* (New York: St. Martin's Press, 1993), 57.

5. Quoted in Mikhail, *Goldsmith*, 83.

6. Washington Irving, *Oliver Goldsmith: A Biography* (London, 1850), 263.

7. See, for example, Melissa Bailes, 'Literary Plagiarism and Scientific Originality in the 'Trans-Atlantic Wilderness' of Goldsmith, Aikin, and Barbauld', *Eighteenth-Century Studies*, 49.2 (2016), 265–79 (266–7). This and the preceding paragraph draw on this article.

8. James Hall Pitman, *Goldsmith's Animated Nature: A Study of Goldsmith* (Hamden, CT: Archon Books, 1924, 1972), 9. These include editions published in London, Dublin, and Philadelphia; the only translation Pitman found is in Welsh.

9. William Smellie's English translation of Georges-Louis Leclerc, Comte de Buffon's *Natural History, General and Particular*, 9 vols. (Edinburgh, 1780) was published after Goldsmith's death, so Goldsmith used Buffon's French volumes; however, where directly referencing Buffon's work in this chapter, I cite Smellie's translation.

10. Katy L. Chiles, *Transformable Race: Surprising Metamorphoses in the Literature of Early America* (Oxford University Press, 2014), 2.

11. Buffon, *Natural History*, 7:394. On Buffon's thoughts about racial transformation and monogenesis, see Andrew S. Curran, *The Anatomy of Blackness: Science and Slavery in an Age of Enlightenment* (Baltimore, MD: Johns Hopkins University Press, 2011), 74–116. For additional commentary on Goldsmith's engagements with race, climate, and Buffon, see Michael Griffin, *Enlightenment in Ruins: The Geographies of Oliver Goldsmith* (Lewisburg, PA: Bucknell University Press, 2013), 31–50.

12. For a list of the main sources Goldsmith employed in writing *Animated Nature*, see the appendix in Pitman, *Goldsmith's Animated Nature*, 137–50. See also Winifred Lynskey, 'The Scientific Sources of Goldsmith's "Animated Nature"', *Studies in Philology*, 40.1 (1943), 33–57.

13. Pitman, *Goldsmith's Animated Nature*, 69.

14. Buffon, *Natural History*, 7:399; see also Melissa Bailes, 'Hybrid Britons: West Indian Colonial Identity and Maria Riddell's Natural History', *European Romantic Review*, 20.2 (2009), 207–17 (212).

CHAPTER 17

War and Empire

Robert W. Jones

Goldsmith's contemporary, the judge and legal theorist William Blackstone, thought that eighteenth-century Britons were 'a nation of freemen, polite and commercial people'.[1] His point was perhaps a more complex one than is now remembered, implying that laws were mutable rather than fixed in their appropriateness, but it remains a gesture of tremendous national and colonial confidence. Britain, self-consciously defined as a maritime nation, had, it was claimed frequently by the mid eighteenth century, remade itself through its commerce. Earlier isolation, restriction, and rudeness had ceased: even the food was better. Addison had said so.[2] Displays of confidence abounded: poems, pamphlets, and speeches extolling Britain as a free, trading nation cannoned from the press – grape-shot in a paper war proclaiming Britain's new commercial strength.[3] Trade was represented as a matter of navigation and amicable distribution:

> By Navigation the whole World is connected, and the most distant Parts of it correspond with each other. And it is this Correspondence which introduces new Commodities, and propagates the most advantageous Manufactures. It not only enables the Inhabitants of those Countries where it flourishes, to export what they have in Abundance . . . but it enables them to procure foreign Commodities, and, after Manufacturing them at Home, to export them again with great Profit. . . . Nature has invested us . . . by our Situation in the Midst of the Ocean. By this Art [of Navigation] every little Port, Inlet and Creek opens a Passage for what we want to send abroad, and an Entrance for what we would bring home. To this we owe the happy Distribution of our Trade; so that every Branch of it is, or may be managed to the utmost Advantage; as it is scarce possible for any Wind to blow, that does not carry Vessels from one Port and bring them to another.[4]

It is hard, reading this triumphant appraisal, not to reflect that had 'Sweet Auburn' been a coastal port, a 'Salty Auburn, safest harbour on the main', perhaps, then its fate would have been happier. But such a response would miss what extollers of British maritime success would most have us overlook: the violence of the enterprise, its reliance on force of arms, as John Entick's dedication to Admiral Edward Vernon, victor of Porto Bello, advertises. Britain seems to have been at war or on the brink of it for much of the eighteenth century. Funded by its great trade and enabled by its considerable armed forces, Britain gained an increasingly large empire, exploiting and curtailing the lives of its own servicemen and many thousands more Native Americans, Indians, and enslaved Africans in the process (see Chapter 14, 'Race'). Trade was rarely innocent of this repeated bloodshed, a fact well understood at the time. Adam Smith believed commerce, rather than allowing abundance merely to circulate for 'great profit', actively promoted war and the creation of empire, a view many historians have since accepted.[5]

Goldsmith could take a still more jaundiced view of all wars and empire building, pointedly refusing to lure readers to the *Bee* with news of battles despite writing in the midst of a successful war. Nor did he find the motives or spoils of trade-driven conflict terribly edifying; the British 'are almost continually at war', he reflects in *Citizen of the World*, and for little more than 'raw silk, hemp, and tobacco' (*Citizen*, 1:58, 62). This chapter examines Goldsmith's awareness of colonial and national conflicts, wars of zealous expansion and disasters in foreign fields, exploring two of Goldsmith's most anxiously repeated complaints: the diminishing nature of the 'event' in the historiographical and political imagination, and the place (he saw decline) of 'great men'. Goldsmith certainly felt the great shifts and expansions of British culture, the flood tides of war and trade, measuring them against the smaller caprices of fashion: such fluxes curtailed, he thought, the possibility for any real distinction or lasting achievement. The terrible effects of war and empire on his fellow citizens, upon their shared culture and community, were keenly felt. Poignant instances abound. The 'broken soldier, kindly bade to stay' in *The Deserted Village* is but one example (*Deserted Village*, 9). Equally keen to show 'how fields were won', though less pitiable, is Mr Hardcastle in *She Stoops to Conquer*, who discourses bountifully on his old campaigns. A more compassionate account of loss through service occurs late in *Citizen of the World*, when the tale is told of a sometime soldier and sailor propelled from parlour comforts to battlefield amputation and destitution by an unthinking state (*Citizen*, 2:217–22). Tales of broken soldiers reappear in Goldsmith's work because their resolution, their suffering, and their stoicism embodied the loss of something of great value that had been idly thrown away.[6]

Given the recurrence of war during the eighteenth century, it is worth being clear about what, where, and when they were. The greatest conflict during Goldsmith's career was undoubtedly the Seven Years' War (1756– 63). Almost all Goldsmith's periodical writing was first published during these war-torn years. But other wars shaped how Goldsmith and his contemporaries responded to what has been acknowledged as the first truly world war.[7] Foremost amongst these are the War of the Austrian Succession (1740–8) into which the War of Jenkins's Ear (1739–42) became subsumed. Despite its eccentric name, the War of Jenkins's Ear conforms to the wider pattern of British maritime assertiveness. Confrontations between Britain, France, and, especially, Spain had grown in the Americas since the War of the Spanish Succession (1701–14). Under the terms of the Treaty of Utrecht (1713), the British South Sea Company gained trade monopolies in South America. This settlement included profitable rights to supply slaves to Spanish colonies, further expanding Britain's involvement in trans-Atlantic slavery, which had grown rapidly since the 1690s. These brutal remunerative arrangements exacerbated longer-standing tensions. An incident in 1731 proved catalytic. Captain Robert Jenkins's ship was boarded by Spanish coastguards who sliced his ear away. Years later, his pickled ear brandished in a jar, Jenkins told the House of Commons of his sufferings. Although the British ministry favoured peace, popular outrage was stirred and war declared in late 1739. The war, though only initially successful for British interests, notably Vernon's triumph at Porto Bello, boosted the popularity of the navy immensely, creating an appetite for conflict. Admirals were suddenly and wonderfully famous, regarded as the defenders of Britain's great freedoms and greater trading interests, including its slave transports.[8]

The War of the Austrian Succession was a grander undertaking, though its impetus was more familial. Emperor Charles VI died in 1740, designat- ing his daughter Maria Theresa heir to the Holy Roman Empire, the Archduchy of Austria, and the Hungarian crown. Doubts as to her claims provided pretext for a war in which Britain with Dutch and Hanoverian allies supported Maria Theresa against France, Bavaria, and Prussia – Spain and Russia were later drawn into the conflict. At issue was the balance of power in Europe and, for some powers, advantages in America and India. France, Austria, and Prussia sought security and control, while George II's loyalty to Hanover gave Britain a stake in these manoeuvres, to the great disquiet of the press. Popular interest focused on fighting France and on victories at sea though George II commanded land forces successfully at Dettingen in June 1743, the last British monarch so to do. Treaties and battles came thick and fast during the conflict, with advantages and acquisitions slipping bloodily from one side to another. It ended at the Treaty of Aix-le-Chappelle in 1748, disliked by almost all the protagonists, few of whom felt they had achieved much by their efforts, though Maria Theresa's claims were upheld. The only nation to achieved unquestionable advantage in Europe was Prussia, which became a great power. The subsequent 'Diplomatic Revolution' of the 1750s saw Prussia and Britain newly allied against France and Austria. Goldsmith's comments in several essays, published in different periodicals, suggest that he doubted that much of moment happened as a result of such bloody campaigning. There was no merit truly in 'battles gained, dominion extended, or enemies brought to submission' (*Citizen*, 1:159). There was little meaning in any of them. Despite such plausible doubts, and largely due to the impressive performance of its naval squadrons (commanded by Vernon, Anson, and Boscawen), Britain had strengthened its position in India, regaining Madras while confirming its commercial claims in the Americas, though France maintained its territories still.

The stage was set for the Seven Years' War. Though it began in North America, Britain and Hanover, newly allied with Prussia, fought France and Austria on the continent, who were later joined by Spain, Sweden, and Russia. Each power had its own ambitions. Prussia sought to enshrine its new status and retain territories captured in the previous war. British soldiers were deployed on the European mainland, notably combining with German forces at Minden in 1759. Ostensibly a victory, the battle was noted more for the misbehaviour of the British cavalry, whose commander was later court-martialled.[9] Even so, Minden formed part of the glorious 'year of victories' that would be crowned with British victory at Quebec in September 1759.[10] Though it cost him his life, the triumph General James Wolfe achieved gave Britain great tracts of Canada, ending French possession there. But the war had not started nearly so well. On the American borders, where tensions with France and between settlers and the Iroquois had been building for some time, Britain endured brutal, ignoble defeats. General Braddock and his men were killed at Fort Duquesne in 1755, and a massacre followed the British surrender at Fort William Henry only months later. Worse came when Admiral Byng could not (or would not) prevent a French fleet from taking Minorca. He was court-martialled and executed. News from India was better and would have longer-lasting implications. East India Company forces under Robert Clive defeated the Nawab of Bengal and his French allies at Plassey in June 1757, limiting French involvement in the subcontinent thereafter and laying the military and mercantile foundations for British rule in India. Engaged in a global conflict, Britain made global gains. These huge successes, secured at tremendous human as well as financial cost, stored trouble as much as they manifested advantage. By 1763, Britain's first empire had reached what would prove an imperfect zenith. It would look very different from the 1770s, a queasy period well reflected in *The Deserted Village*'s presaging of ignominious wasting (see Chapter 21, 'Pastoral Poetry').[11]

Though different in many ways, each conflict raises comparable historiographic questions, often coinciding with debates raging during the period, not least of which those concerned with defining what might have been the aims and purposes of these conflicts. It has been possible to argue that they were driven by clashing dynasties concerned with the balance of power in Europe. George II thought so. It is now more often suggested that conflict was the direct consequence of the aspirations of bellicose nations as they first imagined themselves as communities bent on conquest, with trade the determining factor. These questions pose others, including deciding where the principal theatres of the conflicts lay. It was conceivably at sea, in line with the 'Blue Water' instincts of many British politicians, though equally in Europe (home to the contending powers); or perhaps the Americas, or the East Indies. When the conflict took place outside Europe, the role of and consequence for indigenous people were frequently considerable (though there is scant reflection of that in Goldsmith's work). Colonial and trading aspirations launched Britain into more and more conflicts along its empire's borders, but it was rarely clear where the significance of these recurrent naval and military enterprises ultimately lay. But these wars, most obviously the Seven Years' War, had a cultural impact. Celebrity commanders such as Anson and Vernon were summoned into public view and widely cherished, none more so than Wolfe, whose image would be endlessly elaborated and reproduced.[12] Goldsmith considered that the victories gained by 'our soldiers and sailors' might 'raise our reputation above whatever history can shew; and mark the reign of George the Second, as the great period of British glory', but it was sadly true that a 'COUNTRY at war resembles a flambeaux, the brighter it burns, the sooner it is often wasted'.[13]

It is how that 'flambeaux' flared out and the dubious light it cast that most exercised Goldsmith. War's bright flame established nothing of permanent merit. The nation's cultural spaces had become shrines to very limited accomplishments. Goldsmith, unlike fellow Irishman Edmund Burke, who thought Westminster Abbey a hallowed space of national memory and glory, found both the Abbey and St Paul's cluttered with bloody tat and pointless lumber.[14] Underwritten by his somewhat contradicting his own often-voiced civic humanist ethics, Goldsmith often wrote that war, its victories, and the luxuries it provided and for which it was fought, afforded scant reward, merely laying the groundwork for future crisis.[15] Men are not made great by their endeavours; they are merely popular celebrities, feeders of a tawdry flame kept high on the acclamation of an unthinking populace. The view that war and empire corrode all possibility of real value, especially of 'great men', is best explored when Goldsmith, in an essay, 'On the Instability of Worldly Grandeur', in the *Bee* (10 November 1759), laments a publican who changes the name of his establishment to keep pace with events in Europe. No one is remembered for long:

> An ale-house keeper, near Islington, who had lived at the sign of the French king upon the commencement of the last war, pulled down his old sign, and put up that of the queen of Hungary. Under the influence of her red face, and golden sceptre, he continued to sell ale, till she was no longer the favourite of his customers; he changed her, therefore, some time ago, for the king of Prussia, who may probably be changed, in turn, for the next great man that should be set up for vulgar admiration.

Though seemingly an amiable witness to the shifts of the diplomatic revolution, the ale-house keeper is more keenly the embodiment of cynical, cyclical indifference – the eager representative of and caterer to the may-fly enthusiasms of vulgar opinion: first Louis XIV, then Maria Theresa secure on her throne, and finally Frederick the Great. Amidst this dubious empire of signs, victories and their violence are claimed merely to sell beer and porter. As Goldsmith expresses it: 'Popular glory is a perfect coquet.' It has no lasting merit. Military men seem particularly prone to this seesaw, up-and-down motion, and perhaps they deserve it; theirs are not the 'mild and amiable virtues' that make society. A later Duke of Marlborough, Goldsmith confides, was a better man than his forbear. So that it is without much regret that he notes: 'I have lived to see generals who once had crowds halloing after them wherever they went, who were bepraised by news papers and magazines, those echoes of the voice of the vulgar, and yet have long sunk into merited obscurity, with scarce even an epitaph let to flatter' (*Bee*, 186, 188).

The brevity of modern fame and the declining status of the great were perennial concerns for Goldsmith, not least as he confronted his own posterity.[16] This should not obscure his insight into the fate of the once swaggering generals, who slide into obscurity, and, especially, interchangeability. The loquacious Hardcastle in *She Stoops to Conquer* embodies this fickleness verbosely enough: 'There was a time, indeed, I fretted myself about the mistakes of government, like other people; but finding myself every day grow more angry, and the government growing no better, I left it to mend itself. Since that I no more trouble my head about *Hyder Ali*, or *Ali Cawn*, than about *Ally Croker*' (*Stoops*, 25). Ally Croker is a harmless dupe culled from Irish balladry, but Hyder Ali and Mahomed Ali Kahn, who defied British demands, first from Clive then Warren Hastings, were the rulers of Bengal and Mysore respectively. But Hardcastle muddles them up. They are first similar names, but now empty signifiers merely in narratives too easily forgotten. Meaning nothing in the country (save in the bodies of its victims) and only producing trash and waste elsewhere, neither war nor empire receive much in the way of endorsement from the partly civic, partly cosmopolitan Goldsmith – though his final position still seems hard to define. He was, if anything very definite, a Tory patriot, wary of empire and the trade and traffic which propelled it. Not without feeling for common soldiers and other sufferers, but seeing the world as stratified and hierarchal, based on climate, race, and culture, Goldsmith was a fit monitor and censor for a luxurious and conquering people.

Notes

1. William Blackstone, *Commentaries on the Laws of England*, 4 vols. (Oxford: Clarendon, 1765–9), 3:326.
2. Joseph Addison, *Spectator*, no. 69 (19 May 1711), in Joseph Addison and Richard Steele, *The Spectator*, ed. Donald F. Bond, 5 vols. (Oxford University Press, 1965), 1:292–6.
3. Linda Colley, *Britons: Forging the Nation, 1707–1837* (New Haven, CT: Yale University Press, 1992), 68–75.
4. John Entick, *A New Naval History: or, A Compleat View of the British Marine* (London, 1757), i.
5. See John Brewer, *Sinews of Power: War, Money, and the English State 1688–1783* (New York: Alfred Knopf, 1989), 168. See also Linda Colley, *The Gun, the Ship and the Pen: Warfare, Constitutions and the Making of the Modern World* (London: Profile Books, 2021); and Kathleen Wilson, *The Sense of the People: Politics, Culture and Imperialism, 1715–85* (Cambridge University Press, 1995).
6. Michael Griffin, '"What d'ye call him, Tierconneldrago … ": Oliver Goldsmith and the Seven Years' War', in *The Culture of the Seven Years' War: Empire, Identity, and the Arts in the Eighteenth-Century Atlantic World*, ed. Frans de Bruyn and Shaun Regan (Toronto University Press, 2014), 169–87.
7. De Bruyn and Regan, 'Introduction', *Culture of the Seven Years' War*, 3–5.
8. Kathleen Wilson, 'Empire, Trade, and Popular Politics in Mid-Hanoverian Britain: The Case of Admiral Vernon', *Past and Present*, 121 (1988), 74–109.

9. Piers Mackesy, *The Coward of Minden: The Affair of Lord George Sackville* (London: Allen Lane, 1979).

10. See Frank McLynn, *1759: The Year Britain Became Master of the World* (London: Vintage, 2009); and Fred Anderson, *Crucible of War: The Seven Years' War and the Fate of Empire in British North America 1754–1766* (London: Faber and Faber, 2000).

11. See Eliga H. Gould, *The Persistence of Empire: British Political Culture in the Age of the American Revolution* (Chapel Hill: University of North Carolina Press, 2000).

12. Alan McNairn, *Behold the Hero: General Wolfe and the Arts in the Eighteenth Century* (Liverpool University Press, 1997).

13. Goldsmith, *The Busy Body*, 6 (20 October 1759), 31.

14. Edmund Burke, *The Writings and Speeches of Edmund Burke*, gen. ed. Paul Langford, 9 vols. (Oxford: Clarendon, 1981–2015), 3:169–71.

15. See James Watt, 'Goldsmith's Cosmopolitanism', *Eighteenth-Century Life*, 30.1 (2006), 56–75.

16. See also Philip Connell, 'Death and the Author: Westminster Abbey and the Meanings of the Literary Monument', *Eighteenth-Century Studies*, 38.4 (2005), 557–85.

CHAPTER 18

Ghosts

María Losada-Friend

The second volume of James Prior's *Life of Oliver Goldsmith* (1837) includes the catalogue of furniture and books sold at auction in Fleet Street on 11 July 1774 'by order of the administrator of Dr. Goldsmith, deceased' (Prior, *Life*, 2:525). This list reduces the life of the Irish writer to household items and a large catalogue of books. Dictionaries, encyclopaedias, fables, biographies, plays, and poems in folios, quartos, octavos, and duodecimos reveal Goldsmith's curiosity and erudition (see Chapter 7, 'Libraries'). No volume about ghosts is among them, and yet his pamphlet *The Mystery Revealed* (1762), uncovering the hoax of the famous Cock Lane Ghost in London, is a sign – as are the many significant references to ghosts in his works – of his rejection of supernatural occurrences and his defence of rational Enlightenment values.

Press and public had keenly followed the story of the unseen ghost of Fanny Lynes ('Scratching Fanny'), who through knocks and scratches was supposedly accusing her partner, William Kent, of having poisoned and killed her. The accusation came from Kent's former landlord, Richard Parsons, a Methodist who claimed that his twelve-year-old daughter was regularly disturbed by those noises at night. A Methodist priest, John Moore, even dared to interpret the knocks as 'yes' or 'no' answers to the many queries posed to the ghost. After meetings, discussions, and the convening of committees to evaluate the case, the farce was finally exposed when the girl declared her part in her father's plan to accuse Kent of murder.

Public imagination, newspapers, and debates fuelled the fascination for these irrational supposed occurrences. Goldsmith's response to the Cock Lane episode in his pamphlet exposed the cruel effects of public opinion and press coverage upon Kent, accused of murder by an unseen ghost. His narrative, a mixture of serious scorn and subtle satire, appealed for justice and openly denounced false judgement, morbid curiosity, gossip, and ignorance. His incisive commentaries on superstition and credulity proved a clever way to tackle the threat both posed to uneducated minds. Goldsmith's was one of the many voices in a creative countermovement involving periodicals, novels, poems, and artistic productions that questioned and mocked the national ghost mania (see Chapter 23, 'Periodicals and Literary Reviewing'). Collectively, these works contributed to enliven the debate and paved the way to later rebukes against spiritualism in the nineteenth century.

The fondness for spectres and apparitions, documented by several historians, had become common in the credulous England of the eighteenth century. Jerry White points to the popularity of astrologers, occultists, fortune tellers, and famous ghosts, adding to Cock Lane's other famous spectral entities such as those supposedly haunting Sherrard Street or Golden Square in 1755 or Stockwell in 1765.[1] McCorristine explains the popularity of ghost-seeing among the middle classes from 1750 as a response to their own preoccupations with death.[2] Bath and Newton trace the demonological interests of elite groups from the late seventeenth century that later, through a process of democratization, reached the masses and increased their attention for the supernatural.[3] As Ronald Finucane noted, ghosts can have an important cultural value in explaining a particular social milieu.[4] Similarly, Sean Gaston states that 'every eighteenth-century ghost – even an unseen ghost – is part of a quite specific, cultural, religious and political history'.[5] Undoubtedly, literature and art contributed to heightening interest in ghosts in eighteenth-century society. Emma Clery explains the success of supernatural fiction from 1762 as a sign of the rise of capitalism that commercialized popular discourses on spirits.[6] Sasha Handley documents the increase of popularity and flexibility of the literary ghost report genre in pamphlets, chapbooks, ballads, and the periodical press.[7] Oral ghostly tales became the basis for earlier relevant works such as Defoe's *The Apparition of Mrs Veal* (1706) or such popular narratives as William Wagstaffe's *The Story of the St. Alb—s Ghost* (1712). Later, the Gothic romance novel was a crucial element in increasing the contemporary interest in ghosts and the supernatural.[8] Ghosts were even appropriated for the purposes of indoctrination by religious movements, especially by Methodists, whose language of the miraculous was the object of much Anglican disdain (see Chapter 15, 'Religion').[9]

Ghosts infused literary and artistic discourses with wit, humour, and scorn. Journals and newspapers amplified rumours, scandals, and beliefs in apparitions, stimulating the public imagination, a fact that Addison's light-hearted humour had detected as early as 1711. In *The Spectator*, his narrator walks by a supposedly haunted old abbey and describes the place as 'one of the most proper Scenes in the World for a Ghost to appear in'. Recreating the eerie atmosphere, he acknowledges what superstitious fear can do: 'I do not at all wonder that weak Minds fill it with Spectres and Apparitions.' An instructive speech follows on the dangers of imagination and Addison's rational reflection points at its nationwide effect: 'I should not have been thus particular upon these ridiculous Horrours, did I not find them so very much prevail in all Parts of the Country.'[10] Goldsmith's opinion on the excess of imagination in England is similar. Through Lien Chi Altangi, his Chinese mouthpiece in *The Citizen of the World* (1762), he exposes the English fervour to see wonders ('From the highest to the lowest, this people seemed fond of sights and monsters') and to see reality distorted ('instead of desiring to see things as they should be, they are rather solicitous of seeing them as they ought not to be'; *Citizen*, 1:191, 193).

The overflow of imagination related to ghosts was also effectively observed and criticized in the representation of domestic spaces. The narrator of *The Spectator* witnesses a homely scene around the telling of ghost stories and its prejudicial consequences: 'Indeed they talked so long, that the Imaginations of the whole Assembly were manifestly crazed, and I am sure will be the worse for it as long as they live.' These practices move the narrator to give advice: 'Were I a Father, I should take a particular Care to preserve my Children from these little Horrours of Imagination.'[11] Addison's moral indications condemning irrational deviations of the mind align with Goldsmith's writings on credulous people and with Lien Chi's observations on the danger for the gullible superstitious: 'There are some here who, I am told, make a tolerable subsistence by the credulity of their countrymen' (*Citizen*, 2:166).

However, eighteenth-century ghosts were also used as allies to educate the reading public. Readers enjoyed Swift's use of apparitions in Gulliver's episodes at Glubbdubdrib where the famous traveller meets 'domestick Spectres' and gets used to them: 'I soon grew so familiarized to the Sight of Spirits, that after the third or fourth Time they gave me no Emotion at all.' This habituation allows Gulliver to be instructed by 'the modern Dead' on the real nature of the human race, with examples of cruelty, falsehood or cowardice; thus, Swift cleverly deploys ghosts as peculiar agents of education.[12]

Goldsmith seems to follow Swift's idea when, in his only praise of spectral entities, he describes the beneficial possibilities of introducing a ghost in a biography. In his review of *The Ghost of Ernest, Great-Grandfather of Her Royal Highness the Princess Dowager of Wales* (1757),

Goldsmith approves the strategy of the author who 'lets loose his imagin-
ation upon the subject, and introduces the Ghost of his Hero as addressing
the present Prince of Wales'. He even acknowledges benefits for the reader:
'This is certainly a fine way of giving full weight and solemnity to instruc-
tion. It induces an awe upon the mind of the hearer, and disposes him to
pay attention equal to the importance of the subject.'[13] Presenting the ghost
as a model to be imitated and praising him as 'imaginary Instructor',
Goldsmith creates a ghostly prototype that would be seen later in portraits
of Samuel Johnson appearing as a spectre to Hester Piozzi (1788) or to
Boswell (1803).[14]

Eighteenth-century ghosts were also quite successful on stage. As Diego
Saglia observes, they showed the confrontation between critics and intel-
lectuals – who favoured the exclusion of spectres – and the public, who
were fond of the supernatural and helped the diffusion of popular
superstitions.[15] Addison's *Spectator* humorously noted the advantages of
ghosts in the English tragedy despite their inactivity and voiceless presence:
'A Spectre has very often saved a Play, though he has done nothing but
stalked across the Stage, or rose through a Cleft of it, and sunk again
without speaking one Word.' He wittily comments on the spectral theatri-
cality of the ghost in *Hamlet*: 'The Mind of the Reader is wonderfully
prepared for his Reception by the Discourses that precede it: his dumb
Behaviour at his first Entrance, strikes the Imagination very strongly; but
every Time he enters, he is still more terrifying.'[16]

Conveniently, actors such as Garrick helped the propagation of liter-
ary ghosts. Famously captured by Hogarth in the portrait of Richard III
facing his victim's ghosts (1745),[17] Garrick's acclaimed role as a fearful
Hamlet was even recreated by Fielding in *Tom Jones* (1749) where
Partridge's rapture is humorously registered at seeing the actor's per-
formance: 'And during the whole speech of the ghost, he sat with his eyes
fixed partly on the ghost and partly on Hamlet, and with his mouth open;
the same passions which succeeded each other in Hamlet, succeeding
likewise in him.'[18]

Goldsmith, in his turn, also paid special homage to the ghost in
Hamlet. He relied on the audience's complicity and knowledge of
Shakespeare's play when Marlow answers Tony's statement in *She
Stoops to Conquer* (1773):

TONY. Why, gentlemen, if you know neither the road you are going, nor where
    you are, nor the road you came, the first thing I have to inform you is,
    that – you have lost your way.
MARLOW. We wanted no ghost to tell us that. (*Stoops*, 13)

The intended parallel with the original phrase in *Hamlet*, traced by Arthur Friedman ('There needs no ghost, my lord, come from the grave / To tell us thus'), marks Goldsmith's playful sagacity in matters of literary ghostliness.

But when considering sceptical and mocking eighteenth-century approaches to ghosts, the year 1762 is a landmark regarding the different responses to the fraud of the famous aforementioned Cock Lane Ghost.[19] Goldsmith with *The Mystery Revealed* did his part in unveiling a fraud as he argued against credulity, impostures, and supernatural phenomena, but he had worked on those ideas before. He had reworked as 'On Deceit and Falsehood' Thomas Gordon's essays 'Of Witchcraft' and 'Upon the Same' (1720) in the *Bee* (225–34) and more comments to ghosts are scattered in various works.

Goldsmith's first references to the Cock Lane Ghost had been in *The Busy Body* for 13 October 1759. There, in the description of a noisy and chaotic 'Harmonical Society', a gentleman explains the story of the ghost based on his readings of the newspapers. Among the bustle, roar of voices, interruptions, orders, oaths, and bits of other stories, a partial, disconnected version is provided: 'So, Sir, d'ye perceive me, the Ghost giving three loud raps at the bed-post – ', or 'Then what brings you here? says the parson to the ghost . . . ', or 'No ghost, gentlemen, can be murdered; nor did I ever hear but of one ghost killed in all my life, and that was stabbed in the belly with a – '.[20] In a cleverly conceived carnivalesque atmosphere, Goldsmith presents the ghost tale as the talk of the town, including bold, opinionated declarations scornfully stating the irrationality of popular beliefs.

With a similar tone of ridicule Charles Churchill's *The Ghost* (1762) exploited this theme satirically as a sign of an uncultured, illiterate country: 'ENGLAND, a happy land we know, / Where Follies naturally grow, / Where without Culture they arise, / And tow'r above the common size'.[21] The poem acknowledges urban and rural credulity, a topic that Garrick in his turn presented in the interlude *The Farmer's Return from London* (Drury Lane, 1762), which also had its artistic echo in the printing by Zoffany (1762) that followed Hogarth's drawing for the printed edition of the play.[22] Churchill's satire focuses on the human qualities of the ghost ('*Our* FANNY'), scornfully pointing out her noisy actions.[23] As Gaston suggests, it complemented the success of the restaging of Addison's *The Drummer* (1715) in 1762 and criticized popular London beliefs in ghosts.[24]

Churchill humorously displays the democratized fascination for ghosts in the crowd of witnesses: 'GREAT adepts in the fighting trade',

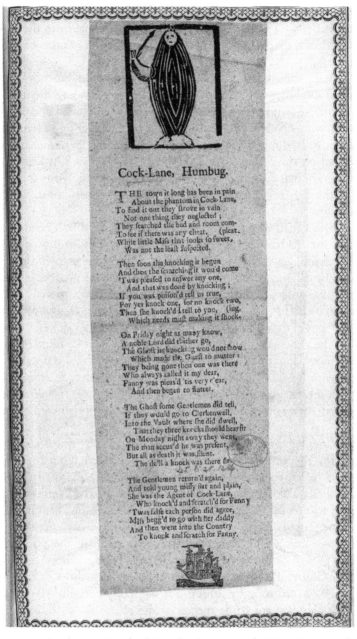

Figure 18.1 'Cock-Lane, Humbug'. British Library, C.20.f.9.(667). Courtesy of the British Library

'She Saints', 'Wits', 'Fools', 'Cowards', 'Men truly brave', 'Courtiers', 'Cits', 'Ladies', 'Lords', 'Physicians, Lawyers, Parsons, Beaux', 'Spruce Temple Clerks', or 'Prentice Fops'.[25] The poet's disdainful tone goes further than Goldsmith's milder rebukes. Churchill mockingly presents Johnson ('Pomposo') as part of the learned committee who in vain visit the vault to test the veracity of the ghost. Churchill even evokes Cervantes's famous squire to laugh at the sages: 'Tho' REASON at the same time cries / *Our* QUIXOTES are not half so *wise*, / Since they with other follies boast / An Expedition 'gainst a *Ghost*'.[26]

Successful as spectacle and poetic subject, the Cock Lane Ghost also became malleable material in Hogarth's hands. *Credulity, Superstition and Fanaticism* (1762) satirized exaggerated religious practices.[27] In *The Citizen of the World*, Goldsmith similarly had scrutinized Methodists as a modern sect of Enthusiasts through Lien Chi Altangi's eyes, insisting on their irrationality ('worshippers who discard the light of reason') and lack of education ('their fears ... increase in proportion to their ignorance'; *Citizen*, 2:184). *Credulity, Superstition and Fanaticism* presents the Cock Lane Ghost in the hands of an enthusiastic congregation, making visible what Goldsmith mockingly registers in *The Mystery Revealed* as reports of the ghost's witnesses: 'the girl saw it without hands, in a shrowd; the other two saw it with hands, all luminous and shining'.[28] Hogarth's grotesque portraits of raptures reveal Goldsmith's description of Methodist practices ('a chorus of sights and groans') in a peculiar cautionary portrait of the dangers of extreme religion (*Citizen*, 2:183).

In his personal crusade against irrational credulity and superstition (and Methodism) Goldsmith sought authorities to support his arguments, surprisingly finding a model in Spain, the country of 'catholic credulity' (*Enquiry*, 64). In the *Bee*, he openly praised the eighteenth-century scholar Benito Jerónimo Feijoo, 'an extraordinary genius now existing in that nation, whose studious endeavours seem calculated to undeceive the superstitious and instruct the ignorant' (*Bee*, 96). Feijoo encompassed the rational approach that the Irish writer pursued, so Goldsmith uses an anecdote in which Feijoo unmasks a miracle as an exemplary story. Similarly, he registers gatherings of multitudes, official processions, or public wonders with scornful disdain ('Whenever the people flock to see a miracle, it is an hundred to one, but that they see a miracle': *Citizen*, 2:186).

Goldsmith observed: 'a Grubstreet writer never thinks his pamphlet succeeds until it is answered' (*Letters*, 61). By this criterion, we might deem this pamphlet a qualified success as it was more than a century later when

Andrew Lang critiqued spiritualism and praised *The Mystery Revealed* in 1894.[29] Considered one of the 'Anti-Spiritualists', Lang defended common sense, following what Goldsmith had done a century earlier with good-humoured scepticism.[30] But other echoes of the Cock Lane Ghost manifested themselves in the literary sphere. The opening of *A Tale of Two Cities* (1859) compares the rappings of spiritualism in England in the 1850s to the knockings of the Cock Lane Ghost.[31] And Scrooge's signature expression of disbelief in *A Christmas Carol* (1843) is a reminder of Goldsmith's scorn and that of the contemporary ballad 'Cock-Lane, Humbug' (1762) (Figure 18.1).[32] In his time, Goldsmith proudly envisioned that future scholars would 'cavil at my productions' (*Letters*, 30). His engagement with the topic of ghosts in *The Mystery Revealed* certainly invites us to do so. The real ghostly terrors for him, ultimately, were blind superstition and a widespread lack of common sense.

Notes

1. Jerry White, *London in the Eighteenth Century: A Great and Monstrous City* (London: Vintage, 2013), 429.
2. Shane McCorristine, *Spectres of the Self: Thinking about Ghosts and Ghost-Seeing in England, 1750–1920* (Cambridge University Press, 2010), 31.
3. Jo Bath and John Newton, 'Sensible Proof of Spirits: Ghost Belief during the Later Seventeenth Century', *Folkore*, 117 (2006), 1–14 (11).
4. Ronald Finucane, *Appearances of the Dead: A Cultural History of Global Ghosts* (London: Junction Books, 1982), 1.
5. Sean Gaston, 'An Event without an Object: The Cock Lane Ghost, London 1762–1763', *Literary London Journal*, 12 (2015), 3–21 (6).
6. Emma J. Clery, *The Rise of Supernatural Fiction, 1762–1800* (Cambridge University Press, 1995).
7. Sasha Handley, *Visions of an Unseen World. Ghost, Beliefs and Ghost Stories in Eighteenth-Century England* (London: Pickering and Chatto, 2007), 12.
8. Carol Davison, *History of the Gothic: Gothic Literature 1764–1824* (Cardiff: University of Wales Press, 2019), 13.
9. Misty G. Anderson, *Imagining Methodism in Eighteenth-Century Britain: Enthusiasm, Belief and the Borders of the Self* (Baltimore, MD: Johns Hopkins University Press, 2012).
10. Joseph Addison and Richard Steele, *The Spectator*, ed. Donald F. Bond, 5 vols. (Oxford: Clarendon, 1965), 1:453, 454, 455.
11. Addison, *The Spectator*, 1:53–4, 54.
12. Jonathan Swift, *Gulliver's Travels*, ed. David Womersley (Cambridge University Press, 2012), 287–8, 297.
13. *Monthly Review* 16 (June 1757), 569.

14. Robert Folkenflik, 'Representations', in *Samuel Johnson in Context*, ed. Jack Lynch (Cambridge University Press, 2014), 62–82 (80).

15. Diego Saglia, 'Staging Gothic Flesh: Material and Spectral Bodies in Romantic-Period Theatre', in *The Romantic Stage: A Many-Sided Mirror*, ed. Lilla Crisafully and Fabio Liberto (Amsterdam: Rodopi, 2014), 161–84 (170).

16. *The Spectator*, 1: 186.

17. William Hogarth, 'Mr. Garrick in the Character of Richard the 3d'. London: The British Museum, 1746. www.britishmuseum.org/collection/object/P_18 68-0822-1569.

18. Henry Fielding, *Tom Jones: A Foundling*, ed. R. P. C. Mutter (London: Penguin Classics, 1985), 709.

19. See Douglas Grant, *The Cock Lane Ghost* (London: St. Martin's Press, 1965); Clery, 'The Case of the Cock Lane Ghost', in *The Rise of Supernatural Fiction*, 13–32; María Losada-Friend, 'Ghosts or Frauds? Oliver Goldsmith and *The Mystery Revealed*' *Eighteenth-Century Ireland* 13 (1998), 159–65; Paul Chambers, *The Cock-Lane Ghost* (Cheltenham: The History Press, 2006).

20. *Essays* (London, 1765), 29–31.

21. Charles Churchill, *The Ghost* (London, 1762), 6.

22. *Painting the Theatre: Garrick in Action*, ed. Véronique Gerard Powell (Durham: The Bowes Museum, 2019), 19.

23. Churchill, *The Ghost*, 19.

24. Gaston, 'An Event without an Object', 7.

25. Churchill, *The Ghost*, 33.

26. Churchill, *The Ghost*, 52.

27. William Hogarth, *Credulity, Superstition and Fanaticism* (London: The British Museum, 1762). www.britishmuseum.org/collection/object/P_1868-0822-1624. *Enthusiasm Delineated* was the title of an earlier version: see Bernd Krysmanski, 'We See a Ghost: Hogarth's Satire on Methodists and Connoisseurs', *The Art Bulletin*, 1998, 80.2 (1998), 292–310. Hogarth also captured the Ghost in *The Times*, Plate II (1762). www.metmuseum.org/art/collection/search/399157.

28. Oliver Goldsmith, *The Mystery Revealed* (London, 1762), 18.

29. Andrew Lang, *Cock Lane and Common-sense* (London: Longmans, Green, and Company, 1894), 163.

30. Tatiana Kontou, 'Anti-Spiritualism', in *Spiritualism 1840–1930*, vol. 4, Patricia Pulham et al. eds. (London: Routledge, 2014).

31. *Charles Dickens. A Tale of Two Cities*, ed. Andrew Sanders (Oxford University Press, 1998).

32. Anonymous, 'Cock-Lane, Humbug' (London, 1762).

PART III

Literary Contexts

CHAPTER 19

Fiction

Ian Campbell Ross

The Vicar of Wakefield is one of the most widely admired, republished, translated, and illustrated works of eighteenth-century English prose fiction, yet Goldsmith's relationship to the 'new species of writing' was remarkably ambivalent.[1] In 1757, as he attempted to make his way in Grub Street, Goldsmith reviewed a French novel translated as *True Merit, True Happiness* for the *Monthly Review*, concluding 'Reader, if thou hast ever known such perfect happiness, as these romance-writers can so liberally dispense, thou hast enjoyed greater pleasure than has ever fallen to our lot. How deceitful are these imaginary pictures of felicity! and, we may add, how mischievous too.'[2] The following year, in a preface to his translation of Jean Marteilhe's autobiographical *Mémoires d'un protestant condamné aux galères de France pour cause de religion* (1757), Goldsmith placed Marteilhe's non-fictional work in the context of the current vogue for 'romance', asserting that the former could not 'be recommended as a grateful Entertainment to the numerous readers of reigning Romance, as it is strictly true. No Events are here to astonish; no unexpected Incidents to surprize, no such high-finished Pictures as captivate the Imagination, and have made Fiction fashionable'.[3] Writing to his brother Henry in January 1759, Goldsmith expressed outright hostility towards fiction: 'Above all things let [your son] never touch a romance, or novel, those paint beauty in colours more charming than nature, and describe happiness that man never tastes' (*Letters*, 42). A year later still, he took aim at the most celebrated fiction of the day, entitling one of his essays in the *Public Ledger*, 'The Absurd Taste for Obscene and Pert Novels, Such as "Tristram Shandy", Ridiculed'.[4]

It may have been the extraordinary popular and commercial success of the first two volumes of Laurence Sterne's novel that prompted Goldsmith's ire, or envy. Two years previously he had written defensively of the status of the hack author in London to his brother-in-law Daniel Hodson in Ireland, suggesting that there was not 'one single writer, who has abilities to translate a french novel, that does not keep better company wear finer cloaths and live more genteely than many who pride themselves for nothing else in Ireland' (*Letters*, 37). In 1761 he would himself translate just such a novel: the anonymously published *Mémoires de Miledi B* ... (1760).⁵ Long believed lost, the translation has been identified as *Memoirs of Lady Harriot Butler* (1761). Goldsmith treated his text with considerable skill and linguistic verve but also freely, adapting aspects of the work's Roman Catholic sentiments for a Protestant audience, sentimentalizing the relationships between the narrator and her father and lover, and even making small but significant changes to the plot.⁶

This translation aside, Goldsmith's early engagement with fiction comprised several short narratives. 'The Story of Alcander and Septimius', a reworking of a tale from Boccaccio's *Decameron* that first appeared in the first number of Goldsmith's short-lived journal the *Bee* (1759), advances the moral 'That no circumstances are so desperate, which Providence may not relieve', so anticipating *The Vicar of Wakefield*. Similarly proleptic of Goldsmith's most celebrated fiction is 'The History of Miss Stanton', which appeared in the *British Magazine* and concerns a country vicar, from 'H. a town in the north of England', whose only daughter is seduced by one of her father's guests, a character not unlike Mr Thornhill. Strikingly, this narrative is prefaced by reflections on 'fictitious stories of distress' which, the author suggests, may help promote moral behaviour 'by example' more successfully than didactic writers 'vainly attempt by maxim or reproof', though Goldsmith's continuing unease regarding fiction is suggested by the stark warning that such stories are unnatural because they 'want the sanction of truth'.⁷

It was in the pages of the daily newspaper, the *Public Ledger*, that Goldsmith made his earliest attempt at extended prose fiction with 'Letters from a Chinese Philosopher in London', subsequently collected as *The Citizen of the World* (1762). Modelled on Marana's *L'espion turc* (1684–97), Montesquieu's *Lettres persanes* (1721), the Marquis d'Argens's *Lettres chinoises* (1739–40), Fougeret de Monbron's *Le cosmopolite ou le citoïen du monde* (1750), and the works of English imitators, including George Lyttleton's *Letters from a Persian in England* (1735) and Horace Walpole's *Letter from Xo-Ho* (1757), Goldsmith's essays, published over a period of nineteen months, are bound together both by the person of the letter-writing 'Chinese philosopher', Lien Chi Altangi, and such recurring figures as The Man in Black and the author Beau Tibbs. The result is a work that recalls Montesquieu's description of his *Lettres persanes* as 'un espèce de roman' (see Chapter 11, 'Cosmopolitanism', and Chapter 26, 'Orientalism').[8]

Though it is unlikely Goldsmith consciously regarded his work as 'a kind of novel', the writing of the 'Chinese Letters' seems to have turned his thoughts to a more extended fiction. It was in 1761 or the following year that he began to draft the work that would become *The Vicar of Wakefield*. By the end of 1762, the draft was sufficiently advanced for Samuel Johnson to read the manuscript and rescue the impoverished author from imprisonment by his landlady by taking it to the bookseller John Newbery, obtaining an advance from him to relieve Goldsmith's immediate needs. Composition continued in 1763 and into 1764, at which point, according to a friend, Goldsmith considered his work ready for the press.[9] John Newbery was evidently less certain for *The Vicar of Wakefield* would not be published until 27 March 1766, by which time the popular and critical success of *The Traveller* (1764) had brought Goldsmith's name to the attention of readers. When his fiction did appear it was indicated as having been printed by Benjamin Collins of Salisbury, who had purchased a third share of the copy, for publication in London by Francis Newbery, John Newbery's nephew.

The form the first edition took offers several insights into Goldsmith's view of contemporary fiction. With the printer dexterously expanding the text by means of blank versos, short line counts, and generous spacing to fill out two small duodecimo volumes, Goldsmith's work appeared under the full title, *The Vicar of Wakefield. A Tale. Supposed to Be written by himself.* While the autobiographical nature of Dr Charles Primrose's narrative recalls the subtitle of Jean Marteilhe's memoir in Goldsmith's translation, the generic alignment of the work as 'A Tale' suggests an attempt by Goldsmith to dissociate himself not merely from the 'pert and obscene' element of contemporary fiction but from the very idea of the 'novel' as it was coming to be understood. In the quarter of a century that had passed since Samuel Richardson's extraordinarily successful *Pamela* (1740) stimulated the mid-century appetite for prose fiction, only a single extended work of fiction had appeared with the subtitle 'A Tale'. This was *The Prince of Abissinia. A Tale* (1759), Samuel Johnson's prose fiction now commonly called *Rasselas* (though not published under that title in England until 1787). The fact that Johnson was both the first reader of Goldsmith's tale and the first author to designate an extended fiction as 'A Tale' powerfully suggests the influence of the writer and his work on Goldsmith, with the parallelism of the titles – *The Prince of Abissinia: A Tale* and *The Vicar of Wakefield: A Tale* – allowing us to read the latter as a domestic counterpart to the earlier exotic tale. Just as Johnson avoided 'the representational priorities and techniques that he elsewhere praises as a critic', so Goldsmith eschewed the kind of realism associated with the mid-century novel as practised by Richardson, Fielding, Smollett, and other contemporaries.[10] The (sometimes disconcerting) play of moral idealism and comedy, combined with a detachment from certain kinds of verisimilitude, characteristic of both *The Prince of Abissinia* and *The Vicar of Wakefield*, might even raise the possibility that it was Johnson who suggested the subtitle of the latter to the often diffident Goldsmith.

Like *The Prince of Abissinia*, *The Vicar of Wakefield* brings to mind the French *conte*, then popular in England. The remarkable similarity of *Rasselas* to Voltaire's philosophical tale *Candide* (1759) has often been noted, not least by Johnson himself.[11] Goldsmith's fiction, meanwhile, may be aligned with the 'moral tale' of other contemporary French authors, such as Marmontel, whom Goldsmith considered a 'fine modern writer',[12] and whose *Contes moraux* (1755–9) appeared in three separate English translations in 1763 and 1764 (see Chapter 30, 'France and French Writing'). In France, the *conte moral* was already well established and the words of Thomas-Simon de Gueullette, author of *Les Sultanes de Guzarate, contes mogols* (1732) – 'THE grand Moral of these ingenious Tales is contained in this Sentence. *True Virtue alone is capable of standing all trials, and persisting therein, is the only means of attaining solid Happiness*' – might serve equally for *The Vicar of Wakefield*.[13] Certainly, the growing popularity of Goldsmith's fiction, which appeared in a fourth London edition in 1769, encouraged other writers to attempt to emulate his success in near identical terms. The year 1771 saw the anonymous publication of both *The Vicar of Bray: A Tale* and *The Curate of Coventry: A Tale*. Others evidently thought there was some value in the previously unfamiliar subtitle, with Francis Newbery selling *The Younger Brother, A Tale* (1770–2) on behalf of an anonymous author, while the year 1771 also saw the appearance of *The Samians, A Tale*.

If Goldsmith had intended to distinguish between the more general run of contemporary fiction and his own work, he was only partly successful. Though the writer of the very first notice of *The Vicar of Wakefield* described it, in the *Monthly Review*, as 'this very singular tale', he added: 'Through the whole course of our travels in the wild regions of romance, we never met with any thing more difficult to characterize, than the *Vicar of Wakefield*.'[14] The review was undoubtedly positive but the difficulty in characterizing the work was echoed in the *Critical Review*, whose exceptionally laudatory account described it as 'this very singular novel' and asserted that Goldsmith possessed 'a manner peculiar to himself ... what the French would term *naïveté*.[15] The *Monthly Review* concurred, suggesting that Goldsmith displayed 'such palpable indications of the want of a thorough acquaintance with mankind' that, were it not for the author's 'extraordinary natural talents', he would be totally unqualified from attempting 'this species of composition'.[16] Towards the century's end, Goldsmith's tale was included in such popularizing collections of prose fiction as *The Novelist's Magazine* in 1790 and Cooke's *Select Novels* (1795), which also included such 'novels' as Voltaire's *Zadig* and *Candide*, John Langhorne's oriental tale *Solyman and Almena*, and Marmontel's *Belisarius*. Subsequently, *The Vicar of Wakefield* appeared in Anna Barbauld's canon-forming, fifty-volume collection, *The British Novelists* (1810), though Barbauld, a great admirer of the work, could not avoid noting that it was 'full of improbabilities and absurdities'.[17] Sir Walter Scott went still further in *Ballantyne's English novelists* (1821-4), and, evidently judging the work against the prevailing realism of early nineteenth-century fiction, admitted that the work contained 'impossibilities'. The question of what kind of composition – 'tale'? 'novel'? 'romance'?[18] – Goldsmith had written has been at the heart of critical discussion of *The Vicar of Wakefield*, with its apparent sentimental benevolence taken with complete seriousness, for at least a century and a half, most notably by Goethe, until the second half of the twentieth century, when academic critics began to favour readings of the tale that posit Goldsmith as an explicit 'anti-benevolist' and the work as a 'sustained satire' (see Chapter 27, 'Satire and Sentiment', and Chapter 34, 'Afterlives 1: The Victorian *Vicar*').[19]

Whether Goldsmith wrote other fictions than those mentioned has proved a question equally problematic and long-lasting. The writer's association with John Newbery led him to produce works of many kinds. Today, Newbery is most closely associated with children's literature and his most famous title, *The History of Little Goody Two-Shoes* (1765), has been frequently attributed to the pen of Goldsmith, not least in the nineteenth century by the writer's dogged biographer Washington Irving, and the historian of the Newbery printing house, Charles Welsh, in his 1881 edition of the children's work. Though modern historians of children's literature are generally unconvinced by the attribution, the British Library continues, reasonably enough, to suggest that 'there is no decisive evidence to confirm or refute this' – and the possibility that Goldsmith wrote, if not the fiction, at least the 'Introduction. By the Editor' is a real one.[20]

Still more contentious is the attribution to Goldsmith of the anonymously published *The Triumph of Benevolence; or, The History of Francis Wills* (1772). That Goldsmith might have written the book – which reads today as part insipid sentimental novel, part weak imitation of the more robust fiction of Tobias Smollett – was first suggested by the publisher of a French translation, *Histoire de François Wills, ou le Triomphe de la bienfaisance; par l'auteur du Ministre de Wakefield* (1773), republished the following year in Neuchâtel.[21] In 1786, an English-language edition appeared in Berlin, its title page declaring it to be 'By the Autor [*sic*] of The Vicar of Wakefield'.[22] Nineteenth-century writers, including James Northcote and William Hazlitt – the latter drawing on the work of the former – reported that Mary Gwyn, née Horneck, Goldsmith's 'Jessamy Bride', told the story that Goldsmith had read her several chapters of a novel he was writing shortly before his death (the dating already making the attribution problematic). Doubters were not far behind, with Robert Southey lamenting that 'A fraud has been practised in France on Goldsmith's reputation' in attributing *The Triumph of Benevolence* to him.[23] Even so, Sir James Prior offered more circumstantial evidence for Goldsmith's authorship, writing that, following the (very modest) financial success of the first three editions of *The Vicar of Wakefield*, John Newbery, 1786 offered Goldsmith a substantial advance of £200 or £300 for a new novel, only for the manuscript Goldsmith submitted to prove to be a reworked version of his play *The Good Natur'd Man* (1768), which Newbery rejected. It was from a putative second attempt at a novel, Prior suggested, that Goldsmith supposedly read aloud to a gathering at which Mary Horneck was present. Both Washington Irving and John Forster rejected this idea and Robert Browning savagely – but accurately – dismissed the novel as 'a miserable, two volume, twaddling story' in which 'Malevolence triumphed with a vengeance, in giving the paternity of the book to Goldsmith!'.[24] Among later Goldsmith scholars, only A. Lytton Sells seriously attempted to reconsider the question of authorship, though his admirably thorough '*The History of Francis Wills*: A Literary Mystery' finally rejected the idea, tentatively suggesting Goldsmith's fellow countryman Arthur Murphy as a possible author.[25]

It is, then, on *The Vicar of Wakefield* that Goldsmith's reputation as an author of fiction rests. Alongside the three London editions of 1766, the tale was published in three Dublin editions the same year, and an American edition appeared in 1767. So too did the first French translation, *Le ministre de Wakefield*, by Madame de Montesson, which went through five editions and was followed by five different French translations published between 1796 and 1802, before the exceptionally successful and long-lived translation by the novelist Charles Nodier appeared in 1838. Goldsmith's fiction appeared in translations in other languages also: German in 1768 and 1777, Dutch in 1768, Danish in 1779, Swedish in 1782, Russian in 1786, Italian in 1809, and Spanish in a translation published in 1825 in New York. Later translations included those into Welsh, Hungarian, Bohemian, Romanian, Hebrew, Icelandic, Chinese, Catalan, and Irish.

The popularity of *The Vicar of Wakefield* has lasted for more than 250 years to the present day, as evidenced by the plethora of popular editions in print, including dozens in ebook form in different languages. That popularity serves to suggest that regardless of the remarkable critical disagreement over two and a half centuries about how the work might be or should be read, Goldsmith's demonstrably ambivalent attitude to fiction has allowed readers of all kinds to shape *The Vicar of Wakefield* in ways that continue to please or intrigue them. That fiction is not only, as Robert Southey wrote, 'a puzzler for the critic', but a work characterized, in Henry James's enigmatic words, by an 'incomparable amenity' that requires 'scarcely anything else'.[26]

Notes

1. See Francis Coventry, *An Essay on the New Species of Writing Founded by Mr. Fielding* (London, 1751).

2. [Oliver Goldsmith], 'Art. 6, True Merit, True Happiness', *Monthly Review*, 16 (May 1757), 453.

3. [Jean Marteilhe], *The Memoirs of a Protestant Condemned to the Galleys of France for His Religion. Written by Himself*, 2 vols. (London, 1758), v–vi.

4. *Public Ledger*, 30 June 1760, reprinted as Letter LI in *The Citizen of the World*, 2 vols. (London, 1762), 1:232–6.

5. The novel is now known to be the earliest work of Charlotte-Marie-Anne Charbonnier de La Guesnerie (*c.*1710–85).

6. The identification was made by Arthur Freeman, who was wrong, however, to describe Goldsmith's work as a 'direct and quite literal translation'; see 'New Goldsmith?', *Times Literary Supplement* (15 December 2006), 15–16.

7. *British Magazine*, 3 (July 1760), 128–32.

8. Charles-Louis de Secondat, baron de la Brède et de Montesquieu, 'Quelques réflexions sur Les Lettres persanes', *Œuvres de Monsieur Montesquieu*, 3 vols. (Amsterdam, 1758), 3:[3]–6 ([3]).

9. Thomas Percy, 'The Life of Dr. Oliver Goldsmith', in *The Miscellaneous Works of Oliver Goldsmith, M. B.*, 4 vols. (London, 1801), 1:62; the friend was Dr William Farr.

10. Samuel Johnson, *Rasselas*, ed. Thomas Keymer (Oxford University Press, 2009), xxvi.

11. See James Boswell, *The Life of Samuel Johnson, LL.D*, 2 vols. (London, 1791), 1:185.

12. *Critical Review*, 9 (January 1760), 14.

13. [Thomas-Simon de Gueullette], *Mogul Tales, or, The Dreams of Men Awake. Being Stories Told to Divert the Sultana's of Guzarat, for the Supposed Death of the Sultan. Written in French by the Celebrated Mr. Gueullette, Author of the Chinese Tales, &c.*, 2 vols. (London, 1736), 1:xvi.

14. *Monthly Review*, 34 (May 1766), 407.

15. *Critical Review*, 21 (June 1766), 439–41.

16. *Monthly Review*, 34 (May 1766), 407.

17. Anna Barbauld, ed., *The British Novelists*, 50 vols. (London, 1810), 23:[i], xi.

18. All three terms appear in the earliest magazine reviews of *The Vicar of Wakefield*.

19. Ricardo Quintana, '*The Vicar of Wakefield*: The Problem of Critical Approach', *Modern Philology* 71.1 (1973), 62; Robert H. Hopkins, 'Fortune and the Heavenly Bank: *The Vicar of Wakefield* as Sustained Satire', in *The True Genius of Oliver Goldsmith* (Baltimore, MD: Johns Hopkins University Press, 1969), 166–230.

20. www.bl.uk/collection-items/the-history-of-little-goody-two-shoes.

21. *Histoire de François Wills, ou le Triomphe de la bienfaisance; par l'auteur du Ministre de Wakefield* (Rotterdam, 1773 and Neuchâtel, 1774).

22. *The Triumph of Benevolence; or, The History of Francis Wills. By the Autor [sic] of The Vicar of Wakefield*, 2 vols. (Berlin, 1786).

23. *Omniana; or, Horæ otiosiores*, 2 vols. (London, 1812), 1:296.

24. John Forster, *The Life and Times of Oliver Goldsmith*, 2 vols. (2nd ed. London, 1854), 2:338n.

25. 'The History of Francis Wills: A Literary Mystery', *Review of English Studies*, 11.41 (January 1935), 1–27; a revised version of the essay is reprinted as Appendix 1, '*The History of Francis Wills* and the Mystery of Goldsmith's Lost Novel', in Lytton Sells, *Oliver Goldsmith: His Life and Works* (London: Allen & Unwin, 1974), 383–96.

26. *Southey's Common-Place Book: Third Series. Analytical Readings*, ed. John Wood Warter (London, 1850), 3:718 [34:407]; Henry James, 'Introduction', in *The Vicar of Wakefield* (New York: The Century Company, 1900), xiii.

CHAPTER 20

Theatre

Gillian Russell

Oliver Goldsmith's success as a dramatist came comparatively late in his career, after he had made his reputation as a man of letters in many genres. Adding dramatist to the labels of novelist, historian, philosopher, essayist, and critic was not easy, however, as he had to deal with the formidable gatekeepers of the British theatre in the form of David Garrick of Drury Lane and Covent Garden's George Colman. It is likely that Goldsmith was a regular playgoer, familiar with the theatres of Dublin, Edinburgh, and London and most likely Europe, as well as the more ragged performances of travelling companies in the provinces. In *The Vicar of Wakefield*, Primrose encounters a troop of strolling players on the move with their 'scenes and other theatrical furniture' in a waggon and later sees their performance of Nicholas Rowe's tragedy *The Fair Penitent* at 'the play-house, which was no other than a barn' (*Vicar*, 1:212). Goldsmith reviewed the publications of new tragedies, John Home's *Douglas* in 1757 and *The Orphan of China* by Arthur Murphy in 1759, and also made a number of interventions in dramatic criticism, including a chapter on 'the STAGE' in the *Enquiry into the State of Polite Learning* and an influential essay comparing the sentimental and laughing comedy, strategically published in the *Westminster Magazine* as he was negotiating with George Colman over the production of *She Stoops to Conquer*.[1]

The British theatre of the mid eighteenth century was dominated by the twin citadels of Covent Garden and Drury Lane, both royal houses insofar as they held patents or authority from the monarch to perform and had privilege to stage the spoken drama as defined by the 1737 Licensing Act. They were winter theatres, active from September to May. Samuel Foote's theatre in the Haymarket had a patent to stage plays in the summer months while Sadler's Wells Theatre in the rural margins of London in Islington was licensed by local magistrates to perform entertainments such as tumbling shows and dancing dogs. Theatre outside London was growing in towns and cities such as York, Norwich, Bath, Bristol, and Belfast, complementing the established playhouses in the capitals of Dublin and Edinburgh. The growth of the print trade, particularly the mid-century newspaper press, expanded audiences, both real and virtual, for the theatre, making national celebrities of figures such as David Garrick who in 1769 inaugurated the cult of Shakespeare with a multimedia festival, *The Jubilee*, staged at Stratford-upon-Avon and then at Drury Lane (see Chapter 23, 'Periodicals and Literary Reviewing', and Chapter 25, 'Authorship').

The British theatre was also making inroads in the colonies, in conjunction with an expanding print trade, in places such as North America, the Caribbean, and India, meaning that a successful play had the potential to reach a global audience, both in performance and in print. The possibility of a truly national theatre was signified by the success of John Home's *Douglas*, which had its origins in Scotland and endured in the repertory well into the nineteenth century. At the same time, however, becoming a successful dramatist was fraught with difficulty as it potentially exposed the writer to numerous trials – the favour or disfavour of a manager, the commitment or not of the performers, and the whims of a temperamental audience. Moreover, in the 1760s and 1770s, the theatrical milieu was riven with disputes and jealous competition that could sometimes erupt in scandal, especially sexual scandal. In 1772 Goldsmith's long-standing antagonist, William Kenrick, accused David Garrick of a sodomitical relationship with the playwright Isaac Bickerstaff. Garrick's reputation survived, but Bickerstaff's career, like that of the prominent playwright and actor-manager Samuel Foote, was destroyed in the 1770s by the accusations of sodomy, a capital offence. Becoming a successful dramatist was therefore potentially lucrative and prestigious but in the febrile climate of the 'gender panic' of the 1760s and 1770s it could also risk scandal and ignominy (see Chapter 13, 'Gender').

The 'gender panic' of this period took the form of anxiety about the feminization of British culture as a result of the influence of fashion, luxury, and commerce. These developments were part of the complex response to how the Seven Years' War (1757–63) had transformed Britain into a geopolitical colossus, inaugurating the Second British Empire. As Carol Watts argues, 'One consequence of winning the war was the need to make sense of an extraordinary extension of territorial boundaries that troubled the limits of the state.' This was 'a moment too in which new kinds of subjects might emerge, loosed in messy and uncertainly provisional ways from the ties that had traditionally defined their place in the world' (see Chapter 17, 'War and Empire').[2]

Goldsmith began working on his first comedy, *The Good Natur'd Man*, in 1766–7. After an unsuccessful try with Garrick, the play was eventually accepted by George Colman at Covent Garden where it was performed on 29 January 1768. It was up against Hugh Kelly's sentimental comedy *False Delicacy* that had opened to acclaim at Drury Lane just the week before and featured the star actress Frances Abington. The prospect of success for *The Good Natur'd Man* was not helped by a gloomy prologue written by Samuel Johnson that contextualized his friend's fortunes in terms of prevailing tension over the forthcoming General Election, the first for seven years – 'Our anxious Bard, without complaint, may share/This bustling season's epidemic care' (*Good Natur'd Man*, vii).

The Good Natur'd Man can be described as an 'anxious' comedy. The action takes place in London, focused on the house of the eponymous Young Honeywood, whose generosity to others risks his honour and security. His uncle Sir William Honeywood, who has not seen his nephew since the latter was a child, plans to test him by involving him in 'fictitious distress', a mock arrest by bailiffs to prove the danger he is in (*Good Natur'd Man*, 2). Young Honeywood is a friend of the Croakers, who want to use his influence to persuade their son, Leontine, to marry their ward Miss Richland (who is in love with Young Honeywood). Mr Croaker is a miserable man beset by anxieties about the state of the world, while his wife indulges in the new fashionable entertainments of the town. Leontine has been sent to France to bring back his sister who has been living there since childhood, but instead he returns with a woman he has met there and fallen for, Olivia, who masquerades as his grown-up sister. His intention is to comply with his father's plans for him to marry Miss Richland on the assumption that she will refuse him because she loves Young Honeywood. Goldsmith was himself a frequenter of masquerades and named social gatherings at his chambers 'little Cornelys' after the impresario of Carlisle House, Teresa Cornelys (Prior, *Life*, 2:511).[3] Masquerades thrived on the drama of recognition and misrecognition entailed in the formulaic declaration 'I know you.' In *The Good Natur'd Man* the protagonists do not even 'know' their own closest relatives, Sir William Honeywood and his nephew being mutually unrecognizable while Olivia can masquerade as a daughter and a sister. The comedy thus represents a world in which the British 'family' is distended, at risk of not knowing itself.

Goldsmith explores the limits of this distended society in two dramatic-ally innovative episodes in *The Good Natur'd Man*. The first is the bailiff scene at the beginning of Act 3, when Young Honeywood is visited by a 'Bailiff' and his 'Follower'. The Bailiff, who identifies himself as Mr

Twitch, introduces the Follower to Young Honeywood as 'little Flanigan, with a wife and four children' (*Good Natur'd Man*, 32). Honeywood persuades the bailiffs to masquerade as his servants until he can afford to pay off his debts, a performance which becomes more urgent when Miss Richland arrives. Young Honeywood and Miss Richland attempt to conduct polite conversation with the bailiffs, which is sabotaged when the 'Follower', who has hitherto been mute, joins in, initially by commenting 'Very good circuit weather in the country', law being his business, before erupting into an incoherent rant against the French: 'Damn the French, the parle vous, and all that belongs to them' (*Good Natur'd Man*, 34, 35).

While the Bailiff is listed in the dramatis personae of the first edition of the play, there is no mention of the 'Follower' or Flanigan, a name that suggests Irish origins (see Chapter 9, 'Irish London'). Flanigan's subversion of the polite decorum of genteel comedy evokes rumbustious speech beyond the theatre, the tension surrounding the forthcoming General Election and, previously, the Seven Years' War. Flanigan is a sign of Goldsmith's daring in incorporating what Watts calls 'new kinds of subjects', especially the class and ethnic subjects that had become more visible in the 1760s. Polite conversation about taste and criticism is in comic tension with insurgent energies coming from below to the extent that the Bailiff is not given a proper name in the cast list and the Follower/ Flanigan is not even mentioned there. These omissions may have been because first-night audiences did not find this scene to be very funny. There were hissing objections to the bailiffs as too 'low' and coarse, to the extent that the success of the comedy, and Goldsmith's venture as a dramatic author, were seriously threatened. The bailiff scene was excised from later performances, though Goldsmith kept it in the published edition that appeared on 5 February 1768. It was not restored in performance until 1773, in the light of the success of *She Stoops to Conquer*.

The second test of the boundaries of comedy in *The Good Natur'd Man* occurs when Olivia, who is planning to elope to Scotland with Leontine and is too nervous to write to him, delegates the task to her servant Garnet. Croaker accidentally intercepts the badly spelt letter and misinterprets it as 'incendiary', in line with his anxiety about 'damn'd jesuitical pestilential' plots (*Good Natur'd Man*, 51, 65). The use of anonymous, usually threatening letters was a widespread form of social protest, E. P. Thompson describing them as 'the *only* literate expression of the "inarticulate" that has survived'.[4] Their significance as articulating voices from below is highlighted by Croaker's seizing of an innocent 'post-boy' – a post-boy was a letter and a newspaper carrier – as the letter's author: 'Hold him fast, the dog; he has the gallows in his face. Come, you dog, confess! confess all, and hang yourself' (*Good Natur'd Man*, 64). Croaker's paranoia is ludicrous but Goldsmith is also seriously engaging with a world beyond genteel comedy in which communication is more complicated and its lower-class inter-mediaries increasingly visible as subjects in their own right.

Though it had a respectable run of ten nights, earning Goldsmith £400 from author benefit nights and £50 for the copyright of the text, *The Good Natur'd Man* was not a runaway success, nor did it become part of the dramatic canon. It was more than five years until Goldsmith made another attempt as a dramatist, partly because the manager of Covent Garden, George Colman, delayed in putting his new comedy into production. *She Stoops to Conquer* was staged late in the season on 15 March 1773. Some of the actors who played in *The Good Natur'd Man* also appeared in *She Stoops to Conquer*. Edward (Ned) Shuter, who was Croaker, was the first Hardcastle, while Mrs Hardcastle was played by a Covent Garden stalwart, Jane Green, who had performed as Olivia's servant Garnet in *The Good Natur'd Man*. Kate Hardcastle, the heroine of *She Stoops to Conquer*, was played by Mary Bulkeley, the first Miss Richland. The role of Tony Lumpkin, Mrs Hardcastle's son by her first marriage, was taken by John Quick, who had played the post-boy nearly throttled by Croaker in *The Good Natur'd Man*. Lumpkin was Quick's breakout role, making him a comic star for decades. He was reputed to be George III's favourite actor. Tony Lumpkin is socially anomalous, having rights to the wealth and status of a country family while consorting with the 'shabby fellows' of the local tavern and his 'amour' Bet Bouncer. He has not lost his social status so much as he is carelessly forging his own flexible class identity, making him a fascinating figure to Georgian audiences of all ranks. Later in the twentieth century he was played by actor-singer Tommy Steele in 1960 and the 1970s heartthrob David Essex in 1993, indicating the character's enduring cross-class, even 'pop' appeal (see Chapter 35, 'Afterlives 2: Theatre').

While the locale of Goldsmith's first comedy is London, with reference also to France and Italy, *She Stoops to Conquer* is set somewhere in the country, specifically the '*old-fashioned*' house of the Hardcastles (*Stoops*, 1). After two visiting London gentlemen, Marlow and Hastings, insult Tony Lumpkin, he tricks them into thinking that their destination, Hardcastle's house, is an inn. A marriage between Marlow and Kate Hardcastle has been arranged by their parents but Marlow is extremely diffident before polite women, partly because his education has been confined to the male homosocial world of university and the milieu he is part of in London (see Chapter 12, 'Marriage'). He is more comfortable with servants and prostitutes than he is with women of his own class, Hastings commenting, 'If you could but say half the fine things to them that I have heard you lavish upon the bar-maid of an inn, or even a college bed maker–' (*Stoops*, 21).

Both Marlow and Hastings are linked in the play with the 'macaroni' phenomenon, the fashion in the 1760s and 1770s for elaborate clothing for men, high hairstyles, and heels, associated with male members of the elite who spent big and lived high on the Italian Grand Tour – to whom the term 'macaroni' was applied. When Marlow realizes his mistake in taking the Hardcastle house for an inn he bemoans the fact that he will be notorious in 'town' as the stupid 'Dullissimo Maccaroni', a reference to the successful series of caricatures of macaronis marketed by Matthew and Mary Darly (*Stoops*, 82). 'Macaroni' was shorthand for a concern in the 1770s about effeminized masculinity and its risk to a greatly expanded and less secure British empire that would be tested further in the conflict with the American colonies just two years after *She Stoops* was first performed. The adoption by men of fashionable style and behaviour associated with women was paralleled by an increasing visibility for women in the sphere of fashionable sociability – masquerades held in Cornelys's Carlisle House and the Pantheon (opened in 1772), entertainments at home known as routs, attendance at auctions, and the takeover of spaces previously the preserve of men in the form of elite gambling clubs. When he is seducing Kate Hardcastle, in her guise as the inn barmaid, Marlow boasts that he is well known 'at the Ladies Club in town', a reference to a club or association for both women and men also known as the 'Female Coterie' set up in 1770 and the object of much commentary in newspapers, journals, and the satirical prints (*Stoops*, 61).

Marlow may not be a fully fledged macaroni, only boasting of being one to a woman he thinks is his inferior, but the macaroni phenomenon serves to contextualize the difficulty he has in dealing with women of his own class. His encounter with Kate Hardcastle as herself in Act Two inverts the conventions of courtship and hierarchies of gender as he finds himself unable to speak or even look at her, forcing her to take charge of the conversation and to coach him in the clichés he should be using – 'You were observing, Sir, that in this age of hypocrisy' [getting desperate] 'something about hypocrisy, Sir' (*Stoops*, 36). Macaroni manners, Goldsmith suggests, were distorting 'normal' life to the extent that gentlemen such as Marlow, who in the comic tradition were usually carefree rakes, were incapable of playing their proper part. They were too like the women who were in effect feeding them their lines.

The rise of fashionable sociability in the 1760s and 1770s represented a challenge to the pre-eminence and cultural and social prestige of the London theatre. Alternative entertainments and spaces such as the masquerade and the Pantheon were competing for audiences, especially polite ones, by offering novel forms of theatricality and arenas of display. The theatre responded by critiquing and satirizing these trends in plays such as *The Clandestine Marriage* (1766) by Garrick and Colman, Colman's own *The Man of Business* (1774), Garrick's *Bon Ton* (1775), and *The School for Scandal* (1777) by Richard Brinsley Sheridan. Fashionable sociability in these plays is associated with the tastes of older women such as Mrs Croaker in *The Good Natur'd Man* and Mrs Hardcastle in *She Stoops*, who were initially played by the same actress, Jane Green. Mrs Hardcastle is a dedicated follower of the London fashions who yearns to visit the Pantheon and adapts her 'head' – that is, her hairstyle – from a 'print in the Ladies Memorandum-book for last year' (i.e. she is desperately behind the times: *Stoops*, 39). Goldsmith draws attention to how, like the Darly Macaroni prints, metropolitan fashion was being commodified for the country as a whole, thereby orienting his comedy as another form of mediation by which such fashion could be objectified and scrutinized. Covent Garden theatre was as much a part of the metropolitan world as the Pantheon and the Ladies Coterie but for the time of performance it could pretend not to be, thereby asserting its value as a theatre for and of the British nation.

The fate of Mrs Hardcastle is relevant in this respect. The Hardcastles are an unusual family insofar that for Mr and Mrs Hardcastle this is a second marriage and the children are half-siblings (if Kate is Mrs Hardcastle's daughter by blood). Mrs Hardcastle desires Tony Lumpkin, still in his minority, to marry Kate's friend Constance Neville, of whose fortune Mrs Hardcastle has 'sole management', meaning that she has unusual authority for a married woman. Tony Lumpkin tricks his mother into thinking that she has successfully escaped with Miss Neville in order to thwart a marriage with Hastings and keep Miss Neville for Tony, who would rather marry Bet Bouncer. Tony bamboozles his mother into thinking that she has endured a rough journey across country when she has never left the garden of the Hardcastle house. At one level Mrs Hardcastle's 'journey' across what she thinks are bandit-ridden commons populated by gibbets satirizes the London in-crowd's view of the country beyond Westminster. On another level, however, like Flanigan and the post-boy, this episode introduces into the comedy another social reality, the darker side of the landscape, even if we know that this 'place' is a fiction, like indeed the play we are watching. When Mr Hardcastle interrupts Lumpkin's trick, Tony pretends to his mother that her husband is a highwayman, at which Mrs Hardcastle panics into misrecognition, causing her husband to declare: 'I believe the woman's out of her senses. What, Dorothy, don't you know *me?*'. The episode is a temporary break-down of the most familiar of social relations (*Stoops*, 105).

The Hardcastles' knowledge of each other is restored, of course, and the multiple marriage plots are successfully resolved. *She Stoops to Conquer* was a hit both in the theatre and as a book of the play. It was customary for the text of plays to be produced very quickly after the first performance, Newbery publishing an edition on 25 March, ten days after the premiere. The orange-women in Covent Garden theatre were unable to keep up with the demand, while in Ireland, where play texts were normally pirated, *She Stoops to Conquer* appeared in the booksellers before it was even performed. The *Belfast News Letter* advertised the book of the play on 16 April 1773 but it was not staged in the city until 17 September of the same year.[5] *She Stoops to Conquer* continues to be performed in theatres across the world and is read and studied as part of the canon of dramatic literature, like another comedy of the 1770s, Sheridan's *The School for Scandal*. The topical contexts of both plays, their references to Carlisle House, the Pantheon, macaronis, and high hair, have lost their meaning for twenty-first-century audiences, but what remains is the fact that both plays rely on the humili-ation of women – Lady Teazle's exposure in the famous screen scene of *The School for Scandal* and Mrs Hardcastle being dragged through the mud and nearly losing her senses. In Sheridan's play the last word is given to a penitent Lady Teazle who speaks the epilogue whereas Mrs Hardcastle's last words are a grumpy or shattered acknowledgement of her 'undutiful offspring', Tony (*Stoops*, 114). The epilogue to *She Stoops* was given by Tony Lumpkin not, as would have been customary, Mary Bulkeley, who had played Kate. Lumpkin announces the fact that he is going to 'take the town' in company with Bet Bouncer, avoiding plays as 'they say it a'n't polite' in favour of Sadler's Wells and the opera. For Tony, cultural distinctions are irrelevant – '*We know what's damn'd genteel, as well as they*' (*Stoops*, Epilogue). Played by John Quick, who had been the post-boy of *The Good Natur'd Man*, Tony Lumpkin signifies a new kind of subject, someone who in class terms is unconscious of hierarchies, who doesn't give a 'damn'. He is the audience's and the King's darling: he is the future.

Notes

1. 'DOUGLAS; a Tragedy', *Monthly Review*, 16 (1757); 426–39; 'Art. IX. The Orphan of China', *Critical Review*, 7 (1759), 434–40; 'An Essay on the Theatre', *Westminster Magazine*, 1 (1773), 4–6.
2. Carol Watts, *The Cultural Work of Empire: The Seven Years' War and the Imagining of the Shandean State* (Edinburgh University Press, 2007), 11, 12.
3. At the behest of Cornelys, Goldsmith wrote 'Threnodia Augustalis' to commemorate the death in February 1772 of Augusta, Princess Dowager and mother of George III, performed at Carlisle House with music by Mattia Vento. Goldsmith also wrote an oratorio, *The Captivity* (1764). See Mollie Sands, 'Oliver Goldsmith and Music', *Music & Letters*, 32.2 (1951), 147–53.
4. E. P. Thompson, 'The Crime of Anonymity' in *Albion's Fatal Tree: Crime and Society in Eighteenth-Century England*, ed. Douglas Hay et al. (New York: Pantheon Books, 1975), 378–431 (420).
5. *Belfast News Letter*, 16 April 1773, 17 September 1773.

CHAPTER 21

Pastoral Poetry

Dustin Griffin

For much of the nineteenth and twentieth centuries, *The Deserted Village* (1770) was read as an emotionally charged semi-autobiographical poem in which sentiment softens the description of the vanished Auburn and strong feeling colours the bold analysis of the causes of the village's disappearance. But more than fifty years ago a new generation of critics saw a carefully controlled rhetorical performance, suggesting in passing that the poem was not an autobiographical utterance, but was generically a pastoral: a 'historical pastoral', or a 'redefinition' or 'renewal' of pastoral elegy.[1] These suggestions, however, were not developed. Then came what is still the most influential reading of *The Deserted Village*, Raymond Williams's *The Country and the City* (1973), which directed attention to 'the real social pressures of the time'.[2] Over the next quarter century other generic frames were suggested: anti-pastoral (the idyllic village is gone),[3] georgic (the poem deals more with agricultural labour than leisurely herding), an inverted country-house poem (the abandoned village is now the site of a rich man's 'seat', 'park', and 'lake'), a topographical poem (describing a particular place), and a retirement poem (the speaker longs to 'retire' to Auburn).[4] But attention to the thematic content of the poem obscured sustained attention to its genre. Critics filled in the picture of the 'real' countryside, noticing that Goldsmith seems more disturbed by the building of country estates than by the rise of small industry and the changes wrought by agricultural 'improvement'. Others focused on Goldsmith's distress over emigration, trade, and empire.[5] In the course of the last generation a new wave of self-styled 'ecocritics' has focused on Goldsmith's reflections on the relationship between human beings and the natural environment (see Chapter 36, 'Afterlives 3: Poetry').[6] Little critical attention is now paid to the poem's *form*.

It is timely, then, to develop the brief suggestions from the 1960s about *The Deserted Village* as 'pastoral' into a full consideration of the role played in shaping the poem by the conventions of pastoral poetry, as founded by

Theocritus and Virgil and reinterpreted by English pastoral poets from Milton to William Shenstone. This will involve teasing out both textual and subtextual connections between Goldsmith's poem and the pastoral poems he knew.

Pastoral as Goldsmith's model has been largely disregarded because most literary historians still commonly assume that the last notable pastorals were published by Pope in 1709, and that pastoral poetry thereafter declined, or was turned into a mock form by Gay and Swift. In retrospect, we can see that the old genre system was breaking down. But that was not yet clear in 1750, when Goldsmith began his literary career and was looking about for models. (Within a generation Wordsworth was to find new uses for pastoral and pastoralism.)

Other literary historians citing Samuel Johnson's famous remark about Milton's *Lycidas* – 'Its form is that of a pastoral, easy, vulgar, and therefore disgusting . . . In this poem there is no nature, for there is no truth' – hastily assume that by 1779, when Johnson wrote, no good critic or poet could take pastoral seriously. They overlook Johnson's serious consideration of pastoral poetry in his earlier essays: 'There is scarcely any species of poetry that has allured more readers or excited more writers than the pastoral' (*Rambler* 36).[7] Virgil provides a 'distinct and exact idea of this kind of writing' (37). And in *Adventurer* 92 Johnson comments on Virgil's *Eclogues*, particularly admiring the first of them, in which Meliboeus, forced to leave his land, compares his fate with that of Thyrsis, who luckily remains in place: 'The complaint of the shepherd, who saw his old companion at ease in the shade, while himself was driving his little flock he knew not whither, is such as . . . misery always utters at the sight of prosperity.'[8] And when Johnson notes that the first eclogue was produced by an event 'that really happened' – i.e., the seizure of farms by Augustus to award his veteran soldiers – he finds that pastoral poems are not always 'fictions' but can be based on 'truth', a hint that Goldsmith may well have seized.[9] When Johnson wrote that 'Whatsoever . . . may . . . happen in the country, may afford a subject for a pastoral poet', Goldsmith perhaps saw an opening – to write a pastoral poem about the end of a pastoral village.

In the minds of Goldsmith's fellow poets, pastoral, despite Johnson's strictures, still seemed to be a viable literary form. Numerous new pastorals were published between 1740 and 1770, including the *Persian Eclogues* of William Collins (1742), Thomas Warton's *Five Pastoral Eclogues* (1745), Shenstone's 'Pastoral Ballad' (1743) and very popular *School-Mistress* (1742), and John Langhorne's 'Genius and Valour: A Scotch Pastoral' (1763). Goldsmith would have known others, including Thomas Parnell's

'Health; an Eclogue', in the 1747 edition of Parnell's *Works*, Charlotte
Lennox's *Philander, a Dramatic Pastoral* (1758), Churchill's 'Scots Pastoral'
(1763), and Colley Cibber's *Pastoral Farce* (1767), as well as poems by
Stephen Duck, Thomas Blacklock, and James Woodhouse.[10]

Furthermore, Virgil's pastorals were published repeatedly, at least
thirty-five times between 1700 and 1770. Goldsmith had first-hand know-
ledge of Virgil's Latin and Theocritus's Greek, having studied Greek and
Latin poetry at Trinity College (see Chapter 6, 'Universities').[11] In an
essay in the *Bee* he cites Virgil's second eclogue. And Virgil continued to
be translated into English. Dryden's well-known translation reached
a seventh edition in 1748. A new translation by Joseph Warton appeared
in 1753, with a second edition in 1763. The 1731 blank-verse translations of
Joseph Trapp, Professor of Poetry at Oxford, appeared in a fourth edition
in 1755. Dryden's well-known translations appeared again in 1763 and
1769 (see *Bee*, 179).

Goldsmith's *Beauties of English Poesy* (1767), a compilation of what he
and his publisher regarded as the best English poems of various kinds,
makes clear that for Goldsmith the traditional genre system was still in
place and provided an idea of what he regarded as appropriate for the
pastoral 'kind'. Included are Milton's 'L'Allegro' and 'Il Penseroso' and
poems written as late as the 1740s, among them pastorals by Gay, Collins,
and John Byrom, along with Shenstone's *School-Mistress*. In his notes
Goldsmith prefers that a modern poet not use 'obsolete antiquity'. As he
says, 'I dislike the imitations of our old English poets in general,' though he
puts up with the Spenserian language in Gay and Shenstone. He remarks
that Gay 'has hit the true spirit of pastoral poetry', 'rustic pleasantry, which
should ever distinguish this species of composition', though there is little
'pleasantry' in *The Deserted Village*, where the prevailing mood is
melancholic.[12] In his *Enquiry into the Present State of Polite Learning*, he
mocks 'modern Arcadians' who continue to write about nymphs and
swains (*Enquiry*, 50), and *The Citizen of the World* laughs at the ossified
conventions of pastoral elegy, in which two shepherds retire to sing in
alternate verse about the death of a third: 'I am quite unaffected in all this
distress: the whole is liquid laudanum to my spirits' (*Citizen*, 2:163).
Goldsmith elsewhere calls for 'local' images in pastoral, suggesting that
pastoral should be tied to particular places.

He modestly commends the 'simplicity' of Thomson's 'Palemon and
Lavinia' (from 'Autumn' in *The Seasons*) and the 'natural simplicity' of
Shenstone. His portraits of the 'village preacher' and 'village master' in
The Deserted Village (8–12) derive from Shenstone's portrait of 'the

School-mistress'. What Goldsmith means by 'simplicity' – a slippery eighteenth-century critical term[13] – is not made explicit, but he appears to adopt the view of Thomas Purney's *Full Inquiry into the True Nature of Pastoral* (1717), and follows Gay and others in associating it with the plain and artless manner of Theocritus.[14] And although Gay 'more resembles Theocritus than any English pastoral writer', even Gay makes too much use of 'antiquated expressions', and Goldsmith wishes that he had preserved the 'simplicity' of Theocritus without them.

Although intimately familiar with classical and English pastoral poems, with pastoral's generic requirements, and with the genre system that sustained them, Goldsmith himself wrote no poem that he called a 'pastoral' or an 'eclogue'. (By contrast, in his small poetic corpus are found poems he calls 'epitaph', 'sonnet', 'elegy', 'ode', 'song', 'epitaph', and 'poetical epistle', and his *Traveller* is recognizably a 'prospect poem'; see Chapter 22, Prospect Poetry'). But in *The Deserted Village*, which he simply calls 'a long poem', he in effect remembers Virgil and the roots of English pastoral. He sets out not to write a 'pastoral' himself, but to adapt the well-established conventions of this ancient literary form to shape an observer's response to a contemporary rural scene in which shepherds have virtually disappeared. Although there are various traces in the poem of Goldsmith's wide reading in eighteenth-century English verse and prose, including Gray's *Elegy Written in a Country Churchyard*, the several pastoral notes are telling.

The first pastoral note to strike the reader of *The Deserted Village* is probably Goldsmith's diction. He deploys the traditional pastoral language of *bowers, copse, field, floods, gale, grove, lay, lawns, meadow, murmuring, plain, rill, rustic, shade, springs, streams, swain, sylvan, vale, verdant*, and *woods* – words found in *Lycidas*, in Pope's *Pastorals*, and throughout the poems of dozens of minor eighteenth-century pastoralists – to describe the remembered Auburn.

The speaker, a former denizen of Auburn, now a 'deserted' village, is here an urban sophisticate and a poet who has returned to the scene of his youth. This enables Goldsmith to finesse the issue of the proper language for a pastoral poem. As a man who has travelled 'this world of care', Goldsmith's poet speaks appropriately, in language plain, measured, sober, sometimes delicate and plaintive, but not rustic. His diction includes Latinate polysyllabic terms – *desolation, accumulates, counterfeited, insidious, participate, devastation* – that would sound foreign in a countryman's mouth but appropriate in his own. In this respect Goldsmith proceeds on a principle Johnson had laid down in *Rambler*

37, that pastoral 'admits of all ranks of persons, because persons of all ranks inhabit the country. It excludes not ... any elevation or delicacy of sentiment'. Because pastoral, says Johnson, is properly a 'representation of rural nature', it may exhibit 'the ideas and sentiments of those, whoever they are, to whom the country affords pleasure', or, as Johnson acknowledges elsewhere, affords either 'sorrow' or 'joy'. In *The Deserted Village*, the joy consists of nostalgic remembrance of the past, the sorrow of regret at the desolation of the present. Making his speaker an urban refugee also enables Goldsmith to broaden his range of reference. Johnson had insisted that 'those ideas only are improper [in pastoral] which, not owing their original to rural objects, are not pastoral'. Goldsmith evades Johnson's objection by making his speaker plausibly acquainted with great cities as well as country villages. He also evades Johnson's objection to the intrusion of satire in pastoral – 'complaints of errors in the church and corruptions in the government' of the kind found in Spenser and Milton – by making clear that his worldly poet is acquainted with the ruinous effects of 'luxury' and 'improvement' on the rural scene.

Virgil's *Eclogues* in effect provide a model for Goldsmith's use of a first-person speaker. As Trapp notes in his 'Introductory Remarks', Virgil in Eclogue I 'introduces *himself* under the Person of *Tityrus*'. As Quintana was the first to notice, Virgil also provides a model for the devastation that Goldsmith laments: just as Meliboeus has been dispossessed of his land and must go into exile, so Goldsmith's peasants are forced to leave their village.[15]

Goldsmith's villagers emigrate to 'distant Climes', as do Virgil's (in the translations by Trapp and Warton),[16] 'equinoctial fervours' and 'polar world' (*Deserted Village*, 19, 23) that echo the 'scorching or the freezing zone' in Dryden's translation. The contrast in Virgil between what Trapp calls the 'happy Condition of *Tityrus* and the quite contrary one of *Meliboeus*' is transformed by Goldsmith into the contrast between the Auburn of the poet's youth and the Auburn of the present day. When Virgil (in Trapp's translation) has Meliboeus imagine that one day he might 'see / After long Absence ... / My country's Coasts ... / See to what Extremes / Our wretched Natives are reduc'd', he in effect provides a model for the return of Goldsmith's poet to Auburn to behold the 'wretched Matron' (*Deserted Village*, 8) and the village's devastation.

Among modern pastoralists Goldsmith seems to draw most on Milton, not only on *Lycidas*, but also on 'L'Allegro' and 'Il Penseroso' – Goldsmith thought 'the imagination shewn in them is correct and strong'.[17] Building *The Deserted Village* around the contrast between past and present,

Goldsmith could have found in 'L'Allegro' a model for the device of the thoughtful urbanite, wandering alone on an excursion from the city, who takes note of rural charms. But Goldsmith's solitary wanderer does not actually see rural 'charms': he only remembers them from his youth. In 'Il Penseroso' Goldsmith could have found a sober and pensive observer, contemplating the rural scene and prompted by it to philosophical reflection.

In *Lycidas* too Goldsmith could have found a model for a poem comparing a rich rural past and a bleak rural present. Milton's poet remembers when, 'Under the opening eye-lids of the morn', he and his fellow shepherd 'drove a-field', then battened 'our flocks', all the while listening to 'the rural ditties'. What has intervened is the death of Lycidas: 'But O the heavy change now thou art gone!' Goldsmith's similarly laments a loss, not of a shepherd but of an entire village. And like Milton's poem, Goldsmith's engages in topical protest that is linked to the pastoral world.

How to end his long poem seems to have presented Goldsmith with some difficulties. He opts for a Virgilian note. Just as Virgil's Meliboeus at the end of the first eclogue prepares to leave his fields and his pastoral songs – 'carmina ulla canam' (l. 77, 'No more songs shall I sing') – Goldsmith's poet bids farewell to Poetry: 'And thou, sweet Poetry, thou loveliest maid, / . . . Thou guide . . ., / Thou nurse of every virtue, fare thee well' (*Deserted Village*, 22).

Virgil's poem ends with the invitation from Tityrus to spend a final night before he leaves. For his conclusion Goldsmith appears to have looked elsewhere, to the typical resolution of pastoral elegy established in Theocritus's first idyll and Virgil's fifth eclogue, when the death of Daphnis is lamented but, in a sudden reversal, mourning yields to consolation and celebration, as Daphnis has become a god. Goldsmith too ends his poem on a reassuring note. He laments the 'death' of Auburn and the exile of Poetry itself, but at the close imagines that the 'voice' of poetry will survive: 'Still let thy voice prevailing over time, / Redress the rigours of the inclement clime; / Aid slighted truth', and 'teach erring man . . . / . . . that states of native strength possesst, / Tho' very poor, may still be very blest' (*Deserted Village*, 23) His elegiac consolation does not depend as in classical pastoral on deification or as in Christian pastoral on resurrection but on a kind of sturdy self-reliant endurance.

In what way the exiled peasantry may ultimately be 'blest' is left vague. (Apparently not in the same way Milton's Lycidas dwells now 'in the blest kingdoms'). And what can it mean to 'prevail' over time? Perhaps to resist what Shakespeare called time's 'wrackful siege'. The conclusion, supplied by Johnson, makes an even stronger claim. His four lines, based on hints earlier in the poem about the 'decay' of 'trade's proud empire', extend the lesson that Poetry teaches – that 'self-dependent power' can not only 'prevail' over Time but 'defy' it (an echo of two pastoral poets), perhaps hinting at a transformed version of the permanence that pastoral elegy promises.[18]

Notes

1. Ricardo Quintana, *Oliver Goldsmith: A Georgian Study* (New York: Macmillan, 1967), 135; Earl Miner, 'The Making of *The Deserted Village*', *Huntington Library Quarterly*, 22.2 (1959), 125–41; Roger Lonsdale, *The Poems of Gray, Collins, and Goldsmith* (London: Longman, 1969), 673.

2. Raymond Williams, *The Country and the City* (New York: Oxford University Press, 1973), 79.

3. John Barrell and John Bull, eds., *The Penguin Book of English Pastoral Verse* (London: Penguin, 1974), 7–8.

4. Leo Storm, 'Literary Convention in Goldsmith's *Deserted Village*', *Huntington Library Quarterly*, 33.3 (1970), 243–56.

5. Stuart Curran, 'The Pastoral', in *Poetic Form and British Romanticism* (Oxford University Press, 1986); Suvir Kaul, *Poems of Nation, Anthems of Empire* (Charlottesville: University of Virginia Press, 2000); Samuel Baker, 'Britannia's Pastorals', in *Written on the Water: British Romanticism and the Maritime Empire of Culture* (Charlottesville: University of Virginia Press, 2009), 115–52.

6. Terry Gifford, 'Pastoral, Anti-pastoral, post-Pastoral', in *The Cambridge Companion to Literature and the Environment*, ed. Louise Westling (Cambridge University Press, 2013), 17–30; and *Pastoral* (Abingdon: Routledge, 2nd ed., 2019), especially 201–7.

7. Samuel Johnson, *The Rambler 36: The Works of Samuel Johnson*, ed. W. J. Bate and Albrecht Strauss (New Haven, CT: Yale University Press, 1968), 3:203.

8. Samuel Johnson, *The Adventurer 92: The Works of Samuel Johnson*, ed. John M. Bullitt, W. J. Bate, and L. F. Powell (New Haven, CT: Yale University Press, 1963), 2:422.

9. Goldsmith's *Roman History* (London, 1769) reports that Virgil successfully 'begged permission to retain his patrimonial farm' (2:64).

10. In *The Life of Thomas Parnell* (London, 1770), Goldsmith quotes a letter from Pope, remarking that the 'eclogue on health' is one of 'the most beautiful things I ever read' (19).

11. Brian Arkins, 'All You Need to Know: Greek and Roman Themes in Goldsmith', *Études Irlandaises*, 16.2 (1990), 27–32.

12. Goldsmith, *The Beauties of English Poesy*, 2 vols. (London, 1767), 1:133, 69, 133.

13. See Raymond Dexter Havens, 'Simplicity: A Changing Concept', *Journal of the History of Ideas*, 14 (1953), 3–32.

14. See Gay's 'Proem' to *The Shepherd's Week* (1714), and Thomas Purney's *Pastorals: After the Simple Manner of Theocritus* (1717).

15. Quintana, *Oliver Goldsmith*, 132–4.

16. *The Works of Virgil: Translated into English Blank Verse* (1731), line 82, 1:13. In the 1753 edition Trapp revised 'Climes' to 'Shores' (l. 82); Joseph Warton, *The Works of Virgil* (1753), 1:59.

17. Goldsmith, *Beauties*, 1:39.

18. Compare Allan Ramsay's *Gentle Shepherd* (1735), 'my Love shall Time defy' (31) and Shenstone's 'Elegy II', 'your blooming praise shall time defy', *Works* (1764), 1:14.

CHAPTER 22

Prospect Poetry

Katherine Turner

This chapter will situate Oliver Goldsmith's poem *The Traveller, or A Prospect of Society* (1764) at the confluence of various literary genres and show how its hybridity contributes to its novelty. The poem's dyadic title reflects its melding of the so-called prospect poem, usually focused on a British locale, with the genre of the epistle (whether in prose or verse) from abroad. The pan-European scope of the poem's sociopolitical commentary also reflects Goldsmith's work in other genres while he was composing the poem and further enlarges its prospects. Finally, the poem's projection of a complex and melancholy textual persona opens up new vistas for poetic identity at this moment in literary history.

The 'prospect' or 'loco-descriptive' or 'topographical' tradition in English poetry derives from Virgilian pastoral and georgic. It characteristically entwines description of a rural place with moralized reflections upon historical, social, and political issues, usually with a politically conservative tone.[1] The tradition begins with Sir John Denham's Royalist poem *Cooper's Hill* in 1642, which opens with a self-deprecating comparison between Parnassus and Cooper's Hill (in Egham, Surrey – just west of London), but gathers in confidence as the poem describes historical sites within the Thames valley. The speaker surveys Windsor, London, Chertsey Abbey, and Runnymede, and meditates in dignified couplets upon British history, celebrating periods of tranquil harmony between monarchs and subjects and lamenting the various eruptions of 'lawless power' (l. 332) which have threatened the natural order.[2]

Alexander Pope's *Windsor-Forest* (1713) is the most brilliant of Denham's successors. It contrasts various turbulent periods in British history with the present glories brought about by the Peace of Utrecht under Queen Anne – 'rich Industry sits smiling on the Plains, / And Peace and Plenty tell, a Stuart reigns' (ll. 41–2). Pope signals his debt to Denham at various points – 'On Cooper's Hill eternal Wreaths shall grow, / While lasts the Mountain, or while Thames shall flow' (ll. 265–6) – but is also more complex and ambitious. He embeds his own life within the landscape (he grew up near Windsor) and echoes Virgil's *Georgics* (and his own earlier poem 'Spring') in the poem's closing lines, thus signalling his claim to the role of national poet in this new Augustan age: 'Enough for me, that to the listning Swains / First in these Fields I sung the Sylvan Strains' (ll. 433–4).[3]

Other prospect poems are more concerned with nature and philosophy. James Thomson's great four-book poem *The Seasons* (1726–40) is the most ambitious example. The poem is global in its visionary range, describing in Miltonic blank verse the seasonal wonders of divinely ordered nature. It may in fact be too vast to qualify as a 'prospect poem' in the terms explored here. However, it clearly influenced Goldsmith; his scope in *The Traveller* is similarly ambitious, as he looks from the Alps 'downward where an hundred realms appear', and he uses the seasons (as well as geographical movement) to structure his poem. The Swiss are associated with winter, the Italians with luxurious summer, the French with sprightly spring, and the Dutch with autumnal ideas such as 'treasure, wealth, gain', even as the poem complains that their good husbandry has been corrupted by greed.[4]

Similarly stretching the boundaries of 'prospect poetry' into more philosophical territory is Samuel Johnson's *The Vanity of Human Wishes* (1749), which opens 'Let observation with extensive view, / Survey mankind, from China to Peru.' The universalizing mode of Johnson's poem clearly influenced Goldsmith, and of course Johnson himself supplied most of the final paragraph of *The Traveller*. The more philosophical passages within *The Traveller*, especially the idea that 'Though patriots flatter, still shall wisdom find / An equal portion dealt to all mankind' (ll. 77–8), also recall Pope's *Essay on Man* (1733–4), the most generalized prospect poem of its age, which declares its intention to 'Expatiate free o'er all this scene of Man; / A mighty maze! But not without a plan' (ll. 5–6).

Goldsmith's poem departs strikingly from the prospect tradition in placing its observing 'I' abroad as a wanderer or exile. Here, *The Traveller* draws upon the emerging genre of the verse epistle from abroad, of which Joseph Addison's *Letter from Italy, to the Right Honourable Charles Lord Halifax* (1703) is the earliest and most influential example. We know that Goldsmith admired Addison's work, since he had written in *The Beauties of English Poesy* that it contained 'a strain of political thinking that was, at that time, new in our poetry'.[5] Most such epistles (for instance, Lord Lyttelton's 1730 'Epistle to Mr Pope' and George Keate's 1755 *Ancient and Modern Rome*) follow Addison in lamenting over 'the proud Ruins of immortal Rome' (Keate, l. 11) and drawing political comparisons between ancient Rome and modern Britain.[6] Addison's poem celebrates Liberty as 'thou Goddess heavenly bright' (l. 119) whom '*Britannia*'s Isle adores' (l. 127). Finding in the ruins of Rome an emblem of Liberty betrayed by tyranny and luxury, in a move reminiscent of Pope's depiction of Windsor Forest as the place from which peace and prosperity will radiate across the globe, Addison proclaims that Britain, unlike Rome, will maintain her imperial role:

> 'Tis Britain's care to watch o'er Europe's fate,
> And hold in balance each contending state,
> To threaten bold presumptuous kings with war,
> And answer her afflicted neighbours' pray'r.   (ll. 145–8)

Another notable example of the European verse epistle is John Dyer's *The Ruins of Rome* (1740), written as a companion poem to his own *Grongar Hill* (1726), an endearingly local prospect poem which describes an obscure Welsh landscape of rivers, mountains, and ruined 'ancient towers' (l. 71). Unlike Denham's *Cooper's Hill*, *Grongar Hill* eschews political moralizing in favour of landscape description, although it does celebrate rural virtues as opposed to 'the proud and mighty' (l. 91), a sentiment which likely influenced Gray's famous *Elegy Written in a Country Churchyard* (1751). *The Ruins of Rome* opens by declaring 'Enough of Grongar' (l. 1) and bidding the Muse 'soar a loftier flight; / Lo the resistless theme, imperial Rome!' (ll. 14–15).[7]

The poem then describes in vivid detail real walks around the sites of ancient Rome, some in ruins, others still splendid. There is no reference to the modern city beyond the occasion mention of a 'pilgrim' (line 38) or 'hoary monk' (line 337). This resolute focus on 'classic ground' had also characterized Addison's *A Letter from Italy* (1703), which views '*Virgil's Italy*' (line 54; italics in original) through the lens of ancient history, looking for 'streams immortaliz'd in song' (line 32), but is otherwise uninterested in landscape. Dyer's poem reflects upon Roman greatness and hopes that Britain may attain similar creative heights while avoiding the tyranny and luxury which Rome's ruins now symbolize: 'O Britons, O my countrymen, beware, / Gird, gird your hearts; the Romans once were free, / Were brave, were virtuous' (lines 510–12).

Aside from such works, there are surprisingly few eighteenth-century poems about European travel until the era of Wordsworth and Byron, whereas hundreds of prose travel narratives were published in the eighteenth century. Goldsmith's unusual poem echoes, and is in turn echoed by, many important eighteenth-century travel writers as well as poets.[8] *The*

Traveller is as indebted to the prolific tradition of prose travel narrative as to poetic antecedents; indeed, Goldsmith initially drafted the work as prose, which perhaps explains the great 'concentration of ideas' in the poem.[9] In his 1759, *Enquiry into the Present State of Polite Learning in Europe*, Goldsmith had remarked that 'Countries wear very different appearances to travellers of different circumstances. A man who is whirled through Europe in a post chaise, and the pilgrim who walks the grand tour on foot, will form very different conclusions' (181). The tone here is that of many a contemporary travel writer, although the rather solitary and pedestrian mode of his travels differentiates Goldsmith from most other British travellers at this time.

There is a long gap between Goldsmith's own European travels in 1755 and the poem's publication in 1764. Goldsmith had time to reflect upon his own experiences and to modify his ideas in response to the many works he read and reviewed during these years. He also wrote a lot himself, in many different genres. *The Vicar of Wakefield*, although not published until 1766, was likely written in 1761–2 and contains a sequence of European travel (see Chapter 19, 'Fiction'). Goldsmith reviewed poetry, drama, philosophy, and history; translated French Protestant memoirs; wrote books of history (including the two-volume *History of England, in a Series of Letters*), cultural history (*An Enquiry into the Present State of Polite Learning*), and biography; and contributed comic and moral essays to various periodicals, including the *Chinese Letters* (collected in 1762 as *The Citizen of the World*).[10] In these essays in particular, Goldsmith explores topics such as national identity and stereotypes, develops the trope of the observant or naïve traveller, and reflects upon the folly of expecting to find happiness 'somewhere else but where we are' (*Citizen*, 1:186; see Chapter 11, 'Cosmopolitanism', and Chapter 26, 'Orientalism').

Many of these works borrow (often silently) from other texts, especially French works of social and political theory by Voltaire, Diderot, and Montesquieu (see Chapter 30, 'France and French Writing'). From these Enlightenment thinkers, who (following Tacitus) tended to view the Mediterranean south as degenerate and sensual and the Nordic north as ascetic and rational, Goldsmith derives the national and racial stereotyping that informs *The Traveller* (see Chapter 14, 'Race').[11] Leo Storm has noted Goldsmith's 'habitual dependence upon themes and topics of discourse taken from his own small stock of ideas and those ideas he found in the conventional literary genres of the eighteenth century'; he was not an original thinker, but a good distiller of common ideas, thus embodying

Pope's definition of True Wit – 'what oft was thought, but ne'er so well exprest' ('An Essay on Criticism', l. 298).[12]

Unusually for the European verse epistle, Goldsmith's does not describe Rome, doubtless because he himself never got that far on his own actual travels.[13] This frees him to characterize other nations at greater length and to reflect in more generalized ways upon the poem's broad network of themes – solitude, society, patriotism, national character, liberty, and happiness. The dedication to his brother, Henry, emphasizes the unusually philosophical scope of the poem, especially the closing assertion that 'I have endeavoured to show that there may be equal happiness in states, that are differently governed from our own' (*Traveller*, iii–iv). Like many prose travelogues of this period, Goldsmith's poem purports to depict other nations with sympathetic tolerance, yet often falls back upon national stereotyping; his accounts of France, Italy, Switzerland, and Holland are entirely conventional.

Readers would likely have expected the survey of European nations which takes up the central section of the poem to build up to a climactic celebration of British liberty, but Goldsmith does not take that road. The ongoing Wilkes controversy meant that 'liberty' had been co-opted as a rallying cry against the government and king (see Chapter 10, 'Liberty'). Goldsmith therefore sidesteps into a highly topical complaint about the degeneration into 'ferments' and 'factions' of British civic and political life (ll. 339–48). The speaker's apparent distaste for politics is important to his melancholy alienation; however, the anti-Wilkes agenda of these lines is clear, and it compromises the poetic traveller's posture of lofty disengagement. As I have noted elsewhere, the poem 'provides a poetic shorthand for a number of tensions which are then worked out with greater complexity within the prose travel writing of the period: between individual and national identity, patriotism and dissidence, travel and domestic yearning. It is not until Wordsworth's *Prelude* that poetry ventures again into this problematic territory'.[14]

Another of the poem's innovations is its modification of the trope found in the related genre of the 'progress of poetry' text, by which civilization and empire move westwards from ancient Rome to modern Britain.[15] *The Traveller* goes far beyond British horizons in its closing geographical sequence, describing the forced emigration of the poor and dispossessed from Britain to North America, 'Where wild Oswego spreads her swamps around, / And Niagara stuns with thundering sound' (ll. 411–12). Britain's 'useful sons' are exchanged for 'useless ore', and 'opulence, her grandeur to maintain', leads 'stern depopulation in her train' (ll. 397–401). Goldsmith had developed these ideas in an essay, 'The Revolution in Low Life', published in 1762, and was to explore them further in *The Deserted Village*. His Irish identity, never explicit in *The Traveller*, doubtless informs the poem's scepticism about empire; various critics (most recently Norma Clarke) have located the poem's depiction of depopulation in Ireland (see Clarke, *Brothers of the Quill*, 99–100). Several of the prospect poem's notable practitioners were not in fact English. Thomson was a Scot and Dyer a Welshman, for instance; however, unlike Goldsmith, they used the genre to assert their status as British poets. *The Traveller* is startling here in its critique of empire, and, further, in the connection suggested between the poem's speaker and the unhappy 'pensive exile', who 'Casts a long look where England's glories shine, / And bids his bosom sympathize with mine' (ll. 421–2).[16] For nation and poet alike, the prospect is bleak.

At this point, the first draft of the poem had ended. However, *The Traveller* adds sixteen lines (largely contributed by Johnson) which reflect upon the pointless 'weary search' for happiness, 'That bliss which only centres in the mind' (ll. 423–4).[17] Here, the world of the literal prospect poem gives way to the moral universe of Johnson's own *The Vanity of Human Wishes*, with an emphasis on 'reason, faith and conscience' (l. 438), yet the closing paragraph also echoes the sentiments of the poem's opening paragraph, in particular 'Where'er I roam, whatever realms to see, / The heart untravell'd fondly turns to thee' (ll. 7–8), thus framing the work with the poet's own situation. Johnson's closing lines rework the same idea of pointlessness into the more objective and ironic query, 'Why have I stray'd, from pleasure and repose / To see a good each government bestows?' (ll. 425–6).

Here, the poem again draws upon a tradition from prospect poetry. Rachel Crawford has recently reminded us of 'the *double entendre* of the word "prospect", in which the viewer's apprehension of space presupposes an analogue in the viewer's expectations or fortune'.[18] In *Cooper's Hill*, in lines which became widely loved and quoted long after the rest of the poem had fallen into obscurity – in 1779 Samuel Johnson said that 'almost every writer for a century past has imitated them'[19] – the speaker interrupts a description of the Thames to express hopes for his own poetic voice:

> O could I flow like thee, and make thy stream
> My great example, as it is my theme!
> Though deep, yet clear, though gentle, yet not dull,
> Strong without rage, without ore-flowing full.   (ll. 189–92)

Addison performs a more sycophantic version of this manoeuvre in *A Letter from Italy*, addressing his epistle's recipient Lord Halifax (hardly a well-known poet then or now) as the model for such inspiration:

> Oh, could the Muse my ravished breast inspire
> With warmth like yours, and raise an equal fire,
> Unnumbered beauties in my verse should shine,
> And Virgil's Italy should yield to mine!   (ll. 51–4)

A similar sentiment appears in Dyer's *The Ruins of Rome*, where he hopes that the sights of Rome's ruins and the site of Virgil's 'humble tenement' (l. 371) may 'inflame' him to 'high ambitious thoughts . . . / Greatly to serve my country' (ll. 128–9). The intertwining of the poet's own 'prospects' with those that are the ostensible subject of the poem occurs too in Goldsmith's poem; yet here, again, he performs a variation on the theme, by characterizing himself less as a poet and more as a man of feeling. The opening lines would likely have struck readers as highly unusual for a self-proclaimed 'prospect' poem, with their arresting and sentimental focus on the 'heart untravelled'. This aspect of the poem has become so central to its appeal that it's worth registering how arresting it would have been in 1764. The importation from more introspective poems (such as Gray's *Elegy*), and from sentimental fiction, of the melancholy wanderer into the philosophic-prospect mode was a stroke of genius. It enabled Goldsmith to position himself as the inheritor of Augustan vision as well as the harbinger of a new sensibility. The poem was the first work to which Goldsmith put his name, and it transformed him from 'journalist to poet, from hack to literary celebrity'.[20] John Montague describes the publication of *The Traveller* as Goldsmith's 'deliberate attempt to take his place in the tradition of the Augustan essay-poem', a capacious label which clearly includes the genre of the prospect poem but reminds us that Goldsmith, like his visionary traveller, was creatively unconfined by boundaries (see Chapter 36, 'Afterlives 3: Poetry').[21]

Notes

1. See Robert Arnold Aubin, *Topographical Poetry in XVIII-Century England* (London: Milford, 1936), David Fairer, *English Poetry of the Eighteenth Century 1800–1789* (London: Longman, 2013), and John Dixon Hunt, *The Figure in the Landscape: Poetry, Painting, and Gardening during the Eighteenth Century* (Baltimore, MD: Johns Hopkins University Press, 1976).
2. Quotations from Denham are from *The Poetical Works of John Denham*, ed. T. H. Banks (Hamden, CT: Archon Books, 1969).

3. Quotations from Pope are from *The Poems of Alexander Pope*, ed. John Butt (London: Routledge, 1963).
4. See Pat Rogers, 'The Dialectic of The Traveller', in *The Art of Oliver Goldsmith*, ed. Andrew Swarbrick (London: Vision and Barnes & Noble, 1984), 107–25.
5. Oliver Goldsmith, *The Beauties of English Poesy*, 2 vols. (London, 1767), 1:111.
6. Lyttelton's epistles, 'To the Rev. Dr Ayscough' (1728), 'Epistle to Mr Pope' (1730), and 'To My Lord Hervey' (1730), were first published in *Dodsley's Collection of Poems, by Several Hands*, 4 vols. (London, 1748–9).
7. Quotations from Dyer are from *The Poetical Works of Armstrong, Dyer, and Green*, ed. George Gilfillan (Edinburgh: James Nichol, 1858).
8. See Katherine Turner, *British Travel Writers in Europe 1750–1800: Authorship, Gender and National Identity* (Aldershot: Ashgate, 2001), 13–17, and Ingrid Horrocks, '"Circling Eye" and "Houseless Stranger": The New Eighteenth-Century Wanderer (Thomson to Goldsmith', *English Literary History*, 77.3 (Fall 2010), 665–87 (683).
9. John Montague, 'Exile and Prophecy: A Study of Goldsmith's Poetry', in *Goldsmith: The Gentle Master*, ed. Sean Lucy (Cork University Press, 1984), 50–65 (53).
10. Peter Dixon usefully charts connections between Goldsmith's periodical writing and *The Traveller* in *Oliver Goldsmith Revisited* (Boston, MA: Twayne, 1991), 97–117.
11. Rogers, 'The Dialectic of *The Traveller*', 108–9.
12. Leo Storm, 'Conventional Ethics in Goldsmith's *The Traveller*', *Studies in English Literature*, 7 (1977), 463–76 (464).
13. On what little we know of Goldsmith's actual travels, see Wardle, 39–69.
14. Turner, *British Travel Writers in Europe*, 16.
15. James Thomson's 'Liberty' (1735–6) and Thomas Gray's 'The Progress of Poesy' (1757) are important such works. See Michael Meehan, *Liberty and Poetics in Eighteenth-Century England* (London: Routledge, 1986).
16. See Suvir Kaul, *Poems of Nation, Anthems of Empire: English Verse in the Long Eighteenth Century* (Charlottesville: University of Virginia Press, 2000), 92–121.
17. On the poem's composition and Johnson's contributions, see Roger Lonsdale's magisterial editorial work in *Gray, Collins & Goldsmith: The Complete Poems* (London: Longman, 1969), 622–57, and Roger Lonsdale, '"A Garden, and a Grave": The Poetry of Oliver Goldsmith', in *The Author in His Work: Essays in a Problem in Criticism*, ed. Louis Martz and Aubrey Williams (New Haven, CT: Yale University Press, 1978), 3–30.
18. Rachel Crawford, *Poetry, Enclosure, and the Vernacular Landscape* (Cambridge University Press, 2002), 26.
19. Samuel Johnson, *Lives of the Poets*, ed. Roger Lonsdale, 4 vols. (Oxford: Clarendon, 2006), 1:238.
20. Kaul, *Poems of Nation*, 117.
21. Montague, 'Exile and Prophecy', 51.

CHAPTER 23

Periodicals and Literary Reviewing

Manushag N. Powell

In 1757, when thirty-something Oliver Goldsmith was hired by Ralph Griffiths, an important bookseller and the printer of the *Monthly Review*, he must have seen his interval as a Grubstreet reviewer – labouring literally under the Sign of the *Dunciad* in St Paul's – as a stopgap, for he still intended to support himself in the medical profession. Stephen Gwynn, among later biographers, argues Goldsmith must have nursed professional literary ambitions from an earlier point, but in any case Goldsmith's plans to travel to India as a physician for the East India Company were real. In 1758, the French were assailing Chennai/Madras with significant hope of success, and it is unclear what reception would have awaited Goldsmith.[1] In December 1758, he would fail to qualify as a naval surgeon, and he never made the voyage he intended as a ship's surgeon to the Coromandel Coast. But his hack work for the *Monthly*, for which he received room and board as well as a reasonable salary – £100 per annum – turned out to be fated. Griffiths, who was both discrete and upwardly mobile, in general seems to have treated his authors better than the stereotype of the Grubstreet sharp might suggest. Although his relationship with Griffiths soured, Goldsmith found himself to be more or less permanently one of those eighteenth-century figures with 'a long habitude of writing for bread' (*Enquiry*, 145).

Goldsmith was a periodicalist from start to finish. Yet his vacillation about that fact is reflected in our critical tendency to see him as a dramatist, a novelist, perhaps an essayist – with seldom more than a nod to the actual format in which much of his work was done, and without which he quite possibly would have starved. Goldsmith's wide-ranging periodical and reviewing work allows us to theorize the development of his interest in the stage, in French literature, in aesthetic theory, in orientalized subjects, and, though in more indirect ways, in fiction as well. But for scholars of eighteenth-century culture more broadly, his career is an exceptional window into the importance of periodical writing to individual careers as well as the culture of reviewing writ large (see Chapter 25, 'Authorship'). 'I have as much pride as they who have ten times as many readers,' he wrote in his failing *Bee*, perhaps coldly comforted to know he was writing to spec for some of those more successful ventures as well (*Bee*, 98).

There is a paradox to British periodical writing in the eighteenth century: periodicals, which, unlike most other publications, could enable a steady income, allowed authors to survive as educated and educating professionals displaying the power of their brains. But having any profession at all conflicted with the preferred periodical voice of the genteel, disinterested, high-status male. Far from trying to hide this conflict, many periodical essay writers grumble about it constantly, Goldsmith among them. He is a part of the essay 'we' *and* the magazine 'we', the periodical 'we'. He is interested in what he does as the work of a professional, even a labourer, as he simultaneously tries to build a reputation for himself as something more exalted.

Part of his conflictedness comes from the neophyte magazine form itself: it was the mid-century growing-together of the essay and magazine that enabled Goldsmith to launch his career. While the claim that the magazine form suffocated the essay periodical is now understood to be an oversimplification, the heterogeneity of miscellanies drew much contemporary critique. Even so, the popularity of magazines allowed serial essays to continue thriving within their copious pages even when slimmer single-essay ventures flailed; some, like the *Monthly*, also nurtured a strong taste for literary and theatrical reviewing among the wider reading public. Goldsmith's career underscores this wider cultural tension around both wanting and resenting magazine publication, as his career nicely encapsulates the uneasy coexistence of the essay periodical and the magazine in the periodical marketplace. He wrote in both forms simultaneously, while apparently fending off personal ambivalence about each. His *Enquiry into the Present State of Polite Learning* lambasted periodical writing: when an aspiring author signs on with a bookseller, says Goldsmith, 'There cannot be ... a combination more prejudicial to taste. ... It is the interest of the one to allow as little for writing, and of the other to write as much as possible; accordingly, tedious compilations, and periodical magazines, are the result of their joint endeavours' (*Enquiry*, 144).

And yet, at essentially the same time, Goldsmith was writing for the *Critical Review* and musing in his own miscellany periodical the *Bee*. By 1762, in *Lloyd's Evening Post*, writing as 'The Indigent Philosopher', he was poking fun at miscellanies, as though he had not contributed to many: 'We essayists, who are allowed but one subject at a time, are by no means so fortunate as the Writers of Magazines, who write upon several ... I have some thoughts ... of making this Essay a Magazine in Miniature.'[2] The resulting concoction includes an advertisement for a new '*Infernal Magazine*', rules on social decorum, thoughts on war with Spain, and a detailed explanation of how to summon Satan. One might conclude Goldsmith meant to elevate the essay over the magazine form that he knew actually published his essays. In fact, though, he is signalling he knows the extent to which the two modes were part of a 'diverse but contiguous group' of contemporary periodical forms; magazines and essay serials were and are often opposed to each other rhetorically, but in practice they were mutually inoculated with each other and grew together.[3]

Disavow as he might, Goldsmith was, in fact, an accomplished magazine worker as well as essayist, contributing many types of short pieces to many, many such ventures. From 1757 to 1762, he worked on the *Monthly Review*, the *Critical Review*, the *Bee*, the *Lady's Magazine*, the *Busy Body*, Newbery's *Public Ledger* (where, of course, he first ran the letters that would be collected as the *Citizen of the World* essays), the *Weekly Magazine*, the *Royal Magazine*, *Lloyd's Evening Post*, and the *British Magazine*. And later in his career, even after fame had come, he had durable periodical contributions, such as the often-taught 'Essay on the Theatre, or, A Comparison between Laughing and Sentimental Comedy', first published in the *Westminster Magazine* for 1 January 1773.

Periodical writing meant periodic income, which virtually no other mode of writing permitted; meanwhile, it was a mode for which Goldsmith's talented but imperfectly attentive temperament was suited. As Norma Clarke succinctly put it, Goldsmith's 'career was short ... and crammed' (Clarke, *Brothers of the Quill*, 2). It was crammed because by any and all accounts, Goldsmith, though a preternaturally gifted and eventually very popular writer – and more than that, one who was often paid fairly for his labours – was wretched at managing his finances. His professional abilities meant that he had to keep writing because his personal vice was that he could not stop spending; he could not write his way out of Grub Street – and, socially awkward, he either would not or could not flatter his way out by begging for pensions. Writing in periodicals '*for bread*' in the *Lloyd's Evening Post*, Goldsmith's Indigent Philosopher laments, 'But I must write, or I cannot live.' He adds, 'I shall take no shame to myself for endeavouring to enforce morals or improve good humour.'

The *Monthly Review* (1749–1845), the first periodical entirely devoted to reviews of literary works very broadly defined (Griffiths covered everything from novels to political pamphlets) in London, was a popular venture as well as a prolific employer; if it was not precisely neutral or beloved by authors, still its durability is a testament to its importance. The *Monthly* is often called the first review periodical in English. It is very far from it; abstracting and reviewing periodicals with various interests had been around since the 1714 *Memoirs of Literature*. The *Monthly* did not begin seriously taking on the task of criticism as its main function until later in the century. Goldsmith's tendency to offer thoughtful criticism of what he read was not unique, but it did stand out. Moreover, the *Monthly* was unrivalled in its degree of comprehensiveness. Goldsmith's relationship with the *Monthly*, and with Griffiths, lasted only a little over half the contracted period. According to Thomas Percy, Goldsmith told him that Griffiths and his wife, Isabella, were interfering editors, and not only over-corrected his prose but also wanted him to keep regular hours, writing from 9 a.m. to 2 p.m.[4] It may simply have been a terrible personality mismatch. It probably did not help matters that Goldsmith owed money and pawned some of Griffiths' books, and Griffiths held a grudge. Goldsmith, his abilities obvious but his name still unmade, turned briefly to teaching and medicine, and more permanently to writing, soon taking up with the rival *Critical Review*. Hired work for a journal like the *Monthly* or *Critical* may not sound like the kind of shining foray into the *belles lettres* that most men would brag about – but it was not obviously a matter for shame, either; acclaimed writers did it often and well.

Samuel Johnson himself reviewed Goldsmith's *The Traveller* in the *Critical*'s pages.[5] And while Smollett and Goldsmith would soon be at loggerheads, the latter's review of the former's *Compleat History of England* (1748) in the *Monthly* was undeniably, although not uniformly, positive. (He praises the doctor's style and judgement, but not the character summaries.) Goldsmith's reviews show literary talent, and whether or not scholars agree with his takes, he does at least tend – much of the time, anyway – to include actual reviews in his reviewing, instead of providing only lengthy excerpts.

Goldsmith's work for the *Critical*, then principally edited by Smollett, overlapped with his work on the *Bee*. The *Bee* has had a stronger afterlife than most of Goldsmith's magazine work, but, as Graham points out, the form of its afterlife has misled readers: 'since its essays are most often reprinted, the *Bee* is usually thought of as an essay serial'. It was really a thirty-two-page miscellany (well, thirty-two pages at first – it got shorter).[6] In the *Bee*, Goldsmith was hoping for a durable commercial success. In the *Monthly* he had fawningly reviewed a collection of Bonnell Thornton and George Colman the Elder's influential *Connoisseur* essays (1754–6). However, only eight *Bee*s ever appeared, and although their leading essays were issued together in book form, they were positively but slightly reviewed. The 'Preface' to Goldsmith's 1765 collected essays joked that the *Bee* essays 'have already appeared at different times, and in different publications ... I can by no means complain of their circulation. The magazines and papers of the day have, indeed, been liberal enough' by plagiarizing them.[7] Goldsmith complains of the chaos of the periodical culture that has slightingly reviewed his work while rewarding the voracity of the magazines.

From the start, Goldsmith's own reviewing covered all genres, including theatre criticism. He was a creative thinker, and his critical takes were often contrary to the majority view. His reading of Burke's treatise *A Philosophical Enquiry into the Origin of Our Ideas of the Sublime and Beautiful* – which he views as a foundational conversation starter, rather than the final word on aesthetic theory – is perceptive as well as a skilful digest of the author's argument. His first theatrical review, for the May 1757 issue of the *Monthly*, was of the Scotsman John Home's *Douglas: A Tragedy*. Little remembered now, *Douglas* was a massive hit and remained an important part of the repertory for decades. Goldsmith's review of the playtext, which could not have been ignorant of the performance's success, nonetheless accurately predicts the eventual critical assessment: 'Let candour allow this Writer mediocrity now; his future productions may probably entitle him to higher applause.' He also facetiously condoles with David Hume for sacrificing taste for friendship in endorsing the play.[8]

When it comes to what he calls 'modern Romances' – novels – Goldsmith can be glib, preferring to leave happy couples in their marital 'felicity' rather than inquire too far into how they got there.[9] His review – it was likely his – of the epistolary *Jemima and Louisa* offers a dimly sexist view of novel authorship: 'The female muse, it must be owned, has of late been tolerably fruitful ... Yet let not the ladies carry off all the glory of the late productions ascribed to them; it is plain by the stile, and a nameless somewhat in the manner, that pretty fellows, coffee critics, and dirty-shirted dunces, have sometimes a share in the atchievement.'[10] But our paradoxical essayist who knew he needed miscellanies would soon try his hand at the novel form he'd disdained. *The Vicar of Wakefield* long outlasted the unfortunate *Jemima and Louisa* (see Chapter 19, 'Fiction').

Goldsmith's skill at adopting personae when he wrote, obvious in *Vicar*, particularly adapted him for periodical essay writing, which by mid-century accepted without much question the utility of the constructed eidolon for developing an audience. But in the clubbish eighteenth-century London world of letters, written skill was not enough. It was controversial even among his friends whether the agreeable Dr Goldsmith were truly as genteel as one might like such an acclaimed author to be; Boswell's *Life of Johnson* critiques him for attempting to shine beyond his parts – yet clearly all the same he is well liked, applauded for good nature (an idealized version of his Irishness, posits Clarke), and his writing is universally admired (Clarke, *Brothers of the Quill*, 35; see Chapter 3, 'Friendships and Feuds'). 'It is not difficult to conceive . . . that for many reasons a man writes much better than he lives,' wrote Johnson in the *Rambler*, anticipating his later friendship with Goldsmith: 'Nothing is more unjust . . . than to charge with hypocrisy him that expresses zeal for those virtues, which he neglects to practice; since he may be sincerely convinced of the advantages of conquering his passions, without having yet obtained the victory.'[11] The passion Goldsmith is generally decried for not conquering is his tendency to overspend; he may have been equally concerned with his recurring passion for writing himself out of debt.

In his reviewing and other periodical work, Goldsmith is consumed by the question of how long any of this can last, and whether his professional writing, done 'for bread', a phrase he returned to often, would be affirmed by popular applause. He is still working through this early crisis of authorial identity in the widely acclaimed *Vicar of Wakefield* (1766, but composed earlier, during Goldsmith's most periodical period). George Primrose relates of his time on his own in town that he was

> obliged to . . . write for bread. . . . I could not suppress my lurking passion for applause; but usually consumed that time in efforts after excellence which takes up but little room, when it should have been more advantageously employed in the diffusive productions of fruitful mediocrity. My little piece would therefore come forth in the mist of periodical publication, unnoticed and unknown . . . My essays were buried among the essays upon liberty, eastern tales, and cures for the bite of a mad dog. (*Vicar*, 2:9–10)

George echoes his creator's stance in *An Enquiry into the Present State of Polite Learning* (1759), where Goldsmith had warned his audience and perhaps himself that, 'A long habitude of writing for bread, thus turns the ambition of every author at last into avarice. He finds, that he has wrote many years, that the public are scarcely acquainted even with his name; he despairs of applause and turns to profit, which invites him' (*Enquiry*, 316).

Yet it would be a mistake to take Goldsmith's professed disdain for periodical work too seriously; it is his conflict over anonymity rather than the demands of genre that probably rankled. This was a necessary evil for magazine work, as the convention in first runs was to publish anonymously or pseudonymously. Moreover, Friedman suggests that given his brutal attack on the state of critics in general in *An Enquiry into the Present State of Polite Learning*, Goldsmith found it awkward to allow his own work as a critic to be publicly known.[12] Before the novel brought him the applause he longed for, Goldsmith had made a serious bid for periodical fame, implying at least a quondam belief that such a thing was plausible.

Notes

1. See Stephen Gwynn, *Oliver Goldsmith* (New York: Haskell, 1976 / reprint of 1935), 88–9; see also Clarke, *Brothers of the Quill*, 100–1.
2. '*The* Indigent Philosopher', *Lloyd's Evening Post*, 4 (8–10 February 1762), 142.
3. Jennie Batchelor and Manushag Powell, *Women's Periodicals and Print Culture in Britain 1690–1820s* (Edinburgh University Press, 2018), 8; Powell, *Performing Authorship in Eighteenth-Century English Periodicals* (Lewisburg, PA: Bucknell University Press, 2012), 192.
4. Memorandum dictated to Thomas Percy, 1773; British Museum Add. MS. 42516, ff. 15v–16v.
5. More Tory than the *Monthly*, the *Critical* had as its motto, 'Nothing extenuate, nor set down in malice', a motto 'which, unfortunately, they could not quite live up to', as Walter Graham put it. See *English Literary Periodicals* (New York: Thomas Nelson & Sons, 1930), 213.
6. Graham, *English Literary Periodicals*, 132.
7. *Essays by Mr Goldsmith* (London, 1765), i–iii.
8. *Monthly Review*, 16 (May 1757), 426–9 (427).
9. *Monthly Review*, 17 (July 1757), 82.
10. *Critical Review*, 8 (August 1759), 165–6. It should be noted that Friedman found Goldsmith's authorship of this piece plausible but uncertain: see *The Collected Works of Oliver Goldsmith*, ed. Arthur Friedman, 5 vols. (Oxford: Clarendon, 1966), 1:205n.
11. 'Rambler 14, 5 May 1750', in *The Yale Edition of the Works of Samuel Johnson*, ed. W. J. Bate and Albrecht Strauss, 23 vols. (New Haven, CT: Yale University Press, 1969), 3:75–6.
12. Friedman, 'Introduction' to the *Critical Review*, in the *Collected Works*, 1:145.

CHAPTER 24

History Writing

Ben Dew

Oliver Goldsmith was a prolific writer on historical themes. His first book-length foray into the field came in 1764 with *An History of England, in a Series of Letters from a Nobleman to His Son*; this was followed by *Roman History* (1769), *The History of England* (1771), and the posthumously published *Grecian History* (1774).[1] Despite such endeavours, Goldsmith did not, in the main, conceive of himself as a historian. Rather he viewed his works as 'compilations', 'epitomes', and 'abridgements', and himself as a 'compiler'. As such, he sought to condense and adapt the often prolix accounts of other writers for a general, non-scholarly audience.[2] The aim here was utility; while history was a high-status form which provided opportunities, if practised successfully, for literary immortality, the humble compiler was obliged to decline 'all attempts to acquire fame satisfied with being obscurely useful'.[3]

Goldsmith's status as a compiler did much to shape his relationship with the dominant trends in Enlightenment historiography. The historical writing of the period, as the commentaries of Arnaldo Momigliano and J. G. A. Pocock have demonstrated, can be conceived of as a union between erudition, classical narrative, and philosophy, the latter term associated with the 'philosophical disposition' through which historians sought to distance their writing from partiality and controversy.[4] The compiler, however, self-consciously rejected one element of this triumvirate. As Goldsmith noted in the preface to *The History of England*, he had been obliged to forego erudition – and the discovery of new 'books' and 'anecdotes' that it entailed – because his aim was 'not to add to our present stock of history, but to contract it'.[5] Such an approach also had significant consequences for his handling of narrative. The ongoing importance of classical ideals ensured that, as a genre, history in the eighteenth century continued to be conceptualized as a linear, narrative account of the public actions of public men, which could provide clear lessons for future political leaders.[6] Despite this focus, however, there was also a growing awareness

that activities which lay beyond the explicit control of the political elite –
commerce and finance, manners and mores, learning and literature – acted
as both symptoms and potential drivers of historical development.[7] These
concerns led not only to the emergence of new types of conjectural history
that used innovative narrative forms to discuss man's social development,
but also to shifts in approach from writers working in the classical trad-
ition. Indeed, the major historians of the period – Edward Gibbon, David
Hume, and William Robertson foremost among them – all supplemented
their political narratives with an array of erudite prefaces, footnotes, and
appendices which sought to evidence and explain processes of societal
change. Goldsmith's relationship with these traditions was a complex
one. On the one hand, like many of his contemporaries, he assumed that
political actions could be understood only when placed in the context of
a wider social and economic backdrop. As a consequence, he was clearly
interested in the 'new' directions Enlightenment history had taken. On the
other hand, however, he maintained a commitment to the didactic func-
tion of history and, through eschewing the scholarly apparatus of his
sources, was able to develop a series of tight and focused, neoclassical-
style narratives. Such an approach had consequences for his handling of
both English and classical history.

Goldsmith presented his major works on England's past in contrasting
formats. The *Letters*, as their title implies, were epistolary in structure; the
History was a more conventional historical narrative with chapters provid-
ing a chronologically organized account of the reign of a particular English
king or queen. Despite such differences, however, the approach of the two
accounts, and much of the actual content, were the same. Both works were
aimed at a younger audience, and both were self-consciously didactic in
focus. Indeed, underpinning the narratives was the notion, expressed in the
first of the 'letters', that 'to understand history is to understand man'. As
a consequence, this was a mode of writing from which 'every advantage
that improves the gentleman, or confirms the patriot, can be hoped for'.[8]

The similarities between the two works were further exacerbated by
Goldsmith's engagement with other historians. While he drew on a range
of sources when constructing his accounts – Paul Rapin Thoyras, Tobias
Smollett, and Voltaire – both the *Letters* and the *History* were essentially
condensed versions of one account: David Hume's *History of England*. This
reliance on Hume did much to shape the core narrative and political
orientation of his work. Two points are significant here. First, Goldsmith
accepted Hume's judgement on the most politically divisive area of
England's history – the reigns of the Tudor and Stuart monarchs – and,

as Hume had done, developed a moderate, Tory analysis of English history. For both writers James I and Charles I were not the despots of parliamentarian and Whig myth, but rather victims of circumstance. The reigns of the Tudors, particularly that of the avaricious Henry VII, had seen a series of reforms which caused the balance of property, and with it the balance of power, to tilt away from the nobility and towards 'the middle rank of men'.[9] It was this group, driven by new ideas of commercial, political, and religious liberty, who had come to question and ultimately resist Stuart rule. James I's and Charles I's crime, if it could be so labelled, lay in their fundamental misinterpretation of the circumstances with which they were confronted. The monarchical prerogatives the Stuarts claimed were, for the most part, in line with well-established precedents; what both monarchs failed to realize – with tragic consequences in the case of Charles – was that the political climate had fundamentally shifted. Second, and largely as a consequence of this, Goldsmith followed Hume in conceiving English liberty as a relatively modern invention. For both writers, Whiggish ideas about an ancient constitution that had underpinned English political practices since time immemorial were fundamentally inaccurate. Rather, the liberties the country currently enjoyed were a product, entirely unintended by the any of the participants, of the events of the sixteenth and seventeenth centuries. As Goldsmith noted: 'many were the miseries sustained in bringing [Charles I] to the block'. However, 'those struggles in the end were productive of domestic happiness and security ... all became more peaceable as if a previous fermentation in the constitution were necessary for its subsequent refinement'.[10]

In spite of Goldsmith's broad endorsement of Hume's analysis, however, there were a number of areas in which he diverged from the Scot. This was partly a matter of chronology and partly a matter of tone. While, as noted, Hume saw the origins of English modernity as rooted in early sixteenth-century changes in landownership, he was at pains to point out that these developments took time to affect British political, economic, and cultural life. He conceived, for example, of Elizabeth I's much celebrated government as bearing 'some resemblance to that of Turkey' (a byword for despotism in eighteenth-century writing) and emphasized that Elizabethan commerce was both badly managed and primitive. The period's literature, meanwhile, a key gauge in Enlightenment thought of social development, was for Hume uninspiring. Perusal of the work of Edmund Spenser, the finest 'writer of his age', was said to be 'so tedious, that one never finishes it from the mere pleasure it affords'.[11] Goldsmith considerably tempered such judgements.

Although he acknowledged that Elizabeth 'knew her own power, and often stretched it to the very limits of despotism', he emphasized the ways in which England was already emerging as a major commercial power. During her reign international trade and manufactures flourished, and the polite arts, literature among them, enjoyed an Augustan age. Spenser and Shakespeare were, in Goldsmith's estimation, writers for whom 'all praise must be too low for their merits'.[12] Importantly, therefore, just as Hume stressed the differences and disjunctions between contemporary and Tudor and Stuart practices, Goldsmith focused on the ways in which characteristically modern forms of behaviour were coming into existence.

Both the similarities and the differences between Hume's and Goldsmith's analysis are also in evidence with regard to Irish historiography. On publication, the Scotsman's account had received criticism from Irish historians for being overly biased against Irish Catholics.[13] However, while Goldsmith expressed some sympathy for the Irish in his discussions of the country's early history, in relation to the key events of the seventeenth century, he extended and hardened Hume's censures.[14] With regard to the massacres of 1641, for example, Hume conceived of the violence against 'British Protestants' as a product of both the ignorance and barbarity of the Catholic populace and a consequence of the increasingly extreme Puritan politics of the Protestants. Goldsmith, however, ignored the latter aspect of Hume's analysis and focused entirely on the former. It was the Catholic Irish hatred of the riches and religion of the Protestants, he argued, that had caused the violence and the 'savage' state of development in which the populace lived that made it particularly severe. A similar pattern can be observed in relation to Goldsmith's handling of the Siege of Derry/Londonderry in 1689, albeit this time the source material comes from Tobias Smollett.[15] Although Goldsmith followed the outlines of Smollett's account both the material he failed to include and the material he added are significant. Thus he decided not to include Smollett's observation that the Protestant garrison in the city was pushed to such extremity that 'they began to talk of killing the popish inhabitants and feeding off their bodies'.[16] He added, however, an aside of his own highlighting the 'bigotry and cruelty' of the Catholics.[17] Such features of the narrative might, of course, be seen as straightforward products of Goldsmith's own Irish Protestant background. Equally significant here, however, are the historiographical differences. Hume's account and, to an extent that of Smollett, emphasized the remoteness of past events; their aim was to explain a form of political enthusiasm – part Catholic, part Protestant – which, they hoped, was at odds with the attitudes of their readers. Goldsmith's discussion served to substantially reduce the historical distance between present and past and conceived of both the Elizabethan population and Irish Protestants as a prototype for the polite, civilized commercial people of the mid eighteenth century (see Chapter 9, 'Irish London', and Chapter 15, 'Religion').

Goldsmith's writing on classical history was also shaped by his sources. In relation to Rome, he drew principally on the work of Laurence Echard; with regard to Greece, it was Temple Stanyan and Charles Rollin.[18] These authors were not proponents of Humean philosophical history and, in following them, Goldsmith both repeated many of their judgements and drew on their broad historiographical frameworks. His accounts of Greece and Rome, therefore, are primarily focused on high politics and military endeavours, and these subjects are used to develop a series of paeans to liberty and warnings about the corrupting influence of luxury.[19] However, these claims, as they had been in the writing of Echard, were moderated by a broadly Tory political sensibility. Whiggish accounts of the classical world, particularly in relation to Rome, had sought to distinguish between heroic defenders of liberty (Cicero, Cato, Brutus, and Cassius) and traitors and self-seeking politicians (Tiberius Gracchus and Caesar).[20] Echard, in contrast, was much more sympathetic to monarchical government and provided a rigorous defence of Caesar as 'the greatest Soul, the most magnanimous Spirit ... Rome, or perhaps the world ever saw'.[21] Goldsmith was unwilling to go quite so far, but offered praise for the Gracchi reforms and an account of Caesar which acknowledged his fortune and his scheming, but expressed admiration for his 'great abilities'. Moreover, while he saw the Commonwealth's fall as entailing the abandonment of all 'just patriotic principles', he also maintained, in Tory style, that monarchy was the best form of government that could be found to unite the diverse group of peoples who now constituted the empire (see Chapter 10, 'Liberty').[22]

Despite such debts to his sources, Goldsmith framed his accounts using a distinctively mid eighteenth-century conceptual framework. The principal concern in earlier works had been with tracing the rise of Roman and Greek power; in Echard's words: the transformation of a 'Troop of Vagabond Shepherds' into 'an Universal Empire' that 'became the Metropolis of the whole Word'. Goldsmith, however, when outlining these developments, paid far more attention than his predecessors to the wider social context, giving particular prominence to changes in manners and mores. One example will suffice to illustrate this. Echard concluded his chapter on the fifth Roman king, Tarquinius Priscus, by noting that during his reign 'Roman greatness and magnificence began to appear much more'.[23] While Goldsmith's discussion of Tarquinius followed Echard closely, he stressed that the king helped 'to introduce the polite arts [to Rome]', and concluded with the observation that while the Romans were not yet 'civilized', 'they were much more so than any of the barbarous nations around them'.[24] Goldsmith's method here was, therefore, in a sense the opposite of that he had utilized when discussing English history. Whereas with regard to England he had transformed Hume's work into a more conventional, classically inflected linear narrative, in relation to Greece and Rome, he had added a few Humean tweaks to give the narrative a distinctively 'modern' feel. The result, however, was that his works of history shared a common approach; all offered a moderate Tory vision of the past that sought to balance exemplary, didactic forms of history with a series of enlightened narratives of progress and decline.

Goldsmith's historical writing received mixed reviews from critics. And underpinning the analyses of the various commentators who dealt with these compositions was a distinctly ambivalent attitude towards historical compilation. On the one hand, the genre was frequently characterized as a low, commercial form of writing which had more in common with Grub Street journalism and tawdry political polemic than true 'history'. Indeed, one particularly damning review of the *Grecian History* noted that 'it was a bookseller's job, probably *first* undertaken by the author to relieve a temporary exigence'. As a consequence, it was a work that had been put together 'with hurry, carelessness and reluctance'.[25] On the other hand, however, there was an awareness that this mode of writing could, in stylistic terms, achieve true success. The *Monthly Review*, in an account of the *History* which offered sharp criticism of both Goldsmith's politics and his skills as a historian, acknowledged his work had 'a degree of dignity, which [was] perfectly suitable to historical composition'.[26] A rather more positive account of the *Roman History* commented that 'the performance is seasonable, and well executed' and that it provided an 'excellent and elegant digest'. As such, while it may not have been of value to 'a scholar or a critic', it was 'the best and most suitable work for the use of gentlemen . . . that has yet been published'.[27] There was a sense, therefore, that despite its lowly associations, the manageable length, clear linear narrative, and high style of the compilation made it better adapted to the needs of polite, high-status audiences and their offspring than 'real' history.

Such features helped to ensure that Goldsmith's history achieved considerable and long-lasting commercial success. A version of the *History of England*, for example, restyled for school use by William Pinnock, had run to forty-six editions by 1858; adaptations of the Grecian and Roman histories ran to twenty-nine and thirty-three editions respectively by the 1860s. There were also American editions and translations into German, French, and Polish. The success of these publications gives Goldsmith's historical writing an important position within the eighteenth-century canon. While his works may lack the historiographical innovations of Hume and Voltaire, they form a key conduit through which the ideas of these writers were communicated. Indeed, the nineteenth century's encounter with Enlightenment historiography cannot be fully understood without considerations of the work of compilers – Goldsmith foremost among them (see Chapter 33, 'Critical Reception after 1900').

Notes

1. Oliver Goldsmith, *History of England, in a Series of Letters from a Nobleman to His Son*, 2 vols. (London, 1764); *The Roman History*, 2 vols. (London, 1769); *The History of England*, 4 vols. (London, 1771); *The Grecian History* (London, 1774).
2. Paul Rapin Thoyras, *History of England*, tr. Nicholas Tindal, 15 vols. (London, 1725–31); David Hume, *The History of England*, 6 vols. (Indianapolis, IN: Liberty Fund, 1983).
3. Goldsmith, *Roman History*, i.
4. Arnaldo Momigliano, 'Gibbon's Contribution to Historical Method', *Historia: Zeitschrift für Alte Geschichte*, 2.4 (1954), 450–63; J. G. A. Pocock, *Barbarism and Religion, Volume 2: Narratives of Civil Government* (Cambridge University Press, 1999).
5. Goldsmith, *History of England*, 1:vi.
6. On the neoclassical forms, see Philip Hicks, *Neoclassical History and English Culture, from Clarendon to Hume* (Basingstoke: Macmillan, 1996).
7. On these developments, see Mark Salber Phillips, *Society and Sentiment: Genres of Historical Writing, 1740–1820* (Princeton University Press, 2000).
8. Goldsmith, *History of England*, 1:3.
9. David Hume, *The History of England*, 6 vols. (Indianapolis, IN: Liberty Fund, 1983), 4:384.
10. Goldsmith, *History of England*, 3:315–16.
11. Hume, *History*, 4:360, 386.
12. Goldsmith, *History of England*, 1:299, 298.
13. For example, Charles O'Connor and John Curry. On Hume's account of Ireland, see David Berman, 'David Hume on the 1641 Rebellion in Ireland', *Studies: An Irish Quarterly* 65.258 (1976), 101–12.
14. On Goldsmith's views on Ireland, see Yuhki Takebayashi, 'The Grounded Patriot: Oliver Goldsmith As Historical Compiler', unpublished PhD Thesis, Trinity College, Dublin (2019).

15. Hume's account concluded with the events of 1688. Tobias Smollett, *A Complete History of England*, 4 vols. (London, 1757–8).

16. Smollett, *History of England*, 4:24.

17. Goldsmith, *History of England*, 4:59.

18. Laurence Echard, *The Roman History*, 2 vols. (London, 1696); Temple Stanyan, *The Grecian History*, 2 vols. (London, 1707, 1739); Charles Rollin, *Histoire Ancienne*, 12 vols. (Paris, 1730–8).

19. See, for example, his discussion of Sparta in the *Grecian History* (1:13–44).

20. On the political issues at stake with regard to classical history, see Addison Ward, 'The Tory View of Roman History', *Studies in English Literature, 1500–1900*, 4.3 (1964), 413–56.

21. Echard, *Roman History*, 1:373.

22. Goldsmith, *Roman History*, 2:27, 95.

23. Echard, *Roman History*, 1:Preface, 38.

24. Goldsmith, *Roman History*. 1:40.

25. *Westminster Magazine*, December 1774, 648.

26. *Monthly Review* (December 1771), 45, 436–4 (440).

27. *Critical Review* (June 1769), 27, 433–9.

CHAPTER 25

Authorship

Maureen Harkin

The poet's poverty is a standing topic of contempt. His writing for bread is an unpardonable offence. Perhaps of all mankind an author in these times is used most hardly.

Enquiry, 139–40

The nature and status of authorship was a topic that consumed Oliver Goldsmith throughout his career, a matter of pressing practical as well as intellectual concern for the impecunious writer. Right up to the final year of his life a financially strapped Goldsmith engaged in producing the kind of low-level translation and compilation work for money he had begun on his arrival in London in 1756, even though by this point he had also attained the heights of success in multiple genres, with the publication of *The Traveller* in 1764, *The Vicar of Wakefield* in 1766, and *The Deserted Village* in 1770, and the staging of *She Stoops to Conquer* in 1773 (see Chapter 4 and, 'Booksellers and the Book Trade', and Chapter 23, 'Periodicals and Literary Reviewing').[1] The gap between his extraordinary literary accomplishments and his still precarious social and economic position was dramatic, and this experience clearly feeds into Goldsmith's pessimistic conclusions about the consequences of the increasing commercialization of British literary production over the preceding decades.

The standard mid-century narrative of the book trade and authors' position in it is, as Dustin Griffin puts it, one of a fall, from a transparently idealized earlier era of enlightened patronage for a select company of learned and worthy authors to a contemporary scene featuring literary marketplaces overcrowded by 'hordes of [under-educated] hacks', the consequent devaluing of all authors' work – even the deserving – by harsh critics and indifferent audiences, and hostility between rival authors.[2] Goldsmith of course is simply one of many expressing concern about the mid-century literary field and the role it assigns to the author in the period. James Ralph, lamenting the treatment of authors by a literary world now dominated by booksellers in his *Case of Authors* (1758), anticipates many of Goldsmith's critiques, as does Adam Smith in his commentary on the travails of modern authorship in *The Theory of Moral Sentiments* (1759).[3] Samuel Johnson expresses many of the same criticisms as his friend in the *Adventurer* No. 115, though in a less embattled, more Johnsonian tone. Describing 'the present age [as] The Age of Authors', he deplored the fact that 'men of all degrees of ability . . . were posting with ardour so general to the press' as an 'intellectual malady' and an 'evil'.[4]

Goldsmith's complaints are, then, part of this very well-established story, although it is safe to say that no one among this group of observers exceeded Goldsmith in the sense of profound alarm he expressed at where all this had left authors.[5] Where he *differs* from contemporary commentators is mostly in the intensity, even panic, detectable in his assessments. Throughout his career Goldsmith expresses the deepest unease about the quantities of commodified prose produced for the market in books and journals and the correspondingly low status of those generating it, and is left doubtful about what, if any, socially useful role an author might claim in this society. That the respect he felt should be due, but was seldom forthcoming, to the author is a recurring theme in *An Enquiry into the Present State of Learning in Europe, The Citizen of the World*, and numerous other periodical essays. Moreover his anxieties about how authorial impact ultimately depends on or defers to social power turns out to be a dominating theme in Goldsmith's *The Vicar of Wakefield*, and key to its problematic ending.

Goldsmith introduces his project in the *Enquiry into the Present State of Polite Learning in Europe* as an ambitious one: an impartial, dispassionate attempt 'To mark out . . . the corruptions that have found way into the republick of letters, to attempt the rescuing of genius from the shackles of pedantry and criticism . . . and . . . to attempt . . . improvement' (*Enquiry*, 4). The *Enquiry*'s reflections on the state of British literary culture are certainly wide-ranging, though their tone is often one of angry condemnation and rebuke rather than that of the calm detachment implied by the Introduction, with many accounts of the precarious finances and petty humiliations of contemporary writers.[6] Chapter XI ('Upon Criticism') describes the persecution of writers by critics applying rigid rules, while Chapter X ('Of the Encouragement of Learning') describes other authorial mortifications, tracing the difficulties for writers created by both failure and success. The account of the lack of encouragement given to authors uses the example of Voltaire as exemplar, and indeed Goldsmith imports a large piece of

Voltaire's 'Lettre à M. Lefebvre' to make his case. Goldsmith's free borrowings from other authors for his opinions here and elsewhere is in keeping with contemporary practice, but it does create a problem for him, presenting as it does an apparent contradiction to his claim that authors are deserving of honour because of their wit and merit. The argument that wit or merit are the special contributions of the writer evidently references a concept of originality just beginning to emerge as a fundamental literary value in the period, yet Goldsmith's own frequent practice of freely adapting or borrowing the work of other writers makes perfectly clear that he cannot consistently lay claim to these elements as his own authorial contribution.[7]

In any event the poverty, contempt, and unfair attacks to which the modern writer is subjected lead Goldsmith to conclude at last that it is not possible to make an honourable living from writing:

> every author at last . . . finds that money procures all those advantages, that respect, and that ease which he vainly expected from [literary] fame. Thus the man, who under the protection of the Great might have done honour to human nature, when only patronized by the bookseller, becomes a thing little superior to the fellow who works at the press. (*Enquiry*, 145–6)

Goldsmith's putative solution to the problems he diagnoses is to look back to a system of patronage as the best way to support writers and literature and to raise the quality of output. Yet, as Adam Rounce has suggested, Goldsmith's backwards look at the age of patronage is undermined by its manifestly wishful, nostalgic elements, with scant evidence of 'the Great' offering support when most needed, the obvious instance of such neglect being Lord Chesterfield's recent failure to give assistance to Johnson's Dictionary.[8]

The Citizen of the World (1762) returns to many of the same concerns with the state of the author and the literary marketplace and continues the narrative of decline (see Chapter 11, 'Cosmopolitanism', and Chapter 26, 'Orientalism'). The figure of Lien Chi Altangi, ostensibly visiting England from China to conduct a broad-ranging examination of England's 'opulence, buildings, sciences, arts and manufactures', is Goldsmith's device here for creating a distanced, impartial view of the scenes he describes (*Citizen* 1:3). The series devotes at least 19 of the 123 Citizen's letters to writers, reviewers, books and booksellers, newspapers and periodicals, and English reading habits, and we are soon plunged back into Goldsmith's familiar concerns: the oversupply of authors/texts relative to paying readers in Letter 30; the mean-spirited attacks of authors ('every member of this fancied republic [of letters] looks upon his fellow as a rival ... they calumniate, they injure, they despise, they ridicule each other' (*Citizen* 1:67); the particular sufferings of great writers at the hands of envious rivals, including Pope, Dante and Voltaire; and the constant reduction of works of imagination to mere commodities like any other.[9]

In short, in both the *Enquiry* and the *Citizen of the World* Goldsmith is emphatic that the recent emergence of a literary marketplace where booksellers like Ralph Griffiths had displaced aristocratic patrons as the primary source of economic support for writers was demeaning to writers and destructive to literature. To be sure, Goldsmith is not completely consistent on this score. Occasional glimmers of acceptance of the changed situation of the eighteenth-century writer, and even of some Johnsonian optimism for the economic possibilities this changed situation opens, appear in his work.[10] In a late letter from *The Citizen of the World*, for example, Lien Chi Altangi essays an Adam Smith-style argument that, as literature (or 'wit') is in fact a commodity like any other, one should seek it from those who specialize in this kind of production. These thinkers indeed develop their talent by employing it:

> were I to buy an hat, I would not have it from a stocking-maker, but an hatter; were I to buy shoes, I should not go to the taylor's for that purpose. It is just so with regard to wit: did I, for my life, desire to be well served, I would apply only to those who made it their trade, and lived by it ... wit is in some measure mechanical: and ... a man long habituated to catch at even its resemblance, will at last be happy enough to possess the substance: by a long habit of writing he acquires a justness of thinking, and a mastery of manner, which holiday-writers, even with ten times his genius, may vainly attempt to equal. (*Citizen*, 2:119–20)

Similarly, in one of his 'Indigent Philosopher' essays for *Lloyd's Evening Post* Goldsmith tells a different story about writing for the market, attacking the notion that being paid for their work is degrading to authors: 'shall I be ashamed of being paid a trifle for doing this, when Bishops are paid for scarce preaching on Sundays! ... This power, if I have any power, was the only patrimony I received from a poor father! ... *By Heavens I ... glory in it*'.[11] Here one sees a glimmer of a different narrative, where the shift from a patronage-based to a market-based model for literary production gets read as a logical effect of the division of labour, and one potentially supportive of writers' professional freedom. This enables the narrative of historical change to be considered not as a decline, but rather as a development enabling the rise of the independent author.[12] Yet despite these sporadic attempts to see his historical situation as offering opportunity rather than a loss, Goldsmith much more frequently finds the status of writer for pay insulting and expresses contempt for the way in which the literary marketplace has treated authors. These occasional attempts to reconcile the harsher aspects of the literary system at mid-century with Goldsmith's longing for respect and authority remain isolated and largely disconnected from the main current of his arguments, and sit awkwardly at odds with his nostalgic vision of an age of patronage.

What distinguishes Goldsmith's comments on the position of the author at mid-century, then, is less their originality or consistency than the special, personalized force of his plaints, and the way this anxiety persists as a topic of discussion across his works. It is this note of personal distress, this affective quality, that gives Goldsmith's comments on authorship their significance and peculiar force.

A good example of this characteristically Goldsmithian treatment of the pathos of the author is found in his comments in the first issue of the *Bee* (6 October 1759). Here Goldsmith as author introduces himself to the reader by asserting the identity between a shy man affecting a social confidence he does not feel and a writer facing his first audience who is stunned into nervous flippancy:

> There is not, perhaps, a more whimsically dismal figure in nature, than a man of real modesty who assumes an air of impudence; who, while his heart beats with anxiety, studies ease, and affects good humour. In this situation, however, a periodical writer often finds himself, upon his first attempt to address the public in form. All his power of pleasing is damped by solicitude, and his chearfulness dashed with apprehension. Impressed with the terrors of the tribunal before which he is going to appear, his natural humour turns to pertness, and for real wit he is obliged to substitute with vivacity. (*Bee*, 1–2)

The authorial self-portrait here is a good sample of Goldsmith's complicated, tormented vision of the position of the author at mid-century. Visibly looming in the background is the imposing, authoritative figure of Samuel Johnson, confident arbiter of all questions of literary and cultural merit and model of the kind of 'ease' valued by these daunting judges. But there is and can only be one Samuel Johnson, a figure whose authority derives precisely from his magisterial singularity. Goldsmith's picture here makes clear that this example cannot furnish the model for the practice of the representative professional writer. In fact the opposite is the case: Goldsmith emphasizes the strain on the typically diffident subject who puts himself forward as author. His intense sensitivity to the interior struggles of a figure whose professional obligation is precisely to try to appear at ease and authoritative in the Johnsonian manner, while actually sinking under 'the terrors of the tribunal', indicates a deeply personal connection. This kind of vividly rendered account of the *average* working writer's experience, one of high emotion, anxiety, and dread, is Goldsmith's distinctive contribution to the discourse on authorship and another indicator of how profoundly these concerns are embedded in his thinking.

This sketch of the marginalized, frightened, and demoralized writer finds its culminating expression in Goldsmith's *The Vicar of Wakefield* (see Chapter 19, 'Fiction'). Goldsmith's concerns about authorship, and especially the social powerlessness of the writer, are dominant issues in the novel from the outset. Goldsmith sets the scene with the notably defensive comments of his 'Advertisement':

> The hero of this piece . . . is drawn as ready to teach . . . simple in affluence, and majestic in adversity. In this age of opulence and refinement whom can such a character please? Such as are fond of high life, will turn with disdain from the simplicity of his country fireside. Such as mistake ribaldry for humour, will find no wit in his harmless conversation; and such as have been taught to deride religion, will laugh at one whose chief stores of comfort are drawn from futurity. (*Vicar*, 'Advertisement', n.p.)

Goldsmith's opening gambit is to describe the current historical moment as the wrong one for his project, identifying its refined audiences as hostile to any representations that lack the spice of sophistication or vulgarity, and, fed on the works of Fielding or Sterne, quite resistant to moral argument. This publication begins, thus, with a strikingly self-defeating, if by now familiar, image of author-reader relations.

The narrative, interspersed with multiple references to varieties of authorship, continues the exploration of the indignities of the writer's lot. There are brief references to Doctor Burdock distributing verses in manuscript and Lady Blarney publishing 'things in the Lady's Magazine' (*Vicar*, 1:105), instances of supposedly wealthy amateurs circulating texts for their circle's amusement. These sketches of writing as elite aristocratic pastime are of course fictional, comic inventions. Much more important are the examples of the vicar and his eldest son, George. Primrose early on identifies himself as author, albeit an unsuccessful one, with the discussion of his (unsold) publications on clerical monogamy and the Whistonian controversy in chapter 2, and consistently articulates his ambition and his confidence about reforming audiences through his texts and sermons. Later in the text we have the elaboration of George Primrose's humiliating foray into Grub Street. George's misadventures there describe a scene already quite familiar from the *Enquiry* and the *Citizen*. The well-meaning though perhaps not very talented George attempts a writing career as one of several failed efforts to make his fortune, and he meets with the neglect, disappointment, and abuse that he relates is the standard lot of 'disappointed authors' (*Vicar*, 2:10). Though his travails are sympathetically described, the point is clearly made that George is merely seeking income rather than aspiring to true literary greatness, so that his failure can be seen as an acceptable, and indeed appropriate outcome – a mismatch, not an indictment of the literary field. In the middle of his account George pauses to assure his father that, despite his experience, 'true' poets *will* find their level and their reward: 'A true poet can never be so base; for wherever there is genius there is pride ... The real poet, as he braves every hardship for fame, so he is equally a coward to contempt, and none but those who are unworthy protection condescend to solicit it' (*Vicar*, 2:9).

At this stage, 1762, Goldsmith might then seem to have adopted a rather softer stance than in his earlier work. Yet this confident assertion of the essential fairness of the literary marketplace is given no other support in the course of the novel's action, and, as the novel proceeds to its conclusion, a dramatically dark representation of the complete social powerlessness of authors and of the brutal facts of social life overtakes both George's and Primrose's prior optimism.

By chapter 28 of the novel almost every attempt of the vicar to reach an audience with his texts and sermons has failed, and Primrose's idea of the author's role to form and instruct has been revealed as completely misguided by precisely the kind of audience indifference Goldsmith had predicted in his Advertisement. The vicar is sick and imprisoned; one daughter, Olivia, is seduced and abandoned; her sister, Sophia, is abducted; and George is condemned to death: all due to the machinations of the powerful and ruthless local squire, a figure immune to any form of moral persuasion or instruction. The complete shipwreck of the family's fortunes indicates the chasm between Primrose's concept of a world in which writing and preaching shape audiences and the one in which he actually finds himself. Though the novel has mildly satirized the vicar's belief in the social impact of his works from the beginning, the pathos of the complete breakdown of his belief system and of his absolute vulnerability is the dominant feature at this late point in the narrative. Into this breach steps Lord Thornhill.

The well-known problem of the ending, in which Lord Thornhill steps forward to take control of the action and dole out the proper fates to characters in a narrative that is otherwise backed into a corner, actually has to take the shape that it does in order to make the novel's fundamental points: the self-delusiveness of the vicar's belief in the impact of authors on audiences, and the fact of the complete social powerlessness of the writer.[13] What counts, what compels proper response, is the titled man of property and legal power. Lord Thornhill makes this point most effectively in his letter to two of the texts' minor villains, Miss Skeggs and Lady Blarney, where he confidently threatens the miscreants that any further misdeeds will be attended with 'dangerous consequences', not just muttered disapproval (*Vicar*, 1:147). Using the language of power, which can 'prevent' crime by summoning real punishments, Thornhill succeeds where the vicar had failed, in a message whose origins and meaning the vicar only fully grasps at the novel's finale. This final jarring demonstration of raw social power obliterating Primrose's fantasies of authorial influence aligns the novel with Goldsmith's other writings on authorship, and shows once again how these concerns drive his work.

Notes

1. See Simon During on Goldsmith's resentment in 'Charlatanism and Resentment in London's Eighteenth-Century Literary Marketplace', in *Bookish Histories: Books, Literature, and Commercial Modernity, 1700–1900*, ed. Ina Ferris and Paul Keen (Basingstoke: Palgrave Macmillan, 2009), 253–71 (266–8). See also Dustin Griffin on Goldsmith's reputation as compiler, in *Authorship in the Long Eighteenth Century* (Newark: University of Delaware Press, 2014), 179.
2. Griffin, *Authorship*, 4. See also Linda Zionkowski, 'Territorial Disputes in the Republic of Letters: Canon Formation and the Literary Profession', *The Eighteenth Century*, 31.1 (1990), 3–22, especially 5–8.
3. James Ralph, *The Case of Authors by Profession or Trade* (London, 1758, 1762); Adam Smith, *Theory of Moral Sentiments*, ed. D. D. Raphael and A. L. Macfie (Oxford University Press, 1976), III.2.18–23.
4. Samuel Johnson, *The Adventurer* 115 (11 December 1753).
5. See Zionkowski, 'Territorial Disputes', 5.
6. See Adam Rounce, 'Young, Goldsmith, Johnson and the Idea of the Author in 1759', in *Reading 1759: Literary Culture in Mid-Eighteenth Century Britain and France*, ed. Shaun Regan (Lewisburg, PA: Bucknell University Press, 2013), 95–112 (101–2). Alfred Lutz elaborates on the class anxieties that drove Goldsmith's frequent attempts to write from a position 'above the fray', as gentleman observer rather than professional writer, in 'The Poet and the Hack: Goldsmith's Career as a Professional Writer', *Anglia: Zeitschrift für Englische Philologie/Journal of English Philology*, 123.3 (2005), 417–21. Clarke sees Goldsmith as trying to come up with a solution to the problem of writer's status via the figure of 'the man of taste', occupying a position somewhere between scholar and gentleman (Clarke, *Brothers of the Quill*, 73–6).

7. See Edward Young's *Conjectures on Original Composition* (London, 1759). See also Martha Woodmansee's discussion in 'On the Author Effect: Recovering Collectivity', in *The Construction of Authorship: Textual Appropriation in Law and Literature*, ed. Martha Woodmansee and Peter Jaszi (Durham, NC: Duke University Press, 1994), 16–17.

8. 'The burden of the sentence falls on the "might have".' Rounce, 'Young, Goldsmith, Johnson and the Idea of the Author in 1759', 105.

9. See Megan Kitching, 'The Solitary Animal: Professional Authorship and Persona in Goldsmith's *The Citizen of the World*', *Eighteenth Century Fiction* 25.1 (2012), 175–98 (178).

10. An optimism most succinctly expressed in Johnson's well-known comment on Andrew Millar, publisher of the *Dictionary*: 'I respect Millar, Sir; he has raised the price of literature'. *LOJ*, 1:288.

11. *Lloyd's Evening Post*, 20–22 January 1762, 78. Zionkowski, though, notes that Goldsmith's 'tone in his pieces that advocate writing for pay appears curiously defensive, as if he is espousing ideas whose truth he himself doubts' ('Territorial Disputes', 7).

12. Griffin, *Authorship*, 5.

13. Marshall Brown, *Preromanticism* (Stanford University Press, 1991), 113, 141–2.

CHAPTER 26

Orientalism

Eun Kyung Min

Goldsmith's most important oriental fiction and first major literary achievement is *The Citizen of the World; or Letters from a Chinese Philosopher, Residing in London, to His Friends in the East*, first serialized between 24 January 1760 and 14 August 1761 in John Newbery's *Public Ledger* (see Chapter 11, 'Cosmopolitanism'). Although this work is sometimes referenced as a novel, we should note that it was originally published in serial form in the *Public Ledger* newspaper before it appeared in book form in 1762 under the title *Citizen of the World*. Goldsmith's Chinese letters clearly grew out of different strands of his journalism: in particular, his interest in the comparative analysis of different national cultures (as exemplified by 'Comparative View of Races and Nations' serialized in four numbers of the *Royal Magazine* in June–September 1760); his debt to French writers such as Voltaire, Montesquieu, and d'Argens whom he cited and referenced widely in his periodical writings; and his experiments with oriental fiction (as evidenced in 'The Proceedings of Providence Vindicated. An Eastern Tale', in the December 1759 issue of the *Royal Magazine* – see Chapter 14, 'Race', and Chapter 30, 'France and French Writing'). By the time Goldsmith embarked on his Chinese letters, there were already so many literary precedents for the oriental travelogue that Goldsmith would have been well aware of the challenge of doing something new with the genre. Goldsmith nonetheless did manage to do something new with the seriality of the pseudo-oriental letter.[1]

From his earliest writings in the *Monthly Review*, Goldsmith clearly indicated his awareness of and interest in the genre of pseudo-oriental letters – in Hamilton Jewett Smith's definition, 'Works in which a foreigner is pictured satirizing the country he visits in a series of letters, made public in alleged translation from the original tongue'.[2] Given his strong interest in geography, history, and the comparative study of cultural and national differences, he no doubt saw in pseudo-oriental letters an opportunity to dwell on these subjects in an entertaining form. We see

Goldsmith proffering general principles governing this epistolary subgenre in the opening paragraph of his review of *Letters from an Armenian in Ireland, to His Friends at Trebisonde, & c. Translated in the Year 1756* in the August 1757 number of the *Monthly Review*:

> THE Writer who would inform, or improve, his countrymen, under the assumed character of an Eastern Traveller, should be careful to let nothing escape him which might betray the imposture. If his aim be satirical, his remarks should be collected from the more striking follies abounding in the country he describes, and from those prevailing absurdities which commonly usurp the softer name of fashions. His accounts should be of such a nature, as we may fancy his Asiatic friend would wish to know, – such as we ourselves would expect from a Correspondent in Asia.[3]

Goldsmith notes here that writing letters 'under the assumed character of an Eastern Traveller' can enable the writer to satirize national 'follies' and 'fashions' in a genial manner. He cautions such a writer to be careful so as not to 'betray the imposture'. However, by the mid-eighteenth century the genre of pseudo-oriental letters had become familiar enough that the informed reader would have immediately suspected that the 'Eastern traveller' was a fictional character. The imposture involved in pseudo-oriental letters was an open secret. The genre of pseudo-oriental letters thus involved a complex literary pact between writer and reader. The reader understood that the author was in oriental disguise; the author did his best to offer something of novel interest while not straying too far from the reader's expectations or 'fancy' about the oriental character. Both reader and writer knew that the orient in question was a fictive one, and the success of the genre turned on how successfully the writer could mobilize and renew the literary trope of the oriental traveller for an audience already familiar with it.

To borrow Srivinas Aravamudan's terms, the 'transcultural fiction' of pseudo-oriental letters can be described as an example of 'imaginative Orientalism'. The 'experimental, prospective, and antifoundationalist' imagination of eighteenth-century orientalism was propelled by 'a strong desire to understand civilizational differences both relativistically and universally'. Unlike nineteenth-century orientalism, it did not propagate a systematic discourse of European domination over the orient; rather, it was characterized by playful parody, 'translocality' and 'intercitationality'. Generically, eighteenth-century orientalism tended to split into the oriental tale sequence or pseudo-oriental letter-writing. In choosing to take up the latter genre, which turned on the premise of the synchronic comparison of east and west, Goldsmith was following an already established tradition of cross-cultural oriental satire. Pseudo-oriental letters flaunted their fake reality; oriental tales, in contrast, were 'Artificially distressed in the manner of fake period furniture'.[4] We know from Goldsmith's translation of Voltaire's remarks about Montesquieu's *Persian Letters* (1721) in another article of the August 1757 *Monthly Review* that he was well aware of such literary precursors of pseudo-oriental letter writing as Giovanni Paolo Marana's *Turkish Spy* (1684–6) and Montesquieu's *Persian Letters* (see Chapter 30, 'France and French Writing'). *Letters from an Armenian in Ireland, to His Friends at Trebisonde* (1756), possibly by the Irish author Edmund Sexton Pery, was only the latest example of many English imitations of these works; other examples included George Lyttleton's *Letters from a Persian in England to His Friend at Ispahan* (1735) and Horace Walpole's *A Letter from Xo-Ho, a Chinese Philosopher at London, to His Friend Lien Chi at Pekin* (1757).

In his own attempt at pseudo-oriental letters, Goldsmith easily could have followed the lead of Marana and Montesquieu and chosen to write under the guise of a Turk or Persian. His biographer James Prior in fact stated that Goldsmith's original plan was to impersonate 'a native of Morocco or Fez' (Prior, *Life*, 1:360). So why did Goldsmith ultimately choose a Chinese native instead? And what does his choice of a Chinese man tell us about the nature of his orientalism? Although we cannot be certain why, several important events in 1759 may have influenced Goldsmith's decision. In February of that year, Goldsmith met Thomas Percy, who was in London to find a publisher for *Hau Kiou Choaan*, his 'translation' of a Chinese novel hitherto unknown in Europe. Through Percy, who secured a contract with Robert Dodsley, Goldsmith no doubt was alerted to the literary market for Chinese characters in the London publishing sphere. A few months later in April, Goldsmith reviewed David Garrick's production of Arthur Murphy's play *The Orphan of China, a Tragedy* at Drury Lane. This play, which ran a total of nine nights and brought Murphy considerable money, may have also influenced Goldsmith's choice of a Chinese man.

However, China would have been an attractive choice for Goldsmith not simply because it represented a more unfamiliar Orient than Turkey, Persia, and the Levant. The 'craze for all things Chinese' – including tea, porcelain, furniture, wallpaper, and silk – had reached its height in mid-eighteenth-century England. The eighteenth-century *chinoiserie* fad–the 'prevalence of fashion in favour of all that came from China', as Goldsmith put it in his review of Murphy's play – combined with the lack of accurate information about 'Chinese manners' created a unique opportunity for the pseudo-oriental letter writer.[5] Moreover, the very format in which Goldsmith's pseudo-letters were to appear argued strongly against merely following in the footsteps of Montesquieu or Marana.[6] Unlike the pseudo-letters of these writers, Goldsmith's Chinese letters were destined for serial publication in the *Public Ledger*, the first continuously published daily newspaper in England. This meant that the letters necessarily would appear in close spatial and temporal proximity to the events reported in the newspaper; they would need to make sense within the context of diurnal news. In other words, Goldsmith needed a modern oriental who would perform well in the company of other anonymous foreign correspondents supplying intelligence from abroad; his letter-writer had to make sense in the bustling public sphere represented by the newspaper (see Chapter 23, 'Periodicals and Literary Reviewing').

Goldsmith's Chinese philosopher Lien Chi Altangi is thus a narrator character who differs substantively from the spy narrators of conventional pseudo-oriental fiction – the 'fearful, paranoid, and subjugated' spies scribbling secret missives to Eastern despots while hiding themselves from the European public.[7] Unlike Marana's silent, solitary, and unhappy Turkish spy Mahmut who finds himself in uncomfortable exile in Paris, Goldsmith's Lien Chi Altangi is an extroverted, cheerful, and sociable character on a leisurely tour of London and its vicinities. Entrusted with no political secrets or schemes, he writes to his friends back in China letters which are sent via a merchant friend in Amsterdam. In the second of the published letters, Altangi tells this merchant friend, 'I shall send them open, in order that you may take copies or translations, as you are equally versed in the Dutch and Chinese languages' (*Citizen*, 1:5). This fiction of open letters provides a narrative pretext for the serial publication of the translated letters in London and underscores their public, as opposed to secretive and private, interest.

It is likely that the writer who had the greatest influence on Goldsmith's choice of a Chinese narrator was Jean-Baptiste de Boyer, Marquis d'Argens, best known for his *Philosophical Correspondence*, a vast pseudo-letter collection of supposedly Jewish, Cabalist, and Chinese letters.[8] In their important study of d'Argens's influence on Goldsmith, Ronald S. Crane and Hamilton Jewett Smith note that Goldsmith liberally and silently borrowed, paraphrased, and lifted passages from d'Argens's *Chinese Letters*, often substituting England for France.[9] A. Lytton Sells indeed calls Goldsmith's work 'a patchwork of imitations and plagiarisms' of d'Argens.[10] D'Argens's book was not simply useful as a rich mine of information about China, however. D'Argens's pseudo-oriental correspondence, like Goldsmith's, was published in serial form, as 'bi-weekly *Lettres* in the form of periodical "demi-feuilles", issued from the Hague'. A 'demi-feuille' was 'a folder or pamphlet consisting of four sheets containing eight pages of print'.[11] When d'Argens later collected his fictional letters in book form, he simply had these 'demi-feuille' papers bound together, preserving the original periodical form in which they had been published. The publication format of d'Argens's *Chinese Letters* thus helped him frame his letters as semi-serious contemporary philosophical pamphlets aimed at promoting the ideas of anticlericalism, deism, and cosmopolitanism. D'Argens's choice of Jewish and Chinese, rather than Turkish or Persian, pseudo-letter writers is closely connected to the form and content of his *Philosophical Correspondence*. His Chinese letter writers, like the Jews in *Jewish Letters*, represent not an exotic and alien orient mired in a premodern past but rather a modern and enlightened orient that represents a cultural alternative to a Europe riven by religious turmoil.[12] D'Argens's letter writers are oriental yet worldly figures; their oriental difference functions not as a sign of political subjugation or absolute religious difference but rather as enlightened cosmopolitanism.[13] This is why they can function as plausible writers of philosophical pamphlets.

Goldsmith follows d'Argens's lead in making Lien Chi Altangi a modern Chinese philosopher who has had extensive former contact with the English and the Dutch in Canton.[14] Like d'Argens's seven Chinese scholars who, having had much contact with both Jesuit missionaries and English merchants in China, are well acquainted with European learning, Lien Chi Altangi is a worldly and sophisticated traveller. However, whereas d'Argens's Chinese philosophers spend considerable time seriously debating the difference between eastern and western religion, Altangi touches only lightly on Chinese thought. Another key difference is that d'Argens's *Chinese Letters* features the correspondence between one Chinese traveller and his numerous correspondents in China, Muscovy, Persia, and Japan, while Goldsmith streamlines the narrative structure of his Chinese letters, limiting Lien Chi Altangi's correspondents to his friend Fun Hoam and his son Hingpo. Underscoring and exploiting the serial and diurnal format of his publication, Goldsmith uses Lien Chi Altangi primarily as a witty, urbane, and comic observer of contemporary English social life.

Far from using Altangi as a figure of oriental difference, Goldsmith thus dismantles the oppositional dynamic between the orient and Europe, turning the Chinese observer into a modern metropolitan and updating the motif of the foreign traveller. An experienced and seasoned city-dweller, Altangi records his initial 'disappointment on entering London, to see no signs of that opulence so much talked of abroad' (*Citizen*, 1:4). He quickly adapts to London life, however, and energetically sets about exploring the city. He is, in his own words, 'often found in the centre of a crowd'; 'wherever pleasure is to be sold', he is 'always a purchaser' (*Citizen*, 1:233–4). Hailing from Canton, he is clearly used to the pleasures of urban commerce. He goes shopping in bookshops and silk shops, dawdles in coffee-houses watches plays at Covent Garden and Drury Lane, visits Westminster Abbey and St Paul's, and diverts himself in Vauxhall Gardens. He is not merely a polite tourist. The pleasure he takes in London life has a Hogarthian edge to it. He has close encounters with London's mixed social classes – its beggars, prisoners, porters, soldiers, and prostitutes. He notices the English fondness for ogling at 'sights and monsters' at fairs (*Citizen*, 1:191), amuses himself at the cart races at Newmarket (*Citizen*, 2:90–4), and marvels at the drunkenness at an election (*Citizen*, 2:186–90). Altangi's letters accurately represent 'the particular experiences of physical crowding, social indiscriminacy, and especially spatial mobility characteristic of the modern metropolis'.[15] In Goldsmith's Chinese letters, the Chinese man is far from a figure of insurmountable difference. Jocosely declaring himself 'almost become an Englishman' (*Citizen*, 2:85), he walks about 'dressed after the fashion of Europe' rather than China (*Citizen*, 1:48), chafes in the presence of fake *chinoiserie* – 'sprawling dragons, squatting pagods, and clumsy mandarins . . . stuck upon every shelf' (*Citizen*, 1:50), and makes a joke of English ideas of Chineseness. More eidolon than alien, Altangi's cosmopolitan and metropolitan modernity is wittily formalized through his appearance in the quotidian space of the English newspaper.[16]

The modern, metropolitan, and cosmopolitan Chinese man, however, is a slippery and unstable, challenging concept. When Altangi declares that 'you must not expect from an inhabitant of China the same ignorance, the same unlettered simplicity, that you find in a *Turk, Persian*, or native of *Peru*', and argues that the Chinese are 'masters of several arts unknown to the people of Europe' (*Citizen*, 1:139), he cites notions of China's comparative modernity not only in relation to Turkey, Persia, and Peru, but also in relation to Europe. At times China is described as a monumental 'empire as large as Europe, governed by one law, acknowledging subjection to one prince' (*Citizen*, 1:178), boasting an advanced civilization acquainted with 'the secrets of gunpowder, and the mariner's compass' long before Europe

(*Citizen*, 2:170). However, Altangi himself undercuts the image of China's advancement or modernity when he admits that China is now 'imperceptibly degenerating from her antient greatness; her laws are now more venal, and her merchants are more deceitful than formerly': 'There was a time when China was the receptacle of strangers, when all were welcome who either came to improve the state, or admire its greatness; now the empire is shut up from every foreign improvement; and the very inhabitants discourage each other from prosecuting their own internal advantages' (*Citizen*, 1:276). Even 'Our manufactures in porcelaine too are inferior to what we once were famous for; and even Europe now begins to excel us' (*Citizen*, 1:276). China's reputed urbanity receives a similarly ambiguous treatment in the Chinese letters.

Goldsmith appears to have taken the idea of Altangi's representative modernity and urbanity from the descriptions of Chinese cities in Louis Le Comte's *Memoirs and Observations Made in a Late Journey through the Empire of China* (1697) and Jean-Baptiste Du Halde's *A Description of the Empire of China and Chinese-Tartary* (1738–41).[17] Le Comte opined in his *Memoirs* that 'our most populous Cities are Wildernesses' in comparison to the Chinese ones.[18] Du Halde popularized the utopian image of geometrical and well-ordered Chinese cities, 'celebrated on account of their Situation and Extent; the Multitude of their Inhabitants; the extraordinary Concourse of the *Chinese* drawn thither for sake of Trade; the Beauty of the publick Buildings, and Plenty which reigns therein'.[19] However, the sublimity of Chinese cities was also a function of the frightening size of their crowds, the 'infinite Multitudes' with their 'surprizing Number of Horses, Mules, Asses, Camels, Carts, Waggons, and Chairs', all milling around on the dusty streets in mighty 'Confusion'. In a picturesque sketch of urban Peking, Du Halde describes 'the various Crowds of Men, 100 or 200 in a Cluster', gathered about fortune tellers, 'Players at Cups and Balls', ballad singers, and quacks.[20] Ultimately, Goldsmith uses these contrastive reports on China not so much to enter in earnest into the controversial debate about Chinese modernity as to turn them strategically into reflective mirrors on London's putative modernity.[21]

Goldsmith's indiscriminate citational style and playful rehearsal of multiple, contradictory stances make it admittedly difficult to gauge the seriousness with which he approached oriental difference. It is not always easy to tell when Goldsmith is exemplifying or criticizing the orient, and when he is just having fun. For instance, when Altangi's friend Fum Hoam informs him that his departure from China, so 'contrary to the rules of our government, and the immemorial custom of the empire' (*Citizen*, 1:21), has caused the angry emperor to incarcerate his family, should we take this as a criticism of China or as a parody of the oriental pseudo-letter genre? The experienced reader of the genre will be wary of reading too much into such passages. By the time Altangi's son Hingpo, fleeing from the despotism of the Chinese emperor, ends up a slave in Persia, it becomes quite clear that Goldsmith's weak attempt at a plot parodies the narrative sequence in *Persian Letters*. In lieu of a coherent narrative and argument about China, Goldsmith supplies an endlessly slippery stance. For this reason, it is not uncommon to find critics protesting Goldsmith's 'exploitative' use of China. For instance, Donna Isaacs Dalnekoff states that 'Goldsmith exploits the associations of China with extreme formality, pedantry, and ceremonialism to turn his philosopher into a figure of ridicule'; Tao Zhijian argues that in Goldsmith's work 'China as the Other is often frivolously appreciated as the ideal' and 'is also tacitly the butt of criticism'. Christopher Brooks asserts that Goldsmith 'victimizes Altangi and the Orient' and 'demonstrates the depths of emulative silliness and the exploitative "use" of the Orient'.[22] However, Goldsmith's allusive, comic, and imaginative orientalism, like much eighteenth-century orientalism, was deliberately unsystematic and inconclusive rather than aggressively exploitative. Altangi indeed warns against systematic, prejudicial orientalism when he declares himself 'amazed at the ignorance of almost all the European travellers, who have penetrated any considerable way into Asia'; as he says, 'their accounts are such as might reasonably be expected from men of very narrow or prejudiced education, the dictates of superstition or the result of ignorance'. As always, it is not easy to judge Goldsmith's tone here, but surely he is not being systematically and prejudicially orientalist. The corrective Goldsmith offers against 'exploitative' orientalism is a flexible and mobile, metropolitan cosmopolitanism. 'As for myself, the world being but one city to me, I don't much care in which of the streets I happen to reside,' says Altangi (*Citizen*, 2:238). While this may not sound particularly Chinese, it says a great deal about the way in which Goldsmith understood his Chinese observer.

Notes

1. Further development of some of the issues raised here can be found in my *China and the Writing of Literary Modernity, 1690–1770* (Cambridge University Press, 2018), 125–63.
2. Hamilton Jewett Smith, *Oliver Goldsmith's* The Citizen of the World: *A Study* (New Haven, CT: Yale University Press, 1926), 39.

3. *Monthly Review* 17 (August 1757), 150–1.

4. Srinivas Aravamudan, *Enlightenment Orientalism: Resisting the Rise of the Novel* (University of Chicago Press, 2012), 4, 4–5, 17.

5. *Critical Review* 7 (May 1759), 434.

6. Dawn Jacobson, *Chinoiserie* (London: Phaidon, 1993), 125. As Jacobson points out, *chinoiserie*, or decorative objects created in the Chinese style, developed out of an insatiable market demand for Chinese goods in modern Europe. By the eighteenth century, the taste for *chinoiserie* was 'ubiquitous and affected every area of the decorative arts from complete interiors to needle-cases' (7).

7. Ros Ballaster, *Fabulous Orients: Fictions of the East in England, 1662–1785* (Oxford University Press, 2005), 148.

8. D'Argens's *Correspondance philosophique*, comprising *Lettres juives, ou Correspondance philosophique, historique, et critique, entre un Juif voyageur en différens états de l'Europe, et ses correspondants en divers endroits* (1736–8), *Lettres cabalistiques, ou, Correspondance philosophique, historique, et critique entre deux cabalistes, divers esprits élémentaires et le Seigneur Astaroth* (1738), and *Lettres chinoises, ou, Correspondance philosophique, historique et critique, entre un Chinois voyageur à Paris et ses correspondants à la Chine, en Moscovie, en Perse, et au Japon* (1739–40), was originally issued in periodical format by Pierre Paupie in the Hague. In the preface to the third edition of the *Lettres cabalistiques*, d'Argens noted that all three books contained the subtitle '*Correspondance philosophique, historique, et critique*' and declared that they ought to be considered in total as forming a single work. The three works were never published as a single work, however. The first English translation of d'Argens's *Lettres chinoises* appeared in 1741 under the title *Chinese Letters*. A subsequent translation, *The Chinese Spy*, appeared in 1752. *The Jewish Spy* appeared in English translation in 1739, 1744, and 1753. *Lettres cabalistiques* was not issued in English. See Newell Richard Bush, *The Marquis d'Argens and His Philosophical Correspondence: A Critical Study of d'Argens' Lettres juives, Lettres cabalistiques and Lettres chinoises* (Ann Arbor, MI: Edwards Brothers, 1953), 52, 234–7. In keeping with d'Argens's understanding of the continuity between the three works, I will refer to the collection as *Philosophical Correspondence*.

9. Ronald S. Crane and Hamilton Jewett Smith., 'A French Influence on Goldsmith's "Citizen of the World"', *Modern Philology*, 19.1 (1921), 83–92. For an extensive discussion of Goldsmith's general debt to French writers, see Arthur Lytton Sells, *Les sources françaises de Goldsmith* (Paris: Édouard Champion, 1924).

10. Arthur Lytton Sells, *Oliver Goldsmith: His Life and Works* (New York: Barnes and Noble, 1974), 248.

11. Bush, *The Marquis d'Argens and His Philosophical Correspondence*, 2, 64–5.

12. Commenting on Adam Sutcliffe's *Judaism and Enlightenment*, Catherine R. Power points out, 'The figure of the Jew could be both familiar and cosmopolitan in ways that the Muslim "oriental" figure could not'. See

'Figural Judaism and Political Thought in the Marquis d'Argens' *Lettres juives*', *Review of Politics*, 81 (2019), 363–80 (371).

13. Adam Sutcliffe, *Judaism and Enlightenment* (Cambridge University Press, 2003), 210.

14. In the preface to his *Chinese Letters*, d'Argens describes his Chinese correspondents as 'very well instructed in the Learning of the Europeans', having 'had a long intimacy with the Missionary Jesuits' and 'Aquaintance with several English Merchants at Pekin': Marquis d'Argens, *Chinese Letters. Being a Philosophical, Historical, and Critical Correspondence between a Chinese Traveller at Paris, and His Countrymen in China, Muscovy, Persia and Japan* (London, 1741), xi.

15. Laura Brown, *Fables of Modernity: Literature and Culture in the English Eighteenth Century* (Ithaca, NY: Cornell University Press, 2001), 29.

16. On the figure of the eidolon, see Manushag N. Powell, *Performing Authorship in Eighteenth-Century English Periodicals* (Lewisburg, PA: Bucknell University Press, 2012), 13–48.

17. Louis Le Comte's book was originally published in 1696 under the title *Nouveaux mémoires sur l'état présent de la Chine*. Du Halde's massive, encyclopaedic compendium of European knowledge of China, originally published as *Description géographique, historique, chronologique, politique et physique de l'Empire de la Chine et de la Tartarie chinoise* in 1735, appeared first in English in John Watt's 1736 edition, soon to be surpassed by Edward Cave's luxurious folio edition of 1738–41.

18. Louis Le Comte, *Memoirs and Observations Made in a Late Journey through the Empire of China* (London, 1697), 57.

19. Jean-Baptiste Du Halde, 'The Author's Preface', in *A Description of the Empire of China and Chinese-Tartary*, 2 vols. (London, 1738), 1:iii.

20. Du Halde, *A Description of the Empire of China and Chinese-Tartary*, 1:66.

21. For a detailed discussion of the place of China in the English quarrel between the ancients and the moderns, see the first chapter of my *China and the Writing of English Literary Modernity*.

22. Donna Isaacs Dalnekoff, 'A Familiar Stranger: The Outsider of Eighteenth-Century Satire', *Neophilologus*, 57 (1973), 121–34 (124); Tao Zhijian, 'Citizen of Whose World? Goldsmith's Orientalism', *Comparative Literature Studies*, 33.1 (1996), 15–34 (21); Christopher Brooks, 'Goldsmith's *Citizen of the World*: Knowledge and the Imposture of 'Orientalism', *Texas Studies in Literature and Language*, 35.1 (1993), 124–44 (133, 139).

CHAPTER 27

Satire and Sentiment

Lynn Festa

Essayist, poet, novelist, playwright, critic – lauded stylist and sometime Grub Street hack – Oliver Goldsmith was attuned to the shifting sensibilities and interests of the reading public, his adroit negotiation of various genres, mediums, and modes a reflection both of his literary talents and of the commercialization of print culture in the 1760s and 1770s. The subtle slippage between sentimental and satiric registers in Goldsmith's oeuvre reflects the professional writer's grasp of – and ambivalent relation to – the literary marketplace as it responded to the shifting sensibilities of the British public in the wake of the Seven Years' War. At a moment in which Britons sought to grapple with an unprecedented influx of wealth and consumer goods and to acclimate to their newfound role as a global imperial power, existing genres strained to reconcile long-standing moral ideals with a changing social, economic, and political landscape (see Chapter 17, 'War and Empire'). While the corrosive language of satire violated the precepts of polite sociability that underwrote the mid-century culture of sensibility, the sympathetic solidarity with suffering others and the naïvely benevolent humanity celebrated in sentimental literature proved a fragile bulwark against the commercial energies shaping the period. Even as Goldsmith satirized sentimentality – its pathos, its clichés, its cardboard characters, its unreflecting altruism, and its inefficacy in effecting material change – he incorporated a sentimental strain into works that railed against injustice and moral decline. This chapter investigates the ways sentimentality and satire commingle in the narrative, poetic, and dramatic forms that make up Goldsmith's astonishingly diverse oeuvre.

It is a critical cliché that the Augustan Age of Satire gave way at mid-century to an Age of Sentiment, as the newly prosperous middling sort staked their claim to cultural authority through the cultivation of moral sensibility, rejecting the harsh corrective of the Juvenalian lash in favour of a sentimental lamentation at the world's woes.[1] Yet satire persisted even in sentimental texts, both in the smiling Horatian chastisement of human frailty and in an ironizing strain incorporated into sentimental bestsellers such as Sterne's *Tristram Shandy* and Mackenzie's *Man of Feeling*, as writers sought to exploit the power of sensibility to move audiences while preserving the critical distance necessary for the discernment and correction of faults. Thus while Goldsmith mocked sentimentalism as a fashionable abstraction, his work reflects on and exploits the power of emotions to shape belief, thought, values, and action. His plays capitalize on sentimental plots even as they provoke laughter at human folly; poems like *The Deserted Village* (1770) and novels like *The Vicar of Wakefield* (1766) offer pathetic accounts of the misery of the disenfranchised, even as they interrupt sympathetic identification by cultivating perspectives that offer a critical appraisal of the causes of – and pleasures extracted from – suffering (see Chapter 19, 'Fiction', and Chapter 21, 'Pastoral Poetry'). Yet, inasmuch as the loose structure and generic plurality of Goldsmith's works undermine the formal unity that allows for decisive assertions about literary mode or authorial stance, his oeuvre produces spiralling ironies that call into question the opposition between satire and sentiment that has shaped eighteenth-century literary histories.

Inasmuch as satire and sentimentality are discursive modes designated by the responses they elicit from their audiences, attempts to classify Goldsmith's works as one or the other depend on the sensibility of the reader or spectator, the horizon of expectations set by the genre, and the degree to which the narrative voice is deemed ironic – a determination that often depends upon the nebulous question of 'tone'. Defined by I. A. Richards in *Practical Criticism* as the speaker's '*attitude to his listener*', inasmuch as he 'arranges his word differently as his audience varies, in automatic or deliberate *recognition of his relation to them*', tone floats between speaker and implied interlocutor, governed by such difficult-to-pin-down factors as the inflection of the voice and the sensitivity of the ear.[2] As (in Sianne Ngai's apt words) a 'promiscuously used yet curiously underexamined concept', tone eludes precise description: it is 'a materially created semblance of feeling that nonetheless dissolves into static when one attempts to perform a 'micro-analysis', or to break it down into isolated parts'.[3] While tone becomes visible through the affects it elicits, Ngai notes, its identifying traits are often hard to specify ('I don't like your tone'). Dependent upon a readerly projection rather than a fixed feature within the text, the individual sensibilities and collective 'mood' that decide 'tone' govern whether a text is experienced as sentimental or felt to be satiric. Yet tone holds extraordinary sway over critical interpretations, for readers perform a kind of fetishistic inversion in which the feeling the work induces in the reader is treated as a property of the text itself: it is the detection of an ironic tone by the reader that reclassifies a sentimental scene as satiric or unveils satire as sentiment in disguise. Given the multiple publics Goldsmith sought to address and the varying contexts that shaped the reception of his works, it is perhaps unsurprising that his work is alternately characterized as satirical and sentimental.

The fact that both the sentimental and the satiric are defined by the affect they elicit reminds us that neither mode offers an impersonal or empirically objective account of its objects; both single out an *aspect* of an individual or a situation in order to shape audience responses. Given the lack of a formal feature that decisively classes (e.g.) an effusion of tears as sentimental or satiric, critics have sought to class Goldsmith's works as one or the other by isolating an authorial stance through Goldsmith's essays and criticism (presumed to reflect his true convictions) and his paratexts (advertisements, prefaces, footnotes, epilogues).[4] Yet no Fieldingesque narrator or Richardsonian footnote instructs the reader on the appropriate (sentimental or satiric) response. The fluctuations in voice in the epistolary *Citizen of the World* (1762) and the intermittent ironizing of the Chinese observer's perceptions suggest that Lien Chi Altangi cannot be identified as Goldsmith's proxy, while the tension between the moral aphorisms trotted out by *The Vicar of Wakefield*'s eponymous narrator and the plot of the novel yield dramatic ironies that undermine any clear-cut classification of the text as sentimental. Despite Goldsmith's asserted preference for 'laughing' over 'sentimental' comedy in his 'Essay on the Theatre', his plays confuse the binaries set forth in his criticism. The impossibility of parsing Goldsmith's texts as sentimental or satiric issues from the difficulty in pinning down Goldsmith's 'own' authorial voice, not to mention his intentions. In what follows, I trace the shifting status of the satiric and the sentimental through Goldsmith's major dramatic, poetic, and prose works.

Capitalizing on – and satirizing – the mid-century Orientalist vogue to which it also belongs, Goldsmith's 1762 epistolary 'spy narrative', *The Citizen of the World*, offers an estranging perspective on British culture through the eyes of a cosmopolitan Chinese traveller (see Chapter 11, 'Cosmopolitanism', and Chapter 26, 'Orientalism'). Both the defamiliarizing point of view and the diverse genres the text embraces – philosophical essay, moral set piece, character sketch, Oriental tale, sentimental vignette, fable, romance – make it hard to determine whether the letter writers artlessly deploy these genres or parody them. The epistolary form, which withholds an authorial proxy, likewise makes it difficult to stabilize the text's myriad ironies. While Lien Chi Altangi at times appears as a naïve observer – mistaking prostitutes for 'daughters of hospitality', for example – elsewhere he offers ironizing reflections on English customs and even on his own position as speaker ('I talked of trifles, and I knew that they were trifles': *Citizen*, 1:26, 2:229). At other moments, the narrative itself seems to satirize Altangi.[5] Thus when the begging soldier Altangi encounters concludes his narrative of the service that has left him maimed and penniless with gushing praise of liberty, property, and Old England, it is not clear whether the veteran is an object of sentiment or satire, nor is it clear whether Altangi's 'admiration of his intrepidity and content' is sincere or ironic (*Citizen*, 2:222). If a purely sympathetic relation to the indigent veteran occludes the essay's satiric point about both the state's failure to care for its veterans and the jingoism that blinds the soldier to his nation's flaws, the rhetorical and affective efficacy of the passage depends upon *both*. Inasmuch as 'this dislocating mixture of ironies leads to several different but simultaneous levels of perception in the reader', Charles Knight argues, the point is to recognize – but not to reconcile – these contradictions.[6]

Although *The Citizen of the World* includes a broad endorsement of what might be called sentimental cosmopolitanism – Altangi singles out the English subscription to relieve starving French prisoners of war as a laudable example of 'national benevolence' towards one's 'fellow creatures' (*Citizen*, 1:88) – Goldsmith criticizes sensibility through the figure of the Man in Black, a philanthropic soul whose shame at his 'natural benevolence' ('even to profusion') leads him to cloak his charitable acts in affected misanthropy (*Citizen*, 1:99). Described as 'rather the effect of appetite than reason' (*Citizen*, 1:103), the Man in Black's altruistic urges are subjected to satiric scrutiny by Altangi, who intimates that his companion is the dupe of impostors, dispensing largesse that underwrites 'idleness, extravagance, and imposture' (*Citizen*, 1:100). While sensibility incites tears at the world's woes, Goldsmith's text exposes the ease with which it may be exploited.

The tension between sentimental pathos and an analytic purchase on the forces behind suffering is apparent in Goldsmith's depiction of rural collective life in poems like *The Traveller* (1764) and *The Deserted Village*. Combining elements of the prospect poem, loco-descriptive verse, pastoral, and idyll, Goldsmith's verses lament the decline of traditional life-ways while dismantling any sentimental vision of a naturally benevolent humanity. '[T]imes are altered; trade's unfeeling train / Usurp the land and dispossess the swain', the speaker in *The Deserted Village* proclaims, as he makes his 'solitary rounds' amid the 'glades forlorn' of the depopulated hamlet Auburn (*Deserted Village*, 4, 5, 5). The depredations wrought by burgeoning commerce are likewise a central concern in *The Traveller*: 'As nature's ties decay, / As duty, love, and honour fail to sway, / Fictitious bonds, the bonds of wealth and law, / Still gather strength, and force unwilling awe' (*Traveller*, 19). That the amassed forces of nascent capitalism extort 'unwilling awe' converts lamentation over the loss of collective bonds into bedazzlement before the forces destroying the rural world. In tracing the miseries inflicted upon rural communities by England's trading policies, the swelling luxury of the rich, and the Enclosure Acts of the 1750s and 1760s, Goldsmith not only pleads for sympathy for the poor but also decries failures in policy. As the 'fictitious bonds . . . of wealth and law' preempt 'nature's ties', the satirist's view of human nature as irremediably corrupt prevails over the sentimental vision of benevolent humanity.

The fancy that sensibility will amend the world's ills is a recurrent satiric target in Goldsmith's oeuvre. His 1768 play, *The Good Natur'd Man*, targets the excessive benevolence and amiable pliancy of the eponymous hero, Honeywell, whose readiness to accommodate others has led him to the brink of ruin (see Chapter 20, 'Theatre'). Like the Man in Black in *The Citizen of the World* and Sir William Thornhill in *The Vicar of Wakefield* (who faults himself for 'a sickly sensibility of the miseries of others': *Vicar*, 1:27), Honeywell bestows his benevolence upon unworthy objects. His quest to please all and sundry leaves the character devoid of a moral centre. His 'charity', as his uncle Sir William points out, proves 'but injustice'; his 'benevolence . . . but weakness; and [his] friendship but credulity'. While Honeywell does not renounce sentimental humanity, he absorbs the play's satiric lesson 'to reserve my pity for real distress [and] my friendship for true merit' (*Good Natur'd Man*, 72, 74).

The sensibilities cultivated – but also satirized – in the play notoriously shaped its reception, as the 'low' humour of the bailiff scene, in which Honeywell endeavours to pass a cluster of debt collectors off as genteel callers, offended the public taste. In the preface to the published version of the play, Goldsmith fears that the 'too delicate' sensibilities and 'too much refinement' of the public have 'banish[ed] humour . . . from the stage' (*Good Natur'd Man*, iii), a theme recapitulated in his famous 1773 'Essay on the Theatre, or, A Comparison Between Laughing and Sentimental Comedy'. Condemning the 'Weeping Sentimental Comedy, so much in fashion at present' as 'a kind of *mulish* production' that confuses the stratification of ranks that separates tragedy and comedy, Goldsmith elevates laughter at folly over grief at distress as an instrument of moral correction.[7] Arguing that the 'Low or Middle Life' should be represented through the 'Exhibition of its Follies' rather than the tearful redemption of transgression, Goldsmith asserts that sentimental comedies invite the audience to applaud facile sentiments and shed cheap tears, palliating rather than ridiculing folly.[8] While the 'Essay on the Theatre' has been frequently educed as proof that the Age of Sensibility had ousted the Age of Satire, Goldsmith's characterization of the contemporary stage as swamped by sentimental treacle has been debunked by Arthur Sherbo, Robert Hume, and Frank Donoghue, who have shown that the repertoire was neither dominated by 'weeping comedy' nor devoid of 'laughing comedy'.[9] Indeed, the sentimental strain against which Goldsmith pits himself, Donoghue argues, is found 'not in the plays themselves but in popular dramatic criticism'.[10] Published two months before the 1773 debut of *She Stoops to Conquer*, Goldsmith's polemic was designed to shape the public and critical discourse to favour the play's reception.

The key points made in the 'Essay on the Theatre' are recapitulated in the prologue David Garrick penned for *She Stoops to Conquer*. Noting that 'The Comic muse, long sick, is now a-dying', the Prologue condemns the 'sententious look, that nothing means', and the 'Faces [that] are blocks, in sentimental scenes', before promising 'a doctor ... to cheer her heart' (*Stoops*, 'Prologue'). The play privileges the comic, relegating the sentimental couple, Hastings and Miss Neville, to the secondary plot and placing the play's Lord of Misrule, Tony Lumpkin, and its comic heroine, Kate Hardcastle, at the heart of the dramatic action. Lumpkin tricks Marlow (the wealthy young man invited to Hardcastle's country house as a suitor of his daughter Kate) and Marlow's friend Hastings into taking their host's house for an inn, while Kate passes herself off as a maid to Marlow in order to cure him of his bashfulness before women of his class. By modifying the frames that render language and behaviour intelligible, Kate and Lumpkin expose the conventions that determine whether a statement will be understood as high or low, polite or rude, sentimental or satiric, pointing to the absence of any stabilizing essence.

Goldsmith's decision to make the wealthy gentleman, Marlow, the target of satiric emendation calls into question the values that align the comic with the 'low' even as it exposes the power relations and hierarchies that underlie sentimental culture. While the performance of deference to ladies dictated by polite society entails for Marlow a paralyzing form of social impotence, his submissive demeanour merely disguises his rakish freedoms with lower-class women, as the satire unveils the material forces behind the sentimental veneer.[11] If the sentimental values that underwrite the companionate marriage between Marlow and Kate secure the comic

ending and the play makes its politically disenfranchised characters –
Lumpkin, believed to be a minor, and Kate, a woman – the agents of the
action, neither the play's sentiment nor its satire dismantle the economic
and political hierarchies that govern the status quo.

While Goldsmith's 'Essay on the Theatre' and his plays were viewed as
a 'satiric reaction against a dominant mode of sentimental playwrighting'
until the 1950s,[12] the reverse is true of *The Vicar of Wakefield*, which was, for
almost two centuries, understood as a sentimental novel, praised (in Sir
Walter Scott's words) for affording 'the best and truest sentiments enforced
in the most beautiful language' (*Critical Heritage*, 276). Although early
readers noted the ironizing discrepancies between Primrose's adages and
his comportment, his self-betraying slips, and the absurdities of the plot,
not until the twentieth-century work of Ricardo Quintana, Robert
Hopkins, and Richard Jaarsma did *The Vicar* come to be read as a satire
of its narrator and a parody of sentimental novels, with their moralizing
excesses, maudlin set pieces, and contrived romances.[13]

The satiric reading of the novel largely hinges on the relation taken to the
first-person narrator. If one understands Primrose as an uncalculating naïf,
blind to the contradictions between his self-characterizations and his actions,
the novel is a sentimental portrait of a lovable, fallible clergyman; viewed
satirically, Primrose becomes a vain hypocrite, 'a fortune-hunter as well as
a professor of optimistic platitudes', whose 'complacency is nauseous'.[14]
While a purely satiric reading helps reconcile the dissonance between the
comic tone and the Job-like afflictions Primrose endures, the relation
between the two modes is perhaps better understood dialectically, for, like
Wittgenstein's duck–rabbit drawing, *The Vicar of Wakefield* admits a shift in
aspect that converts sentiment to satire – and back again. Seen satirically, for
example, the gap between the Primrose family's social-climbing affectations
and their financial straits is risible; seen from a sentimental point of view, the
distance between their former and present circumstances incites pathos at
their suffering. This oscillation between sentiment and satire, as James Kim
has argued, enables the narrative to stabilize the compromised patriarchal
authority of the vicar, for while satiric mortification diminishes Primrose's
authority, his humiliation and suffering sentimentally elevates him, reinstat-
ing the patriarchal values imperilled by a shifting sociopolitical landscape.[15]
The movement between modes also shapes the reader's experience: while the
numerous reversals in the novel's closing chapters burlesque sentimental
fiction, George Haggerty contends, the 'irony is . . . itself sentimental' in that
it licenses 'those feelings that an intellectual approach to the novel makes
unacceptable'.[16]

Readings of the novel as satire depend upon the presence (or perception) of 'another point of view . . . presented through the first-person narration'.[17] Much thus hinges upon the title page of the novel, which states that the text is 'Supposed to be written by HIMSELF'. In admitting daylight between the narrator and the author of the text, the title page suggests a split perspective that affords ironic distance from the vicar's account. There is, John Bender argues, a 'covert impersonality at work here, some tacit collaboration between an implied third-person perspective . . . and an implied reader'.[18] Bender's 'tacit' relation between 'implied' subjects conjures a 'covert impersonality' that seems to transcend the subjective vagaries of the sentimental and the satiric, exposing the text to a relativism that Goldsmith is far from endorsing. If, as Ricardo Quintana notes, Goldsmith's 'art, for all its grace and apparent plasticity, has the strength and firmness of impersonal statement', it is in part because his work, in exposing the insufficiency of each mode on its own, recognizes the possibilities that issue from their confusion.[19] While neither the sentimental nor the satiric alone can register both the bustling energies of the emerging commercial order and the losses incurred by its consolidation, the movement *between* the two modes creates readers able to grieve the eclipse of an earlier order while attaining the critical distance necessary to grasp the new.

Notes

1. See, for example, Ashley Marshall, *The Practice of Satire in England, 1658–1770* (Baltimore, MD: Johns Hopkins University Press, 2013); Ronald Paulson, *Satire and the Novel* (New Haven, CT: Yale University Press, 1967); Stuart Tave, *The Amiable Humorist: A Study in the Comic Theory and Criticism of the Eighteenth and Early Nineteenth Centuries* (University of Chicago Press, 1960); on the persistence of satire, see Simon Dickie, *Cruelty and Laughter: Forgotten Comic Literature and the Unsentimental Eighteenth Century* (University of Chicago Press, 2011).
2. I. A. Richards, *Practical Criticism* (Edinburgh University Press, 1930), 182.
3. Sianne Ngai, *Ugly Feelings* (Cambridge, MA: Harvard University Press, 2005), 41, 81.
4. Thus Jaarsma says that Goldsmith's reviews and his 'Essay on the Theatre' mean he would not present these 'values to the reader for approbation in *The Vicar*', while Arthur Friedman uses the paratextual 'Advertisement' as proof that *The Vicar* is not satiric. Richard Jaarsma, 'Satiric Intent in *The Vicar of Wakefield*', *Studies in Short Fiction*, 5.4 (1968), 331–41 (334); Arthur Friedman, 'Introduction', *Vicar of Wakefield*, ed. Arthur Friedman (Oxford University Press, 1999), xvii. See also Wood, '*The Vicar of Wakefield* and Recent Goldsmith Scholarship', *Eighteenth-Century Studies*, 9.3 (1976), 429–43.

5. See Wayne Booth, '"The Self-Portraiture of Genius": *The Citizen of the World* and Critical Method', *Modern Philology*, 73.4 (1976), 585–96.

6. Charles Knight, 'Ironic Loneliness: The Case of Goldsmith's Chinaman', *Journal of English and Germanic Philology* 82.3 (1983), 347–64 (360). See also Robert H. Hopkins, *The True Genius of Oliver Goldsmith* (Baltimore, MD: Johns Hopkins University Press, 1969), 116–24.

7. Oliver Goldsmith, 'An Essay on the Theatre, or, A Comparison between Laughing and Sentimental Comedy', *Westminster Magazine*, 1.1 (January 1773), 4, 6.

8. Goldsmith, 'Essay on the Theatre', 4.

9. Arthur Sherbo, *English Sentimental Drama* (East Lansing: Michigan State University Press, 1957); Robert D. Hume, 'Goldsmith and Sheridan and the Supposed Revolution of 'Laughing' against 'Sentimental' Comedy', in *The Rakish Stage: Studies in English Drama, 1660–1800* (Carbondale: Southern Illinois University Press, 1983), 312–55 (316).

10. Frank Donoghue, '"He Never Gives Us Nothing That's Low": Goldsmith's Plays and the Reviewers', *English Literary History*, 55.3 (1988): 665–84 (666).

11. James Phillips, 'Oliver Goldsmith's *She Stoops to Conquer*: The Stakes of Shame and the Prospects of Politeness', *English Literary History*, 87.4 (2020): 999–1023 (1007).

12. Donoghue, 'He Never Gives Us Nothing', 665.

13. Ricardo Quintana, *Oliver Goldsmith: A Georgian Study* (New York: Macmillan, 1967); Hopkins, *True Genius*; Jaarsma, 'Satiric Intent'.

14. Hopkins, *True Genius*, 207.

15. James Kim, 'Goldsmith's Manhood: Hegemonic Masculinity and Sentimental Irony in *The Vicar of Wakefield*', *Eighteenth Century: Theory and Interpretation*, 59.1 (2018), 21–44

16. George Haggerty, 'Satire and Sentiment in *The Vicar of Wakefield*', *Eighteenth Century: Theory and Interpretation*, 32.1 (1991), 25–38 (36).

17. Hopkins, *True Genius*, 207.

18. John Bender, 'Prison Reform and the Sentence of Narration in *The Vicar of Wakefield*', in *The New Eighteenth Century*, ed. Felicity Nussbaum and Laura Brown (New York: Methuen 1987), 168–88 (183).

19. Quintana, *Oliver Goldsmith*, 16.

CHAPTER 28

The Sister Arts

Timothy Erwin

The visual approach to literary study today typically involves a knowledge of media culture. Film versions of classic fiction, websites devoted to poetry, and podcasts featuring the author interview reach us by way of mixed media. We absorb their messages through different kinds of interplay, between the dialogue and the film score, say, or the mise en scène and cinematography. Sorting out the mix sometimes requires a special vocabulary. For Goldsmith and his contemporaries, literary pictorialism offered two different ways of merging the verbal with the visual. Academic doctrine looked back to antiquity to fuse together narrative plot and visual arrangement. The analogy was based in a special knowledge of form and craft, as if the reader or beholder were looking over the artist's shoulder. The poet approximated the painter by slowing the narrative flow and describing an object in fine detail, a practice the Greeks called *ekphrasis*. In mastering the *difficulté vaincue* of the French academy, the painter transposed narrative time into visual space. The challenge was to select the right moment, since history painting was limited to the representation of single action, most often the Aristotelian turn or climax. The shared design was vested in classical rhetoric and ancient doctrine, in the *Ars poetica* of Horace, for example, which gave criticism the phrase *ut pictura poesis* (as is painting so is poetry).

Sibling rivalry prompted more forward-looking artists and writers to favour a progressive, scientifically assured analogy likening language to colouring. With the rise of empiricist aesthetics, the reader or beholder stood opposite the artwork to receive and reflect upon streaming sense impressions. The concern was to understand the way individual consciousness registered visual and verbal imagery. The approach focused on the subjective response to the discrete image and promised interpretive freedom. It took impetus from the *Essay concerning Human Understanding* (1690) of John Locke, with its notion of primary and secondary sense impressions, and from advances in science, especially Newtonian optics.

The term *sister arts* was originally rhetorical. Poetry and painting were deemed sisters because they traced a similar creative progress. John Dryden based the sisterhood in the first three parts of classical rhetoric – *inventio*, *dispositio*, and *elocutio*.[1] Invention included canvassing precedent, design meant arranging the parts to best effect, and colouring or stylistic elaboration gave the whole elevated expression. The shared creative sequence made for a sistership readily extended, mutatis mutandis, to the arts of musical composition, architecture, and landscape gardening. Throughout the century a knowledge of design, the middle term of the formal analogy, spoke to the unity and harmony of the artwork. In the academy it elevated painting from manual copying to mental contemplation. Sir Joshua Reynolds recommends that artists study poetry and music for that reason. 'There is no better way of acquiring this knowledge' he says, 'than by this kind of analogy: each art will corroborate and mutually reflect the truth on the other. Such a juxtaposition may likewise have this use, that whilst the artist is amusing himself in the contemplation of other arts, he may habitually transfer the principles of those arts to that which he professes.'[2]

Meanwhile Joseph Addison introduced the linguistic analogy in his papers 'On the Pleasures of the Imagination' from *The Spectator* (411–21; 1712). Addison endorses chromatic beauty at the expense of formal design. The beautiful attracts the gaze not through proportion and symmetry but instinctively by way of colouring. Verbal description can surpass visual depiction and even sense impression because language can make ideas more lively than sight itself: 'The Reader finds a Scene drawn in stronger Colours, and painted more to the Life in his Imagination, by the help of Words, than by an actual Survey of the Scene which they describe.'[3]

In the same spirit James Thomson praises the way Newton's optics 'Untwisted all the shining Robe of day' into its parent colours.[4] The empirical analogy of language to vivid colouring gains further support from the aesthetics of sublimity. Edmund Burke diminishes the power of formal beauty by opposing its inherent weakness to the strength of the sublime. William Collins and Thomas Gray follow suit, Collins by separating the lesser Horatian ode from the greater sublime ode and Gray by taking the Pindaric to ever loftier heights.

Goldsmith has always been considered a pictorial writer. Samuel Johnson commends the way *The Traveller* launches its survey of national custom as if from an alpine summit (see Chapter 22, 'Prospect Poetry'). Goethe gives the character of Parson Primrose his highest praise, while for Henry James the charm of *The Vicar of Wakefield* rests in its fine detail, a feature he credits to its author's irrepressible fancy.[5] Our author himself has little to say about the sources of his imagery, but artists were drawn to his work as to a lambent flame.[6] Before the century was out *The Deserted Village* was reimagined by Francis Wheatley, John Keyse Sherwin, and James Gillray, among others, and early the next Thomas Rowlandson added two dozen colour plates to *The Vicar of Wakefield*. All these images reflect an unusual visual appeal and offer clues to interpretation. They show that Goldsmith found a middle way by blending the unity of design with the poetics of striking imagery, bringing lively description within the compass of Augustan harmony.

Goldsmith largely rejected the sublime aesthetic of Burke, and with it a narrow view of the empirical analogy. In reviewing Burke's *Enquiry into the Origin of Our Ideas of the Sublime and Beautiful* (1757) he questions the opposition of sublimity versus beauty, self-preservation versus society, and pain versus pleasure. Where Burke names the kind of pleasure arising from the cessation of pain 'delight', Goldsmith argues that pleasure is pleasure, sometimes operating in conjunction with pain and sometimes not. Where Burke contends that sublimity depends upon physical exertion and that we experience sublime emotion in darkness because the expanding iris suffers a tension, Goldsmith the physician notes that in darkness the optic nerve in fact relaxes. Where Burke claims that beauty is clear and the sublime obscure, Goldsmith argues on the authority of Virgil that clear bold strokes carry the day for both. 'The term *painting*, in poetry', he writes, 'implies more than the mere assemblage of such pictures as affect the sight': 'sounds, tastes, feeling, all conspire to complete a poetical picture: hence this art takes the imagination by every inlet, and while it paints the picture, can give it motion and succession too. What wonder then it should strike us so powerfully!'[7]

The visual aspect of poetry derives from causes deeper than the mechanical operation of stimuli on the nervous system. Readers bring imagery to life by mixing sense impression with their personal experience, emotion, and taste. Goldsmith held with Horace that a work should be simple and uniform (*simplex dumtaxat et unum*), and he was suspicious of imagery untethered to its subject. When Lien Chi Altangi decries 'a parcel of gaudy images' (*Citizen*, 2:132) in verse, or when Mr Burchell denounces 'a combination of luxuriant images, without plot or connexion' (*Vicar*, 1:69), they speak for their author on the need for textual harmony.

An episode from *The Vicar of Wakefield* reimagined by Rowlandson helps to make the point (see Chapter 19, 'Fiction'). In the chapter 'The family use art, which is opposed with still greater', social ambition leads the Primrose family to commission a family portrait (Figure 28.1).

Figure 28.1 Thomas Rowlandson, 'The Family Picture', from chapter 16 of *The Vicar of Wakefield*, R. Ackermann, 1823. Huntington Library, RB 140485. The Huntington Library, San Marino, California

Sir William Thornhill, masquerading as Mr Burchell, has been dismissed from Primrose family gatherings for presuming to give advice, leaving his nephew their landlord free to seduce Olivia, one of the daughters. When the family fix on an allegorical history painting, the squire offers to sit with them and join the family in art, from which they assume that he is equally ready to join the family in life. In fact, they have exiled their protector and welcomed their undoer, and things will get worse before they get better. The humour involves several different kinds of incongruity: the picture proves too large to move, fails utterly to impress the neighbours, and disappoints one daughter while placing the other in jeopardy.

Rowlandson represents Mrs Primrose as the goddess Venus trying to make a match between Olivia and the squire, who kneels at her daughter's feet as Alexander the Great. She appears seated and surrounded by doves and cherubs. The vicar stands to her left and presents her with his view on clerical monogamy, not a position likely to interest the goddess of love. The family crowd into the image alongside 'as many sheep as the painter could put in for nothing' (*Vicar*, 1:161), as Goldsmith puts it, only to perform roles having little to do with one another. Although Mrs Primrose is pleased with its vivid colouring, the tableau is neither pastoral idyll nor history painting. Academic tradition held that a history painting should display no more than twelve figures in three distinct groups and should maintain unity of action by keeping to a single idea.[8] The family picture instead gives us a jumble of figures and ideas. The irony rests in how little design the squire needs to gain his ends and how much the family requires merely to fail in theirs. Instead of blaming the squire, the vicar owns that his wife laid schemes, as if her artifice were at all comparable. And that 'greater art' of the title? Goldsmith gives the phrase a literal twist so that it refers at once to a canvas too large to leave the kitchen and again to the outsized deception of the squire. Like a later illustration called 'A Connoisseur', not pictured here, the family portrait is a picture about picturing or metapicture. Neither image targets the art of painting or connoisseurship, any more than Goldsmith does.[9] They allow us to see how carefully he knits together text and image in a shared design aimed at the abuse of credulous innocence.

The single work that best represents the way that Goldsmith blends contested approaches to the sister arts is *The Deserted Village* (see Chapter 21, 'Pastoral Poetry'). Dedicated to Reynolds, the poem appeared the year after Goldsmith's appointment as Professor of Ancient History at the Royal Academy, and as we know shuttles back and forth between two time frames. One stretches forward from the medieval era to the time of the speaker's departure and describes a state of rural content. The other recounts the speaker's dismay at the unnatural decline of his native village whilst away. The speaker offers little in the way of narrative to link past to present, and yet pictorial touches are everywhere – in the pained glance that sweeps across the ruined landscape, the vivid characters sketched from memory, and the vignettes of village life then and now – all reimagined in concise verbal sketches. Victorian illustrators adapted several of them to the graphic arts, and one represents the 'hare whom hounds and horns pursue' (*Deserted Village*, 6) returning to its warren (Figure 28.2).

The metaphor is unusual and operates at some distance from the narrative. The tenor is the disappointed speaker and the timid herbivore the vehicle, and there is contrast between the two as well as resemblance. Both seek to return home safely but while the rabbit is hunted the speaker is not, at least not explicitly, and while the rabbit presumably has a safe place return to, the speaker has none. The illustrator Frederick Tayler reimagines the trope in a crisp naturalist style that recalls the linguistic analogy of depiction to lively description. From the time of Addison the linguistic analogy was linked to mercantilism, just as the formal analogy had been to court culture, but by the mid nineteenth century any

Figure 28.2 Frederick Tayler, 'As a Hare . . . ', from *The Deserted Village*, Etching
Club, London, 1841. Huntington Library, RB 292804. The Huntington Library, San
Marino, California

commercial aspect had blurred enough that an illustration like this could
sit comfortably alongside the general censure of trade.

Despite its lack of episodic narrative, the poem also represented the
formal analogy for Goldsmith's close contemporaries. From the 1780s
Gillray, Sherwin, and Wheatley superimposed a dramatic structure upon
the dual time frame. Gillray and Sherwin combine distinct characters from
the opening and close of the poem, the 'bashful virgin' (*Deserted Village*, 2)
and the dutiful daughter, into a single tragic figure. Wheatley portrays the
moment of narrative reversal when she follows her family, leaving behind
her beloved (Figure 28.3):

Figure 28.3 Anker Smith after Francis Wheatley, 'His Lovely Daughter ... ', from
The Poems of Oliver Goldsmith, F. J. Du Roveray, London, 1800. Huntington
Library, RB 108733. The Huntington Library, San Marino, California

His lovely daughter, lovelier in her tears,
The fond companion of his helpless years,
Silent went next, neglectful of her charms,
And left a lover's for a father's arms.

(*Deserted Village*, 20)

The image leads the eye from the church steeple at right to the paternal
figure at left, with his hands clasped in prayer, and then back to the central
dilemma. Her gaze a sentimental mix of blame and entreaty, the heroine at

the centre steps forward to confront the beholder with the acute cost of forced emigration. Even though the narrative turn lacks textual authority, the interpolated tale furnishes the poem with the reversal of history painting. As Reynolds says, 'a painter has but one sentence to utter, but one moment to exhibit', a stricture his fellow academicians understood as licence to create such a moment where it never existed.[10]

John Montague tells us that Goldsmith's aesthetics involve 'a personal development of the classical Augustan doctrine of "ut pictura poesis"'.[11] On this view an art of transition reconciles the parts to the proportions of a larger whole, as in architecture. The verse paragraph pictured here ends by posing the father in the 'silent manliness of grief' (*Deserted Village*, 21). In the next, much as an attorney turns to point an accusing finger at a criminal, the narrator launches his final peroration against the bane of luxury, bringing figural language to bear on poetic form. Who would trade away maternal affection, 'doubly dear' (21) when under duress, he asks, for the 'sickly greatness' (21) of unwieldy wealth? In less skilful hands the transition between a 'splendid and a happy land' (15) might appear abrupt. In Goldsmith the shift underscores the master trope, first by showing how trade makes its victims party to a bad bargain and then by voicing the proper moral response. Separate ligatures mediate between image and apostrophe, mute distress and narrative outrage, fellow feeling and a surfeit of greed, to exemplify the exchange of a divine blessing for a social blight. Strikingly imaginative phrasing is brought into the harmony of a larger design. For Reynolds the genius of his friend lay in an intuitive mastery of mental associations like these, linking what the poem calls the 'busy train' of memory (5) to the creation of a composite whole doubly memorable in its visual aspect.[12]

Notes

1. 'A Parallel betwixt Painting and Poetry', in *The Works of John Dryden: Prose 1691–1698*, ed. A. E. Wallace Maurer, vol. 20 (University of California Press, 1989), 38–77.
2. Sir Joshua Reynolds, *Discourses on Art*, ed. Robert W. Wark (London: Yale University Press, 1975), 234.
3. Joseph Addison, *Spectator* 412, in *The Spectator*, ed. Donald F. Bond, 5 vols. (Oxford: Clarendon, 1965), 3:560.
4. 'A Poem Sacred to the Memory of Sir Isaac Newton', in *James Thomson: Liberty, The Castle of Indolence, and Other Poems*, ed. James Sambrook (Oxford: Clarendon, 1986), 10.

5. Samuel Johnson, *Critical Review; Or, Annals of Literature*, 18 (December 1764), 458; Johann Wolfgang von Goethe, *The Autobiography of Goethe*, trans. John Oxenford, 2 vols. (London: Bell and Sons, 1897), 1:474; Oliver Goldsmith, *The Vicar of Wakefield*, intro. Henry James (New York: Century Company, 1900), xix–xx. For an historical overview of the reception, see *Critical Heritage*.

6. One contemporary claimed that Goldsmith knew nothing of the art of painting. See James Northcote, *Memoirs of Sir Joshua Reynolds* (London: Henry Colburn, 1813), 154.

7. *Monthly Review*, 16 (1757), 477n.

8. See C. A. Du Fresnoy, *The Art of Painting*, trans. John Dryden, 2nd ed., ed. Alexander Pope and Charles Jervas (London, 1716), 137: 'Annibal Carracci believed that a Picture cou'd not be good, in which there were above twelve Figures.' Du Fresnoy's treatise draws throughout on the practice of the Carracci academy.

9. When Mr Burchell prefers the 'erroneous but sublime animations of the Roman pencil' to the 'tame correct paintings of the Flemish school' (*Vicar of Wakefield*, 1:151), he displays his connoisseurship. Goldsmith had compared Italian and French painters in the same way. 'The striking and visible graces of a single piece of Veronese operate more strongly upon us', he explains', than the most finished pieces of the correct Le Brun' (*Critical Review*, 9 (1760), 12).

10. Reynolds, *Discourses*, 60. I've commented on these interrelations further in 'Book Illustration and The Deserted Village', *Studies in Eighteenth-Century Culture*, 52 (2023), 477–90.

11. John Montague, 'Exile and Prophecy: A Study of Goldsmith's Poetry', in *Goldsmith: The Gentle Master*, ed. Sean Lucy (Cork University Press, 1984), 50–65 (56).

12. In composition he knew instinctively 'how one sentiment breeds another in the mind': quoted from *Portraits by Sir Joshua Reynolds*, ed. Frederick W. Hilles (London: Heinemann, 1952), 52.

CHAPTER 29

Music and Song

Moyra Haslett

Oliver Goldsmith enjoyed singing and playing the flute, and music clearly was an integral part of his life. In childhood and adolescence in the rural midlands of Ireland, he played duets with his cousin Jane Contarine (he on the German flute, she on the harpsichord). In his student days in Trinity College Dublin, he may well have written ballads to be sold to printers in Mountrath Street.[1] In Edinburgh he is said to have entertained fellow medical students with 'songs and stories'.[2] When he toured the continent, he did so with his flute in his pocket, and probably procured lodging and food from appreciative peasant audiences by playing it. In the clubs and homes of friends in London, he sang regularly: one particularly noisy musical evening in Brick Court reportedly disturbed the lawyer Blackstone, who lived below, in the midst of writing up his famous legal *Commentaries*; at the Gerrard Street Club, on the evening of the debut performance of his play *The Good Natured Man* (1768), Goldsmith was said to have sung a popular comic song ('The Old Woman who was Tossed in a Blanket') to calm first-night nerves.[3] And, in one of his final essays, Goldsmith noted, simply, that music is 'an art, of which I am so fond'.[4] It is appropriate, therefore, that several portraits of Goldsmith should record this important element of his life and work: Thomas Rowlandson's water-colour of Vauxhall pleasure gardens (*c*.1784) features Goldsmith with others in a supper-box below the orchestra; Edward Matthew Ward's painting of Goldsmith and Samuel Johnson (*c*.1848) depicts Goldsmith's flute lying on the floor beside him; and the bronze sculpture by Éamonn O'Doherty in Ballymahon, Co. Longford (1999) shows him with the satchel and flute he took with him on his tour of the continent.

Musical references are so many and so diffused throughout Goldsmith's varied writings that in reading them we gain an immediate sense of a deeply informed and appreciative musical author who sometimes wrote explicitly on and about music but who more often integrated musical interests and experiences into his work. Foreign opera singers, castrati, and the affected, talentless singing of fashionable ladies; off-stage trumpets at the theatre and horn-playing in pleasure gardens and homes; the organ in St Paul's cathedral and its female organist; a wind-up music-box as tavern entertainment; street ballad-singers and carol singing; airs, minuets, and dance music from opera and pleasure gardens; the music of musical glasses, of the harpsichord, and of pipe and tabor; fiddles, guitars, halfpenny whistles, drums, bells, and the aeolian harp: all of these appear in Goldsmith's writings and testify to the sound-worlds of his contemporary London, his childhood in Ireland, and his experiences in Scotland and on the continent.

Immediately obvious from this list is Goldsmith's awareness of music of many different kinds. Goldsmith's essays on music include detailed considerations of professional music-making – on opera in England and on national 'Schools' of music (Pergolese, Lully, and Handel are judged to lead the Italian, French, and English schools) – and of scientific and philosophical theories of musical sound in two chapters in his *Survey of Experimental Philosophy* (published posthumously in 1776).[5] Among his earliest writings on music is also a short essay on the Irish harp-player Turlough Carolan (1760), a musician who notably blurs apparent boundaries between the 'concert' music of Vivaldi, Geminiani, and other baroque composers and the 'traditional' music of Ireland, between 'professional' music-making and 'recreational' playing (often thought of as 'amateur', though often it is not).[6] When Goldsmith himself came to write songs for his play *She Stoops to Conquer*, he turned to traditional tunes: the Irish air 'The Humours of Balamagairy' for a song to be sung by Kate Hardcastle, and a selection of traditional songs, Irish, Scottish, and ballad opera repertory, for a sung epilogue (see Chapter 20, 'Theatre').[7] But Goldsmith also wrote an oratorio on the theme of the imprisonment of the Israelites in Babylon and a formal cantata-type work performed as a public commemoration of the death of the Princess Dowager in 1772. Unsurprisingly, then, references to music in his works include the dance tune 'Nancy Dawson' and the minuet from Handel's opera *Ariadne*; traditional ballads and popular songs such as 'Ally Croaker' and 'Ballinamona', 'Hark the Thundering Cannons Roar' and 'The Beautiful Shepherdess of Arcadia'. He also refers to operatic singing such as the aria 'Che Farò' from Gluck's *Orfeo ed Eurydice* and the duet 'Lo conosco a quegl' occelli' from Pergolese's *La serva padrone*.

Although we think of these examples as belonging to very different kinds of music-making, there is good evidence that many eighteenth-century listeners enjoyed a wide variety of music and did not think of them as belonging to different spheres. Carolan famously absorbed and fused together continental baroque and native Irish traditions: Goldsmith's essay on the harper-composer recounts a wager in which Carolan composed on the spot a concerto in the style of Vivaldi. The Neals, Dublin publishers of the first printed collection of Irish tunes, arranged these for 'Violin, German Flute and Hautboy' and advertised on its title page the arrangement of one Irish tune in particular, 'Pléaráca na Ruarcach' (or 'O'Rourke's Feast'), as performed with bass and chorus and arranged by the Italian composer Lorenzo Bocchi.[8] Ballad operas and performances in the pleasure gardens mingled operatic arias with traditional melodies to hugely popular effect. Laurence Whyte, in a 1740 poem which opens in a Dublin theatre, depicts its audience listening to Italian music before calling for the bawdy 'Black Joke' and other popular songs as an encore.[9] Musical glasses, because they are fashionable, can be listed with Shakespeare and painting as an example of 'high' art, their repertoire ranging from Handel's 'Water Music' to the same 'Black Joke' (see *Vicar*, 1:84). Appropriately, then, we find Goldsmith noting in his account of the 'Club of Choice Spirits' (1759) that the pimple-nosed gentleman sings 'Gee Ho Dobbin' while a 'fat figure' with a rough voice offers the aria '*Softly Sweet* in Lydian measure' from Handel's musical ode *Alexander's Feast* (1736).[10]

Goldsmith was alert to the differences between the kinds of playing and singing involved here. He was scathing of pretension and lack of talent: Mrs Tibbs's singing, in *The Citizen of the World*, for example, gives 'but little satisfaction to any except her husband', largely because of its tiresome affectation (*Citizen*, 2:29). And Goldsmith was also conscious of the snobberies embedded in contemporary cultural opinions: in *She Stoops to Conquer*, for example, the '3rd fellow' defensively protests: 'What, tho' I am obligated to dance a bear, a man may be a gentleman for all that. May this be my poison if my bear ever dances but to the very genteelest of tunes. Water Parted [an aria from Thomas Arne's English opera *Artaxerxes*], or the minuet in [Handel's] Ariadne.' When the play's epilogue tells the tale of the barmaid's rise through the social ranks, one focus is upon her changing musical tastes:

> The fourth act shews her wedded to the 'Squire,
> And Madam now begins to hold it higher;
> Pretends to taste, at Operas cries *caro*
> And quits her Nancy Dawson, for *Che Faro*.
>
> (*Stoops*, 11 and epilogue, n.p.)

In *The Vicar of Wakefield*, the local girls, the Miss Flamboroughs, do not know 'country dances', which, despite their name, were danced by 'fashionable' ladies, but understand 'the jig and the round-about to perfection'; while George Primrose recounts to his family how his flute-playing was welcomed by peasants but unappreciated (and unrewarded) by 'people of fashion' who treat his performances as a form of begging (*Vicar*, 1:82, 2:25; see Chapter 19, 'Fiction'). And in *The Citizen of the World*, Lien Chi Altangi is impatient with never-ending performances of the period's most popular ballad opera, *The Beggar's Opera*: 'Rest, rest, ye three dear clinking shillings in my pocket's bottom, the music you make is more harmonious to my spirits than cat-gut, rosin, or all the nightingales that ever chirruped in petticoats' (*Citizen*, 2:86; see Chapter 11, 'Cosmopolitanism', and Chapter 26, 'Orientalism').

While these fictional characters may not represent Goldsmith's own views, a number of references – in both Goldsmith's letters and in his literary works – suggest he believed strongly in the emotional power of traditional singing. Most famous of all Goldsmith's references to music is the following from the *Bee* (1759): 'The music of the finest singer is dissonance to what I felt when our old dairy-maid sung me into tears with *Johnny Armstrong's Last Good Night* or *The Cruelty of Barbara Allen*' (*Bee*, 51–2).[11] Closely echoing this is the vicar of Wakefield's comment that 'the most vulgar ballad of them all generally pleases me better than the fine modern odes, and things that petrify us in a single stanza; productions that we at once detest and praise' (*Vicar*, 1:177). When Goldsmith wrote about concert music – what we would now call 'classical music' (although it was not so called then) – similar preferences recur. In his essay on the production of musical sound, for example, the musical glasses are praised above all for their simplicity of tone; in a discussion of baroque music, Pergolese is praised for the 'delicate simplicity' of his music while later Italian imitators are criticized for their 'studied elegance' and 'unaffecting affectation'.[12]

Goldsmith, then, repeatedly stated a preference for simplicity and unaffected singing. These qualities are not typically associated with the two formal, ambitious musical works for which Goldsmith wrote lyrics. However, even here we can see ways in which the texts spoke to the same impulse. The oratorio, known today under the title *The Captivity*, portrays song as a powerful conveyor of nostalgia. The enslaved Israelites sing songs of home and these songs evoke strong feelings of homesickness while also giving them strength to resist their Babylonian captors: 'That strain once more; it bids remembrance rise, / And brings my long-lost country to mine eyes', sings one of the Jewish prophets (Act I, ll.15–16).[13] The Jews in captivity indeed might be thought to resemble the Gaelic bards described

in Goldsmith's essay on Carolan who sing funereally of 'the bondage of
their country under the English government'.[14] And although the unstrung
lyres and harps which hang silently from the willows allude primarily to
biblical imagery, they are also suggestively evocative of Ireland, with the
country's traditional association with both sounding harps and, at times of
political struggle, unstrung harps.[15]

Goldsmith's formal commemoration for the death of the Princess
Dowager, the *Threnodia Augustalis* (1772), is scored for a musical ensemble
of three soloists and a chorus of twelve voices in addition to two speakers.
Its scope thus resembles the formal odes and serenatas performed as
a regular feature of royal ceremonial music in both London and
Dublin.[16] Notwithstanding these signals of a grand style, Peter Dixon's
passing comment that the work is a 'remodelling' of one of Goldsmith's
favourite ballads, 'Death and the Lady', merits a closer look.[17] The ballad
sings of an encounter between a young lady and the figure of Death. The
lady attempts to bribe Death to stay her death with an offer of gold, but the
offer is unavailing and Death remains resolute. In Goldsmith's *Threnodia*,
the woman speaker also directly addresses the figure of Death:

> Relentless tyrant, at thy call
> How do the good, the virtuous fall?
> Truth, beauty, worth, and all that most engage,
> But wake thy vengeance and provoke thy rage.[18]

Death then responds in an arioso, sung by the bass singer Samuel Thomas
Champness in a style both 'staccato' and 'spirited':

> When vice my dart and scythe supply,
> *How great a king of Terrors I!*
> If folly, fraud, your hearts engage,
> *Tremble ye mortals at my rage!*
> Fall, round me fall ye little things,
> Ye statesmen, warriors, poets, kings,
> *If virtue fail her counsel sage*
> Tremble ye mortals at my rage. (6)

This dramatization of the fatal encounter reflects that of Goldsmith's
singing of the ballad, as recalled by Joshua Reynolds: 'In singing ["Death
and the Lady"] he endeavoured to humour the dialogue by looking very
fierce and speaking in rough voice for Death, which he suddenly changed
when he came to the lady's part, putting on what he fancied to be a lady-
like sweetness of countenance with a thin, shrill voice.'[19] In Goldsmith's

adaptation, the lady in this specific encounter speaks; Death sings in reply, in music composed by the Neapolitan composer Mattia Vento.

Threnodia was the result of a commission from the famous 'impresario' Teresa Cornelys and the printer William Woodfall for a work to be performed at Cornelys's rooms in Soho Square, Carlisle House, famous for hosting various kinds of social entertainment for its private members, including dancing, masked balls, gambling, and music concerts. A letter from Woodfall to Goldsmith writes of how the initial plan for the work was that J. C. Bach would adapt some music by Purcell and Handel to fit Goldsmith's text, before Vento, a composer who had worked for Cornelys before, was appointed.[20] Although Vento's score is not known to have survived, from an eyewitness account of the performance we might expect a sombre setting: Cornelys decorated Carlisle House with black crape and curtains, with a central black canopy under which rested a mocked-up 'white tomb'. If Cornelys was aiming for a sombre, reverential occasion, however, the account speaks only of its being 'a most ridiculous whim' and neither Goldsmith nor Vento ever publicly acknowledged their involvement. Here too, then, we can see the mixing of 'high' and 'popular' forms of culture in which a sombre and stately work, a form of ceremonial cantata or ode, is performed in the 'fairy palace' of Carlisle House, albeit a House tricked out with the paraphernalia of mourning.[21]

In his essay 'On the Different Schools of Music', Goldsmith writes that Purcell attempted to 'unite the Italian manner that prevailed in his time with the antient Celtic carrol and the Scotch ballad', adding further that the Scotch ballad 'probably had also its origin in Italy: for some of the best Scotch ballads (the Broom of Cowdenknows, for instance) are still ascribed to David Rizzio'.[22] Later composers would set both Goldsmith's oratorio and his *Threnodia* to music, but neither would achieve the kind of intrinsic 'fusion' of the affecting power of traditional singing combined with the harmonic richness possible within orchestral or choral singing, or the performance of 'serious' music-making in informal, even frivolous settings which was possible within Goldsmith's own century.[23] Goldsmith was critical of the virtuosic flourishes of formal, professional singing, writing, for example, that these were caused by both the vanity of the singer and the 'sterility' of many cantatas.[24] But poor performance practice did not invalidate the essential core in which people singing arias by Pergolese, Purcell, and Handel, or traditional Irish and English songs and ballads, could equally move audiences to tears.

Notes

1. See Hugh Shields, *Goldsmith and Popular Song* (Dublin: Folk Music Society of Ireland / Cumann Cheol Tíre Éireann, 1985), 26; Julie Henigan, *Literacy and Orality in Eighteenth-Century Irish Song* (London: Routledge, 2016), 155.

2. See, for example, Thomas Percy's 'Life' of Goldsmith in *The Miscellaneous Works of Oliver Goldsmith*, 8 vols. (London, 1801), 1:19.

3. Claude Simpson notes that the song was often sung to the tune of 'Lilliburlero': Claude M. Simpson, *The British Broadside Ballad and Its Music* (New Brunswick, NJ: Rutgers University Press, 1966), 455. For more details on how this politically Williamite tune was used in very different contexts, see Moyra Haslett, '"With Brisk Merry Lays": Songs on the Wood's Halfpence Affair', in *Proceedings of the Seventh Münster Symposium on Jonathan Swift*, ed. Hermann J. Real (Munich: Wilhelm Fink, 2019), 217–18.

4. Oliver Goldsmith, *A Survey of Experimental Philosophy*, 2 vols. (London: 1776), 2:160.

5. 'Of the Opera in England', *Bee*, 248–52; 'On the Different Schools of Music', *The British Magazine*, 1 (1760), 74–6, 181–4; 'Of Musical Sounds' and 'Of Sound in General', in *A Survey of Experimental Philosophy*, 2 vols. (London: 1776), 2:148–65 and 166–204 (chapter x). The essay 'Of Musical Sounds' refers to works by Alberti, Tartini, Rameau, Handel, and Corelli.

6. Oliver Goldsmith, 'The History of Carolan, the Last Irish Bard', *The British Magazine* (July 1760), 418.

7. For a detailed consideration of song in *She Stoops to Conquer,* see Ross W. Duffin, '*She Stoops to Conquer* and Its Lost Songs', *Music & Letters*, 99.2 (2018), 159–93.

8. *A Col[l]ection of the Most Celebrated Irish Tunes, Proper for the Violin, German Flute of Hautboy* (Dublin, 1724).

9. See *The Collected Poems of Laurence Whyte*, ed. Michael Griffin (Lewisburg, PA: Bucknell University Press, 2016), 186–92.

10. *The Busy Body* 3 (13 October 1759), 15.

11. Two further sources corroborate this: an earlier letter in which Goldsmith praises Peggy Golden's singing of 'Johnny Armstrong's last good night' by the fireside in Lissoy above the operatic singing of Mattei and Joshua Reynolds's report that Goldsmith's favourite songs were 'Johnny Armstrong', 'Barbara Allen', and 'Death and the Lady'. See *Letters*, 22; *Portraits by Sir Joshua Reynolds*, ed. Frederick W. Hilles (London: Heinemann, 1952), 50. See also *Vicar*, 1:37.

12. Goldsmith, 'Of Musical Sounds', 158; 'Schools of Music', 74.

13. Oliver Goldsmith, 'The Captivity: An Oratorio', in *The Collected Works*, ed. Arthur Friedman, 5 vols. (Oxford: Clarendon, 1966), 4:216. Unpublished in Goldsmith's time, the text of 'The Captivity' is taken by Friedman from the manuscript now held at the Free Library in Philadelphia. It is one of two manuscript versions; the other is held at the New York Public Library.

14. Goldsmith, 'Carolan', 418.

15. 'The Captivity', 4:219: 'Ye sons of Judah why the lute unstrung / Or why those harps on yonder willows hung / Come leave your griefs and Joint our warbling Choir / For who like you can wake the sleeping lyre'. Compare Psalm 137:1–2. For examples of the 'untuned' and the 'unstrung' harp in Ireland, see *Tom Punsibi's Dream* (Dublin, 1724–5), 1, and *The Patriot Soldier; or Irish Volunteer. A Poem; by a Member of the Belfast First Volunteer Company* (Belfast, 1789), 6. The 'new strung' harp would become a prominent image of the United Irishmen in the 1790s, although it was prefigured in the earlier Volunteer movement: see *Flora's Banquet* (Belfast, 1782), viii. For the imagery of harps hanging silently on willows, see Thomas Moore's song 'My Gentle Harp'.

16. For more on this tradition, see Estelle Murphy, 'Ceremonial Song in Eighteenth-Century Dublin: Cousser's and Dubourg's Odes and Serenatas', in *The Oxford Handbook of Irish Song, 1100–1850*, ed. Conor Caldwell, Moyra Haslett, and Lillis O'Laoire (Oxford University Press, forthcoming).

17. Peter Dixon, *Oliver Goldsmith Revisited* (Boston, MA: Twayne, 1991), 68.

18. Oliver Goldsmith, *Threnodia Augustalis* (London, 1772), 6.

19. *Portraits by Sir Joshua Reynolds*, 50. See the Bodleian Ballads Online for eighteenth-century printings of the ballad, including one printed in London between 1736 and 1763: http://ballads.bodleian.ox.ac.uk/view/edition/18672 (accessed 8 June 2022).

20. See Friedman in *Collected Works*, IV:323–5.

21. For the eyewitness account, see James Harris, *A Series of Letters of the First Earl of Malmesbury, His Family and Friends from 1745 to 1820*, 2 vols. (London: Richard Bentley, 1870), 1:253–4 (letter from Elizabeth Harris to her son, 25 February 1772). 'Fairy palace' is Horace Walpole's term for Carlisle House: quoted in Judith Milhouse's entry on Teresa Cornelys in the *Oxford Dictionary of National Biography*.

22. *Collected Works*, III:93.

23. 'The Captivity' was set to music by Richard John Samuel Stevens in England (*c*.1809; British Library Add MS 31815) and by the Irish church musician George William Torrance (1864). *Threnodia* was set to music by Max Vogrich and performed at the Metropolitan Opera House, New York, on 28 April 1891. 'The Hermit' was also set to music by James Hook and published in Dublin in the mid-1780s.

24. Goldsmith, 'Of Musical Sounds', 163–4.

CHAPTER 30

France and French Writing

Amy Prendergast

Oliver Goldsmith's knowledge of the language and literature of France is in evidence across his writing, traversing all the genres he embraced. The author's biographer Washington Irving argued that Goldsmith acquired his 'smattering' of French from 'among the Irish priests at Ballymahon'.[1] His proficiency was secured across various towns in the midlands region, clearly offering him sufficient expertise to produce competent translations, including *The Memoirs of a Protestant, Condemned to the Galleys of France* (1758). In addition to his various paid engagements with translation work, French influences are in evidence throughout Goldsmith's journalism and essays, and are indeed omnipresent across his full body of work, being immediately apparent in his embracing of the sentimental novel with *The Vicar of Wakefield* (1766), for example.[2] This influence of French writing upon Goldsmith's work has long been recognized and dissected, with various authors held up for particular recognition of their import. At the apex of popularity amongst readers of French in Ireland, ranking third behind only dictionaries and grammars, were the writings of Voltaire, and it is unsurprising that Voltaire should be evidently such an omnipresent, irrefutable influence on Goldsmith's work, generating much scholarship.[3] Alongside Voltaire, Marivaux, and the Encyclopaedists, critics – following the influential work of Arthur Lytton Sells in the 1920s – have also highlighted Goldsmith's indebtedness to Justus Van Effen and Montesquieu, his plagiarism of François-Ignace Espiard de la Borde, and the similarities with the works of D'Argens and de Buffon.[4] While acknowledging and respecting these male influences, this chapter will also seek to highlight and explore the intersections with explicitly *female* French influences on Goldsmith's work, as well as detailing his own legacy amongst various French women writers and translators. Interconnections are particularly discernible between Goldsmith and Françoise de Graffigny (1695–1758), Madame de Montesson (1738–1806), and Marie-Jeanne Riccoboni (1713–92).

As well as being influenced by both the language and literature of France, Oliver Goldsmith's work was also clearly impacted by French culture. Goldsmith was not only a clubman, for example, but also a salon participant, and his work is imbued with an ethos of sociability and informed by a salon culture with undisputed origins in France before being embraced by salon hostesses in Britain and Ireland (see Chapter 8, 'The Club'). Goldsmith's oeuvre is imbued with French influence while he himself clearly left a lasting imprint upon the French literary landscape. Cultural transfer theory enables us to identify the degree of influence and cross-fertilization in place between works from different countries, disrupting impressions of 'self contained national cultures' and highlighting the prevalence and intensity of foreign cultural imports.[5] The relationship between Goldsmith and France is very much a symbiotic one, built upon interdependency and dialogue, commencing during Goldsmith's childhood in Ireland and cemented during his travels on the Continent in the 1750s, including his time in Paris in 1755. Goldsmith's embracing of these French influences took place during a period of severe tensions between Britain and France, and the writer's disinclination to share in any of the chauvinistic suspicion of France or of French intellectual culture so widespread in Britain, even in the midst of the Seven Years' War (1756–63), is particularly noteworthy and perhaps aligns him more with those writing from within an Irish tradition, though he was not in fact to return to his country of birth.

French literature had initially found a highly receptive audience in both eighteenth-century Ireland and Britain, with more than fifty booksellers publishing French material over the course of the century in Ireland, for example.[6] Alongside Enlightenment works and treatises were a myriad of French novels that proved extremely popular, both in the original language and in translation, particularly novels of a sentimental nature, such as those written by Antoine-François, Abbé Prévost, Madame de Graffigny, Baculard d'Arnaud, and Marivaux, with Gillian Dow arguing that 'there is a bit of Marivaux in nearly every eighteenth-century English novel'.[7] This pattern was mirrored in the popularity of later Irish and British sentimental writers in France, leading to a circulation of ideas and works between the countries, with transnational comparisons of the various sentimental novels revealing parallels, intersections, and dialogues between the writings emanating from the different countries.[8] Although written by both men and women, by the 1760s when Goldsmith engaged with the mode, sentimental writing had become identified with female authorship. Writers such as Elizabeth Griffith, Frances Sheridan, and Sarah Scott successfully embraced the genre in Ireland and England, with Marie-Jeanne Riccoboni at the forefront in France, leading to comments that 'this branch of the literary trade appears, now, to be almost entirely engrossed by the ladies'.[9] Though he denigrated such sentimental work, these portrayals of suffering and resistance and of challenges met with fortitude as well as emotion, inspired and influenced Goldsmith in his composition of his bestselling *The Vicar of Wakefield*, irrespective of whether the novel itself is now interpreted as parody of the genre or strict adherent to it (see Chapter 19, 'Fiction', and Chapter 27, 'Satire and Sentiment').[10] Goldsmith's widespread knowledge, if not appreciation, of sentimental novels by French women writers is irrefutable and includes his being the paid translator of Charlotte-Marie-Anne Charbonnier de la Guesnerie's *Mémoires de Miledi B.*, for instance, published in 1760 and translated into English the following year.[11] His intimacy with the French sentimental novel through the translation of such a 'little frothy elegant novel' would undoubtedly have shaped and impacted his own iteration of one, particularly given *The Vicar of Wakefield* was composed at this exact time, between 1760 and 1762, though not published until 1766.[12]

Within months of its publication, Goldsmith's *The Vicar of Wakefield* appeared in translation as *Le Ministre de Wakefield, histoire supposée écrit par lui-même* (London and Paris: Chez Pissot, Desaint, 1767). The work was almost immediately translated into French by actress and author Charlotte-Jeanne Béraud de La Haie de Riou, best known as Madame de Montesson, though neither her name nor Goldsmith's appears on the novel's title page. Such was its popularity in France that a twenty-fifth ostensibly new translation and a seventy-fifth reissue were published by 1860.[13] Prior even to its dissemination through the medium of French, *The Vicar of Wakefield* was being sought in the original by epistolary novelist and actress Marie-Jeanne Riccoboni, a French writer who enjoyed immense popularity across Europe, in original and translation, with one of her novels going through four Dublin editions alone.[14] Riccoboni's letter to actor and theatre manager David Garrick from 11 September 1766 indicates her extreme impatience to obtain Goldsmith's novel, and her disappointment when the promised deliverer of the work fails to produce the text:

> O rage! o fureur! le tranquille Écossois n' a ni curé, ni sacristain, ni vicaire; ne sçait ce que c'est, n'y comprend rien; ne connoit ni moi, ni le vicaire, ni l'église, ni ses prêtres,– c'est un grand hasard s'il connoit Dieu: Et moi de jurer comme un payen: sang et furies ! –Patience, disoit Mr. Changuion, eh, mon Dieu, patience! Le vicaire viendra, je vous assure qu'il viendra.[15]

That the novel was so eagerly sought by an author described as 'among the most significant women writers of the French Enlightenment' is an indication of Goldsmith's reach and influence, and of his work's appreciation by one of the most popular sentimental writers of the day.[16]

The links between Goldsmith's essays, published in book form as *The Citizen of the World* (1762), and Montesquieu's *Persian Letters* (1721) are widely recognized, but the work is also in dialogue with a variety of other texts, purportedly written by exotic travellers, which all sought to defamiliarize the eighteenth-century reader's European surroundings. Françoise de Graffigny's only novel, *Lettres d'une Péruvienne* (1747), for example, was translated as *Letters Written by a Peruvian Princess* (Dublin, 1748) and quickly became a bestseller in both Britain and Ireland, as well as further afield, with the author gaining Europe-wide fame.[17] Conveyed through the letters of the abducted Inca heroine, Zilia, the cross-cultural epistolary novel anticipates the major themes of Goldsmith's work, focusing on national difference and reflecting satirically on the life and manners of those in Europe, though centred in Paris rather than London. The complicated naïveté of Goldsmith's Lien Chi Altangi, wherein the traveller both misinterprets or misunderstands situations while conveying wisdom, can be instructively compared with the evolving character of the innocent and ignorant Zilia, whose initial letters convey a naïve young girl wholly ignorant of quotidian objects such as mirrors (Letter X) and, more threateningly, of the dangers of male lust (Letter XII), who then matures and offers insightful opinions over the ensuing pages of one-sided letters (see Chapter 11, 'Cosmopolitanism', and Chapter 26, 'Orientalism').[18]

In addition to her writing, Françoise de Graffigny was a prominent figure in the world of the French salons, both through her participation in the salons of Jeanne Quinault and through her own role as a *salonnière* whose salons attracted writers and journalists along with artists and scientists. Literary salons had been a key feature of French society since the seventeenth century, promoting intellectual exchanges and debate.[19] The gatherings were emulated by hostesses in Britain and Ireland, who espoused the format in order to provide a similar facet of associational life for invited participants. Oliver Goldsmith's attendance at the celebrated Streatham salons of Wales-born diarist and author Hester Lynch Thrale, later Piozzi (1741–1821), has been generally glossed over, seen as secondary to his membership of Dr Samuel Johnson's Club, perhaps owing to the mixed-gender nature of these literary gatherings. Though an avid participant, Johnson himself famously derided these salons and bemoaned his subjection to their 'petticoat government'.[20] Goldsmith lamented how

Johnson, wishing to hold sway with monologues rather than respect the interactive polyvocal nature of the salons, was 'for making a monarchy of what should be a republic'. After Goldsmith's death in April 1774, Johnson remarked to Thrale: 'poor Goldsmith will be much missed at your literary parties'.[21] Whether in France or abroad, the literary salon enabled all participants to engage in conversation and debate on a range of topics, with the coming together of like-minded people to participate in intelligent debate rather than to play cards or gossip. These 'literary parties' were an institution that also permitted the enhancement and, indeed, even the establishment of literary reputations.

An introduction into a salon, whether in France, Britain, or Ireland, secured a professional network and ultimately an influential audience for aspiring authors. Goldsmith's presence at Thrale's salons awarded him additional status, which he constantly sought, as well as permitting the further dissemination of his work.[22] His depiction upon the periphery of James Doyle's well-known group portrait of Johnson's Club members has been discussed as evidence of his failure to fully integrate into that Club of which he was proud to be a member and reminds us of his position as 'a man on the fringes', full of cultural anxiety and a desire to be accepted.[23] However, Goldsmith was afforded equal status in the visual representation of salon sociability, starring in Thrale's three-quarter-length portrait gallery of her salon's most distinguished guests alongside such figures as Johnson, Edmund Burke, Dr Charles Burney, and Sir Joshua Reynolds, who had himself painted the portraits. The mixed-gender emphasis and meritocratic nature at the heart of the salons generally enabled a more democratic sociability to be embraced, and it seems impossible that this would not have informed those aspects of sociability that pervade Goldsmith's work and have contributed to his transformation into a more assertive, confident, and successful author, despite the various difficulties he encountered as a result of his nationality and position in society.

This transnational consideration of a cosmopolitan Irish writer has show-cased instances of cross-fertilization between the work of Oliver Goldsmith and France and French writing. These Franco-Irish and Anglo-French connections and dialogues also gesture towards a wider pan-European Republic of Letters, highlighting writers who were responding to European trends and a wider cultural identity than that represented by national signifiers alone (see Chapter 5, 'Enlightenments'). This broader cultural identity and process of cultural transfer through translation, trans-mission, and the transfer of ideas formed the basis for a 'reciprocity of intercultural exchange' that the eighteenth-century literary world represented.[24] Goldsmith's career is an exemplary case study of the symbiotic relationship that existed between writers across different European countries during this period, responding to developments across a range of genres, from novels to periodical writing to plays. Goldsmith was influenced by his own engagement with the process of translations, as well as informed by French sentimental writing, epistolary novels, and salon sociability. His own impact on French literature is equally palpable, and this chapter has illustrated that these literary and cultural transfers were not exclusively a male preserve. Instead, it is apparent that Oliver Goldsmith's writing was substantively shaped by and in dialogue with the works of French novelists, translators, and playwrights of both genders.

Notes

1. Washington Irving, *Oliver Goldsmith: A Biography* (London, 1850), 75.
2. French idioms and expressions also abound throughout *She Stoops to Conquer* (1773), with clear similarities to contemporary French characters and style immediately evident, alongside the commentary and reflections on French culture and stereotype. See Charlotte Lee, 'Comparison of Marivaux's *Le Jeu de l'Amour et du Hasard* and Goldsmith's *She Stoops to Conquer*' (Unpublished MA dissertation, University of Wichita, 1931).
3. Graham Gargett, 'Plagiarism, Translation and the Problem of Identity: Oliver Goldsmith and Voltaire', *Eighteenth-Century Ireland*, 16 (2001), 81–103.
4. Arthur Lytton Sells, *Les Sources Françaises de Oliver Goldsmith* (Champion, 1924); Michael Griffin, 'Oliver Goldsmith and François-Ignace de la Borde: An Instance of Plagiarism', *Review of English Studies*, 50.197 (1999), 59–63.
5. Stefanie Stockhorst, 'Introduction. Cultural Transfer through Translation: A Current Perspective in Enlightenment Studies', in *Cultural Transfer through Translation: The Circulation of Enlightened Thought in Europe by Means of Translation*, ed. Stefanie Stockhorst (New York: Rodopi, 2010), 7–26 (21).
6. Máire Kennedy and Geraldine Sheridan, 'The Trade in French Books in Eighteenth-Century Ireland', in *Ireland and the French Enlightenment*, ed. Graham Gargett and Geraldine Sheridan (Basingstoke: Macmillan, 1999), 173–96.
7. Gillian Dow, 'Criss-Crossing the Channel: The French Novel and English Translation, 1660–1832', in *The Oxford Handbook of the Eighteenth-Century Novel*, ed. J. A. Downie (Oxford University Press, 2016), 88–104.
8. *Translators, Interpreters, Mediators: Women Writers, 1700–1900*, ed. Gillian Dow (Bern: Peter Lang, 2007); Amy Prendergast, 'Transnational Influence and Exchange: The Intersections between Irish and French Sentimental Novels', in *Irish Literature in Transition, Volume I: 1700–1780*, ed. Moyra Haslett (Cambridge University Press, 2020), 189–206.

9. 'Review of *The History of Pamela Howard*, *Monthly Review, or Literary Journal, Enlarged*, 51 (1773), 154.

10. For overview of such literary debates, see George E. Haggerty, 'Satire and Sentiment in "The Vicar of Wakefield"', *The Eighteenth Century*, 31.1 (1991), 25–38.

11. This novel has frequently been misattributed to Riccoboni. Marijn S. Kaplan, 'Publication, Authorship, and Ownership in Marie Jeanne Riccoboni', *The French Review* 88.1 (2014), 179–91; Arthur Freeman, 'New Goldsmith?', *Times Literary Supplement* (15 December 2006), 15–16. 'Received from Mr. Ralph Griffiths the sum of ten pounds ten shillings, for the translation of a book entitled Memoirs of my Lady B., as witness my hand'. *The Works of Oliver Goldsmith*, ed. J. W. M. Gibbs (London: George Bell and Sons, 1884), 1:478.

12. 'Review of Memoirs of Lady Harriot Butler', *Critical Review*, November 1761.

13. Katrin Van Bragt lists full details of these translations, their translators, and their issue dates in 'The Tradition of a Translation and Its Implications: '"The Vicar of Wakefield" in French Translation', *Dispositio*, 7.19/21 (1982), 63–75 (64).

14. Riccoboni's third novel, *Lettres de Milady Juliette Catesby à Milady Henriette Campley, son amie*, was second in popularity only to Rousseau's *La Nouvelle Héloïse* (1761).

15. *Critical Heritage*, 48–9. 'O rage! O fury! the Scotsman has neither curate, nor sacristan, nor vicar; knows not what it is, understands nothing; knows neither me, nor the vicar, nor the church, nor her priests – it's a long shot that he knows God: And I am left cursing like a pagan, blood and fury! – Patience, says Mr. Changuion, oh, my God, patience! The vicar will come, I can assure you that he will come' [my translation].

16. Marijn S. Kaplan, *Marie Jeanne Riccoboni's Epistolary Feminism: Fact, Fiction, and Voice* (London: Routledge, 2020).

17. David Smith, 'The Popularity of Mme de Graffigny's *Lettres d'une Péruvienne*: The Bibliographical Evidence', *Eighteenth-Century Fiction*, 3 (1990), 1–20.

18. Françoise de Graffigny, *Letters of a Peruvian Woman*, trans. Jonathan Mallinson (Oxford World's Classics, 2009).

19. Dena Goodman, *The Republic of Letters* (London: Cornell University Press, 1994).

20. *The Letters of Samuel Johnson*, ed. Bruce Redford, 4 vols. (Oxford: Clarendon, 1992–4), 3:250.

21. James L. Clifford, *Hester Lynch Piozzi (Mrs Thrale)* (Oxford: Clarendon, 1941), 121.

22. We know that Thrale disseminated the work of Arthur Murphy in manuscript form, sending it to Thomas Percy, for instance. Hester Lynch Piozzi, *The Piozzi Letters*, ed. Edward Bloom and Lillian Bloom, 6 vols. (Newark: University of Delaware Press, 1989–96), 2:46.

23. *Letters*, xlv–xlviii. Griffin and O'Shaughnessy do note that he was 'not always on the periphery of sociability' and discuss his hosting suppers in his rooms as an example (xlix).

24. Stockhorst, *Cultural Transfer*, 20.

PART IV

Critical Fortunes and Afterlives

CHAPTER 31

Editions

Will Bowers

For 100 years after his death in 1774, Oliver Goldsmith was a national, European, and global publishing phenomenon: his major works were continuously in print in English, while editions in other languages disseminated Goldsmith in novel ways. In the past century, however, editions of Goldsmith have been rarer and of an increasingly academic bent, reflecting his movement from popular author with broad appeal to one whose readership is found predominantly in the university. This chapter is concerned with tracing and analysing these two phases in Goldsmith's publishing history. To do so, it predominantly considers collected editions and editions of *The Vicar of Wakefield* (1766) and *The Deserted Village* (1770) to examine how various approaches towards text and paratext shaped readers' experiences.

Two years after Goldsmith's death, Sir Joshua Reynolds opens a portrait of his close friend with editions in mind: 'If anyone thinks that Dr. Goldsmith was a man not worth the investigation, we must refer him to the public advertisements, where he will find the booksellers have lived upon his reputation, as his friends have lived upon his character, ever since his death'.[1] Reynolds is prescient about Goldsmith's print afterlife: booksellers published dozens of editions in the decades following his death, and in the immediate aftermath produced numerous epitaphs and elegies (see Chapter 32, 'Critical Reception before 1900'). Those works still in fourteen-year copyright remained popular, with *The Deserted Village* running to some twenty-six editions up to the end of its copyright in 1784. Eleven of these were by the copyright holder – printed by Griffin and his successors Rivington, Carnan, and Cadell – with the rest piracies published in London or in provincial hubs such as Belfast and Manchester. The last copyright edition of *The Deserted Village*, the eleventh of 1784, begins by claiming itself as a 'Genuine and Correct edition' and castigating 'extremely incorrect' piracies in a notice which, as William B. Todd has rightly argued, is designed to maintain the publishers' privilege and authority over a popular poem now available for any publisher in the marketplace to print.[2] Predictably, the notice had little effect: scores of London editions were published by various publishers after 1784 along with editions from places such as Glasgow (1794, 1796), Philadelphia (1786, 1791), and Boston (1790, 1793). By and large these editions did not embellish the poem with paratexts or explanatory notes: they were simply aimed to satisfy the demand for *The Deserted Village* across the English-speaking world. There is one notable exception: *Villa Deserta, Poema, Oliveri Goldsmith, Latinè redditum, a Gulielmo Humphries* (Londini: Dennett Jacques, 1790). In this edition Goldsmith's text is printed with a parallel Latin translation on the right-hand page by the Hertfordshire author and occasional *Gentleman's Magazine* contributor William Humphries. As had been the case with eighteenth-century Latin translations of Milton and Spenser, the purpose of this edition is twofold: to facilitate a wider European readership for Goldsmith's poem, and, more importantly, to claim that the literary merit of *The Deserted Village* made it worthy of consideration among poems in the European literary lingua franca (see Chapter 21, 'Pastoral Poetry').[3]

Translation into Latin was not the only way an edition could attempt to bestow canonicity: as Michael Gamer has argued, the Romantic-period literary marketplace also saw collecting an author's work as a means of conferring this status.[4] However, the fact that Goldsmith died in his writing prime (aged forty-five), and well within the copyright period for many of his major works, meant something of a lag in the number of collected editions. Rivington and the other holders of copyright produced the first in two volumes: *Poetical and Dramatic Works of Oliver Goldsmith, M. B. Now First Collected. With an Account of the Life and Writings of the Author* (London, 1780, 1786, 1791). This edition contained several paratexts: a dedication to Joshua Reynolds (the original dedicatee of the *Deserted Village*) which hoped the edition would be 'a lasting monument of [Goldsmith's] Genius' (v); William Woty's epitaph to Goldsmith; and a 'Life of Oliver Goldsmith' based on Richard Glover's *Life of Dr. Oliver Goldsmith* (1774). Those who wished to put out a collected Goldsmith before the end of copyright had a few options. One was to break up Goldsmith into quotations, as did *The Beauties of Goldsmith: or, The Moral and Sentimental Treasury of Genius* (published in London by George Kearsley in 1782), to provide a sort of greatest hits compilation, alphabetically ordered for easy consultation. Another was to publish in Dublin, and a large group of booksellers from that city advertised a collected edition of Goldsmith's poems by subscription in 1785 which promised a 'new life of the author' which corrected 'innumerable errors of former biographers'.[5] The proposed Dublin edition, under the management of Thomas Percy, had been in development since Goldsmith's death, and at one time it was hoped Samuel Johnson would write this 'new life' as part of the *Lives of the Most Eminent Poets* (1779–81). Neither the Johnson biography nor the Dublin edition ever came to fruition.[6] It was not until 1802 that Percy's project, under the editorship of Samuel Rose, was published, and by then copyright was no longer a concern.[7] *The Miscellaneous Works of Oliver Goldsmith* was worth the wait: it is the most significant early collected edition containing the greatest range of works printed to date and prefaced by the most detailed biography of Goldsmith based on information Percy collected during their friendship.[8] It became the standard collection of Goldsmith and was reprinted throughout the nineteenth century.

Posthumous editions of the *Vicar* show Goldsmith's influence beyond the English-speaking world (see Chapter 34, 'Afterlives 1: The Victorian *Vicar*'). Goldsmith's best-known prose work was not an instant success, running to only five copyright and a few pirate editions up to his death in 1774, but it then enjoyed a late boom with twenty-three London editions up to 1800. The international market worked with a similar delay: there had been translations in French and German in 1767, and another in Dutch in 1768, but international editions began in earnest near the end of the century. Many took conventional forms, reprinting Goldsmith's text or translating it into a foreign language, but others present the *Vicar* in bibliographically innovative ways.

German readers who wanted more than an English text or a translation could purchase the 1794 Berlin edition, which included a preface on English pronunciation and a text with 'richtigen Accenten versehen' ('correct verse accents').[9] In this edition, the famous opening opinion appears as: 'thê hónest mán whō márried ánd bróught úp à lárge fámily, díd mòre sérvice thán hè whō contínued single, ánd ònly talked óf population' (1). These diacritical marks, familiar to readers of ancient Greek, would be little help with language acquisition, but they do offer the aspiring Anglophile a way to engage with the *Vicar* in the correct tones (and perhaps aid German families wishing to act aloud the conversations of the Primrose family).

Other editors did have English learners in mind. An unremarkable Danish edition of the English text was published in Copenhagen in 1797, but three years later an edition purporting to be published in London (but probably again published in Copenhagen) showed a demand from Danish readers for an explanation of Goldsmith's language.[10] This 1800 edition contained some sixty pages of English–Danish vocabulary clarifying phrases such as 'it matters little', 'staked a counter', and 'minute's warning', and such a vocabulary suggests Goldsmith's novel was used for learning informal English. The case for the novel's pedagogical use is strengthened by looking at one of the more innovative French editions, also published in 1800. The edition is a 'Stereotype edition' published by Firmin and Pierre-Francois Didot, the French publishing family who had made commercially viable printing from metal plates rather than from individual movable types.[11] Like the Danish *Vicar* this edition contains notes, but these go further than simple translation, as these two examples show:

> *Pag.* 19, *lin.* 23. Christmas carols: hymns sung by the common people of England at Christmas (*Cantiques de Noël*)

[. . .]

> *Pag.* 57, *lin.* 6, 9. Blind man's buff, hot cockles, etc: plays of young people, such as *Colin-Maillard, main-chaude*, etc. in France. (232–3)

The Paris edition not only translates but also offers an explanation which informs French readers of English social contexts. All these international paratexts to the *Vicar* are aimed at readers who already have a grasp of English, who wish to augment their appreciation of a novel which was fast becoming a European classic by getting themselves closer to what these editions told them were Goldsmith's intended sounds and meanings.

International editions of Goldsmith were often aimed at educating non-native speakers, those who, as an 1800 Frankfurt edition of the *Vicar* put it, 'apply themselves to the English language'.[12] But, thanks to the steam press and its potential for mass production after 1830, there were also dozens of nineteenth-century editions of Goldsmith aimed at educating British (and imperial) schoolchildren. Goldsmith had long been thought of as an author who 'invited the young mind to the talk of study and improvement' and his works were often printed in portable, short, and cheap editions 'for use in schools'.[13] For the poetry this meant printing Goldsmith's major works and a glossary in small volumes cheaply bound, as exemplified by 'Chambers's English Classics', while school editions of the *Vicar* often provided lengthy explanatory notes, as in the 'Blackwoods' Educational Series', and in some cases abridged the text, as in the edition by the educationalist H. Courthope Bowen for 'Bell's Reading Books'.[14] It is clear from these editions that Goldsmith was popular in schools, but why? *The Vicar* (especially if carefully abridged) could show the virtues of a Christian and family-oriented home, while *The Deserted Village* could warn of losing the communities which allow such families to thrive, and as an introduction to the heroic couplet (the form which had promoted moral improvement for most of the eighteenth century). A list of other titles in the 'Bell's Reading Books' series suggests one other possible reason, as the novel is listed alongside *Great Englishmen: Short Lives for Young Children*, Robert Southey's patriotic *Life of Nelson* (1813), and a life of the Duke of Wellington. Charles Primrose's narrative of good- and ill-natured provincial life, with its exploration of morality, commerce, and class, is situated (in spite of Goldsmith's Irishness) among a list of suitable texts with which to educate the youth of an empire. It is in the context of this national reading of the *Vicar* that we can appreciate the two-part *Annotations on Goldsmith's Vicar of Wakefield* (1881), written by Hira Lal Pal, a teacher at a school in West Bengal.[15] The more than 300 pages of notes can be viewed as functioning purely educationally, as many foreign editions had before, but the colonial context of publication also suggests the recruitment of Goldsmith in a project to inculcate Britishness into a population growing up some 4,500 miles from the imperial centre.

The nature of and reasons for Goldsmith's dwindling popularity in the twentieth century are the subject of other chapters in this volume, but editions of his work from this period show that he still fascinated and engaged his editors. Austin Dobson's *The Complete Poetical Works of Oliver Goldsmith* (1906) is in some senses the final nineteenth-century edition, the last in a long line which aimed to elucidate Goldsmith's life and work in an age when 'fresh Goldsmith facts are growing rare' (see Chapter 36, Afterlives 3: Poetry').[16] But facts were not, or not predominantly, the grounds for the differences between the two most significant twentieth-century editions of Goldsmith: Arthur Friedman's five-volume *Collected Works of Oliver Goldsmith* (1966) and Roger Lonsdale's *The Poems of Gray, Collins and Goldsmith* (1969). They represent a Janus-faced moment in editorial attitudes, with one edition hoping to take us back to the intentions of the 1760s and 1770s while the other attempts to move the text into the 1960s and 1970s. Influenced by the work of Fredson Bowers, Friedman uses the earliest version (including manuscripts) as his copy text (with copious collations of other editions), because he believes this best represents authorial intention on punctuation. He also does not regularize punctuation or spelling, and he does not change things we would now regard as solecisms (e.g. *it's/its* confusions). Lonsdale (and the *Longman Annotated English Poets* series his work is a part of) takes a very different approach: copy texts are usually taken from the last authoritative version, with only occasional collation with earlier editions; spelling and punctuation are modernized; solecisms are corrected; and poetic elisions are removed when they do not change the metre (e.g. *chill'd* becomes *chilled*). The paratexts too are conceived of differently. Lonsdale follows the Longman series's policy laid out by F. W. Bateson '*to supply whatever information the adult reader* (= approximately the undergraduate, English or American, specializing in English literature upwards) *may be expected to require if he is to appreciate the work's original impact and intention*', and his Goldsmith edition includes copious explanation of the meaning of words and allusions to earlier poetry.[17] Each poem also features a headnote to elucidate its composition, genre, themes, sources, contexts, and reception, a beautiful example of which can be found in the *Deserted Village* which discusses '[Goldsmith's] blending of traditional form, content and style with a new sensibility and rhetoric' in three paragraphs on the poem's amalgamation of Virgil and Milton, and the marked musicality of its couplets.[18] Friedman's methodology is less intent on situating texts within a literary tradition, and his introductions to items maintain his textual focus by considering the composition, publication, and publication history of the text. The notes in this edition are infrequent and rarely expansive, provided 'only when some special knowledge is required that could not be gained without at least a minimum of research'; their main use is to compare a line or phrase to other moments in parts of Goldsmith's oeuvre, which means Friedman's *Collected Works* gives an unrivalled sense of Goldsmith's enduring preoccupations and concerns.[19] Indeed, so restrained are Friedman's notes that when Oxford World's Classics updated their edition of the *Vicar* in 2006, using Friedman's text, they felt that the general reader needed additional explanatory notes and an introduction (provided by Robert L. Mack).[20]

A comparison of Friedman and Lonsdale reveals how different two contemporary editions of the same author can be. But the terms of their difference – the choice between an edition which claims accuracy and/or authenticity and one that claims readability, and decisions over what a reader (British or foreign) needs explained to them – are the same as those that Goldsmith's editors and publishers have faced for centuries. The loss of Goldsmith in particular and of eighteenth-century literature in general from 'use in schools', and the various changes in language and reading brought about by the internet, mean any modern edition of Goldsmith would be as much like those editions aimed at foreign readers of the 1790s – explaining changed meanings of words such as *polite* and *pathetic*, and archaic weights and measures – as it would be engaged in textual debates. A new Cambridge University Press edition of Goldsmith is under way, with Michael J. Griffin and David O'Shaughnessy as its general editors; it will bring Goldsmith's histories into his canon for the first time, and it must walk the old tightrope between rigour and utility (see Chapter 24, 'History Writing'). It is fanciful to think a new edition can put Goldsmith back into the schoolroom or much change his general popularity, but just as Friedman and Lonsdale had the opportunity to reassess an author in the light of critical trends, so do Griffin and O'Shaughnessy. The study of eighteenth-century literature is more poly-vocal, international, and interdisciplinary than it was fifty years ago: a new edition of Goldsmith has a brilliant opportunity to reconceive of an Irish author who excelled in drama, history, journalism, poetry, and the novel, in light of these developments.

Notes

1. Joshua Reynolds, *Portraits*, ed. Frederick W. Hilles (New York: McGraw-Hill, 1952), 44–5.
2. William B. Todd, 'The "Private Issues" of *The Deserted* Village', *Studies in Bibliography*, vi (1953–4), 25–44 (35).
3. See Hazel Wilkinson, *Edmund Spenser and the Eighteenth-Century Book* (Cambridge University Press, 2017), 93; Estelle Hann, '"Latinising" Milton: *Paradise Lost*, *Latinitas* and the Long Eighteenth Century', in *Milton in Translation*, ed. Angelica Duran, Islam Issa, and Jonathan R. Olson (Oxford University Press, 2017), 93–113.
4. See Michael Gamer, *Romanticism, Self-Canonization, and the Business of Poetry* (Cambridge University Press, 2017).
5. *Proposals, for Printing by Subscription, the Poetical Works of Dr. Oliver Goldsmith . . . To Which Will Be Prefixed, a New Life of the Author. In This Will Be Corrected Innumerable Errors of Former Biographers* (Dublin, 1785).
6. See Thomas Percy, *Life of Dr. Oliver Goldsmith*, ed. Richard L. Hard (Salzburg: Institut für Englische Sprache und Literatur, 1976), viii–ix. Copyright was a particular problem for Johnson, as the *Lives* were originally prefaced to selected editions of the poet in question.
7. *The Miscellaneous Works of Oliver Goldsmith, M.B. A New Edition . . . To Which Is Prefixed, Some Account of His Life and Writings* (London, 1801 [1802]).
8. For the sources see Katharine C. Balderston, *The History and Sources of Percy's Memoir of Goldsmith* (Cambridge University Press, 1926), 23–50.
9. Oliver Goldsmith, *The Vicar of Wakefield* (Berlin: Gottfried Carl Nauck, 1794).

10. Oliver Goldsmith, *The Vicar of Wakefield* (London [i.e. Copenhagen]: 1800). Both the Scandinavian style of the title page and an advert for books by F. Brummer of Copenhagen suggests Danish publication.

11. Oliver Goldsmith, *The Vicar of Wakefield* (Paris: P. Didot the elder, and F. Didot, Eighth year [1800]).

12. Oliver Goldsmith, *The Vicar of Wakefield* (Frankfurt: 1800).

13. *Novellettes, Selected for the Use of Young Ladies and Gentlemen* (London: Fielder and Walker, 1780), i–ii.

14. *Goldsmith's Traveller,* Deserted Village, *and* The Hermit (London: W. & R. Chambers, [1870]); Oliver Goldsmith, *The Vicar of Wakefield* (London: Blackwood's, 1885); Oliver Goldsmith, *The Vicar of Wakefield* (London: George Bell, 1883).

15. Hira Lal Pal, *Annotations on Goldsmith's Vicar of Wakefield*, 2 vols. (Calcutta: Palmary Press, 1881).

16. *The Complete Poetical Works of Oliver Goldsmith*, ed. Austin Dobson (Oxford University Press, 1906), iii.

17. John Barnard quoting Bateson, 'Longman Annotated English Poets: Policy and Style Sheet', 3pp, type-written document sent to editors in the 1970s, 1.

18. *The Poems of Gray, Collins and Goldsmith*, ed. Roger Lonsdale (Harlow: Longmans, 1969), 672–3.

19. *Collected Works of Oliver Goldsmith*, ed. Arthur Friedman, 5 vols. (Oxford: Clarendon, 1966), 1:xx.

20. Oliver Goldsmith, *The Vicar of Wakefield*, ed. Arthur Friedman, notes and introduction by Robert L. Mack (Oxford University Press, 2006).

CHAPTER 32

Critical Reception before 1900

Megan Kitching

The early history of Oliver Goldsmith's critical reception reveals him to be one of the best known yet least understood writers of his period. Goldsmith helped shape the developing field of British literary criticism; however, many commentators have concluded that he has been ill served by his own critics. G. S. Rousseau in compiling his 1974 *Critical Heritage* despaired of the scarcity of serious responses from eighteenth- and nineteenth-century sources on Goldsmith. Certainly, the range of Goldsmith's literary output makes any summary of his reception difficult. Rousseau omits *The Citizen of the World* from his critical heritage, while Samuel Woods's annotated bibliography omits *An History of the Earth, and Animated Nature*. Taking into account such commissioned works and his popular journalism allows us to expand the landscape and contexts of Goldsmith criticism beyond the reception of his three major publications. Goldsmith wrote widely, and if his biography remains scantily documented, his critical bibliography is hardly as sparse as Rousseau's survey implies.

Many recurring themes of Goldsmith's critical reception up to 1900 are present in the earliest accounts of his prose. The tendency to rank him among contemporary authors appears in a *Court Magazine* piece of 1761 placing 'Oliver Goldsmith, M.D.' sixteenth of fifty-six writers, motivated by 'Taste and understanding'.[1] Although he probably never earned his medical degree, Goldsmith remained 'Dr' for critics; inevitably, for many, he became 'Dr Minor' to Samuel Johnson's 'Dr Major'.[2] Yet these early assessments acknowledge what distinguished Goldsmith from Johnson and other stylists: his ability to treat familiar material with elegant simplicity. William Rider in *An Historical and Critical Account of the Living Writers of Great-Britain* praised him for 'having happily found out the Secret to unite Elevation with Ease'.[3] That the fluid ease of Goldsmith's writing came about fortuitously, without effort or even awareness, was a widely shared opinion in this period.

Goldsmith was himself a reviewer whose ambivalence towards this nascent profession complicated his reception throughout his lifetime. One notice on his first major publication, *An Enquiry into the Present State of Polite Learning*, opens: 'The ingenious author of this little perform- ance sets out with such a contempt for criticism, that he need not wonder if the critics damn his essay in revenge.'[4] The reviews were not damning, but they did note the essay's lack of depth and originality. William Kenrick for Ralph Griffiths's *Monthly Review* was Goldsmith's harshest critic on these grounds. Griffiths had been pivotal in establishing Goldsmith's journalistic career, but by this time Goldsmith was on difficult terms with the *Monthly*'s proprietor and had moved on to the rival *Critical Review*. Kenrick attacked the *Enquiry*'s 'trite commonplace remarks ... thrown together' without sufficient gratitude towards booksellers.[5] Kenrick also found Goldsmith's magazine the *Bee* agreeable but derivative, and was probably the author of a letter accusing him of plagiarism that would later appear in the *St. James's Chronicle*.[6] Goldsmith defended himself on the latter occasion, and more recent studies have shown him to be a clever manipulator of the periodical press.[7] In his prefaces, dedications, and essays he continued to insist on his works' deficiencies and the difficulty of pleasing readers. Reviewers often took his cue and availed themselves of Goldsmith's own terms and judgements (see Chapter 23, 'Periodicals and Literary Reviewing', and Chapter 25, 'Authorship').

Most critics noted that Goldsmith adapted existing models, however felicitously. John Hawkins relates that, 'As he worked for the booksellers', even Goldsmith's friends early in his career 'looked on him as a mere literary drudge, equal to the task of compiling and translating, but little capable of original, and still less of poetical composition'.[8] Samuel Johnson, the century's foremost critic who had his own experience of drudgery, defended the utility and skilfulness of Goldsmith's abridgements and historical works (*LOJ*, 2:236–7). Along with biographies such as *The Life of Richard Nash*, popular histories were a minor yet significant sideline for Goldsmith (see Chapter 24, 'History Writing'). Critical and popular opinion coincided in favour of *The Citizen of the World*. The two major reviews found the 'Chinese letters' insufficiently 'Asiatic' yet full of 'good sense' and variety.[9] Again, the conceit was not new, but the *Critical* made the important point that these newspaper columns were 'necessarily calcu- lated to the meridian of the multitude'. The *Monthly Review*, meanwhile, used half of its brief article to deny that their attack on the *Enquiry* had been 'personal'. The critical reception of Goldsmith's essays in general improved markedly following the publication of the first of three works that established his literary reputation.

The Traveller and *The Deserted Village* ensured that Goldsmith would be known first and foremost as a poet. His achievements in this culturally pre-eminent form were often cited to offset his perceived shortcomings in other genres. Contrary to his practice elsewhere, Goldsmith wrote and carefully revised both long poems over a period of years, providing further justification to critics who read them as the sincerest expressions of his ideas and philosophy. *The Traveller, or A Prospect of Society* (1764) was the first publication to bear Goldsmith's name, allowing the *Gentleman's Magazine* to hail him as a 'new poet' and generating a sense of excited discovery among reviewers who greeted the poem as a relief from the small-minded factionalism of satire.[10] Johnson, by now a friend and key literary influence, participated in the composition of both major poems. His positive review of *The Traveller* set the tone for others by extolling its smooth versification without directly engaging with its geographic or political arguments (see Chapter 22, 'Prospect Poetry'). Instead, Johnson quotes the dedication's account of Goldsmith's position and implies that readers should judge for themselves whether the author's 'sentiments ... discover him to be a just estimator of comparative happiness'.[11]

The Deserted Village, generally considered Goldsmith's finest poem, reinforced his reputation for descriptive verse in smooth, rhyming couplets (see Chapter 21, 'Pastoral Poetry'). Once again, reviewers were less con-vinced by its political philosophy. London-based critics disagreed that rural virtue was preferable to metropolitan civility, although they enjoyed its pastoral vignettes, singling out the portraits of the village schoolmaster and alehouse.[12] As Goldsmith's preface had predicted, the more serious objec-tion to *The Deserted Village* was 'that the depopulation it deplores is no where to be seen' (*Deserted Village*, vi). These objections were themselves political: the poem's insistence that luxury was blighting Britain ran counter to Whig narratives of commercial progress. The following year, Goldsmith's *History of England* saw him 'abused in the newspapers' as 'an arrant Tory' (*Letters*, 99). Some critical essays mobilized the poem's anti-Enclosure sentiments, but the most radical responses came among *The Deserted Village*'s many imitations and rebuttals in verse. These included republican readings in America, where Auburns sprung up in fifteen states. In view of these imitations, John Aikin would later judge *The Traveller* the '*unique*' and superior poem, though 'both are truly original productions', he wrote, a view itself somewhat unique for its time (*Critical Heritage*, 235).

Once reviewers had enshrined Goldsmith as a poet, his new status coloured their reception of his other literary ventures across this decade. Some anonymous verses, conveniently separating poetry from politics, complained that although they liked his 'good natur'd man':

> Yet don't we wish to meet him on the stage,
> 'Twill spoil the foremost poet of our age;
> Nor would we view him in historic path,
> His politics may rouse up patriot wrath.

'Doctor, stick to what we call thy own', the writer concludes, 'And sport in fields of poesy alone'.[13] *The Good Natur'd Man* had roused its own debate because of a scene in which two debt collectors pretend to be cultured guests. Audiences hissed and reviewers objected to the 'coarse characters' and 'low' language.[14] Yet the play did fairly well, and Goldsmith followed it in 1773 with *She Stoops to Conquer*. Goldsmith's best-known play opened to resounding applause and lukewarm reviews. Critics found its humour forced and its incidents improbable, especially when committed to the printed page, but the main debate dividing them was around prevailing definitions of comedy. Horace Walpole refused the word entirely, calling *She Stoops* the 'lowest of all farces', deliberately opposed to the polite comedies in fashion (*Critical Heritage*, 118–19). There is evidence that Goldsmith's own essay contrasting 'laughing' with 'sentimental' comedy helped create and shape such responses to his plays. Sympathetic reviewers too echoed the national terms in which he praised the vigorous English drama over the sentimental French mode. Within the plays, sentimental and comic strains mingled, as they did to greatest effect in Goldsmith's only novel (see Chapter 20, 'Theatre', and Chapter 27, 'Satire and Sentiment').

Published in the middle of Goldsmith's literary career, *The Vicar of Wakefield* was an instant success, selling out edition after edition (see Chapter 19, 'Fiction'). Critics were bemused again: the novel's improbable plot exerted an undeniable appeal. Frances Burney, steeped in sentimental fiction, began reading 'with distaste', was drawn in by its depiction of 'domestic happiness', and was *'surprised into tears'*. The young Burney was also startled by the novel's 'bold and singular' denunciation of the death penalty (*Critical Heritage*, 52–3). The passages on prisons and penal reform were topical and circulated widely in 1760s periodicals, while the ballad *Edwin and Angelina* became an anthology favourite. Responses to *Vicar* often paralleled reactions to Goldsmith's drama. Anna Barbauld, for instance, censured the 'coarse and low' characters but found *Vicar* pleasing and 'irresistibly comic'.[15] As with the plays' humour, epitomized in Tony Lumpkin, *The Vicar of Wakefield*'s domestic narrative was paradoxically read in national terms as typically English.

All Goldsmith's works were published in Ireland, where his plays proved most popular, but where his critical reception largely reflected that of Britain.[16] Goldsmith did not adopt openly Irish perspectives or personae in print, and eighteenth-century reviewers took his Anglocentrism for granted. One reviewer of his plays, after having referred to Goldsmith's 'own countrymen', glibly explains that 'all the subjects of the British government are countrymen'.[17] Until 1900, explicit references to his Irishness largely stop at accounts of his early life and speculations about the location of Auburn. Nevertheless, the increasing tendency to read Goldsmith's biography into his works could not avoid his birthplace. Moreover, as Norma Clarke observes, stereotypically Irish attributes such as 'open-heartedness', 'impecuniousness ... gullibility, and naive unworld-liness' have powerfully shaped Goldsmith's reception.[18] Goldsmith himself commented that he early 'acquird the name of the facetious Irish man', a caricature that would resonate throughout accounts of his unreliable genius (*Letters*, 15).

Goldsmith died relatively young, which fed the myth of genius unful-filled. Johnson's epitaph hailed him as 'Poet, Naturalist and Historian', marking the publication in the year of his death of *An History of the Earth, and Animated Nature* (1774). This commissioned work in a popular genre was a commercial success (see Chapter 14, 'Race', and Chapter 16, 'Natural History and Science'). A substantial notice in the *Critical* welcomed this 'judicious system of natural history, blending entertainment and informa-tion' such as 'has hitherto never appeared in the English language'.[19] The scientist Edward Bancroft dismissed its errors, and Aikin conceded that Goldsmith was 'a Naturalist only of the bookseller's making', though he praised his poetical descriptions highly.[20] Along with his *Roman History* and the posthumous *Grecian History*, *Animated Nature* testified that Goldsmith remained in demand as a systematic and elegant compiler and translator. Yet the general view remained that writing for hire had deprived the world of more literary masterpieces.

Copious anecdotes and tributes followed Goldsmith's death in April 1774. The July–August volume of the *Critical Review* reviewed not only his natural history, but also two elegies, an 'impartial character' of Goldsmith, an account of his final illness, and Richard Glover's brief *Life* (1774) padded out with literary extracts. The previous April, Goldsmith had furnished Thomas Percy with materials for a projected biography;

copyright and various delays meant that this memoir only appeared in 1801. In the meantime, 'his friends', as Reynolds put it, 'lived upon his character' (*Critical Heritage*, 172). The witty *Retaliation* and responses circulated alongside verse tributes enshrining Auburn's 'sweet bard' as a 'Poet of nature', amplifying Celtic imagery of harps and druids (*Critical Heritage*, 165–9). Biographical information about Goldsmith was and remains scarce. Inevitably, episodes from Goldsmith's essays, poems, and novel flowed in to fill the gaps.

What Ricardo Quintana would call the 'Goldsmith legend' soon arose: his most effective and affecting passages were drawn from his life.[21] An early reviewer of *The Deserted Village* had objected to the line 'The sad historian of the *pensive* plain' on the grounds that 'Goldsmith has given to his Plain too much of the sensibility and contemplation of the poet'.[22] By the early 1800s, this line was singled out for praise with the 'sad historian' read as Goldsmith himself, a slip Rousseau repeats to characterize him as 'a lyricist in the Wordsworthian sense, deeply imbued with a sense of specific place' (*Critical Heritage*, 243, 17). Antiquarians and biographers, following this impulse to its logical conclusion, laboured to pinpoint this place in England or Ireland. The Reverend R. H. Newell published an edition of Goldsmith's poetry containing a travelogue of Irish locations he had visited in search of Auburn, illustrated by plates of the tree, inn, and other landmarks, along with pen portraits of possible local models for the village's inhabitants (see Chapter 36, 'Afterlives 3: Poetry').[23] In 1883, Edward Ford would compile a similar list for *The Vicar of Wakefield* (see Chapter 34, 'Afterlives 1: The Victorian *Vicar*').[24]

The nineteenth century displayed a sentimental fascination with Goldsmith's life which privileged autobiographical readings of his works. While his contemporaries had puzzled over the gulf between his demeanour in public and in print, more complacent Victorian critics simply erased this distance. To read him as a 'child of Nature and Genius, whose writings are so clear a mirror of his own actions' required excising his so-called hack work and identifying characters such as George Primrose and the Man in Black as authorial personae.[25] Approached with a post-Romantic faith in innate poetic inspiration, *The Deserted Village* became a poem longing for the seats of Goldsmith's Irish childhood. William Makepeace Thackeray's 1853 portrait of 'the sufferings, the genius, the gentle nature' of Goldsmith epitomises this lachrymose approach.[26]

A larger problem with the nineteenth century's fondness for Goldsmith was that he became ubiquitous, too familiar to need analysis. His personal and literary faults were excusably obvious. His value as 'moral instructor',

Edward Mangin wrote as early as 1808, outweighed the benefits of any 'critical inquisition' (*Critical Heritage*, 111). Rousseau sees his reputation peaking around 1820, before declining towards the 1880s (*Critical Heritage*, 7) Commentators around the middle of the century wrote as if Goldsmith would be popular forever. His histories sold as standard textbooks – read by both Jane Austen and Jane Eyre – and *The Vicar of Wakefield* remained recommended reading for young and old of both sexes. Six editions of his collected works were published in the 1800s, several with memoirs appended. The first major biographies also appeared.

James Prior's meticulously documented *Life of Oliver Goldsmith* (1837) laid the groundwork for successors (see Chapter 1, 'Life'). Perhaps equally important, Prior also offered the first sustained consideration of Goldsmith among Irish writers working in England.[27] Prior's biography was soon overtaken by John Forster's bestselling *Life and Adventures of Oliver Goldsmith* (1848) and its more scholarly revision of 1854. Both publications were welcomed by those who sought to rescue Goldsmith's reputation from obscurity and what they considered the harsh judgements of Johnson's biographers; De Quincey hailed Forster's biography as a 'retribution'.[28] Others felt that Forster had overcorrected in downplaying Goldsmith's faults and exaggerating his distresses.[29] Washington Irving's 1849 biography, which introduced Goldsmith to American readers, indulged fully in the sympathetic approach. Irving's was partly a commercial venture from a professional writer who saw many parallels between his subject's career and his own.

Many of Goldsmith's more influential nineteenth-century critics shared his preoccupation with the position of the writer in society, including William Hazlitt, Leigh Hunt, and Forster, who had written for Hunt's *Examiner*. Although their radical politics differed sharply from Goldsmith's, these journalists and essayists appreciated his versatility and used his career to comment on their own turbulent times. Hazlitt encapsulated their views: Goldsmith was 'more observing, more natural and picturesque' than Johnson, less refined but more genial than Pope, and the schoolmaster in *The Deserted Village* and the opening of *The Vicar of Wakefield* were his masterpieces (*Critical Heritage*, 258). With the exception of Forster, these critics had little sympathy for the view that Goldsmith suffered undue professional hardship. Hunt found even the sentiments of the poems as inauthentic as their arguments. He much preferred Goldsmith's prose, its 'style the most adapted to miscellaneous writing'.[30] He praised Goldsmith as an essayist, particularly in *Citizen of the World*, and his 'dry simplicity of style' in the *Vicar*, which Hunt placed in its own subgenre of 'the simple domestic' novel, 'unexceptional' in its morality.[31]

The Vicar of Wakefield continued to stand at the heart of Goldsmith's posthumous reputation. Yet by 1900, Henry James could offer no new explanation for its attraction other than its 'incomparable amenity' (*Critical Heritage*, 66). *Vicar* had become an innocuous classic of English rural fiction, widely read in America and Europe. The most prominent of its many German admirers was Johann Wolfgang von Goethe. Goethe's first encounter with *Vicar*, read aloud to him by Johann Gottfried Herder, was transformational, and it exerted a lifelong influence. He was fascinated by the plot's inconsistencies and idolized the narrator: 'A Protestant country-clergyman is, perhaps, the most beautiful subject for a modern idyl' (*Critical Heritage*, 309). Thomas Carlyle, eight years earlier, had called the novel 'the best of all modern Idyls; but ... nothing more' (*Critical Heritage*, 280). That was more than enough for Goethe. Goethe also noted the novel's irony, a rare insight which foreshadowed twentieth-century readings (*Critical Heritage*, 310–11).

One term recurs in early commentary on Goldsmith: genius. Throughout the eighteenth and nineteenth centuries critics had sought to account for how 'an author capable of so strangely under-writing himself' could produce such undisputable successes as *The Vicar of Wakefield*.[32] Invoking his genius was a form of admiration without explanation. Locating Goldsmith's genius in the hazy, nostalgic past was also a way of isolating his work from its wider political and economic contexts.[33] His major works resonated beyond his own politics and circles in sometimes surprising ways, such as the republican readings of *The Deserted Village* in America. The major context for criticism in this pre-1900 period remained biographical. Commentators recounted Goldsmith's life in parallel with his works, seeking to unify biography and bibliography into a narrative of struggle leading to success. Such attempts inevitably failed, yet both the character of Goldsmith-the-author and his major works retained a broad and enduring appeal.

Notes

1. [Hugh Kelly], 'The Motives for Writing: A Dream'. *Court Magazine* (December 1761), 167–9.
2. James Boswell, 'The Journal of a Tour to the Hebrides with Samuel Johnson, LL.D', in Samuel Johnson and James Boswell, *A Journey to the Western Islands of Scotland and the Journal of a Tour to the Hebrides*, ed. Peter Levi (Harmondsworth: Penguin, 1984), 209–10.

3. [William Rider], *An Historical and Critical Account of the Living Writers of Great-Britain wherein Their Respective Merits Are Discussed with the Utmost Candour and Impartiality* (London, 1762), 14.

4. 'Review of *An Enquiry into the Present State of Polite Learning*', *Critical Review* 7 (1759), 369.

5. [William Kenrick], Review of *An Enquiry into the Present State of Polite Learning in Europe*, *Monthly Review*, 21 (1759), 381–9.

6. [William Kenrick], 'Review of the BEE: Being Essays on the Most Interesting Subjects', *Monthly Review*, 22 (1760), 38–45 (39). The letter to the *St. James's Chronicle*, 18–21 July 1767, and Goldsmith's reply of 23–25 July are reproduced in *Letters*, 73–5.

7. Frank Donoghue, *The Fame Machine: Book Reviewing and Eighteenth-Century Literary Careers* (Stanford University Press, 1996).

8. John Hawkins, 'Further Remarks on Goldsmith As a Writer and Member of Dr Johnson's Club', in *The Life of Samuel Johnson, LL.D … 1787*' (*Critical Heritage*, 208).

9. 'Review of *The Citizen of the World*', *Critical Review*, 13 (1762), 397–400; 'Review of *The Citizen of the World*', *Monthly Review*, 26 (1762), 477.

10. 'Extract from the *Traveller*', *Gentleman's Magazine*, 34 (1764), 594.

11. [Samuel Johnson], 'Review of *The Traveller*', *Critical Review*, 18 (1764), 458–62 (459).

12. 'Review of *The Deserted Village*', *Critical Review*, 29 (1770), 435–43; [John Hawkesworth], 'Review of *The Deserted Village*', *Monthly Review*, 42 (1770), 440–5.

13. Sir Nicholas Nipclose[pseud.], *The Theatres: A Poetical Dissection* (London, 1772), 34.

14. Frank Donoghue, '"He Never Gives Us Nothing That's Low": Goldsmith's Plays and the Reviewers', *English Literary History*, 55.3 (1988), 665–84 (671).

15. Anna Barbauld, 'Oliver Goldsmith', in *The British Novelists with an Essay, and Prefaces, Biographical and Critical*, vol. 23, 1810, x–xi.

16. Richard C. Cole, 'Oliver Goldsmith's Reputation in Ireland, 1762–74', *Modern Philology*, 68.1 (1970), 65–70.

17. [William Woodfall], 'Review of *She Stoops to Conquer; or, The Mistakes of a Night*', *Monthly Review*, 48 (1773), 309–14 (310).

18. Norma Clarke, *Brothers of the Quill: Oliver Goldsmith in Grub Street* (Cambridge, MA: Harvard University Press, 2016), 11.

19. 'Review of *A History of the Earth, and Animated Nature*', *Critical Review*, 52 (1774), 97.

20. Edward Bancroft, *Monthly Review*, 15 (1775), 310–14; John Aikin, *An Essay on the Application of Natural History to Poetry* (Warrington, 1777), 54.

21. Ricardo Quintana, *Oliver Goldsmith: A Georgian Study* (New York: Macmillan, 1967), 71.

22. *Critical Review*, 29 (1770), 439–40.

23. R. H. Newell, *The Poetical Works of Oliver Goldsmith. With Remarks, Attempting to Ascertain, Chiefly from Local Observation, the Actual Scene of the Deserted Village* (London, 1811).

24. Edward Ford, 'Names and Characters in *The Vicar of Wakefield*', *National Review*, 1 (1883), 387–94.

25. W. J. Courthope, *A History of English Poetry*, vol. 5 (London: Macmillan, 1905), 210.

26. William Makepeace Thackeray, *The English Humourists of the Eighteenth Century* (London: Smith, Elder and Company, 1853), 293.

27. Prior, *Life*, 1:vii. See also Norma Clarke, "More National (to Ireland) than Personal": James Prior's Life of Oliver Goldsmith (1837)', *Biography*, 41.1 (2018), 48–70.

28. Thomas De Quincey, 'Review of *The Life and Adventures of Oliver Goldsmith*', *North British Review* 9 (1848), 187–212 (187).

29. William Black, *Goldsmith* (London: Macmillan, 1878), 2–4; William Spalding, *The Poetical Works of Oliver Goldsmith, With a Memoir* (London: Charles Griffin, 1864), 5–6.

30. Leigh Hunt, 'Goldsmith: Critical Essay on His Writings and Genius', in *Classic Tales: Serious and Lively, with Critical Essays on the Merits and Reputations of the Authors*, 5 vols. (London, 1806), 1:41–80 (56).

31. Hunt, 'Goldsmith: Critical Essay', 77, 79.

32. 'Review of *The Vicar of Wakefield*', *Monthly Review*, 34 (1766), 407.

33. W. J. McCormack, 'Goldsmith, Biography and the Phenomenology of Anglo-Irish Literature', in *The Art of Oliver Goldsmith*, ed. Andrew Swarbrick (London: Vision, 1984), 180–1.

CHAPTER 33

Critical Reception after 1900

James Ward

In the early twentieth century, critics wrestled with an inherited wisdom that put Oliver Goldsmith's works, in Robert L. Mack's words, 'beyond commentary'.[1] Washington Irving's biography of Goldsmith had established these terms in 1849 when it concluded with a refusal to provide 'any critical dissertation on his writings' beyond declaring them possessed of 'that magic charm of style'.[2] Writing about *The Vicar of Wakefield* in 1900, Henry James inaugurated the modern critical tradition by cleaving fast to the old one. To criticize, he protested, would be to spoil 'the old, old miracle of style' (*Critical Heritage*, 66). Echoing these appeals to the magical and miraculous, Virginia Woolf found herself under the 'spell' of *She Stoops to Conquer* in 1934, singling out 'a unity about it which forbids us to dismember it' (see Chapter 20, 'Theatre', and Chapter 35, 'Afterlives 2: Theatre').[3] By 1974 the weight of such demurrals had come crushingly to bear on G. S. Rousseau, who adopted a harried Grub Street persona to reflect on the task of producing a volume on Goldsmith for the *Critical Heritage* series. 'The scarcity of important criticism was so overwhelming', he quavered, 'that those reviewers who would savage me, would have good reason' (*Critical Heritage*, 1). Ironically, Rousseau was writing just at the point that this always-suspect notion had become definitively unsustainable. The 1960s, as Michael Griffin notes, 'saw a substantial burst of editorial and critical work', in turn enabled by a steady stream of editions, biographies, and occasional pieces from the first half of the century.[4] Another work published in 1974, Raymond Williams's *The Country and The City*, showed the potential for political perspectives like cultural materialism to reframe, if not to resolve, the mixed rapture and frustration that held earlier critics spellbound. In *The Deserted Village*, Williams wrote, 'the present is accurately and powerfully seen but its real relations, to past and future, are inaccessible'.[5]

While its terms may have shifted from aesthetic enchantment to ideological mystification, the apprehension of a hermetic stylistic perfection recurs in Goldsmith's modern critical reception. One quarter of the way through the twenty-first century, Goldsmith's writing has nonetheless been successfully integrated into four areas of debate outlined in the rest of this chapter. A revisionist approach to the rhetorical stance and moral seriousness of Goldsmith's work is a new and distinctive feature of his post-1900 critical reception, while postcolonial critique has changed the character and emphasis of work on intercultural and geographical themes. Goldsmith's writing and drama have been prominent in a surge of interest in the Irish Enlightenment, with his work proving important to arguments about the historical character and intellectual context of this era and movement (see Chapter 5, 'Enlightenments'). This reappraisal overlaps with an effort, ongoing throughout the period under consideration, to locate Goldsmith as an Irish writer and in relation to a wider national literature in both Irish and English. Each of these areas will be explored after a summary of major developments in biographical and textual approaches.

The first half of the twentieth century saw a run of popular biographies and of research aimed at putting the study of Goldsmith's works on a serious scholarly footing. Katharine C. Balderston's work is foremost in this latter respect, notably *A Census of the Manuscripts of Oliver Goldsmith* (1926) and *The Collected Letters of Oliver Goldsmith* (1928) while R. S. Crane's *New Essays by Oliver Goldsmith* (1927) added to the known corpus of the author's journalism. Advances in bibliography and attribution are synthesized in Arthur Friedman's five-volume *Collected Works* (1966) and summarized in the entry on Goldsmith in volume two of the *New Cambridge Bibliography of English Literature* (1971). Michael Griffin and David O'Shaughnessy's edition of the correspondence (2018) adds thirteen letters to those published by Balderston; their new *Collected Works* (forthcoming from Cambridge University Press) will be the first complete scholarly edition since Friedman's.

Goldsmith's colourful, short, and tragic life has long supplied biographers with archetypes of the deracinated Irish intellectual, the jobbing writer, and the feckless bohemian. With apocrypha and anecdote making up most of the biographical data, approaches have shifted from an enthusiastic embrace of such material to a determined stripping down of the evidentiary base, and finally back to a recognition that Goldsmith's legacy includes an enduring cultural mythos as well as a body of literary works. Titled simply for its subject, Stephen Gwynn's 1935 biography exemplifies the first approach. Told in a poetic style which revels in accumulated fabulation while acknowledging of it that 'nobody should be asked to credit a word', it joins Richard Ashe King's 1910 life in seriously engaging Goldsmith's Irishness (see Chapter 9, 'Irish London').[6] By mid-century an emphasis on scholarship had begun to displace the kind of pacy, entertaining biographies produced by King, Gwynn, and Frankfort Moore (*The Life of Oliver Goldsmith*, 1910). Ralph M. Wardle's 1957 *Oliver Goldsmith* is, in its author's words, 'the first attempt at a scholarly biography ... published in the twentieth century'. Wardle is concerned to portray his subject judiciously as neither the 'idiot' derided by Horace Walpole nor 'the martyred saint that apologetic biographers have sometimes tried to make him'.[7] A. Lytton Sells's 1974 book builds on this foundation in determining to 'go back to the sources' and consider Goldsmith's 'character afresh'. For Sells this includes a full and honest appraisal of his subject's faults and recurrent problematic relationships, whether with his mother or with his French sources.[8] John Ginger's 1977 biography is the most richly contextualized modern life of Goldsmith and twenty-first-century biographical studies have embraced its wider perspective over the traditional focus on Goldsmith's unique personality by developing a distinctly prosopographic approach. Leo Damrosch's coverage of Goldsmith in *The Club* (2019) is brief but sympathetic while Norma Clarke's *Brothers of the Quill* (2017) is a comprehensive portrait of Goldsmith as creator and product of émigré professional and homosocial networks, as well as his own and others' mythmaking (see Chapter 1, 'Life', and Chapter 3, 'Friendships and Feuds').

Posed in various ways, the question of whether and how far to take Goldsmith straight has been a defining issue in his modern reception. Critics of the post-war generation relished the prospect of Goldsmith as ironist, seeing a chance to finally dispatch the pious sentimentalist beloved of Victorian essayists (see Chapter 27, 'Satire and Sentiment'). Katharine Worth highlights Goldsmith's use of a ludic and 'self-conscious theatricalism to express shifts and divisions in personality', but the dominant ironic reading came from male critics who saw in it a bullish effort at 'defending the finest values of the disintegrating Augustan world'.[9] In this interpretation, as pursued by Ricardo Quintana and Robert H. Hopkins, Goldsmith declares 'war against the sentimentalism of his age', using 'irony to undermine "delicate" sensibility as a primary literary norm', flying in the face of contemporaries who either 'failed to understand his irony', or were 'unable to accept his anti-sentimental attitudes'.[10] Already complicated by the psychological reading of John Dussinger, this position came under strain in the 1980s from Oliver W. Ferguson, who delineates limits to Goldsmith's irony in both the periodical writing and *The Vicar of*

Wakefield, while reasserting the novel's central insistence on the 'worth of good humour and domestic virtues', and 'the sustaining power of Christian submission' (see Chapter 19, 'Fiction').[11] The gendered subtext of the earlier anti-sentimentalist school becomes apparent when juxtaposed with more recent criticism informed by critical masculinity and queer studies (see Chapter 13, 'Gender'). Reframing the repeated references found in earlier criticism to the enigma of Goldsmith's style, James Kim characterizes the novel through 'a style of masculinity harried by a series of emasculating contradictions, none of which can be resolved without generating yet further contradictions'. For Kim the interplay of satire and sentimentality that has troubled readers of the novel for so long merely indexes 'Goldsmith's attempt to smooth out the fissures in an emergent heteropatriarchal order'.[12]

With the late twentieth-century turn from formalist to political criticism, cosmopolitanism began to displace irony as a primary critical concern. Debate continued to turn, however, on the sincerity or otherwise of Goldsmith's authorial stance. Part of a wider body of Irish writing that can encompass, in Joseph Lennon's words, 'both collusive and subversive representations of Empire', Goldsmith's work can be seen either as bound up in both the practical business and ideological project of western colonialism, or as separate from and even critical of it (see Chapter 14, 'Race', and Chapter 17, 'War and Empire').[13] Since the publication of Edward Said's *Orientalism* (1978), *The Citizen of the World* has been a focus for this debate, although critical interest in this work and its contexts stretches back to Hamilton Jewett Smith's 1926 book-length study, as well as Martha Pike Conant's *The Oriental Tale in England in the Nineteenth Century*, published in 1908 and still in print (see Chapter 11, 'Cosmopolitanism', and Chapter 26, 'Orientalism'). Goldsmith's adoption of the oriental pseudo-letter is generally seen as more nuanced and multi-layered than is typical for the time: 'China as topic of expansionist interest gives way', Christopher Brooks writes, 'to China as vehicle for ironic discourse'.[14] The eponymous Lien Chi Altangi is, however, seen more as a rhetorical device than a means to engage seriously or in depth with Chinese culture, which Goldsmith, in Conant's words, merely 'imagines, or pretends to imagine'.[15] Tao Zhijian takes this observation to its logical endpoint, concluding that Goldsmith offered 'nothing more than an ethnocentric European vision, fostered by his own prejudices and colonial sentiments'. Mengmeng Yan's study of Sino-British encounters offers a contrasting position, arguing that Goldsmith's writing was actively informed by Chinese literature and philosophy, while allowing, like

Lennon and Brooks, that China can act as a cipher for an underlying preoccupation with Anglo-Irish cultural tensions.[16] Such duality and ulteriority are shown more generally, as James Watt writes, in the way Goldsmith's cosmopolitanism is 'shadowed by a skeptical commentary on the content and meaning of this elusive term'.[17] Comparable modes of obliquity and paradox also govern Goldsmith's relationship to the historic Enlightenment and to the country of his birth.

Goldsmith's participation in eighteenth-century cultures of secular learning and public debate encompasses both local and transnational models of enlightenment. Work on this theme has often sought to highlight Goldsmith's engagement with French philosophical writing and the extent of his borrowing from these sources.[18] Since 2000, however, his work has become increasingly central to versions of Enlightenment inflected by, if not centred on, Ireland (see Chapter 5, 'Enlightenments'). Describing Goldsmith's first published work, an English translation of Jean Marteilhe's *Memoirs of A Protestant*, as a 'classic Enlightenment denunciation of religious persecution', Bridget Orr joins Michael Brown and Helen Burke in presenting *She Stoops to Conquer* as an exemplary inscription of enlightened sociability via what Burke calls the 'anti-bourgeois popular performance tradition of rural Ireland'.[19] This typically ex-centric and idiosyncratic version of Enlightenment is widened in scope by O'Shaughnessy, who locates Goldsmith's theatre within a larger and more diffuse Irish Enlightenment 'energised by its transnational kinesis and the cosmopolitan environs of London'.[20] Even so, several aspects of Goldsmith's politics, notably his monarchism and appeal to vertical modes of community, seem to militate against easy reception as an enlightened cosmopolite. These apparent elements of counter-Enlightenment, Griffin argues, actually make Goldsmith a 'representative author in enlightenment' by forcing him to 'grapple dialectically with, enlightenment modernity'.[21]

Yet more grappling besets the question of Ireland. This perennial point of contention was sharpened in the twentieth century by enduring ambivalence about an Anglophone cultural inheritance subject to successive waves of cultural nationalist, revisionist, and postcolonial critique. Published in 1935, Stephen Gwynn's assessment is tellingly irenic in the wake of revolution, independence, and civil war, with its insistence that Goldsmith 'never wrote a line that sharpened Irish divisions or added to bitterness between England and Ireland'.[22] Goldsmith's lines were, however, co-opted to underpin the respective patrician and distributist idylls of W. B. Yeats and Éamon de Valera.[23]

Sympathetic criticism offsets Goldsmith's lack of demonstrative assertion with the argument that his homeland was an object of sublimation throughout his career. Though he presents as 'lacking any patriotism', in Gwynn's words, Goldsmith's apparent indifference to such matters was a mask which left him free, Declan Kiberd argues, 'to tell the underlying truth about a deeper self'.[24] Not all critics endorse this sense of identity as a rich if well-concealed subterranean seam, however – Seamus Deane insists on a surface reading, imputing to Goldsmith a stylistic alchemy of 'blandness ... converted to sweetness', which serves to efface 'the drastic effects of English misrule'.[25] Eavan Boland deploys markedly similar terms to contrast Goldsmith's mannered style of 'sweet Augustan double talk', with his alienation from Gaelic culture, characterizing the latter with reference to Goldsmith's 'History of Carolan', where he is in, Boland's words, 'bewildered and fascinated', 'astonished and put off' by his bardic counterparts and their funerary laments (see Chapter 36, 'Afterlives 3: Poetry').[26] Goldsmith viewed such scenes, Deane writes, 'almost with the eyes of a foreigner', reducing Irish culture to 'a slightly exotic variation of the English norm'.[27] This critical position is summarized in Graham Gargett's verdict that Goldsmith 'considered himself to be English' and addressed Irish concerns only in 'an indirect or spasmodic way'.[28]

An opposing current suggests that Goldsmith was in youth deeply immersed in Irish cultural forms and practices and retained a quiet attachment to them throughout his career. In one of the earliest modern considerations of this inheritance, Robert W. Seitz characterizes Goldsmith's palliative 'conservative liberalism' as that of a 'provincial Irish countryman'.[29] Kiberd brought bicultural fluency to the issue, detecting Gaelic poetic topoi in *The Deserted Village* and interpreting Goldsmith's legendary, ruinous generosity as his way to honour the Gaelic tradition of *flaithiúlacht*.[30] Terry Eagleton suggests that Goldsmith achieves in his great pastoral poem something like an 'equitable interaction of cultures', which comes about not through synthesis but rather the revelation of economic exploitation common to English and Irish modes of life. As they inhere in what Eagleton calls the 'oxymoronic quality of easy elegance or polished spontaneity' which in his estimation embodies a typically Anglo-Irish style, such tensions return us to the paradox of style raised at the start of this chapter.[31] Goldsmith's critical reception across the long twentieth century tells the story of how this once-ineffable effect now yields to the apprehension that 'something more is going on', as Kiberd puts it, 'than seems to be the case'.[32]

Notes

1. Robert L. Mack, 'Introduction', in *The Vicar of Wakefield* (Oxford University Press, 2006), xxii.
2. Washington Irving, *Oliver Goldsmith: A Biography* (London, 1850), 420.
3. Virginia Woolf, 'Oliver Goldsmith', in *The Captain's Death Bed and Other Essays* (New York: Harcourt Braces, 1950), 11.
4. Michael Griffin, 'Oliver Goldsmith', *Oxford Bibliographies*. www.oxfordbi bliographies.com. https://doi.org/10.1093/OBO/9780199846719-0026.
5. Raymond Williams, *The Country and the City* (Oxford University Press, 1973, repr. 1975), 78.
6. Stephen Gwynn, *Oliver Goldsmith* (London: Thornton Butterworth, 1935), 62, 282.
7. Ralph M. Wardle, *Oliver Goldsmith* (Lawrence: University of Kansas Press, 1957), vii, 289.
8. A. Lytton Sells, *Oliver Goldsmith: His Life and Works* (London: Allen & Unwin, 1974), 9.
9. Katharine Worth, *Sheridan and Goldsmith* (Basingstoke: Macmillan, 1992), 9.
10. Ricardo Quintana, *Oliver Goldsmith: A Georgian Study* (London: Weidenfeld and Nicolson, 1967), 54; Robert H. Hopkins, *The True Genius of Oliver Goldsmith* (Baltimore, MD: Johns Hopkins University Press, 1969), 9, 11.
11. Oliver W. Ferguson, 'Goldsmith As Ironist', *Studies in Philology*, 81 (1984), 212–28 (228); John Dussinger, '*The Vicar of Wakefield*: A "Sickly Sensibility" and the Rewards of Fortune', in *The Discourse of the Mind in Eighteenth-Century Fiction* (1974; repr. Berlin: De Gruyter, 2011), 148–72.
12. James Kim, 'Goldsmith's Manhood', *The Eighteenth Century*, 59 (2018), 21–44 (35, 22).
13. Joseph Lennon, *Irish Orientalism: A Literary and Intellectual History* (Syracuse, NY: Syracuse University Press, 2004), 123.
14. Christopher Brooks, 'Goldsmith's Citizen of the World: Knowledge and the Imposture of Orientalism', *Texas Studies in Literature and Language*, 35.1 (1993), 124–44 (128).
15. Martha Pike Conant, *The Oriental Tale in England in the Eighteenth Century* (1908; repr. New York: Octagon 1966), 198–9.
16. Tao Zhijian, 'Citizen of Whose World? Goldsmith's Orientalism', *Comparative Literature Studies*, 33.1 (1996), 15–34 (32); Menmeng Yan, *Foreignness and Selfhood: Sino-British Encounters in English Literature of the Eighteenth Century* (Abingdon: Routledge, 2022), 83, 78.
17. James Watt, 'Goldsmith's Cosmopolitanism', *Eighteenth-Century Life*, 30.1 (2006), 56–75 (73).
18. A. Lytton Sells, *Les Sources Françaises de Goldsmith* (Paris, É. Champion, 1924); Joseph E. Brown, 'Goldsmith's Indebtedness to Voltaire and Justus Van Effen', *Modern Philology*, 23.3 (1926), 273–84; Graham Gargett, 'Plagiarism, Translation and the Problem of Identity: Oliver Goldsmith and Voltaire', *Eighteenth-Century Ireland/Iris an dá chultúr*, 16 (2001), 83–103.

19. Bridget Orr, *British Enlightenment Theatre: Dramatizing Difference* (Cambridge University Press, 2020), 233, 236, Michael Brown, *The Irish Enlightenment* (Cambridge, MA: Harvard University Press, 2016), 337–43, Helen Burke, '"Country Matters": Irish "Waggery" and the Irish and British Theatrical Traditions', in *Players, Playwrights, Playhouses: Investigating Performance, 1660–1800*, ed. Michael Cordner and Peter Holland (Basingstoke: Palgrave, 2007), 213–28 (214).

20. David O'Shaughnessy, 'Introduction: Staging an Irish Enlightenment', in *Ireland, Enlightenment and the English Stage, 1740–1820*, ed. David O'Shaughnessy (Cambridge University Press, 2019), kindle edition, 691–3.

21. Michael Griffin, *Enlightenment in Ruins: The Geographies of Oliver Goldsmith* (Lewisburg, PA: Bucknell University Press, 2013), 3.

22. Gwynn, *Oliver Goldsmith*, 282.

23. Michael Griffin, 'Oliver Goldsmith', *The Cambridge Companion to Irish Poets*, ed. Gerald Dawe (Cambridge University Press, 2018), 47–60 (47–8); *Enlightenment in Ruins*, 151.

24. Gwynn, *Oliver Goldsmith*, 62; Declan Kiberd, *Irish Classics* (London: Granta, 2000), 108.

25. Seamus Deane, 'Oliver Goldsmith: Miscellaneous Writings, 1759–74', in *The Field Day Anthology of Irish Writing*, ed. Angela Bourke, Siobhán Kilfeather, Maria Luddy, et al., 5 vols. (Derry: Field Day, 1991–2002), 1:658–60 (660).

26. Eavan Boland, 'Re-reading Oliver Goldsmith's "The Deserted Village" in a Changed Ireland', in *A Woman without a Country* (Manchester: Carcanet, 2014), 64–7 (67); 'Islands Apart: A Notebook'. www.poetryfoundation.org/poetrymagazine/articles/69033/islands-apart-a-notebook.

27. Deane, 'Oliver Goldsmith', 659–60.

28. Gargett, 'Plagiarism', 95, 97.

29. Robert W. Seitz, 'The Irish Background of Goldsmith's Social and Political Thought', *PMLA*, 52.2 (1937), 405–11.

30. Kiberd, *Irish Classics*, 116, 109.

31. Terry Eagleton, *Crazy John and the Bishop and Other Essays on Irish Culture* (Cork University Press, 1998), 115, 102.

32. Kiberd, *Irish Classics*, 116.

CHAPTER 34

Afterlives 1: The Victorian *Vicar*

Jarlath Killeen

In the early 1840s, as part of his attempt to document the lives of some of the poorest Londoners, the pioneering ethnographer and journalist Henry Mayhew interviewed a number of street booksellers to determine what was attracting customers in the thoroughfares of the capital city. He found that the 'readiest sales' were of 'English classics': 'such works as the "Spectator", "Tatler", "Guardian", "Adventurer", "Rambler", "Rasselas", "The Vicar of Wakefield", "Peregrine Pickle", "Tom Jones", "Goldsmith's Histories of Greece, Rome, and England"' drew in the crowds as they all sold 'quick'. A book auctioneer explained that collections of Goldsmith's poetry and *The Vicar of Wakefield* were major pulls, even when printed on 'inferior paper' and with 'ridiculous' frontispieces. They 'gave to the public what is called an "impetus" for reading', and formed an important part of the intellectual life of the city. Where authors like Henry Fielding and Tobias Smollett were represented by a single text, an extensive range of Goldsmith's work – his plays, fiction, journalism, poetry, and histories – was available on the stalls.[1]

The interest of the nineteenth-century reading public in Goldsmith is evident also in the fact that he was the subject of four major biographical studies, by James Prior (in 1837), Washington Irving (in 1849), Thomas Babington Macaulay (in 1856), and, most significantly, by John Forster (in 1848; see Chapter 1, 'Life'). Forster's biography was so popular indeed that it went through five editions in the author's lifetime, appealing to different audiences, outselling even his enormously influential biography of his friend and collaborator, Charles Dickens (published in 1872–4). Forster's deeply romantic *Life and Adventures of Oliver Goldsmith* (later transformed into the much more scholarly *Life and Times of Oliver Goldsmith* in 1854 after Forster was accused by James Prior of egregious plagiarism) took 'an indiscriminate and dead collection of details about a man' and turned these dry facts into 'a living picture of the man himself surrounded by the life of his time', and is one of the towering achievements of Victorian biography (see Chapter 32, 'Critical Reception before 1900').[2]

289

Even while vowing not to review any more art 'inspired' by the *Vicar*,
William Makepeace Thackeray was declaring his love for Goldsmith and
repeating and confirming Walter Scott's view that he was the 'most beloved
of all English writers'.[3] As Goldsmith's significance in English cultural life
grew, *The Vicar of Wakefield* took its place as the most important and
emblematic of his works (see Chapter 19, 'Fiction'). Forster insisted that
when this 'little book' was first published, 'no noise was made about it, no
trumpets were blown for it', but it slowly and 'silently forced its way', and
by the mid nineteenth century had come to be considered as one of the
most important books ever written.[4] 'No book upon record has obtained
a wider popularity than *The Vicar of Wakefield*, and none is more likely to
endure', declares Forster at the start of his chapter on the novel; in his
edition of Goldsmith's *Complete Works* in 1872, William Spalding main-
tained that the *Vicar* had been 'read and liked, oftener than any other novel
in any other European language'.[5] 'Everyone reads *The Vicar of Wakefield*
and *The Deserted Village*', affirmed Macaulay, 'and everyone loves their
author'.[6] In 1808, the Irish writer Edward Mangin described the novel as
'so well-loved' and 'so universally admired' that it had become representa-
tive of England itself: 'In England alone, amongst the nations of the earth,
could such an individual as the vicar be supposed'.[7] The affection for the
novel extended across the Victorian cultural landscape. As the art historian
Marcia Pointon points out, with the *Vicar* 'we are dealing with one of the
most frequently illustrated narratives in the history of modern Western
Art',[8] and prominent artists and illustrators like Daniel Maclise, William
Mulready, and Thomas Rowlandson contributed to an artistic vogue for
the novel (see Chapter 28, 'The Sister Arts').[9]

That *The Vicar of Wakefield* had become 'standard' by the early nine-
teenth century is clear by the way in which it was casually referenced in the
fiction of the period. In Jane Austen's *Emma* (1815), as evidence that her
suitor, the farmer Robert Martin, is a well-read and passingly intellectual
man, Harriet Smith offers the information that as well as being thoroughly
acquainted with Agricultural Reports, 'he has read *The Vicar of Wakefield*'
(though, to her disappointment, he had never even heard of *The Romance
of the Forest* nor *The Children of the Abbey* until informed of their existence
by Harriet herself).[10] Knowledge of the *Vicar* was so taken for granted that
in Mary Shelley's *Frankenstein* (1818), the Swiss Henry Clerval can casually
drop in a reference to 'the Dutch schoolmaster in *The Vicar of Wakefield*',
with the expectation that everyone would be familiar with a minor charac-
ter in Goldsmith's novel.[11] In Charlotte Brontë's *The Professor* (1857), it is
reported that the *Vicar* has become a foundational text in the teaching of

English as a foreign language and is 'much used in foreign schools because it is supposed to contain prime samples of conversational English'.[12]

This love of the *Vicar* was generated, in part at least, by childhood reading experiences as attested by Charles Dickens's semi-autobiographical *David Copperfield* (1849–50), where the protagonist recalls how, as a young boy, he delighted in eighteenth-century literature. David cites the Vicar along with Roderick Random, Peregrine Pickle, Humphrey Clinker, Don Quixote, Robinson Crusoe, and Tom Jones as among his favourite childhood friends.[13] Copperfield was not alone. David Fairer has pointed out that the *Vicar* was one of the most important texts of the eighteenth century for readers and writers of the 1850s, contending that 'Goldsmith's warm-hearted picture of the Primrose family triumphing over malice and misadventure suited the tastes of Dickens' readers at mid-century.'[14]

The *Vicar* did suit their taste, but there were other, pressing contemporary reasons why references to Goldsmith's novel can be found littering the fiction of the period. In his biography, Forster explains that while the *Vicar* was a book first encountered in the nursery, it was not discarded as its readers grew older. 'We read it', he insisted (and note the inclusiveness of Forster's language here), 'in youth and age. We return to it, as Walter Scott has said, again and again'.[15] The *Vicar* became a companion through the life of the reader, because it came to be regarded as the fictional equivalent of texts like the Bible or catechisms and devotional works whose moral lessons could be applied to the challenges everyone must face at different stages of life: '[the novel] is designed to show us that patience in suffering, that persevering reliance on the providence of God, that quiet labour, cheerful endeavour, and an indulgent forgiveness of the faults and infirmities of others, are the easy and certain modes of pleasure in this world, and of turning pain to noble uses'.[16] This devotional element of the novel was confirmed by Washington Irving, who asserted that one of the key strengths of the novel was that within it, Goldsmith presented 'religion under its most enduring forms', with a 'feeling that could only flow from the deep convictions of the heart' (see Chapter 15, 'Religion').[17] The Victorian Vicar was certainly not the ironic or satiric or morally untrustworthy character that many critics now insist he is,[18] but a moral exemplar and one who despite (or because of) his many imperfections, offered a Christian model of endurance and faith in the face of calamity and even disaster, a Job figure who, like his Biblical predecessor, faced the problem of evil squarely, and overcame it.[19] While William Paley's *Natural Theology* (1802) had provided an intellectual response to theodicy (the attempt to reconcile the existence of moral and natural evil in the world with the supposed goodness of an omnipotent God), Goldsmith's novel possessed a broad and *popular* appeal and accrued to itself an enviable cultural authority.[20]

Victorian readers increasingly felt in need of such an authority to address the problem of evil, but it is not clear that *The Vicar of Wakefield* retained its ability to convince and satisfy as the century wore on. Recent historians of religion have pointed out that the Victorian period was a particularly fruitful time for the production of multiple theodicies. The much exaggerated phenomenon of Victorian doubt was generated far more by a cultural conversation about the apparent failure of a perfectly good Creator to prevent not just the kind of human immorality that inflicted pain on others, but also natural evils like earthquakes, floods, and famines, than by scientific challenges to traditional Christianity.[21] Fictional responses to the problem of evil, such as *The Vicar of Wakefield*, were marked by what the critic Thomas Vargish calls a 'providential aesthetic', where, no matter what personal disasters morally upstanding characters experienced, God would ultimately ensure that all worked out well. This aesthetic represented the view that the Almighty cared 'for his creatures . . . supervis[ed] over them, and . . . order[ed] . . . the whole course of things for their good' with the promise that everything 'will all turn out cosmically right'.[22]

Such an aesthetic was under increasing pressure by the middle of the century for a number of reasons, one being the exponential growth in knowledge about the magnitude of suffering and pain in the world. The 'hungry 40s' were dominated by a series of crises, including a cholera pandemic and the great Irish Famine. Alongside these crises, however, and perhaps more important than individual events themselves, was the ability of literate citizens to read about them for the first time. This new stream of information was succinctly captured by an article in *Fraser's Magazine* in January 1851, which pointed out that 'it is not the evils themselves, but our knowledge of them, which is new'.[23] Much of this knowledge of misery and suffering flowed from the series of articles by Henry Mayhew, published in the *Morning Chronicle*, the very same articles in which he charted the continued popularity of Goldsmith's novel on the book stalls of the capital city. In this series, Mayhew chronicled the extraordinary extent of indigence, poverty, and suffering in the everyday life of the masses of men and women who now populated the cities of industrial Britain, articles in which, as one reviewer put it, 'Human misery has at last found tongues and pens to make itself heard.'[24]

The old answers to the problem of evil, the answers found in William Paley and *The Vicar of Wakefield*, seemed rather less persuasive as the modern world was revealed as a crucible of suffering and death. In a number of major mid nineteenth-century novels, the *Vicar* is invoked as what appears to be an ironic counterpoint to what is ultimately a demonstration of the tragic constitution of the world, a sense that the world was not designed for the ultimate happiness of even the most worthy of characters. In George Eliot's *Middlemarch* (1871–2), the virtuous but thoroughly practical Mary Garth describes herself as in possession of a 'dreadfully secular mind' and averse to the kinds of comforts supposedly provided by religion, insisting that she dislikes clergymen in general, excepting Mr Farebrother (the local vicar, more interested in entomology than theodicy) and the Vicar of Wakefield.²⁵ The suggestion here is that in a nineteenth-century world, the only clergymen worth anything are those who are uninterested in justifying the ways of God to men, or who exist only in romantic fiction. In Charlotte Brontë's *Villette* (1853), the afflicted orphan Lucy Snowe is an isolated and struggling teacher in France, disliked by her pupils, treated with disdain by her employer, unlucky in love and friendship, and despairing that her stoic response to almost constant psychological distress will not ultimately be vindicated by the God in whom she believes. She sets two of her weakest students the job of translating from the English classics, and remarks that it was 'hard work ... to get them to translate rationally a page of *The Vicar of Wakefield*'.²⁶ The irony here is that, as Lucy constantly stresses, the lazy, stupid, and immoral students she teaches fare far better in the world than she does. The *Vicar* teaches that reward will (eventually) come to those who, like Dr Primrose, cling to Christian virtues and persevere through even extraordinary degrees of misery. However, as the critic Heather Glen argues, the lesson of *Villette* thoroughly undermines this 'public narrative of optimism'.²⁷ Lucy ends the novel completely alone and all her hopes for a happy ever after are dashed.

Perhaps an increasing sense that the *Vicar* offers an inadequate response to the problem of evil is most apparent in the work of Charles Dickens. Dickens himself was extremely attached to the novel, describing it in 1849 as 'a book of which I think it is not too much to say that it has perhaps done more good in the world, and instructed more kinds of people in virtue, than any other fiction ever written'.²⁸ In Dickens's early fiction, the *Vicar* retains a transformative power. Mr Pickwick is an even more naïve version of Dr Primrose, and in *The Pickwick Papers* (1836–7), he endures trials similar to those of his literary predecessor, and even ends up in prison. All ends well, though, and at the conclusion, the benevolent Pickwick dispenses gifts on everyone, even his enemies (like Alfred Jingle, who has relentlessly persecuted Pickwick since his first appearance in the text).

By *Hard Times* (1854), we have moved to a world in which happy endings are rather more elusive. The *Vicar* is represented as a dangerous text because it provides hope to the inhabitants of the industrial hell that is Coketown, ruled over by the crazed empiricist Thomas Gradgrind, who prefers the kind of theodicy provided by Thomas Malthus (after whom he names one of his children) than that articulated by Dr Primrose:

> There was a library in Coketown, to which general access was easy. Mr. Gradgrind greatly tormented his mind about what the people read in this library: . . . They sometimes, after fifteen hours' work, sat down to read mere fables about men and women, more or less like themselves . . . They . . . seemed to be on the whole more comforted by Goldsmith than by [Edward] Cocker.[29]

While threatening to the kind of mind control embodied by Gradgrind, *Vicar* is presented as a 'fable' and offers an escape from, rather than a genuine confrontation with, suffering and misery. Dickens associates *Vicar* with what he called 'Fancy', since, as Mr Sleary, the circus owner stresses, the 'people mutht be amuthed', and the degree to which it can provide an alternative philosophy to the 'facts' of life is in doubt.[30]

Dickens's fourth Christmas book, *The Battle of Life* (1846), is the closest he came to an extended commentary on Goldsmith's beloved text, and a belated attempt to rework many elements of the *Vicar*'s plot for a mid nineteenth-century audience. In *Battle*, Dickens famously eschewed the supernatural interventions that provided answers to the problems of his other Christmas books – *A Christmas Carol* (1843), *The Chimes* (1844), and later *The Haunted Man* (1848) – and tried to weave a fairy-tale solution out of the petty tragedies of everyday life. The action of the novella takes place on a former battlefield where the blood of hundreds of men has been spilled, which becomes representative of the suffering world in which we all live. It is a field where 'Many a wild flower formed by the Almighty Hand to be a perfumed goblet for the dew, felt its enamelled cup filed high with blood . . . .and shrinking dropped'.[31] Nature and time eventually restore to the field its earlier innocence and beauty, however, while green patches reappear, 'underneath those fertile spots, heaps of men and horses lay buried, indiscriminately, enriching the ground'.[32] On this battleground, the guileless (but finally justified) cosmic Christian optimism of Dr Primrose is transformed into the tragi-comic pessimism of Dr Jeddler, whose awareness of the scope of human misery prevents him from taking what he describes as the 'preposterous and ridiculous business called Life' at all seriously.[33]

While the novel sets out to teach Jeddler to change perspective and to accept that life is both serious and worthwhile through suffering the apparent loss of his daughter to sexual scandal, the novel is widely acknowledged as a failure and the weakest of the Christmas books, precisely because the attempt to make a realist text out of the *Vicar* cannot work in the hungry '40s. The bitter reaction of contemporary critics (and the novel's continued unpopularity today) indicate how difficult Dickens found it to work out a happy ending in which providence delivers a just reward for perseverance without requiring the direct intervention of supernatural agents. The failure to provide adequate realist solutions to the problem of evil may have contributed to Goldsmith's novel falling out of intellectual and literary favour. *Olivia*, the Irishman W. G. Wills's adaptation of the novel for the stage, was an enormous success in 1877 (and starred Ellen Terry in the title role), but the shift of focus away from the stoic protagonist to his wronged daughter is indicative of the sense that Primrose and his beliefs were increasingly out of time and out of place. After a revival of the play in 1897, George Bernard Shaw confessed that while it was 'easy' for him, 'taught my letters as I was by a governess who might have been Mrs. Primrose herself, to understand the Wakefield vicarage', things had dramatically changed, even since his childhood: 'what I want to know is, can it carry any conviction to people who are a generation ahead of me in years, and a century in nursery civilization?'[34] Shaw associates his love of Goldsmith with his childhood immersion in the Bible, his familiarity with traditional stories of good overcoming evil, and wonders whether all this would appear as inadequate nostalgic frippery to younger contemporaries. Shaw received his answer from a 'modern lady' who simply 'dismissed' the play 'as "beneath contempt"'.[35] By the end of the century it certainly seemed as if the Victorians had fallen out of love with Goldsmith and his *Vicar*.

Notes

1. Henry Mayhew, *London Labour and the London Poor*, vol. 1 (London: G. Woodfall and Son, 1851), 293–4 (296, 294).
2. John Forster, *The Life and Times of Oliver Goldsmith*, 2 vols. (London: Bradbury and Evans, 1854), 1:vii.
3. [William Makepeace Thackeray], 'May Gambols; or, Titmarsh in the Picture-Galleries', *Fraser's Magazine*, 29 (June 1844), 706; [William Makepeace Thackeray], *The English Humourists of the Eighteenth Century*, ed. Edgar F. Harden (Ann Arbor: University of Michigan Press, 2007), 97.

4. Forster, *Life and Times*, 2:17.
5. Forster, *Life and Times*, 2:4.
6. Quoted in Robert L. Mack, 'Introduction', in Oliver Goldsmith, *The Vicar of Wakefield* (Oxford World's Classics, 2006), xii.
7. Quoted in Norma Clarke, '"More National (to Ireland) than Personal": James Prior's *Life of Oliver Goldsmith* (1837)', *Biography*, 41.1 (Winter 2018), 53–4.
8. Marcia Pointon, 'On Reading Rowlandson's *The Vicar of Wakefield*: Challenging and Subverting the Narrative', *Journal of Area Studies,* Series 1.7 (1986), 20.
9. For illustrations of Goldsmith's novel, see Robert H. Hopkins, 'Fortune and the Heavenly Bank: *The Vicar of Wakefield* as Sustained Satire', in *The True Genius of Oliver Goldsmith* (Baltimore, MD: Johns Hopkins University Press, 1969), 166–230.
10. Jane Austen, *Emma*, ed. James Kinsley (Oxford World's Classics, 2005), 23.
11. Mary Shelley, *Frankenstein*, ed. M. K. Joseph (Oxford World's Classics, 1980), 60.
12. Charlotte Brontë, *The Professor*, ed. Margaret Smith and Herbert Rosengarten (Oxford World's Classics, 1991).
13. Charles Dickens, *David Copperfield*, ed. Nina Burgis (Oxford World's Classics, 1997), 53.
14. David Fairer, 'Preface', in *The Victorians and the Eighteenth Century: Reassessing the Tradition*, ed. Francis O'Gorman and Katherine Turner (Aldershot: Ashgate, 2004), xv.
15. Forster, *Life and Times*, 2:4.
16. Forster, *Life and Times*, 2:5.
17. Washington Irving, *The Life of Oliver Goldsmith* (London, 1850), 425.
18. For readings of the novel as a satire, and its narrator as unreliable, see Robert H. Hopkins, *The True Genius of Oliver Goldsmith* (Baltimore, MD: Johns Hopkins University Press, 1969), 200–24; Richard J. Jaarsma, 'Satiric Intent in *The Vicar of Wakefield*', *Studies in Short Fiction*, 5 (1967–8), 331–41.
19. For the *Vicar* and Job, see Martin Battestin, 'Goldsmith: The Comedy of Job', in *The Providence of Wit: Aspects of Form in Augustan Literature and the Arts* (Oxford: Clarendon, 1974), 193–214; Henry N. Rogers, 'God's Implausible Plot: The Providential Design of *The Vicar of Wakefield*', *Philological Review*, 28.1 (2002), 5–17.
20. My understanding of the importance of theodicy to the Victorians has been greatly enhanced by the work of my former doctoral student, Paula Keatley, who also helped guide me through the scholarly literature on the subject.
21. Howard R. Murphy, 'The Ethical Revolt against Christian Orthodoxy in Early Victorian England', *American Historical Review*, 60 (1955), 800–17.
22. Thomas Vargish, *The Providential Aesthetic in Victorian Fiction* (Charlottesville: University Press of Virginia, 1985), 18, 33.
23. Anon., 'The First Half of the Nineteenth Century', *Fraser's Magazine* (January 1851), 14.

24. Anon., 'The Distressed Needlewomen', *Westminster Review* (January 1849), 371.

25. George Eliot, *Middlemarch*, ed. David Carroll (Oxford World's Classics, 1997).

26. Charlotte Brontë, *Villette*, ed. Sally Shuttleworth (Oxford World's Classics, 2000), 215.

27. Heather Glen, *Charlotte Brontë: The Imagination in History* (Cambridge University Press, 2002), 257.

28. 'Dickens to Angela Burdett Coutts, 15 November, 1849', in *The Heart of Charles Dickens, As Revealed in His Letters to Angela Burdett Coutts, Selected and Edited from the Collection in the Pierpont Morgan Library*, ed. Edgar Johnson (Boston, MA: Little, Brown, 1952), 144.

29. Charles Dickens, *Hard Times*, ed. Paul Schlicke (Oxford World's Classics, 2006), 52.

30. Dickens, *Hard Times*, 269.

31. Charles Dickens, *The Battle of Life: The Christmas Books*, ed. Ruth Glancy (Oxford World's Classics, 1998), 281.

32. Dickens, *Battle*, 281.

33. Dickens, *Battle*, 285.

34. Bernard Shaw, *Our Theatres in the Nineties*, vol. 3 (London: Constable and Company, 1948), 37. Note that John J. Douglass's sensationalized version of *The Vicar of Wakefield* was staged in November 1870 at the Standard Theatre, London. The critic for the *Observer* complained that Samuel Emery's performance as Dr Primrose failed to 'show with any amount of skill the sweet contentment of the simple country clergyman at the commencement of the play, or the calm resignation of the Christian gentleman at its conclusion' ('Standard Theatre', *Observer*, 6 November, 1870, 7).

35. Shaw, *Our Theatres*, 37.

CHAPTER 35

Afterlives 2: Theatre

David Clare

Since enjoying a successful premiere run in London in 1773, Oliver Goldsmith's comedy *She Stoops to Conquer* has been a fixture on stages across the world (see Chapter 20, 'Theatre'). It has long production histories in Australia's major cities, and has been popular in Russia (formerly the Soviet Union) since a hit run at Moscow's Vakhtangov Theatre Studio in 1956. It has been revived on South African stages no fewer than seventeen times since 1807 – including the first recorded instance of a 'published play [being] performed' by a Black South African company.[1] (It was staged by Herbert Dhlomo's Bantu Dramatic Society at the Bantu Men's Social Centre on 28 April 1933.) In North America, the comedy premiered in New York only four and a half months after its London premiere, and it became a 'mainstay' on American and Canadian stages by the early nineteenth century – in cities of all sizes.[2] It has remained popular there during the twentieth and twenty-first centuries (e.g. there were significant Broadway and Off-Broadway revivals in 1905, 1924, 1949–50, 1960, 1984, 2002, 2005, and 2016). And A. Lytton Sells has written of the play's perennial popularity on the French stage; it has even 'inspired' numerous French 'imitations'.[3] By contrast, Sells informs us, Goldsmith's other full-length play, *The Good Natur'd Man* (1768), 'never appealed much to the French'.[4] It did not appeal much to theatre producers and companies in the other countries just mentioned either.

The Good Natur'd Man has, however, had some purchase on the stages of the two countries where Goldsmith has been most frequently produced: the country where he lived for most of his adult life, England, and the country where he was born and raised, Ireland. While *She Stoops to Conquer* has been revived much more frequently in these two countries than *The Good Natur'd Man*, the widespread love for Goldsmith's drama (and his other writings) in England and Ireland has encouraged theatremakers to also occasionally take a chance on his 'forgotten' comedy. The bulk of this chapter focuses on seminal productions of *She Stoops to Conquer* and *The*

Good Natur'd Man in the two countries most central to Goldsmith's own life.

The Good Natur'd Man has received sporadic, high-profile revivals (as well as numerous amateur stagings) in England ever since its semi-successful debut at Covent Garden over eleven nights in February and March 1768. Two of the more interesting revivals were mounted in 1939 at the Buxton Festival by the Old Vic (while the company was overseen by the English-born Irish director Tyrone Guthrie) and in 1971–2 at the Old Vic itself (in a National Theatre production).

The publicity material fed to newspapers by the Old Vic in advance of the 1939 Buxton production suggested that this was 'the first important revival since the play was first performed 171 years ago'.[5] While this boast might be somewhat excessive, this staging was more adventurous and successful than previous revivals, and a key aspect of the play's improved reception was ascribable to Guthrie's belief in the script (and what he could do with it). Guthrie felt that the antipathy that critics and audiences felt for *The Good Natur'd Man* upon its premiere was due to their misguided 'dislike [for its] Irish humour'; he also felt that subsequent productions had been marred by the theatremakers' unwillingness to properly engage with the script's politically charged commentary on English high society.[6] Convinced that English audiences had grown to understand and appreciate riskier (and allegedly cruder) forms of Irish humour by 1939, Guthrie restored the play's most 'Irish' scene: the appearance of the two bailiffs, including the (presumably) Irish character Flanagin the Follower. This scene had been dropped from the play after its opening night in 1768, as audience members, squeamish at lowborn bailiffs intruding into a polite society drawing room, hissed 'low, low'.[7] Guthrie, as the critic for *The Times* of London notes, also drew out the 'sly' sociopolitical 'satire' in the script, though not in a heavy-handed way that killed the audience's enjoyment of the piece.[8] Indeed, the same critic observes that the director 'add[ed]' to the 'fun' of the 'strong comic passages … by mocking the sentimentalities of the piece'.[9] Goldsmith famously claimed to dislike 'sentimental comedy'; as such, this was a knowing and interesting move on Guthrie's part (see Chapter 27, 'Satire and Sentiment').

The Good Natur'd Man had its Irish premiere at Dublin's Capel Street Theatre on 17 May 1770. It was subsequently performed at Dublin's Crow Street Theatre nine times between 1773 and 1811.[10] The play also drew the attention of actor-manager Michael Atkins in Belfast, who produced it at the New Theatre in Mill Gate during his tenure there between 1773 and 1778.[11] Over the ensuing centuries, the play was sporadically revived across the island, with the most interesting production taking place in Dublin. I refer to the late 1974–early 1975 Gate Theatre production mounted to mark the bicentennial of Goldsmith's death. Director Hilton Edwards attempted to 'Hibernicise' the play by casting *both* bailiffs as Irish and adding three new interludes in which these characters behave like slapstick 'Stage Dubs'.[12] The production was a success, running for three months.

In England, *She Stoops to Conquer* was an instant sensation. After its initial run of twelve shows at London's Covent Garden, mounted between March and May 1773, it was revived by Samuel Foote for six performances that summer at the Haymarket, and was presented eight more times at Covent Garden that autumn. James Ogden informs us that, during that year, the play was also staged 'successfully at most towns in England'.[13] Over the following two and a half centuries, it was 'revived in London over sixty times' and also played 'at most provincial theatres' and was tackled by 'most' of the serious 'amateur dramatics societies'.[14] It spawned numerous operatic and musical adaptations, as well as popular 'sequels' written by important theatremakers such as the actor/dramatists John O'Keeffe (his *Tony Lumpkin in Town* had a one-night premiere run in Dublin in 1774 but enjoyed much greater success at London's Haymarket in 1778), John Quick (whose *Tony Lumpkin's Adventures in a Trip to Liverpool* premiered at Liverpool's Theatre Royal in 1784), and Charles Mathews (a creator of popular one-man shows featuring characters from plays he'd starred in, including *She Stoops to Conquer*). As Ogden notes, during the late eighteenth century and throughout the nineteenth, there was an ever-increasing tendency in England to play up the farcical elements of the play, even when it was being used as a star vehicle for aspiring or established 'serious' actors such as Ellen Terry and Lillie Langtry; but this was corrected to a certain (admittedly limited) degree during the twentieth and twenty-first centuries, including in high-profile productions at the Old Vic in 1960 and at the National Theatre in 2012.[15]

Although the 1960 Old Vic production arguably retained too much of the 'high-spirited[ness]' common to English productions through the centuries, director Douglas Seale still managed to include enough light and shade in the production to please both audiences *and* critics. In the eyes of many, Judi Dench's 'kittenish' turn as the heroine was the production's 'real success', but this staging was also noteworthy for the fact that Tony Lumpkin was played by rock 'n' roller Tommy Steele.[16] While only new to acting, Steele was – in the opinion of *The Times* of London reviewer – 'eminently satisfactory in the role, despite 'shout[ing] his way through . . . "The Three Pigeons"' and 'not yet [being] sufficiently adept' as an actor 'to make it clear that Lumpkin is a country and not a town lout'.[17]

The 2012 National Theatre production of *She Stoops to Conquer* also arguably emphasized fun and liveliness at the expense of Goldsmith's social satire. However, as Libby Purvis notes in her review, the fact that British aristocrats like young Marlow are taught to believe that it is 'OK to treat the lower orders insolently' was implicitly condemned in the production.[18] Additional satire was generated by heavily emphasizing Mrs Hardcastle's social-climbing tendencies, with the actor playing the role – Sophie Thompson – stealing the show in the opinion of many critics.

This production was also noteworthy in other key ways. First, the casting process was colour-blind, which resulted in Black British actor Cush Jumbo playing Constance Neville, and, as the *Evening Standard* reviewer stated, she 'dazzle[d]' audiences.[19] Also, on this occasion, the production's 'liveliness' was carefully and brilliantly choreographed (and therefore more visually and intellectually satisfying) thanks to director Jamie Lloyd's wise decision to enlist Ann Yee as movement director. Finally, while the celebrity casting of Steele in the 1960 production had mixed results, casting a figure from popular culture on this occasion proved beneficial to the show. The star turn that garnered the most attention, aside from Thompson's, was Katherine Kelly's as Kate Hardcastle. Back in 2012, Kelly was famous for her role as working-class Becky McDonald from the television serial *Coronation Street*, so when she switched from posh young lady to barmaid in this production, those in attendance were delighted to see a very 'Becky'-like persona suddenly make an appearance. Even better, as Purvis notes, Kelly's transformations were sudden and complete: she 'is too skillful [an actor] not to keep the two personalities going, just as she has heart enough to convince us when real love dawns'.[20]

She Stoops to Conquer premiered at Dublin's Smock Alley Theatre less than a month after its London debut. The first performance, which took place on 13 April 1773, featured John O'Keeffe as Tony Lumpkin, initiating his strong association with that role. In addition to performing the role of Lumpkin many times on London and Dublin stages, O'Keeffe wrote two 'sequels' to *She Stoops to Conquer*: the aforementioned *Tony Lumpkin in Town*, which had its world premiere at Smock Alley on 13 April 1774 and which was revived there in 1785, and a one-man show entitled *Tony Lumpkin's Rambles thro' Cork*, which premiered in Cork City in 1773 and which was retitled *Tony Lumpkin's Frolics through Dublin* when it was first performed at Smock Alley in 1776. (*Tony Lumpkin's Frolics through Dublin* was subsequently revived at the Crow Street and Smock Alley theatres 'several times' between that spring and 1781).[21] However, Ireland's interest in the play was not confined to the comedy provided by Tony Lumpkin – a character known in Ireland to have been based on Goldsmith's Irish cousin (and scion of the Pallas estate) Bob Bryanton. There were several other reasons, aside from the obvious one of Goldsmith's Irish nationality, which piqued Irish interest in the play and caused it to be revived regularly in Ireland.

The script is often described as having an Irish 'flavour', thanks to its rollicking plot and the seeming Hibernicisms in the dialogue—for example, when Mrs Hardcastle exclaims, 'Oh, Tony, I'm killed' after emerging from the lake, or when Tony says, in a phrase first coined here by Goldsmith, 'Ask me no questions, and I'll tell you no fibs' (*Stoops*, 94, 51). There are also numerous Irish references surreptitiously seeded into the script that have often gone unnoticed by commentators outside of Ireland. These include the references to 1) Derry-born playwright George Farquhar, 2) the Dublin ballad 'Allie Croker' (including the implicit link Goldsmith makes between that ballad and anti-colonial agitation in India), 3) the extravagances of Irish absentees in England (through the allusions to Lady Killdaylight and the Countess of Sligo and possibly through the characterisation of Mrs Hardcastle), 4) the possibly Irish cookmaid Bridget (unseen on stage but vividly described), and 5) a central English character (young Marlow) depicted as a hypocrite, which, as I have discussed elsewhere, is a common trope in Irish literary works featuring English characters.[22]

Between the late eighteenth and early twentieth centuries, the Irish aspects of the play merely meant that it was revived frequently across the island (especially in Dublin, Cork, and Belfast) and often on special occasions. For example, a survey of the 120 performances of the play mounted in Dublin's Smock Alley, Crow Street, and Fishamble Street theatres between 1773 and 1818 reveals how many times it was used to celebrate big occasions such as royal birthdays and jubilees, visits to the Irish capital by British aristocrats, and the reopening of theatres.[23] (Indeed, later in the nineteenth century – in 1871 – it would be the play chosen to open Dublin's new Gaiety Theatre).[24] It seems as if the play's Irish 'flavour' combined with its English setting made it a work that could appeal to both Irish nationalists and Irish unionists.

It was only after the twenty-six counties gained their independence from Britain that a tendency to 'Hibernicise' the play began to prevail in the Irish Free State/Republic. For example, the play was reset in Ireland for the productions at the Abbey Theatre in 1969, 1982, and 2014–15 and at the Gate Theatre in 1995. In that same 1995 production, the Gate also restored a song set to an Irish melody ('The Humours of Balamagairy') included in the original draft of the play. Another common 'Hibernicising' technique was to keep the play set in England but to have certain English characters played as Irish. Arguably going even further, Piaras Béaslaí translated the play into the Irish language in 1929. This version was entitled *Ísliú Chun Buadha* and produced by An Comhar Drámaíochta that year on the Abbey Theatre's Peacock stage.

By contrast, theatremakers working in Northern Ireland post-partition have found it easier to retain the play's essential Irish-British hybridity in their productions. A high-profile production at the Grand Opera House in Belfast in 2008 kept the play's setting in England but allowed the play's multiple Irish references and resonances to speak for themselves.

In addition to the productions of his two major plays just discussed (including the various adaptations, 'imitations', and 'sequels' popular in France, England, and Ireland), one might also note the numerous stage adaptations of Goldsmith's classic 1766 novel, *The Vicar of Wakefield*. In England, the most successful adaptation to date has been *Olivia*, by W. G. Wills, 'which ran for 138 nights in its original production in 1878 and 135 more when it was revived by [Henry] Irving in 1885' (see Chapter 34, 'Afterlives 1: The Victorian *Vicar*').[25] In Ireland, the most famous adaptation (aside from the one that Richard Brinsley Sheridan is reputed to have created while still a student at Harrow) is Tom Murphy's. It was a script that the Tuam-born Murphy laboured over for many years. At various points, it was produced and published under two different titles: *The Vicar of Wakefield* (in 1974 and 2010) and *She Stoops to Folly* (in 1996). Versions under both titles generated significant interest and excitement when produced at the Abbey Theatre.

Dublin was also the site for two other notable stage works based on the writings of Oliver Goldsmith. On 25 April 1781, a short play entitled *The Knabbers* and attributed to 'the late Doctor Goldsmith' was produced at Smock Alley.[26] The script for this play remains untraced. It is possible that this was a misnamed version of *The Grumbler*, Goldsmith's very short farce based on Sir Charles Sedley's translation of a scene from David-Augustin de Brueys's *Le Grondeur* (1691) and produced once (for the benefit of John Quick, the original Tony Lumpkin) at Covent Garden in 1772. The second curious and notable Dublin production is an operatic version of Goldsmith's poem 'The Hermit', which was created by the composer Sir John Stevenson and librettist John Charles Clifton and which debuted at the Crow Street Theatre in 1816.[27] This is an example of Irish-based composers departing from the more common practice of adapting

Goldsmith's dramatic masterpiece, *She Stoops to Conquer*, for the operatic stage. Goldsmith has managed to capture the attention of theatremakers and audiences across the world – but especially in England and Ireland – over the course of two and a half centuries. As all of these productions indicate, Goldsmith's work (whether intended for the stage or not) is particularly well suited to theatrical presentation. And it is likely that productions of his dramatic scripts, as well as stage adaptations of his other writings, will continue to feature on the world's stages for the foreseeable future.

Notes

1. Yvette Hutchison, 'South Africa', in *A History of Theatre in Africa*, ed. Martin Banham (Cambridge University Press, 2004), 312–79 (345). See also Anon., '*She Stoops to Conquer*', *Encyclopaedia of South African Theatre, Film, Media and Performance* (*ESAT*), last edited 10 May 2021. https://esat.sun.ac .za/index.php/She_Stoops_to_Conquer (accessed 21 May 2021).
2. Marlies K. Danziger, *Oliver Goldsmith and Richard Brinsley Sheridan* (New York: Ungar, 1978), 161.
3. A. Lytton Sells, *Oliver Goldsmith: His Life and Works* (London: George Allen & Unwin, 1974), 398 (see also 397–405).
4. Sells, *Oliver Goldsmith*, 398 (see also 404).
5. Anon., 'The Theatres', *The Times* [of London], 21 August 1939.
6. Anon., 'The Theatres'.
7. 'Special Correspondent', 'Buxton Festival: "The Good-Natured Man" by Oliver Goldsmith', *The Times* [of London], 12 September 1939.
8. 'Special Correspondent', 'Buxton Festival: "The Good-Natured Man" by Oliver Goldsmith'.
9. 'Special Correspondent', 'Buxton Festival: "The Good-Natured Man" by Oliver Goldsmith'.
10. See John C. Greene, *Theatre in Dublin, 1745–1820: A Calendar of Performances*, 6 vols. (Bethlehem, PA: Lehigh University Press, 2011), vols. 2–6.
11. Roy Johnston with Declan Plummer, *The Musical Life of Nineteenth-Century Belfast* (New York: Routledge, 2017), 41.
12. David Clare, 'Goldsmith, the Gate, and the "Hibernicising" of Anglo-Irish Plays', in *The Gate Theatre, Dublin: Inspiration and Craft*, ed. David Clare, Des Lally, and Patrick Lonergan (Dublin: Carysfort Press / Oxford: Peter Lang, 2018), 239–59 (256–8).
13. James Ogden, Introduction to *She Stoops to Conquer*, by Oliver Goldsmith (London: Black / New York: Norton, 2001), xi–xxxix [xxxiv].
14. Ogden, *Introduction*, xxxiv.
15. Ogden, *Introduction*, xxxiv–xxxviii; Michael Billington, '*She Stoops to Conquer*, Olivier, London', *The Guardian*, 1 February 2012.

16. Anon., 'High-Spirited Evening with Goldsmith', *The Times* [of London], 9 November 1960; Ogden, *Introduction*, xxxvi.

17. Anon., 'High-Spirited Evening with Goldsmith'.

18. Libby Purvis, 'Theatre: *She Stoops to Conquer*, Olivier', *The Times* [of London], 2 February 2012.

19. Anon., '*She Stoops to Conquer*, National (Olivier) – Review', *The Evening Standard*, 10 April 2012.

20. Libby Purvis, 'Theatre: *She Stoops to Conquer*, Olivier'.

21. John C. Greene, *Theatre in Dublin, 1745–1820: A History*, 2 vols. (Bethlehem, PA: Lehigh University Press, 2011), 2:495.

22. For extended discussions of these Irish aspects of the play, see Clare, 'Goldsmith, the Gate, and the "Hibernicising" of Anglo-Irish Plays', 239–59.

23. See Greene, *Theatre in Dublin, 1745–1820*, vols. 2–6.

24. Smock Alley also celebrated its grand reopening in 2012 with a production of the play.

25. James F. Stottlar, 'A Victorian Stage Adapter at Work: W. G. Wills "Rehabilitates" the Classics', *Victorian Studies*, 16.4 (1973), 401–32 (403).

26. Greene, *Theatre in Dublin, 1745–1820: A Calendar of Performances*, 3:1973.

27. Greene, *Theatre in Dublin, 1745–1820: A Calendar of Performances*, 6:4152.

CHAPTER 36

Afterlives 3: Poetry

Alfred Lutz

Of the small number of Oliver Goldsmith's poems, only a handful – *The Deserted Village, The Traveller, Retaliation, Edwin and Angelina,* and *The Haunch of Venison* – have been frequently anthologized. Only the first two have received sustained critical attention, and only *The Deserted Village* (1770) has had the kind of afterlife this chapter attempts to trace.

The poem's originality lies in its understanding of the village – 'Sweet Auburn, loveliest village of the plain' (line 1) – as a community representing moral, economic, and political values capable of sustaining arguments about the larger social whole (see Chapter 21, 'Pastoral Poetry'). Later writers influenced by Goldsmith's poem either dismiss the possibilities this synecdochic relationship between the village and the wider world offers, or they make it the centre of their work. The former approach, the more popular one, views the village as a self-contained, inward-looking entity, as a natural growth embedded in the seasonal cycle and, as a result, strips Goldsmith's poem of its critical potential. The less popular approach conceives of the village as socially constructed and embedded in linear history. It places Auburn's decline in a larger political and social context to read the poem as addressing a wide range of political and cultural dispossessions (see Chapter 10, 'Liberty').

The former perspective resurrects the rural idyll Goldsmith's poem relegates to the past and celebrates the village community as an organic embodiment of traditional values. Writers following this lead tend to lavish their praise on the character sketches (the village preacher, the schoolmaster), the description of the ale house, and the villagers' leisure activities – that is, the parts of the poem that would become the oft-anthologized 'beauties'.[1] Examples of this approach in the early decades after the poem's publication include Anthony King's *The Frequented Village: A Poem. Inscribed to Dr. Oliver Goldsmith* (1771) and James Hurdis's *The Village Curate* (1788). George Crabbe's *The Village* (1783), the best and best-known early response to *The Deserted Village*, dismisses Goldsmith's poem as a purely literary – and thus unrealistic – representation of rural life, as a nostalgic construction of an ahistorical paradise.

In the nineteenth century, *The Vicar of Wakefield* (1766) became Goldsmith's most popular work (see Chapter 34, 'Afterlives 1: The Victorian *Vicar*'). While the focus of *The Deserted Village* is the village community, the focus of the novel is the Primrose family. Nineteenth-century writers influenced by Goldsmith often populate the village community offered by Goldsmith's poem with the type of characters offered by his novel. This perspective finds its culmination in the mid nineteenth-century interest in domestic realism, the favoured location of which is the village community. The most successful example in this tradition is Mary Russell Mitford's *Our Village*, which was issued in a series of five volumes from 1824 to 1832, and which, according to Ronald Blythe, inaugurated the 'national village cult'.[2] Her character sketches – 'The Talking Lady', 'An Old Bachelor', 'A Village Beau', and so on – are embedded in an essentially timeless village.

The blending of *The Deserted Village* with *The Vicar of Wakefield* remained popular throughout the nineteenth century in both Britain and the United States, and it was buttressed by biographical readings of Goldsmith's work and various biographies, especially those by John Forster and Washington Irving, which, as Richard D. Altick points out, 'wrapped the figure of Goldsmith in a thick aura of sentimental affection'.[3] The many illustrated editions of *The Deserted Village*, created by and reinforcing this reading, take this perspective well into the twentieth century (see Chapter 28, 'The Sister Arts'). While the poem presents the idyllic and organic village community as belonging to the past, illustrated editions, which tend to focus on the sections of the poem addressing the Auburn of old, inevitably – by the sheer power of pictorial representation – turn the absence of 'Sweet Auburn' into a presence.[4] The staying power of this reading of the poem is illustrated by Éamon de Valera's vision of an ideal Ireland – the noble peasant living in an organic village community – memorably expressed in his 1943 St Patrick's Day radio broadcast during which he imagines 'a land whose countryside would be bright with cosy homesteads, whose fields and villages would be joyous with the sounds of industry, with the romping of sturdy children, the contests of athletic youths and the laughter of comely maidens, whose firesides would be forums for the wisdom of serene old age'.[5]

The Deserted Village's conceptualization of the village community as an organic entity also influenced writers in the British colonies in North America and the early United States. These writers replace the *temporal* relationship between the Auburn of old and the deserted village of the present with a *spatial* relationship. They present the deserted village as a contemporary *English* village, while the Auburn of the poem's past now represents a contemporary *American* village. Whereas the temporal, deeply nostalgic presentation of Goldsmith's poem measures an enormous loss in one place, this spatial reading reconstitutes the nostalgic vision as contemporary American reality, symbolizing the promise offered to the new nation by agrarian nationalism.

Timothy Dwight's *Greenfield Hill* (1794) is a fine example. Part II of the poem ('The Flourishing Village') is an imitation of *The Deserted Village*. The happy American village is located in the present – 'Thrice bless'd the life, in this glad region spent, / In peace, in competence, and still content; / Where bright, and brighter, all things daily smile, / And rare and scanty, flow the streams of ill' – and it is clear that the future will be even better.[6] The past is marked by Indian savagery, which is presented, not surprisingly, by an attack on a village, a scene also painted in David Humphreys's *A Poem, On the Happiness of America; Addressed to the Citizens of the United States* (1786). Similar arguments are made in Philip Freneau's *The American Village* (1772), Oliver Goldsmith's, great-nephew of the poet, *The Rising Village* (1825), William Ray's *Village Greatness* (1821), Samuel Deane's *The Populous Village* (1826), John Howard Bryant's *My Native Vale* (1826), and Charles Wheeler Denison's *The American Village* (1845).

The second major response to *The Deserted Village* aligns the village community with radical political perspectives. Rather than focusing on the village of the past as an idyllic, inward-looking community, this reading focuses on the radical possibilities offered by the temporal separation of sweet Auburn from the deserted village, teasing out the potentially radical implications of the poem's nostalgia. This view is reflected in imitations published in the decades immediately following the publication of Goldsmith's poem, such as John Robinson's *The Village Oppress'd: A Poem* (1771), an attack on luxury and commerce dedicated to Goldsmith, and Thomas Bachelor's *Village Scenes, The Progress of Agriculture, and Other Poems* (1804).

In addition to these minor figures, several major poets draw on a radical reading of Goldsmith's poem. John Clare's indebtedness to Goldsmith runs deep, though not in the field where Clare's specific genius shines. His focus on the particular – bird nests, for example, rather than the village as corporate entity – is fundamentally different from Goldsmith's neoclassical focus on the general. Still, Goldsmith was an abiding presence in Clare's poetry, especially early on when Clare worked through the poetic styles

available to him. 'Helpstone', the most important poem in his first collec-
tion, *Poems Descriptive of Rural Life and Scenery* (1820), draws on
Goldsmith's *The Deserted Village* for its major themes: nostalgia for the
village of his youth, the opposition between past and present, and the
destruction of the village. Other Clare poems that show the influence of
The Deserted Village are 'Elegy on the Ruins of Pickworth, Rutlandshire',
'Helpstone Green', 'The Village Minstrel', and his long poem *The Parish:
A Satire*. Ebenezer Elliott is similarly indebted to Goldsmith, most obvi-
ously in 'The Splendid Village', which, like *The Deserted Village*, operates
on two temporal planes and is nostalgic for an earlier time, which is
conjured up in language echoing Goldsmith's rather closely: 'Ere
England's wrongs began, and labour's woes'.[7]

The Deserted Village is also regularly mentioned in pro- and anti-
enclosure tracts, in the writings of both the radical agrarians of the late
eighteenth and early nineteenth centuries as well as their opponents, and in
the work of political economists and their critics.[8] In almost all of these
texts – poetry as well as prose – *The Deserted Village* is not understood as
a serious and sustained argument in favour of particular political or
economic positions; rather, it is used as shorthand for such positions. It
figures as a *moral* perspective on economic and political issues.[9] The large
number of such references and the reliability with which *The Deserted
Village* serves in this illustrative function speak to both the popularity of the
poem and its role as representative of a position most readers would be
expected to recognize.

Such political readings of Goldsmith's work largely disappear in the
nineteenth century. Rhetorics of resistance developed in the late eighteenth
and nineteenth centuries replace the language Goldsmith's poem offers
and, more importantly, make it more difficult to recognize the poem's
radical potential. In addition, the development of the field of economics
offered a 'scientific' vocabulary deemed more appropriate for the discus-
sion of economic matters than the language of poetry. Rejecting
Goldsmith the philosopher but praising Goldsmith the poet, this view,
to quote Thomas Babington Macaulay, dismisses the 'theory' but argues
that 'the poem, considered merely as a poem, is not necessarily the worse
on that account'.[10] Still, references to Goldsmith in the context of eco-
nomic and political debates do not disappear entirely. For those writers
who reject the idea of the economy as a self-contained system following
internal laws that make it impermeable to outside influence, the poem
retains its function as easily recognizable shorthand for a particular kind of
moral economy. For example, the organic husbandry movement between

the 1930s and 1950s addressed some of the same concerns Goldsmith's poem tackles.[11] More recently, Tony Judt's *Ill Fares the Land* (2011), a defence of social democracy against neoliberalism, announces its allegiance in the title.

The radical Goldsmith also appeals to writers in colonial settings. Writing about Goldsmith's *The Deserted Village*, John Montague argues: 'For although the idea of an Irish literature in English was outside his experience, *The Deserted Village* rehearses one of the most Irish themes of all, a forecast of the downfall of Britain through imperial greed. He produced the first anti-imperialistic poem in the period of England's greatest imperial expansion' (see Chapter 17, 'War and Empire').[12] Locating the setting of Goldsmith's poem outside a specifically Irish geography, Montague's argument implies that the poem becomes available to any colonial context, where Goldsmith's nostalgia could be transferred to a pre-colonial time. Sol T. Plaatje's *Native Life in South Africa, before and since the European War and the Boer Rebellion* (1916), an argument against the 1913 Natives Land Act, quotes several British writers, presumably to appeal to his book's intended audience. The passages he quotes from *The Deserted Village* – one quotation is made up of lines 5–18; 29–38; 49–52; the other of lines 57–8; 63–4; 69–74; 83–6 – focus on the Auburn of the past and, in the context of Plaatje's revision, oppose a precolonial past to the colonial present, thus mourning, as does Goldsmith's poem, the disappearance of a way of life and, more important in a colonial context, a material and cultural dispossession. The transplanted poetic ideal becomes the utopian vision of political independence. Rēweti Tūhorouta Kōhere, the Māori translator and author (1871–1954), uses Goldsmith's poem in a series of newspaper articles for similar purposes. Goldsmith also crops up in quite unexpected contexts. The foreword to the final report of the Human Rights Violations Investigation Commission (2002), charged with investigating human rights violations in Nigeria between 1966 and 1999, written by the commission's chairman, Chukwudifu A. Oputa, begins with an epigraph taken from *The Deserted Village* ('Ill Fares the Land . . . '). These examples suggest the wide availability of the poem in British colonial contexts.[13]

Although recent scholarship has reclaimed Goldsmith for a specifically Irish context, this perspective was not prominent in much of the nineteenth century. In their introduction to *A Treasury of Irish Poetry in the English Tongue*, Spofford A. Brooke and T. W. Rolleston argue that 'Goldsmith and other Irishmen had written poems in the English tongue before the close of the eighteenth century, but they were English in matter and manner, and belonged to the English tradition.'[14] William Butler Yeats, though he includes two passages from *The Deserted Village* – lines 83–96 and 137–62 – in his anthology *A Book of Irish Verse*, writes in the introduction to that volume that 'English-speaking Ireland had meanwhile no poetic voice, for Goldsmith had chosen to celebrate English scenery and manners'.[15] Later in his career, in 'The Seven Sages', included in *The Winding Stair and Other Poems* (1933), Yeats regards him, along with Swift, Berkeley, and Burke, as one of the 'four great minds that hated Whiggery', but he still views him as someone who 'never saw the trefoil stained with blood'.[16] The pastoral Goldsmith highlighted by his nineteenth-century biographers becomes a minor member of Yeats's Protestant tradition.

Despite his relegation to the sidelines as a writer not centrally concerned with the most pressing problems Ireland faced – the national question, most prominently – Goldsmith's major poem nevertheless remains a presence in Irish culture (see Chapter 33, 'Critical Reception after 1900'). Voted #15 by the readers of *The Irish Times* among their favourite Irish poems, *The Deserted Village* also still attracts the attention of major poets, who rely on his popularity as a widely recognized reference point to pursue their own complex concerns.[17] John Montague's interest in Goldsmith spans his entire career. In an early essay on Goldsmith, he calls Patrick Kavanagh's *The Great Hunger* 'a repudiation of the traditional rustic idyll, a sort of anti-Goldsmith'. Published ten years before the publication of his major poem, *The Rough Field* (1972), this essay reads *The Deserted Village* as 'one of the first statements of a great modern theme, the erosion of traditional values and natural rhythms in a commercial society: the fall of Auburn is the fall of a whole social order'. Montague has argued that the admiration T. S. Eliot, who supported the organicist movement, had for *The Deserted Village* 'may be partly due to the fact that it represents an anticipation of certain aspects of his own work: a sort of rural *Waste Land*'.[18] Montague's essay recognizes the synecdochic function Goldsmith's organic village community serves.[19] *The Rough Field*, like *The Deserted Village*, addresses rural decay, the return home to the place of birth, and radical changes in the present. Montague is fully aware that the rural past was not like that described in Goldsmith's poem. After all, 'Only a sentimentalist would wish/to see such degradation again.'[20] Yet Montague also mourns the loss of a social ideal, commemorated by, for example, 'Chagall's lovers/floating above a childhood village/remote but friendly as Goldsmith's Auburn'.[21]

Another contemporary poet who relies on *The Deserted Village* to think through one of her major concerns is Eavan Boland in her poem

'Rereading Oliver Goldsmith's *The Deserted Village* in a Changed Ireland'. She draws on Goldsmith's poem at a time when Ireland was undergoing rapid change. Responding specifically to the construction of Dundrum Town Centre, a shopping mall opened in 2005, Boland's poem, like Goldsmith's, addresses the destruction of a particular place and the community associated with it. Prompted by these developments in her community, she returns to Goldsmith's poem because she remembers 'Goldsmith's old lament'.[22] In Boland's reading of Goldsmith's place in that tradition, though, *The Deserted Village* becomes a tool to erase Irish history. In Goldsmith's poem, according to Boland, 'the small town of Lissoy / Sinks deeper into sweet Augustan double-talk and disappears'. Goldsmith's erasure of actual history, of a particular place, is something 'A subject people knows': 'the first loss is through history. / The final one is through language'.[23] In contrast to writers who draw on the geographical non-specificity of Auburn to transmute the village into their colonized locality, that same non-specificity Boland reads as a deliberate erasure of Ireland, so that Goldsmith's poem becomes an example of the process of anglicizing Ireland during the eighteenth century.

Although Goldsmith's poem no longer has the cultural presence it had in the late eighteenth and nineteenth centuries, it retains its appeal for the general reader and for poets, and it remains useful as a reference point in political debates.[24] The poem's continued appeal may well be based on what many readers of Goldsmith's work have responded to for more than 250 years: his appeal to the heart, an appeal that can be both sentimentalized and politicized. As the anonymous author of *An Impartial Character of the Late Doctor Goldsmith* wrote in the year of the poet's death: 'He wrote from the heart to the hearts of mankind.'[25]

Notes

1. See, for example, *The Beauties of Goldsmith: or, The Moral and Sentimental Treasury of Genius* (1782).
2. Ronald Blythe, *Akenfield: Portrait of an English Village* (Pleasantville, NY: Akadine Press, 2000), 16. Other examples are Elizabeth Hamilton's *The Cottagers of Glenburnie* (1808), John Galt's *The Annals of the Parish* (1821), Harriet Martineau's *Deerbrook* (1839), and Elizabeth Gaskell's *Cranford* (1853).
3. Richard D. Altick, *Paintings from Books: Art and Literature in Britain, 1760–1900* (Columbus: Ohio State University Press, 1985), 158. Goldsmith's influence on Washington Irving is profound. See, for example, Irving's 'Rural Life in England', a chapter in *The Sketch-Book of Geoffrey Crayon, Gent.* (1819–20).

4. See, for example, the 1885 Cassell & Company edition of *The Deserted Village*; the Harper & Brothers 1902 edition, edited by Austin Dobson, which includes Edwin A. Abbey's illustrations; and a Dodd, Mead & Company 1909 edition, including W. Lee Hankey's illustrations.

5. Éamon de Valera, 'The Undeserted Village Ireland', in *The Field Day Anthology of Irish Writing*, ed. Seamus Deane, 3 vols. (Derry: Field Day, 1991), 3:748.

6. Timothy Dwight, *Greenfield Hill* (New York: Childs and Swaine, 1794), 49–50.

7. Ebenezer Elliott, *The Splendid Village: Corn Law Rhymes; And Other Poems* (London, 1833), 26.

8. Examples are Robert Potter's *Observations on the Poor Laws, on the Present State of the Poor, and on Houses of Industry* (London, 1775), John Howlett 's *An Examination of Dr. Price's Essay on the Population of England and Wales* (London, 1781), George Dyer's *The Complaints of the Poor People of England* (London, 1793), and Thomas Spence's *Pigs' Meat; or Lessons for the Swinish Multitude*, 3 vols. (London, 1795).

9. The passages usually quoted from *The Deserted Village* are lines 51–2 ('Ill fares the land, to hastening ills a prey,/Where wealth accumulates, and men decay'), 57–8 ('A time there was, ere England's griefs began,/When every rood of ground maintained its man'), and, less frequently, 55–6 ('But a bold peasantry, their country's pride,/When once destroyed, can never be supplied') and 63–4 ('But times are altered; trade's unfeeling train/Usurp the land and dispossess the swain').

10. Thomas Babington Macaulay, 'Oliver Goldsmith', in *Critical, Historical, and Miscellaneous Essays and Poems*, 3 vols. (Chicago, IL: Belford, Clarke and Company, 1888), 3:274.

11. Jeremy Diaper, '*Ill Fares the Land*: The Literary Influences and Agricultural Poetics of the Organic Husbandry Movement in the 1930s–50s', *Literature & History*, 27.2 (2018), 167–88. Goldsmith is mentioned in Friend Sykes's *Humus and the Farmer* (London: Faber, 1946) and H. J. Massingham 's *The English Countryman: A Study of the English Tradition* (London: B. T. Batsford, 1942).

12. John Montague, 'Oliver Goldsmith: The Sentimental Prophecy', in *The Figure in the Cave and Other Essays*, ed. Antoinette Quinn (Dublin: Lilliput Press, 1989), 61–77 (75).

13. See Nikki Hessell, 'Antipodean Auburn: "The Deserted Village" and the Colonized World', *Modern Philology*, 112.4 (May 2015), 643–60.

14. Spofford A. Brooke and T. W. Rolleston, *A Treasury of Irish Poetry in the English Tongue* (London: Macmillan, 1900), x.

15. William Butler Yeats, *A Book of Irish Verse* (London: Methuen, 1895), xii–xiii.

16. William Butler Yeats, *The Poems*, ed. Richard J. Finneran, 2nd ed. (New York: Scribner, 1997), 245.

17. *The Irish Times Book of Favourite Irish Poems* (Dublin: Irish Times Books, 2000), 18–20.

18. Montague, 'Oliver Goldsmith: The Sentimental Prophecy', 64, 74–5, 75.

19. Seamus Heaney referred to this essay as a 'premonition of *The Rough Field*': Heaney, *Stepping Stones: Interviews with Seamus Heaney*, ed. Dennis O'Driscoll (New York: Farrar, Straus and Giroux, 2008), 51.

20. John Montague, *The Rough Field in Collected Poems* (Winston-Salem, NC: Wake Forest University Press, 1995), 80.

21. Montague, *The Rough Field*, 80–1.

22. Eavan Boland, 'Rereading Oliver Goldsmith's *The Deserted Village* in a Changed Ireland', in *A Woman without a Country* (New York: Norton, 2016), 74.

23. Boland, 'Rereading Oliver Goldsmith', 77.

24. In addition to the poets discussed, Vona Groarke, whose poem 'Or to Come' occupies a Goldsmithian landscape, should be mentioned as the editor of a recent edition of *The Deserted Village* (2002). Her collection *Flight and Earlier Poems* (2004), in which 'Or to Come' appears, begins with an epigraph from *The Deserted Village*. English examples of twentieth-century poems that draw on *The Deserted Village* are John Betjeman's 'The Dear Old Village' and Donald Davie's 'West Virginia's Auburn'.

25. Anon., *An Impartial Character of the Late Doctor Goldsmith* (London, 1774), 11.

Further Reading

Publisher details given only for post-1850 works.

1 Life

Clarke, Norma, *Brothers of the Quill: Oliver Goldsmith in Grub Street* (Cambridge, MA: Harvard University Press, 2016).
'"More National (to Ireland) than Personal": James Prior's *Life of Oliver Goldsmith* (1837)', *Biography*, 41.1 (2018), 48–70.
Dussinger, John A., 'Goldsmith, Oliver (1728?–1774), author', in *Oxford Dictionary of National Biography*. 23 September 2004; Accessed 16 September 2022. https://doi.org/10.1093/ref:odnb/10924.
Forster, John, *The Life and Adventures of Oliver Goldsmith*, 2 vols. (London, 1848).
Irving, Washington, *Oliver Goldsmith: A Biography* (London, 1850).
Percy, Thomas, 'The Life of Dr. Oliver Goldsmith', in *The Miscellaneous Works*, 4 vols. (London, 1801), I:1–118.
Prior, James, *The Life of Oliver Goldsmith, M. B.*, 2 vols. (London, 1837).
Sells, Arthur Lytton, *Oliver Goldsmith: His Life and Works* (London: George Allen & Unwin, 1974).
Wardle, Ralph, *Oliver Goldsmith* (Lawrence: University Press of Kansas, 1957).

2 Letters

Burke, Edmund. *The Correspondence*, ed. Thomas W. Copeland et al., 10 vols. (Cambridge University Press, 1958–78).
Clarke, Norma, *Brothers of the Quill: Oliver Goldsmith in Grub Street* (Cambridge, MA: Harvard University Press, 2016).
Curran, Louise. *Samuel Richardson and the Art of Letter-Writing* (Cambridge University Press, 2016).
Damrosch, Leo, *The Club: Johnson, Boswell, and the Friends Who Shaped an Age* (New Haven, CT: Yale University Press, 2019).
Garrick, David, *The Letters*, ed. David M. Little and George M. Kahrl, 3 vols. (Cambridge, MA: Belknap Press of Harvard University Press, 1963).

Goldsmith, Oliver, *The Collected Letters*, ed. Katharine Balderston (Cambridge University Press, 1928).

The Letters, ed. Michael Griffin and David O'Shaughnessy (Cambridge: Cambridge University Press, 2018).

Johnson, Samuel, *The Letters*, ed. Bruce Redford, 3 vols. (Princeton University Press, 1992).

Nelson, Taylin, 'Labouring Bodies: Work Animals and Hack Writers in Oliver Goldsmith's Letters', in *Letters and the Body, 1700–1830: Writing and Embodiment*, ed. Sarah Goldsmith, Sheryllynne Haggerty, and Karen Harvey (New York: Routledge, 2023), 212–35.

3 Friendships and Feuds

Clarke, Norma, *Brothers of the Quill: Oliver Goldsmith in Grub Street* (Cambridge, MA: Harvard University Press, 2016).

Damrosch, Leo, *The Club: Johnson, Boswell, and the Friends Who Shaped an Age* (New Haven, CT: Yale University Press, 2019).

Ginger, John, *The Notable Man: The Life and Times of Oliver Goldsmith* (London: Hamish Hamilton, 1977).

Prior, James, *The Life of Oliver Goldsmith, M. B.*, 2 vols. (London, 1837).

4 Booksellers and the Book Trade

Basker, James. *Tobias Smollett, Critic and Journalist* (Newark: University of Delaware Press, 1988).

Bertelsen, Lance, *The Nonsense Club: Literature and Popular Culture, 1749–1764* (Oxford University Press, 1986).

Brewer, John, *Party, Ideology, and Popular Politics at the Accession of George III* (Cambridge University Press, 1976).

Justice, George, *The Manufacturers of Literature: Writing and the Literary Marketplace in Eighteenth-Century England* (Newark: University of Delaware Press, 2002).

Kent, Elizabeth Eaton, *Goldsmith and His Booksellers* (Ithaca, NY: Cornell University Press, 1933).

Ralph, James, *The Case of Authors by Profession or Trade* (London, 1758).

Raven, James, *Bookscape: Geographies of Printing and Publishing in London before 1800* (London: British Library, 2014).

The Business of Books: Booksellers and the English Book Trade 1450–1850 (New Haven, CT: Yale University Press, 2007).

Spector, Robert, *English Literary Periodicals and the Climate of Opinion during the Seven Years' War* (The Hague: Mouton, 1966).

Suarez, Michael F., SJ, and Michael L. Turner, eds., *The Cambridge History of the Book in Britain, Volume V: 1695–1830* (Cambridge University Press, 2009).

Taylor, Richard C., *Goldsmith As Journalist* (Madison, WI: Fairleigh Dickinson University Press, 1993).

5 Enlightenments

Brown, Michael, *The Irish Enlightenment* (Cambridge, MA: Harvard University Press, 2016).
Ferrone, Vincenzo, *The Enlightenment: History of an Idea* (Princeton University Press, 2010).
Israel, Jonathan, *A Revolution of the Mind: Radical Enlightenment and the Intellectual Origins of Modern Democracy* (Princeton University Press, 2009).
Ní Chuanacháin, Deirdre, *Utopianism in Eighteenth-Century Ireland* (Cork University Press, 2016).
Siskin, Clifford, and William Warner, eds., *This Is Enlightenment* (University of Chicago Press, 2010).

6 Universities

Allan, David, *Virtue, Learning and the Scottish Enlightenment* (Edinburgh University Press, 1993).
Anderson, Robert D., Michael Lynch, and Nicholas Phillipson, *The University of Edinburgh: An Illustrated History* (Edinburgh University Press, 2003).
McDowell Robert B., and David A. Webb, *Trinity College Dublin, 1592–1952* (Dublin: Trinity College Press, 2004).
Ridder-Symoens, Hilde de, *A History of the University in Europe, Volume II: Universities in Early Modern Europe, 1500–1800* (Cambridge University Press, 1996).
Van Strien, Kees, 'Oliver Goldsmith and the University of Leiden', *Notes and Queries*, 50.2 (2003), 208–14.

7 Libraries

Amory, Hugh, ed., *Sale Catalogues of Libraries of Eminent Persons, Volume 7: Poets and Men of Letters* (London: Mansell, 1973).
Dobson, Austin, 'Goldsmith's Library', *Eighteenth Century Vignettes* (London: Chatto and Windus, 1892), 166–75.
Ellis, Markman, 'Coffee-House Libraries in Mid-Eighteenth-Century London', *The Library*, 10.1 (2009), 3–40.
Lynskey, Winifred, 'The Scientific Sources of Goldsmith's *Animated Nature*', *Studies in Philology*, 40.1 (1943), 33–57.
Mandelbrote, Giles, and Keith A. Manley, eds., *The Cambridge History of Libraries in Britain and Ireland, Volume II: 1640–1850* (Cambridge University Press, 2006).

8 The Club

Boswell, James. *The Correspondence and Other Papers of James Boswell relating to the Making of the 'Life of Johnson'*, ed. Marshall Waingrow (New Haven, CT: Yale University Press, 2016).

Life of Johnson, ed. George Birkbeck Hill and Lawrence F. Powell (Oxford University Press, 1934–64).

Clark, Peter, *British Clubs and Societies, 1580–1800: The Origins of an Associational World* (Oxford University Press, 2001).

Damrosch, Leo, *The Club: Johnson, Boswell, and the Friends Who Shaped an Age* (New Haven, CT: Yale University Press, 2019).

Fifer, Charles N., 'The Founding of Dr Johnson's Literary Club', *Notes & Queries*, 3.7 (1956), 302–3.

Grant Duff, Mountstuart E., *The Club, 1764–1905* (London: Printed for private circulation, 1905).

Mee, Jon, *Conversable Worlds: Literature, Contention, and Community, 1762 to 1830* (Oxford University Press, 2011).

Newman, Ian, *The Romantic Tavern: Literature, Politics and Conviviality* (Cambridge University Press, 2019).

Piozzi, Hester Lynch Thrale, *Anecdotes of the Late Samuel Johnson, LLD during the Last Twenty Years of His Life* (London, 1786).

9 Irish London

Bailey, Craig, *Irish London: Middle Class Migration in the Global Eighteenth Century* (Liverpool University Press, 2013).

O'Shaughnessy, David, ed., 'Networks of Aspiration: The London Irish of the Eighteenth Century', a special issue of *Eighteenth-Century Life*, 39.1 (2015).

Prior, James, *The Life of Oliver Goldsmith*, 2 vols. (London, 1837).

Rodgers, Nini, *Ireland, Slavery and Anti-slavery, 1612–1865* (Basingstoke: Palgrave Macmillan, 2009).

White, Jerry, *London in the Eighteenth Century* (London: Random House, 2012).

10 Liberty

Ashcraft, Richard, and M. M. Goldsmith, 'Locke, Revolution Principles, and the Formation of Whig Ideology', *The Historical Journal*, 26.4 (1983), 773–800.

Bataille, Robert A., 'City and Country in *The Vicar of Wakefield*', *Eighteenth-Century Life*, 3 (1977), 112–14.

Carson, James P., '"The Little Republic" of the Family: Goldsmith's Politics of Nostalgia', *Eighteenth-Century Fiction*, 16.2 (2004), 174–96.

Cuttica, Cesare, 'Reputation versus Context in the Interpretation of Sir Robert Filmer's "Patriarcha"', *History of Political Thought*, 33.2 (2012), 231–57.

Gargett, Graham, 'Oliver Goldsmith and Voltaire's "Lettres Philosophiques"', *The Modern Language Review*, 96.4 (2001), 952–63.

Helgerson, Richard, 'The Two Worlds of Oliver Goldsmith', *Studies in English Literature, 1500–1900*, 13.3 (1973), 516–34.

Horrocks, Ingrid, '"Circling Eye" And "Houseless Stranger": The New Eighteenth-Century Wanderer (Thomson to Goldsmith)', *English Literary History*, 77.3 (2010), 665–87.

Levine, William, 'Collins, Thomson, and the Whig Progress of Liberty', *Studies in English Literature, 1500–1900*, 34.3 (1994), 553–77.

McNally, David, 'Locke, Levellers and Liberty: Property and Democracy in the Thought of the First Whigs', *History of Political Thought*, 10.1 (1989), 17–40.

Tarlton, Charles D., 'Reason and History in Locke's *Second Treatise*', *Philosophy*, 79.308 (2004), 247–79.

11 Cosmopolitanism

Gargett, Graham, 'Cosmopolitanism in Action: Voltaire's Influence on Goldsmith in *The Citizen of the World*', in *Reverberations: Staging Relations in French since 1500*, ed. Phyllis Gaffney, Michael Brophy, and Mary Gallagher (University College Dublin Press, 2008), 365–78.

McMurran, Mary Helen, 'The New Cosmopolitanism and the Eighteenth Century', *Eighteenth-Century Studies*, 47.1 (2013), 19–38.

Min, Eun Kyung, *China and the Writing of English Literary Modernity, 1690–1770* (Cambridge University Press, 2018).

Porter, David, 'Sinicizing Early Modernity: The Imperatives of Historical Cosmopolitanism', *Eighteenth-Century Studies*, 43.3 (2010), 299–306.

Simpson, David, 'The Limits of Cosmopolitanism and the Case for Translation', *European Romantic Review*, 16.2 (2005), 141–52.

Watt, James, 'Goldsmith's Cosmopolitanism', *Eighteenth-Century Life*, 30 (2005), 56–75.

Williams, Laurence, 'Anglo-Chinese Caresses: Civility, Friendship and Trade in English Representations of China, 1760–1800', *Journal for Eighteenth-Century Studies*, 38.2 (2015), 277–96.

12 Marriage

Bannet, Eve Tavor, 'The Marriage Act of 1753: "A Most Cruel Law for the Fair Sex"', *Eighteenth-Century Studies*, 30.3 (1997), 233–54.

Carson, James P., '"The Little Republic" of the Family: Goldsmith's Politics of Nostalgia', *Eighteenth-Century Fiction*, 16.2 (2004), 173–96.

Hopkins, Robert H., 'Matrimony in *The Vicar of Wakefield* and the Marriage Act of 1753', *Studies in Philology*, 74.3 (1977), 322–39.

Kim, James, 'Goldsmith's Manhood: Hegemonic Masculinity and Sentimental Irony in *The Vicar of Wakefield*', *The Eighteenth Century*, 59.1 (2018), 21–44.

Lemmings, David, 'Marriage and the Law in the Eighteenth Century: Hardwicke's Marriage Act of 1753'. *The Historical Journal*, 39.2 (1996), 339–60.

Zomchick, John, *Family and the Law in Eighteenth-Century Fiction: The Public Conscience in the Private Sphere* (Cambridge University Press, 1993), 154–76.

13 Gender

Barr, Rebecca Anne, Sean Brady, and Jane McGaughey, 'Ireland and Masculinities in History: An Introduction', in *Ireland and Masculinities in History*, ed. Rebecca Anne Barr, Sean Brady, and Jane McGaughey (London: Palgrave, 2019), 1–17.

'Brightest Wits, and Bravest Soldiers: Ireland, Masculinity, and the Politics of Paternity', in *Irish Literature in Transition, 1700–1780*, ed. Moyra Haslett (Cambridge University Press, 2020), 263–83.

'Crossing Acts: Irish Drama from George Farquhar to Thomas Sheridan', in *The Blackwell Companion to Irish Literature*, ed. Julia M. Wright (Chichester: Blackwell, 2010), 127–41.

Evans, James, '"The Dullissimo Maccaroni": Masculinities in *She Stoops to Conquer*', *Philological Quarterly*, 9.1 (2011), 45–65.

'*She Stoops to Conquer*: An Irish Expatriate Comedy', *Restoration and Eighteenth-Century Theatre Research*, 32.1 (2017), 7–19.

Kavanagh, Declan, *Effeminate Years: Literature, Politics, and Aesthetics in Mid-Eighteenth-Century Britain* (Lewisburg, PA: Bucknell University Press, 2017).

Kim, James, 'Goldsmith's Manhood: Hegemonic Masculinity and Sentimental Irony in *The Vicar of Wakefield*', *The Eighteenth Century*, 59.1 (2018), 21–44.

14 Race

Eze, Emmanuel Chukwdui, ed., *Race and the Enlightenment: A Reader* (London: Blackwell, 1997).

Hart, William, 'Africans in Eighteenth-Century Ireland', *Irish Historical Studies*, 33.129 (May 2002), 19–32.

Lovejoy, Arthur O., *The Great Chain of Being* (Cambridge, MA: Harvard University Press, 1936).

Mills, Charles, *The Racial Contract* (Ithaca, NY: Cornell University Press, 1997).

Morgan, Jennifer L., *Laboring Women: Reproduction and Gender in New World Slavery* (University of Pennsylvania Press, 2011).

Vartija, Devin J., *The Color of Equality: Race and Common Humanity in Enlightenment Thought* (University of Pennsylvania Press, 2021).

Wheeler, Roxann, *Complexion of Race: Categories of Difference in Eighteenth-Century British Culture* (University of Pennsylvania Press, 2000).

15 Religion

Anderson, Misty, *Imagining Methodism in Eighteenth-Century Britain: Enthusiasm, Belief & the Borders of the Self* (Baltimore, MD: Johns Hopkins University Press, 2012).

App, Urs, *The Birth of Orientalism* (University of Pennsylvania Press, 2010).

Clark, J. C. D., *English Society, 1660–1832: Religion, Ideology and Politics during the Ancien Régime*, 2nd ed. (Cambridge University Press, 2000).

Hempton, David, *The Church in the Long Eighteenth Century* (London: I. B. Tauris & Company, 2011).

Lewis, Jayne Elizabeth, ed., *Religion in Enlightenment England: An Anthology of Primary Sources* (Waco, TX: Baylor University Press, 2017).

Lewis, Simon, *Anti-Methodism and Theological Controversy in Eighteenth-Century England: The Struggle for True Religion* (Oxford University Press, 2022).

Reeves, James Bryant, *Godless Fictions in the Eighteenth Century: A Literary History of Atheism* (Cambridge University Press, 2020).

Rivers, Isabel, *Reason, Grace, and Sentiment: A Study of the Language of Religion and Ethics in England, 1660–1780*, 2 vols. (Cambridge University Press, 1991).

Taylor, Charles, *A Secular Age* (Cambridge, MA: Harvard University Press, 2007).

16 Natural History and Science

Barrow, Barbara, '"Shattering" and "Violent" Forces: Gender, Ecology, and Catastrophe in George Eliot's *The Mill on the Floss*', *Victoriographies: A Journal of Nineteenth-Century Writing, 1790–1914*, 11.1 (2021), 38–57.

Gray, Beryl, '"Animated Nature": *The Mill on the Floss*', in *George Eliot and Europe*, ed. John Rignall (Aldershot: Scolar, 1997), 138–55.

Jones, Claude E., 'Goldsmith's "Natural History": A Plan', *Notes and Queries*, 191 (1946), 116–18.

Lovejoy, Arthur O., 'Goldsmith and the Chain of Being', *Journal of the History of Ideas*, 7.1 (1946), 91–8.

Lynskey, Winifred, 'Goldsmith and the Chain of Being', *Journal of the History of Ideas*, 6.3 (1945), 363–74.

'Pluche and Derham: New Sources of Goldsmith', *PMLA*, 57.2 (1942), 435–45.

Parsons, Coleman O., 'Tygers before Blake', *Studies in English Literature, 1500–1900*, 8.4 (1968), 573–92.

Seeber, Edward D., 'Goldsmith's American Tigers', *Modern Language Quarterly: A Journal of Literary History*, 6.4 (1945), 417–19.

17 War and Empire

Anderson, Fred, *Crucible of War: The Seven Years' War and the Fate of Empire in British North America 1754–1766* (London: Faber and Faber, 2000).

Baugh, Daniel, *The Global Seven Years War, 1754–1764: Britain and France in a Great Power Conflict* (London: Longman, 2011).

Brewer, John, *Sinews of Power: War, Money, and the English State 1688–1783* (New York: Alfred Knopf, 1989).

Colley, Linda, *Britons: Forging the Nation*, 2nd ed. (New Haven, CT: Yale University Press, 2005).

Conway, Stephen, *War, State, and Society in Mid-Eighteenth-Century Britain and Ireland* (Oxford University Press, 2006).

Greene, Jack P., *Evaluating Empire and Confronting Colonialism in Eighteenth-Century Britain* (Cambridge University Press, 2013).

Schumann, Matt, and Karl Schweizer, *The Seven Years War: A Transatlantic History* (London: Routledge, 2008).

Watts, Carol, *The Cultural Work of Empire: The Seven Years' War and the Imagination of the Shandean State* (Edinburgh University Press, 2007).

Wilson, Kathleen, *The Island Race: Englishness, Empire and Gender in the Eighteenth Century* (London: Routledge, 2003).

18 Ghosts

Barry, Jonathan, *Raising Spirits: How a Conjuror's Tale Was Transmitted across the Enlightenment* (Basingstoke: Palgrave Macmillan, 2013).

Bennett, Gillian, *Alas, Poor Ghost! Traditions of Belief in Story and Discourse* (Logan: Utah State University Press, 1999).

Brooks, John A., *The Ghosts of London: East End, City and North* (Peterborough: Jarrold, 1982).

Davies, Owen, *The Haunted: A Social History of Ghosts* (New York: Palgrave Macmillan, 2007).

Finucane, Ronald C., *Ghosts: Appearances of the Dead and Cultural Transformation* (Amherst, NY: Prometheus Books, 1996).

Fleischhack, Maria, and Elmar Schenkel, eds., *Ghosts – or The (Nearly) Invisible Spectral Phenomena in Literature and Media* (Frankfurt: Peter Lang, 2016).

Hudson, Martyn, *Ghosts, Landscapes and Social Memory* (London: Routledge, 2017).

Marshall, Peter, *Invisible Worlds: Death, Religion and the Supernatural in England, 1500–1700* (London: Society for Promoting Christian Knowledge, 2017).

McGill, Martha, *Ghosts in Enlightenment Scotland* (Woodbridge: Boydell Press, 2018).

Young, Francis, *English Catholics and the Supernatural, 1553–1829* (Farnham: Ashgate, 2013).

19 Fiction

Bäckmann, Sven, *This Singular Tale: A Study of* The Vicar of Wakefield *and Its Literary Background* (Lund: C. W. K. Gleerup, 1971).

Battestin, Martin C., *The Providence of Wit: Aspects of Form in Augustan Literature and the Arts* (Oxford: Clarendon, 1974), 193–214.

Freeman, Arthur, 'New Goldsmith?', *Times Literary Supplement* (15 December 2006), 15–16.

Grenby, Matthew O., ed., *Little Goody Two-Shoes and Other Stories, Originally Published by John Newbery* (Basingstoke: Palgrave Macmillan, 2013).

Hopkins, Robert H., *The True Genius of Oliver Goldsmith* (Baltimore, MD: Johns Hopkins University Press, 1969), 166–230.

Min, Eun Kyung, *China and the Writing of English Literary Modernity 1690–1770* (Cambridge University Press, 2018), 125–63.

Mullan, John, *Sentiment and Sociability: The Language of Feeling in the Eighteenth Century* (Oxford: Clarendon, 1988), 136–46.

Paulson, Ronald, *Satire and the Novel in Eighteenth-Century England* (New Haven, CT: Yale University Press, 1967).

Quintana, Ricardo, *Oliver Goldsmith: A Georgian Study* (London: Weidenfeld and Nicholson, 1967), 119–214.

Taylor, Richard C., 'Goldsmith's First Vicar', *Review of English Studies*, New Series XLI.161 (1990), 191–9.

20 Theatre

Evans, James, '"The Dullisimo Maccaroni": Masculinities in *She Stoops to Conquer*', *Philological Quarterly*, 90.1 (2011), 45–65.

McNeil, Peter, *Pretty Gentlemen: Macaroni Men and the Eighteenth-Century Fashion World* (New Haven, CT: Yale University Press, 2018).

Milhous, Judith, and Robert D. Hume, *The Publication of Plays in London 1660–1800* (London: British Library, 2015).

Phillips, James, 'Oliver Goldsmith's *She Stoops to Conquer*: The Stakes of Shame and the Prospects of Politeness', *English Literary History*, 87.4 (2020), 999–1023.

Ritchie, Leslie, *David Garrick and the Mediation of Celebrity* (Cambridge University Press, 2019).

Russell, Gillian, *Women, Sociability, and Theatre in Georgian London* (Cambridge University Press, 2007).

Straub, Kristina, *Sexual Suspects: Eighteenth-Century Players and Sexual Ideology* (Princeton University Press, 1992).

Wahrman, Dror, '*Percy*'s Prologue: From Gender Panic to Gender Play in Eighteenth-Century England', *Past & Present*, 159.1 (1998), 113–60.

21 Pastoral Poetry

Alpers, Paul, *What Is Pastoral?* (University of Chicago Press, 1996).

Barrell, John, *English Literature in History, 1730–80: An Equal, Wide Survey* (London: St Martin's Press, 1983).

McKeon, Michael, 'The Pastoral Revolution', in *Refiguring Revolutions: Aesthetics and Politics from the English Revolution to the Romantic Revolution*, ed. Kevin Sharpe and Steven Zwicker (University of California Press, 1998), 267–89.

Patterson, Annabel, *Pastoral and Ideology: Virgil to Valery* (University of California Press, 1987).

Sambrook, James, *English Pastoral Poetry* (Boston, MA: Twayne, 1983).

22 Prospect Poetry

Aubin, Robert Arnold, *Topographical Poetry in XVIII-Century England* (London: Milford, 1936).

Dixon, Peter, 'Public Wrongs and Private Sorrows: "The Traveller" and "The Deserted Village"', *Oliver Goldsmith Revisited* (Boston, MA: Twayne, 1991), 97–117.

Fairer, David, *English Poetry of the Eighteenth Century 1800–1789* (London: Longman, 2013), especially chapter 7, 'Economies of Landscape', 192–214.

Horrocks, Ingrid, '"Circling Eye" and "Houseless Stranger": The New Eighteenth-Century Wanderer (Thomson to Goldsmith)', *English Literary History*, 77.3 (2010), 665–87.

Hunt, John Dixon, *The Figure in the Landscape: Poetry, Painting, and Gardening during the Eighteenth Century* (Baltimore, MD: Johns Hopkins University Press, 1976; repr. 1989).

Kaul, Suvir, *Poems of Nation, Anthems of Empire: English Verse in the Long Eighteenth Century* (Charlottesville: University of Virginia Press, 2000).

Lonsdale, Roger, ed., *Gray, Collins & Goldsmith: The Complete Poems* (London: Longman, 1969).

'A Garden and a Grave: The Poetry of Oliver Goldsmith', in *The Author in His Work: Essays in a Problem in Criticism*, ed. Louis Martz and Aubrey Williams (New Haven, CT: Yale University Press, 1978), 3–30.

Montague, John, 'Exile and Prophecy: A Study of Goldsmith's Poetry', in *Goldsmith: The Gentle Master*, ed. Sean Lucy (Cork University Press, 1984), 50–65.

Rogers, Pat, 'The Dialectic of *The Traveller*', in *The Art of Oliver Goldsmith*, ed. Andrew Swarbrick (London: Vision and Barnes & Noble, 1984), 107–25.

Storm, Leo, 'Conventional Ethics in Goldsmith's *The Traveller*', *Studies in English Literature, 1500–1900*, 17.3 (1977), 463–76.

Turner, Katherine, *British Travel Writers in Europe 1750–1800: Authorship, Gender and National Identity* (Aldershot: Ashgate, 2001).

23 Periodicals and Literary Reviewing

Batchelor, Jennie, and Manushag N. Powell, *Women's Periodicals and Print Culture in Britain 1690–1820s* (Edinburgh University Press, 2018).

Donoghue, Frank, *The Fame Machine: Book Reviewing and Eighteenth-Century Literary Careers* (Stanford, CA: Stanford University Press, 1996).

Italia, Iona, *The Rise of Literary Journalism in the Eighteenth Century: Anxious Employment* (New York: Routledge, 2005).

Taylor, Richard C., *Goldsmith as Journalist* (London: Associated University Presses, 1993).

24 History Writing

Berman, David, 'David Hume on the 1641 Rebellion in Ireland', *Studies: An Irish Quarterly*, 65.258 (1976), 101–12.

Hicks, Philip, *Neoclassical History and English Culture, from Clarendon to Hume* (Basingstoke: Macmillan, 1996).

Momigliano, Arnaldo, 'Gibbon's Contribution to Historical Method', *Historia: Zeitschrift für Alte Geschichte*, 2.4 (1954), 450–63.

Phillips, Mark S., *Society and Sentiment: Genres of Historical Writing, 1740–1820* (Princeton University Press, 2000).

Pocock, John G. A., *Barbarism and Religion, Volume 2: Narratives of Civil Government* (Cambridge University Press, 1999).

Takebayashi, Yuhki, 'The Grounded Patriot: Oliver Goldsmith As Historical Compiler', unpublished PhD Thesis, Trinity College, Dublin (2019).

Ward, Addison, 'The Tory View of Roman History', *Studies in English Literature, 1500–1900*, 4.3 (1964), 413–56.

25 Authorship

Bender, John, *Imagining the Penitentiary: Fiction and the Architecture of Mind in Eighteenth-Century England* (University of Chicago Press, 1987).

Brown, Marshall, *Preromanticism* (Stanford, CA: Stanford University Press, 1991).

During, Simon, 'Charlatanism and Resentment in London's Eighteenth-Century Literary Marketplace', in *Bookish Histories: Books, Literature, and Commercial Modernity, 1700–1900*, ed. Ina Ferris and Paul Keen (Basingstoke: Palgrave Macmillan, 2009), 253–71.

Gargett, Graham, 'Oliver Goldsmith and Voltaire's *Lettres Philosophiques*', *Modern Language Review*, 96.4 (October 2001), 952–63.

'Translation and the Problem of Identity: Oliver Goldsmith and Voltaire', *Eighteenth-Century Ireland / Iris an dá chultúr*, 16 (2001), 83–103.

Griffin, Dustin, *Authorship in the Long Eighteenth Century* (Newark: University of Delaware Press, 2014).

'Fictions of Eighteenth-Century Authorship', *Essays in Criticism*, 53.3 (1993), 181–94.

Kitching, Megan, 'The Solitary Animal: Professional Authorship and Persona in Goldsmith's *The Citizen of the World*', *Eighteenth-Century Fiction*, 25.1 (2012), 175–98.

Lutz, Alfred, 'Goldsmith on Burke and Gray', *Papers on Language and Literature*, 34.3 (Summer 1998), 225–49.

'The Poet and the Hack: Goldsmith's Career As a Professional Writer', *Anglia: Zeitschrift fur Englische Philologie / Journal of English Philology*, 123.3 (2005), 414–40.

Powell, Manushag N., *Performing Authorship in Eighteenth-Century English Periodicals* (Lewisburg, PA: Bucknell University Press, 2012).

Rounce, Adam, 'Young, Goldsmith, Johnson and the Idea of the Author in 1759', in *Reading 1759: Literary Culture in Mid-Eighteenth Britain and France*, ed. Shaun Regan (Lewisburg, PA: Bucknell University Press, 2013), 95–112.

Smith, Adam, *Theory of Moral Sentiments*, ed. D. D. Raphael and A. L. Macfie (Oxford University Press, 1976).

Woodmansee, Martha, 'On the Author Effect: Recovering Collectivity', in *The Construction of Authorship: Textual Appropriation in Law and Literature*, ed. Martha Woodmansee and Peter Jaszi (Durham, NC: Duke University Press, 1994), 15–28.

Zionkowski, Linda, 'Territorial Disputes in the Republic of Letters: Canon Formation and the Literary Profession', *The Eighteenth Century*, 31.1 (1990), 3–22.

26 Orientalism

Aravamudan, Srinivas, *Enlightenment Orientalism: Resisting the Rise of the Novel* (University of Chicago Press, 2012).

Ballaster, Ros, *Fabulous Orients: Fictions of the East in England, 1662–1785* (Oxford University Press, 2005).

Conant, Martha Pike, *The Oriental Tale in the Eighteenth Century* (London: Frank Cass, 1966).

Lennon, Joseph, *Irish Orientalism: A Literary and Intellectual History* (Syracuse, NY: Syracuse University Press, 2004).

Min, Eun Kyung, *China and the Writing of English Literary Modernity, 1690–1770* (Cambridge University Press, 2018).

Porter, David, *The Chinese Taste in Eighteenth-Century England* (Cambridge University Press, 2010).

Smith, Hamilton Jewett, *Oliver Goldsmith's The Citizen of the World: A Study* (New Haven, CT: Yale University Press, 1926).

27 Satire and Sentiment

Dickie, Simon, *Cruelty and Laughter: Forgotten Comic Literature and the Unsentimental Eighteenth Century* (University of Chicago Press, 2011).

Haggerty, George, 'Satire and Sentiment in *The Vicar of Wakefield*', *The Eighteenth Century: Theory and Interpretation*, 32.1 (1991), 23–38.

Marshall, Ashley, *The Practice of Satire in England, 1658–1770* (Baltimore, MD: Johns Hopkins University Press, 2013).

Paulson, Ronald, *Satire and the Novel* (New Haven, CT: Yale University Press, 1967).

Rawson, Claude, *Satire and Sentiment, 1660–1830* (Cambridge University Press, 1994).

Tave, Stuart, *The Amiable Humorist: A Study in the Comic Theory and Criticism of the Eighteenth and Early Nineteenth Centuries* (University of Chicago Press, 1960).

28 The Sister Arts

De Bolla, Peter, *The Education of the Eye: Painting, Landscape and Architecture in Eighteenth-Century Britain* (Stanford, CA: Stanford University Press, 2003).

Erwin, Timothy, 'Ut Rhetorica Artes: The Rhetorical Theory of the Sister Arts', in *Haydn and the Performance of Rhetoric*, ed. Sander Goldberg and Tom Beghin (University of Chicago Press, 2007), 61–79.

Gadamer, Hans-Georg, 'The Speechless Image', in *The Relevance of the Beautiful and Other Essays*, tr. Nicholas Walker, ed. Robert Bernasconi (Cambridge University Press, 1986), 83–91.

Hagstrum, Jean H., *The Sister Arts: The Tradition of Literary Pictorialism and English Poetry from Dryden to Gray* (University of Chicago Press, 1958).

Jaarsma, Richard J., 'Ethics in the Wasteland: Image and Structure in Goldsmith's *The Deserted Village*', *Texas Studies in Language and Literature*, 13.3 (1971), 447–59.

Lee, Rensselaer W., *Ut Pictura Poesis: The Humanistic Theory of Painting* (New York: Norton, 1967).

Lessing, Gotthold Ephraim, *Laocoön*, tr. Edward Allen McCormick (Baltimore, MD: Johns Hopkins University Press, 1984).

Mitchell, W. J. Thomas, *Picture Theory: Essays on Verbal and Visual Representation* (University of Chicago Press, 1994).

Stafford, Fiona, 'Striking Resemblances: National Identity and the Eighteenth-Century Portrait', *Eighteenth-Century Ireland / Iris an dá chultúr*, 19 (2004), 138–62.

Woods, Samuel H., Jr, 'Images of the Orient: Goldsmith and the Philosophes', *Studies in Eighteenth-Century Culture*, 15 (1986), 257–70.

29 Music and Song

Brook, Geoffrey, 'Goldsmith and the Flute', *Pan: The Flute Magazine*, 27.4 (2008), 45–7.

Duffin, Ross W., '*She Stoops to Conquer* and Its Lost Songs', *Music & Letters*, 99.2 (2018), 159–93.

Henigan, Julie, *Literacy and Orality in Eighteenth-Century Irish Song* (London: Routledge, 2016).

McGeary, Thomas, '"Music and the Man of Sentiment"', in Musique et littératures: Intertextualités, ed. Andrée-Marie Harmat', *Anglophonia/ Caliban: French Journal of English Studies*, 11 (2002), 7–18.

Paterson, Adrian, 'Harps and Pepperpots, Songs and Pianos: Music and Irish Poetry', in *Irish Literature in Transition, 1780–1830*, ed. Claire Connolly (Cambridge University Press, 2020), 122–47.

Sands, Mollie, 'Oliver Goldsmith and Music', *Music & Letters*, 32.2 (April 1951), 147–53.

Shields, Hugh, *Goldsmith and Popular Song* (Dublin: Folk Music Society of Ireland / Cumann Cheol Tíre Éireann, 1985).

30 France and French Writing

Dow, Gillian, 'Criss-Crossing the Channel: The French Novel and English Translation, 1660–1832', in *The Oxford Handbook of the Eighteenth-Century Novel*, ed. J. A. Downie (Oxford University Press, 2016), 88–104.

Gargett, Graham, 'Plagiarism, Translation and the Problem of Identity: Oliver Goldsmith and Voltaire', *Eighteenth-Century Ireland / Iris an dá chultúr*, 16 (2001), 81–103.

Gargett, Graham, and Geraldine Sheridan, eds., *Ireland and the French Enlightenment* (Basingstoke: Macmillan, 1999).

Kennedy, Máire, *French Books in Eighteenth-Century Ireland* (Oxford: Voltaire Foundation, 2001).

Prendergast, Amy, 'Transnational Influence and Exchange: The Intersections between Irish and French Sentimental Novels', in *Irish Literature in Transition, Vol. 1: 1700–1780*, ed. Moyra Haslett (Cambridge University Press, 2020).

Stockhorst, Stefanie, ed., *Cultural Transfer through Translation: The Circulation of Enlightened Thought in Europe by Means of Translation* (New York: Rodopi, 2010).

31 Editions

Bateson, F. W., *The Scholar-Critic: An Introduction to Literary Research* (London: Routledge & Kegan Paul, 1972).

Bonnell, Thomas, *The Most Disreputable Trade: Publishing the Classics of English Poetry 1765–1810* (Oxford University Press, 2008).

Bowers, Fredson, *Bibliography and Textual Criticism* (Oxford University Press, 1964).

Friedman, Arthur, 'Oliver Goldsmith', in *The New Cambridge Bibliography of English Literature, Vol. 2: 1660–1800*, ed. George Watson (Cambridge University Press, 1971), 1191–1209.

'Principles of Historical Annotation in Critical Editions of Modern Texts', in *English Institute Annual 1941* (New York: Columbia University Press, 1942), 115–28.

Richards, Jeffrey, ed., *Imperialism and Juvenile Literature* (Manchester University Press, 1989).

Willinsky, John, 'Recalling the Moral Force of Literature in Education', *Journal of Educational Thought*, 22.2 (1988), 118–32.

32 Critical Reception before 1900

Cole, Richard C., 'Oliver Goldsmith's Reputation in Ireland, 1762–74', *Modern Philology*, 68.1 (1970), 65–70.

Crane, Ronald S. 'Oliver Goldsmith, M.B.', *Modern Language Notes*, 48.7 (1933), 462–5.

Donoghue, Frank, *The Fame Machine: Book Reviewing and Eighteenth-Century Literary Careers* (Stanford, CA: Stanford University Press, 1996).
'"He Never Gives Us Nothing That's Low": Goldsmith's Plays and the Reviewers', *English Literary History*, 55.3 (1988), 665–84.
Golden, Morris, 'Goldsmith's Reputation in His Day', *Papers on Language & Literature*, 16.2 (1980), 213–38.
Rousseau, G. S., ed., *Goldsmith: The Critical Heritage* (London: Routledge & Kegan Paul, 1974).
Woods, Samuel H., *Oliver Goldsmith: A Reference Guide* (Boston, MA: G. K. Hall, 1982).

33 Critical Reception after 1900

Griffin, Michael, *Enlightenment in Ruins: The Geographies of Oliver Goldsmith* (Lewisburg, PA: Bucknell University Press, 2013).
Kiberd, Declan, 'Nostalgia As Protest: Goldsmith's *Deserted Village*', *Irish Classics* (London: Granta, 2000), 106–24.
Kim, James, 'Goldsmith's Manhood: Hegemonic Masculinity and Sentimental Irony in *The Vicar of Wakefield*', *The Eighteenth Century*, 59.1 (2018), 21–44.
O'Shaughnessy, David, ed., *Ireland, Enlightenment and the English Stage, 1740–1820* (Cambridge University Press, 2019).
Quintana, Ricardo, *Oliver Goldsmith: A Georgian Study* (London: Weidenfeld and Nicolson, 1967).
Yan, Menmeng, *Foreignness and Selfhood: Sino-British Encounters in English Literature of the Eighteenth Century* (Abingdon: Routledge, 2022).

34 Afterlives 1: The Victorian *Vicar*

Dickens, Charles, *The Battle of Life*, in *The Christmas Books*, ed. Ruth Glancy (Oxford World's Classics, 1998).
Hunt, Leigh, 'Selections from Goldsmith, with Critical Notice', in *Wit and Humour: Selected from the English Poets* (London, 1846), 338–49.
O'Gorman, Francis, and Katherine Turner, eds., *The Victorians and the Eighteenth Century: Reassessing the Tradition* (Aldershot: Ashgate, 2004).

35 Afterlives 2: Theatre

Clare, David, 'Goldsmith, the Gate, and the "Hibernicising" of Anglo-Irish Plays', in *The Gate Theatre, Dublin: Inspiration and Craft*, ed. David Clare, Des Lally, and Patrick Lonergan (Dublin: Carysfort Press, 2018), 239–59.
Greene, John C., *Theatre in Dublin, 1745–1820: A Calendar of Performances*, 6 vols. (Lanham, PA: Lehigh University Press, 2011).
Ogden, James, 'Introduction', *She Stoops to Conquer* (London: Black, 2001), xi–xxxix.

Swindells, Julia, and David Francis Taylor, eds., *The Oxford Handbook of the Georgian Theatre, 1737–1832* (Oxford University Press, 2014).
Worth, Katharine, *Sheridan and Goldsmith* (Houndmills: Macmillan, 1992).

36 Afterlives 3: Poetry

Hessell, Nikki, 'Antipodean Auburns: 'The Deserted Village' and the Colonized World', *Modern Philology*, 112.4 (2015), 643–60.
Lutz, Alfred, 'The Politics of Reception: The Case of Goldsmith's *The Deserted Village*', *Studies in Philology*, 95.2 (1998), 174–96.
Shields, Juliet, 'From Auburn to Upper Canada: Pastoral and Georgic Villages in the British Atlantic World', in *The Edinburgh Companion to Atlantic Literary Studies*, ed. Leslie E. Eckel and Clare F. Elliott (Edinburgh University Press, 2016), 31–44.

Index